The Scottish Provincial
Banking Companies

The Scottish Provincial Banking Companies 1747–1864

CHARLES W. MUNN

BA PhD DipIB(Scot)

Department of Economic History
University of Glasgow

JOHN DONALD PUBLISHERS LTD
EDINBURGH

For my former colleagues at
81–14–48
and
81–14–88

ISBN 0 85976 071 5

Typeset by Hewer Text Composition Services.
Printed in Great Britain by Bell & Bain Ltd., Glasgow.

Acknowledgements

IN writing this book I have incurred many debts, thankfully not of a monetary but of a personal nature. In particular I am grateful to Professor S. G. Checkland and Mr T. Hart of the Department of Economic History in the University of Glasgow who provided advice, guidance and encouragement throughout and to Dr M. C. Reed who helped at an early stage.

The Scottish banks have kindly granted me access to their archives, and debts of gratitude are due to W. T. Liddle at the Bank of Scotland, R. N. Forbes at the Royal Bank of Scotland, and W. Chinn and R. Sim at the Clydesdale Bank. The librarians of these banks have also been of considerable assistance – notably D. Burns, R. Perkins and W. McLeod at the Bank of Scotland and Miss C. H. Robertson at the Royal Bank. Many bank officers throughout Scotland have given their time to show me their historical material. The staff of the Royal Bank of Scotland in Dundee, the Bank of Scotland in Aberdeen and A. Scott of the Bank of Scotland, Chief Glasgow Office, have been particularly helpful in this respect.

A special vote of thanks is due to Mrs E. O. A. Checkland who has transcribed the board minutes of the major Scottish banks and who has maintained a strong interest in the progress of this book. Professor A. Slaven of the University of Glasgow, Professor R. H. Campbell of the University of Stirling, Professor J. Butt, Dr T. Devine, Miss B. Thatcher of the University of Strathclyde and Mr M. Moss of the University of Glasgow have provided information and assistance with source material at various stages of this study. Miss Thatcher was responsible for kindling my interest in the history of banking.

Former colleagues in the British Linen Bank and in the Glasgow College of Technology have assisted in clarifying my thoughts on the more technical aspects of banking. In this respect Mr R. Wallace of Glasgow College of Technology and Mr H. S. Cathcart, now of Hill, Samuel & Co. Ltd., have been particularly helpful.

Mr J. K. Bates and Mr J. Sime of the National Register of Archives (Scotland) have been especially kind. I am grateful to them for the period spent in their employment working on the survey of the archives of the Bank of Scotland and on the preparation of source lists. Access to a number of the private manuscripts consulted was smoothed by these gentlemen and by Miss D. Hunter.

The staff of the Scottish Record Office, Public Record Office, National Library of Scotland and the Signet Library, Edinburgh have shown unfailing courtesy, as have the staffs of the Universities of Glasgow, Edinburgh and Dundee. Numerous public libraries met my requests with speed and efficiency – these include Aberdeen, Perth, Dundee, Stirling, Dumfries, Ayr, Greenock and the Mitchell Library, Glasgow. Staff of Baillie's Library, Glasgow, in particular Mrs Manchester, provided a standard of service beyond that which the researcher has a right to expect.

My thanks are also due to the staff and graduate student seminar of the University of Glasgow's Department of Economic History and to the Monetary History Group under the chairmanship of Professor L. S. Pressnell who provided constructive criticism of an earlier draft of the conclusion.

The Social Science Research Council provided the necessary finance in the form of a research studentship and met all of my requests and queries promptly and courteously.

It is an axiom of research and writing that an author's greatest debt is to his wife. I am no exception. Not only has Andrea suffered the normal hazards of marriage to a researcher, she also typed my work – from the earliest drafts to the final product.

Charles W. Munn
1981

Contents

List of Tables

List of Abbreviations

B.H.	*Business History*
B.L.	British Linen Bank
B.S.	Bank of Scotland
C.B.S.	Commercial Bank of Scotland
D.M.B.	Directors' Minute Books
Ec.H.R.	*Economic History Review*
Ex.E.H.	*Explorations in Entrepreneurial History*
J.Ec.H.	*Journal of Economic History*
J.W.H.	*Journal of World History*
N.B.S.	National Bank of Scotland
N.L.S.	National Library of Scotland
N.R.A.(S)	National Register of Archives (Scotland)
P.P.	Parliamentary Papers
R.B.S.	Royal Bank of Scotland
S.B.M.	*Scottish Bankers' Magazine*
S.H.R.	*Scottish Historical Review*
S.J.P.E.	*Scottish Journal of Political Economy*
S.M.	*Scots Magazine*
S.R.A.	Strathclyde Regional Archives
S.R.O.	Scottish Record Office
T.B.R.	*Three Banks' Review*
U.B.S.	Union Bank of Scotland
W.B.S.	Western Bank of Scotland

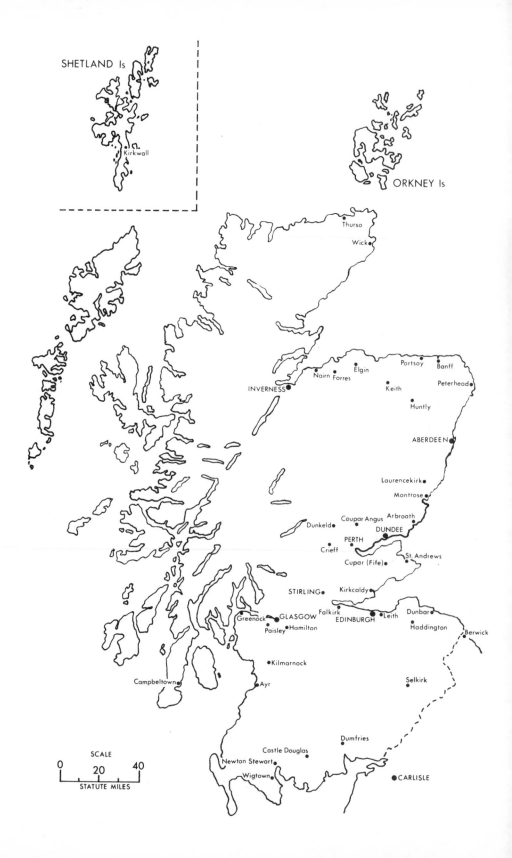

SHETLAND Is

Kirkwall

ORKNEY Is

Thurso
Wick

Portsoy
Banff
Elgin
Nairn Forres
Peterhead
INVERNESS
Keith
Huntly

ABERDEEN

Laurencekirk
Montrose

Coupar Angus Arbroath
Dunkeld
DUNDEE
PERTH
Crieff
St. Andrews
Cupar (Fife)

STIRLING
Kirkcaldy
Falkirk
Dunbar
Greenock GLASGOW
EDINBURGH Leith
Paisley Hamilton
Haddington
Berwick

Kilmarnock

Campbeltown
Ayr
Selkirk

Dumfries

Castle Douglas
Newton Stewart
Wigtown
CARLISLE

SCALE
0   20   40
STATUTE MILES

Introduction

Scotland in 1750

THIS book traces the origins and life cycles of the Scottish provincial banking companies from the first formation in 1747 to the last takeover in 1864. The chronology of erection and closure is outlined in Part One, which also relates the activities of these banks to the banks in Edinburgh. Their business organisation and practice is analysed in Part Two, and their contribution to capital formation in various sectors of the economy is examined in Part Three. The Conclusion gauges the performance of the companies in four respects – active survival, profitability, customer satisfaction, and the contribution to economic growth. These four criteria are examined in terms of the extent to which they contributed towards or undermined the stability of the economy.

The trade of banking which these companies were formed to conduct was thought (in 1763) to encompass

> Issuing and Circulating Notes of hand, . . . lending money on Cash Accompts, Bills or Personal Securities, . . . purchasing Bills of Exchange and discounting Inland Bills or Notes . . .[1]

It later developed to include accepting deposits, investing in public funds and lending on heritable securities.

1. The Scottish Economy

At the time of the Union with England in 1707 Scotland was an economically backward country. Its export trade, with the important exception of linen cloth, was essentially in primary products – notably cattle, coal, wool, hides, fish and salt. The main trading areas were the Baltic countries, France, Spain, Ireland and England, but 'what seems quite clear is that the changes gradually taking place during the seventeenth century had steadily moved Scotland towards greater economic dependence upon England'.[2] The main commodities in the English trade were cattle and linen in return for which Scotland received manufactured goods.

The total circulating coin in Scotland in 1707 was calculated by David Hume to

1

be just under £1m. sterling[3] and by Adam Smith to be just over £1m.[4] This was equivalent to about £1 per head of population.

It has been said that,

> The Union of 1707 effected an internal change in the means of remedying Scotland's economic backwardness by ensuring that Scottish economic policy aimed at rivalling the achievements of the English economy through complementary rather than competitive action.[5]

The principle of comparative advantage was made to work. The effect of the Union was to admit Scotland to a free trade area comprising Great Britain and the colonies. In this Scotland's woollen industry suffered badly because of competition from England, certainly in the finer grades of cloth. On the other hand the linen industry developed successfully especially after the formation of the Board of Trustees for Manufactures in 1727, and it was this industry which in some ways provided a basis for the future development of the cotton industry and therefore of the industrial revolution in Scotland. The trade in black cattle was the second major growth point after 1707.

Perhaps the most important aspect of the Union for Scotland's economic growth was the opening of trade possibilities with the colonies. Daniel Defoe claimed that, 'Several ships were laden for Virginia and Barbadoes the very first year after the Union'.[6] Certainly there had been some trading in these areas beforehand which was, strictly speaking, illegal although some of it had been done through the English port of Whitehaven, which had given it a semblance of legality. The admission of Scotland to the Navigation Laws created the opportunity for further development of this trade, and the natural and other advantages which Scotland enjoyed led to the eventual domination of the tobacco trade by merchants from the West of Scotland. Demand for manufactured goods from the colonies in addition to home demand encouraged the Scottish merchants to develop their own productive capacities. The West of Scotland therefore became the main growth area of the Scottish economy by 1750.

2. Banking Services, 1695–1750

The provision of formal banking services in Scotland began with the formation of the Bank of Scotland in 1695. The twenty-one years' monopoly granted to that concern was infringed for a short time by the ill-fated Company of Scotland and was ultimately allowed to lapse. The Royal Bank of Scotland was founded in 1727. Its 'legitimate parent' was the Equivalent Company[7] which had arisen from the complicated financial settlement necessitated by the Act of Union in 1707. The shares in both of these banks were freely transferable. They were legal corporations which could sue and be sued. They existed in perpetuity and the liability of the shareholders was limited to their subscribed capital. Therefore they shall be referred to as the Public Banks.

The Bank of Scotland came to be known as the 'Old Bank' and the Royal as the 'New'. Relations between these two companies were anything but cordial and the hostilities have been characterised as 'wars'.[8] Each collected the notes of the other and presented them in bulk for payment in specie in the hope that the enemy would be forced out of business. This action persuaded the directors of the Bank of Scotland that, in order to survive, they would have to devise a method of delaying payment of their notes. Consequently they included an 'option clause' in the £5, and later in the £1, notes whereby payment could be deferred, at the option of the directors, for a period of up to six months during which interest would accrue at the rate of five per cent. Seemingly the Royal Bank did not include this clause in its notes until 1761. It is not certain what use was made of the option in the 1730s and 1740s but with the spread of banking companies in the provinces during the 1750s and 1760s, most of which included the clause in their notes, it came to be regarded as a nuisance and as a contributory factor to the inflation which was then widespread. The hostility between the public banks in the 1730s had given rise to a system of potentially inconvertible paper money.

Nevertheless the public banks, despite the problems – which were largely of their own making – built the twin pillars which were to support the Scottish banking system throughout the industrial revolution period. These were the issue of bank notes, particularly those of small denomination, and the cash credit system.

Note-issuing banks made most of their profits by keeping their notes in circulation, and the history of Scottish banking, certainly until the 1830s, is replete with examples of the manner in which the banks pushed their notes into the 'circle' and contrived to keep them there. The maintenance of a paper currency was of crucial importance to the development of the Scottish economy. Gold and silver coins were constantly in short supply both because of the inadequacies of the mint and, more importantly, because Scotland had a constantly recurring balance of payments deficit for most of the period under consideration. An acceptable surrogate for a metal circulating medium was essential. Paper money filled that need but it was not to achieve any great success until the threat of inconvertibility, embodied in the option clause, was removed by legislation in 1765.

The cash credit system was inaugurated by the Royal Bank of Scotland in 1728 and the Old Bank copied it almost immediately. This was a form of advance, roughly analogous to the modern overdraft in which a bond was signed by the borrower and usually two others who guaranteed the credit. No security, other than this personal bond, was required. The borrower could draw on the account at will and paid interest only on the amount which was overdrawn, interest being calculated on the daily balance. These accounts served to circulate the bank notes and, so long as the account was actively used, helped to keep them in the circle. The further advantage of these accounts from the customers' point of view was that the credit was given without limit of time although if the account was found to be unsatisfactory it could be withdrawn at the bank's option.

The public banks also made advances on heritable securities but the discounting of inland trade bills and bills of exchange was not a vigorous aspect of their business in the first half of the 18th century. Indeed for a time they prohibited the lending of money against inland bills.

The British Linen Company was founded in 1746 and was intended to provide organisational and financial aid for the linen industry. By the 1760s it had begun to develop a more specific banking function and consequently to compete for business with the public banks.

Furthermore a number of private bankers had begun to establish themselves in Edinburgh:

> Many, if not most of these, were simply merchants, who besides their usual business carried on the negotiation of bills of exchange, but who, attracted by the profits of banking, and the facilities afforded by the old banks in the shape of cash credits, gradually drew away from merchandise to adopt the profession of banking.[9]

Towards the end of the century some of these even began to issue their own notes.

All of these developments had taken place in Edinburgh but the provincial areas of Scotland were slower to develop formal banking services. Certainly the Bank of Scotland had opened branch offices in Dundee, Montrose, Aberdeen and Glasgow in 1696 but had closed them all by 1699. Further attempts were made in these towns, with the exception of Montrose, in 1731 but all were closed in 1733, leaving the provinces once again bereft of formal banking services. It seems likely that the unprofitability of the branches was caused by the refusal to discount bills.

Informal banking services, however, were provided in the major towns. In Glasgow in the 1730s the Murdoch family 'had a stock employed with them in their Banking Business and other Trades'.[10] Groups of merchants and several companies, notably soapworks, sugar works and tanneries, were prepared to provide some banking services. Mostly these quasi-bankers dealt in bills of exchange and accepted deposits by private bargain. There is no evidence to suggest that they were lending very much money to the public and it seems likely that they were using the deposit money to prosecute their own particular trade. Nevertheless, the economic system had generated a financial network which was sufficiently sophisticated to require brokers. In the *Edinburgh Evening Courant* of July, 1730 John Blair, whose shop was in Glasgow's Saltmarket, advertised that

> all persons who have occasion to buy or sell bills of exchange, or want money to borrow, or have any sort of goods to sell, or want to buy any kind of goods, or who want to buy sugar house notes, or other good bills, or desire to have such notes or bills discounted, or want to have policies signed, or incline to underwrite policies in ships or goods, may deliver their instructions.[11]

Other Scottish towns might not have been able to provide such a wide range of financial services but merchants who dealt in bills of exchange could be found in most areas.[12] With only one exception, in Glasgow, none of these quasi-bankers developed into private bankers of the type found in Edinburgh. Most tended to become involved in the provincial banking companies.

Despite the fact that neither of the public banks maintained branch offices it remained possible for customers in provincial areas to negotiate and, with some difficulty, to operate cash accounts from Edinburgh. Although several people managed to do this, the numbers and the total credit involved were not large because before being awarded a cash account a potential customer had to be well known in the Capital and to be thought credit-worthy. This was not possible for most provincial merchants as communications between the provinces and Edinburgh were still very poor.

Generally the provision of formal banking services was concentrated in Edinburgh. Traders and manufacturers in other areas usually had to make do with informal services. It was always possible to have bills negotiated for payment, but to have them discounted was sometimes a difficult task. There remains a large, and as yet unresearched, area of private credit between individuals but it seems likely that much of it was long-term finance on fixed securities. Bank credit, when available, had advantages in its flexibility and in the accompanying provision of a generally acceptable circulating medium – bank notes. The fact that it was usually short-term, particularly in the case of discounts, was not the disadvantage which has sometimes been supposed. Recent research has shown that working, rather than fixed, capital was the prime requirement of industry during the industrial revolution[13] and the demand for the former was subject to seasonal fluctuations. Therefore bank credit was cheaper than private credit because bank borrowers paid only for what they required whereas private borrowers paid interest over a fixed period of time on the whole sum.

It was against this background of industrial and commercial development and facing these requirements that traders and manufacturers in the Scottish provinces began to look for new ways to satisfy their monetary requirements. The years between 1750 and 1772 were a period of experimentation.

3. The Provincial Banking Companies – a Definition

Sir John Clapham has stated that the banks which were founded in the Scottish provinces were 'joint-stock companies, co-partneries of many partners with unlimited liability'.[14] Comments of this type have largely confused the issue because they are partially inaccurate. It was certainly true that there was no limitation on the liability of shareholders, and many bankers pointed this out to their potential customers in the hope that public faith in their banks would be enhanced by the knowledge that the whole property of the partners could be attached in cases of failure. This knowledge encouraged people to hold banknotes especially if the partners in the bank were men of substance.

On the other hand the contention that these banks were joint-stock companies was wrong. A majority of the bank formations between 1749 and 1830 were in fact simple partnerships. The remainder were co-partneries. For the purposes of this book, partnerships have been defined as organisations of less than 13 partners; co-partneries had 13 or more shareholders. This is a somewhat arbitrary definition but seems justified in terms of management structures. Even quite small co-partneries such as the Glasgow Bank with 14 shareholders were controlled by a committee of management whereas partnerships were usually managed by all the partners acting in concert. Both types, however, were partnerships in law.

In the 1830s large-scale joint-stock banks were formed throughout Scotland but these are only an indirect concern of this book. Nevertheless a word of definition must be said about these firms. The co-partneries have often been confused with these joint-stock concerns, but apart from the differences of scale the major distinguishing factor was that joint-stock shares were often freely transferable whereas co-partnery shares were not. Furthermore co-partneries were founded with a specific period of trading in view, usually 7 or 21 years, although contracts were often renewed upon successful completion of the first period. Joint-stock banks on the other hand were usually founded in perpetuity.

In England the monopoly enjoyed by the Bank of England founded in 1694, was protected by legislation which prohibited the country banks in that country from having more than six partners.[15] The partners in Glasgow's first bank, the Ship Bank, believed that this law also applied to Scotland – it did not, as the founders of the Arms Bank, which was set up within months of the Ship, proved.[16] The Ship Bank had six partners while the Arms Bank had 31 and was never challenged. The inapplicability of this law to Scotland was a major distinguishing feature between the English country banks and the Scottish provinicials which were nevertheless similar responses to similar problems – the need for credit and a reliable circulating medium.

The shortage of good coin with which to pay wages occasioned a number of manufacturers to issue notes of small denominations. In the early 1760s these small note issuers were to be found in 'Dunkeld, Auchtermuchty, Montrose, Linlithgow, Kirkliston, Falkirk and elsewhere'.[17] An Act of 1765, however, prohibited the issue of notes under £1[18] and the practice largely ceased, although throughout the industrial revolution there were occasional examples of this type of note issue being made. Stephen Maberly in Aberdeen issued notes between 1816 and 1818, as did J. A. S. McKenzie in Stornoway between 1822 and 1824.[19] A trader in Tobermory, Isle of Mull, issued 5/- notes in 1825. They bore the inscription:

> For want of change I owe you five shillings and for four of these tickets I will give you a one pound note.[20]

With the exception of the early 1760s, these small note issuers were of little consequence to the economy other than as nuisances. They were not bankers in that their notes were only issued by way of trade and there is no evidence to suggest that they were lending money. Consequently they have been excluded from all statistical tables.

NOTES

1. C. W. Boase, 1867, P. xvii, Contract of Co-partnery of the Dundee Banking Co., 1763
2. T. C. Smout, 1963, p. 238
3. D. Hume, Essay on Banks and Paper Money, in J. R. McCulloch ed., 1857, p. 64
4. A. Smith, 1970, p. 394
5. R. H. Campbell, 1971, p. 3
6. D. Defoe, 1709, Appendix 1, p. 36
7. N. Munro, 1928, p. 32
8. S. G. Checkland, 1975, chapter 3
9. W. Graham, 1886, pp. 56–7
10. S.R.A. B10/15/7145, Discharge by Peter Murdoch, Jnr. to Peter and John Murdoch
11. Quoted in J. Buchanan, (Glasguensis), 1862, p. 2
12. C. W. Boase, 1867, p. xvii
13. F. Crouzet, ed., 1972, *passim*
14. Sir J. H. Clapham, 1944, vol. 2, p. 91
15. 7 Anne ch. 7, clause 61
16. Fettercairn Papers, Accession 4796, Second deposit, Box 24, f81, Mr Dunlop to Sir Wm. Forbes, n.d.
17. Graham, 1886, p. 64
18. 5 George III ch. 49, clause 7
19. *Bankers Magazine*, 1845, p. 426
20. Report from the Select Committee on Promissory Notes in Scotland and Ireland, 26/5/1826, evidence of Thomas Kinnear, p. 123

Part One

THE RISE AND FALL,
1747 – 1864

1

The Formative Years, 1747–1772

1. First Formations and the Response of the Public Banks

THE first provincial banking companies were formed in Aberdeen (1747) and Glasgow (1749 and 1750). The four partners in the Banking Company in Aberdeen were engaged in the hosiery trade while the men involved in the Glasgow Ship and Arms Banks were principally tobacco merchants. Their main reason for forming themselves into banking companies must be sought in the refusal of the public banks to discount their trade bills. The balance sheets of the Ship Bank show that discounts grew rapidly and constituted 50 per cent of total advances by 1761.[1] A desire to participate in the profits of banking must also have been a powerful stimulus.

The initial hostility of the Royal Bank to the formation of these new companies was soon overcome and both public banks encouraged the development of these banking initiatives in the provinces. They did not see the provision of direct finance for trade and industry as a major part of their own business policy. This task they left to the private bankers who borrowed on cash account from them. So it was in this light that they viewed the new provincial banking companies, and they imagined that the Aberdeen and Glasgow men would fulfil the same functions as the Edinburgh private bankers, who were

> merchants, men of substance, who obtain from the banks very extensive credits upon the joint real and personal security of themselves and friends. With this assistance from the banks, and with money borrowed from private people, repayable on demand, something below the common rate of interest, they support the trade of Scotland, by giving credit to the merchants and manufacturers.[2]

It seems that the public banks hoped to reproduce the Edinburgh pattern of banking in Aberdeen and Glasgow but they underestimated the development possibilities of the situation.

The attitude of the public banks towards the Ship Bank when it was projected in 1749 was ambivalent. The Royal Bank consulted its legal advisers with a view to a 'declarator, that no private banking companies have the privilege of banking without public authority', just as they had done two years earlier when the banking company in Aberdeen was formed.[3] In this they sought the co-operation of the Bank of Scotland which replied that the Ship Bank 'did not appear . . . to be an affair of such consequence as to engage them to lay out their money or venture their interest as to the legality of such erections'.[4] The studied nonchalance of this reply concealed the Bank of Scotland's support for the new concern. In July, 1749 the Old Bank had granted cash credit facilities of £10,000 to the Ship Bank proprietors who were led by John Graham of Dougalstoun. That credit, however, was never used as Graham died shortly afterwards and the account had to be re-negotiated. This was achieved in October, 1749 by which time Wm. McDowall of Castle Semple had agreed to join the partnership in place of Graham.[5] It is significant that the names of Graham and McDowall, who were, successively, the major landowners in the projected bank, should appear most prominently in the records of these transactions. It would seem that it was the landholdings of Graham and then McDowall which the Bank of Scotland understood to be the main security for the advance. The actual security was of course on personal bond and did not require a disposition of the land or any other asset. This supposition concurs with the view expressed by Sir James Steuart on the nature of inter-bank relations which is quoted above.

The Royal Bank of Scotland, having been the victim of smart trading by the Bank of Scotland, readily agreed to a proposal for a cash credit of £6,000 in the name of the Glasgow Arms Bank shortly after its opening in November, 1750. The fact that this credit was applied for and granted after the Arms Bank had opened for business contradicts the claim of the historian of the Royal Bank that the Royal had 'initiated the Glasgow Arms Bank, with Cochrane, Murdoch and Company as its representatives'.[6] The minute books of the Royal Bank give the impression that it was the proprietors of the Arms Bank and not the directors of the Royal who were the prime movers in this affair. It was proposed that in return for a cash credit of £6,000 the Arms Bank would promote the circulation of the Royal in the West of Scotland. It was also agreed that the two parties would exchange their notes on a regular basis.[7] The fact that the Arms Bank had responsibilities for the circulation of its own notes and those of the Royal Bank meant that there were clear grounds for a clash of interest built into the situation.

The reasons why there should be two formations in Glasgow and a division of Scottish banking in the lowlands into two camps, with the Bank of Scotland and Ship Bank on one side and the Royal Bank and Arms Bank on the other, are not inmediately apparent. Politics is one possible reason. The Bank of Scotland with its Jacobite sympathies and the Royal Bank with its Hanoverian ties may well have given credit to groups of Glasgow men with similar political dispositions. Andrew Cochrane, sometime Lord Provost of Glasgow, and one of the promoters of the Arms Bank, was certainly no Jacobite. It was he who had tried to get compensation from Parliament for the City of Glasgow for the damage caused by the Prince's army whilst it had been in the city during 1745. More simply the reason for the division may have been a factor of existing business relationships. Cochrane had been a customer of the Royal Bank since its foundation. Whatever the reasons, the ties between these banks and the resultant balance of power which existed for a time between the two groupings was of short duration.

The situation in Aberdeen was rather different. Only one bank had been formed there and this was befriended by the Bank of Scotland. Although the banking company itself did not have an account with the Old Bank, three of its partners did. Alex. Livingstone and John Dingwall and Co. each obtained credits for £500 in 1749. Wm. Mowat was awarded a credit for £1,000 in November, 1750.[8]

The breach in these alliances arose over the question of note circulations. Clearly the public banks had either misunderstood the provincials' intentions with respect to their issue or they had underestimated their potential ability to maintain sizeable circulations. The successes achieved, particularly by the two Glasgow banks, posed a threat to the note issues and therefore to the profitability of the public banks. By 1752 the directors of the Bank of Scotland,

> taking into consideration the circumstances of the country with regard to the great circulation of paper credits occasioned by private persons erecting themselves into Banking Companies without any public authority, particularly the two Banking Companies lately set up in Glasgow . . . were of the opinion that some measure should be speedily taken for preventing the dangerous consequences that might arise not only to this company in particular but to the credit of the nation in general from too great a circulation of paper.[9]

Seemingly someone at the Old Bank had read the proofs of David Hume's *Essays Moral, Political etc.*, published in 1752.[10] The Royal Bank directors held similar opinions. The question of banks requiring public, i.e. parliamentary, authority was one which was raised frequently in the next fifty years.

The incident which had provoked the public banks into action was the withdrawal in 1751 by the Glasgow bankers of their agents in Edinburgh whose function had been to exchange their notes. The Royal Bank directors thought that

> the giving up these correspondents suddenly and without proper notice to the country seems to be ensnaring and could not miss to be attended not only with inconvenience but with loss, to such as had taken them with a view to make payments at Edinburgh.

The public banks, faced with a common enemy, closed ranks. They agreed

> mutually to support, maintain and defend each of them their own, and the others interests against all attacks that may be made by other societies that now subsist, or that hereafter may be set up or pretend to carry on the business of banking in other parts of Scotland than Edinburgh.[11]

They further agreed to withdraw all cash credits from the Glasgow and Aberdeen areas, and anyone in Edinburgh who circulated provincial notes was to suffer a similar fate. More than this; they used their influence with the Boards of Customs and Excise to ensure that only Edinburgh notes would be accepted in payment.[12] The bank war had begun in earnest and the lines were redrawn.

The effect of these actions was to withdraw £15,000 of authorised cash credits from the Glasgow region and £6,700 from Aberdeen. At this time cash credits authorised by the Glasgow banks were probably in the region of £100,000 and discounts were about £20,000 so that the removal of public bank credit represented a withdrawal of about 12.5 per cent of total bank credit from the Glasgow area.[13]

No attempts at negotiation with the Glasgow or Aberdeen banks took place. It would seem, therefore, that the action of the public banks was rather precipitate.

If the removal of the Edinburgh agents by the Glasgow bankers had been the sole reason for their action it seems likely that some negotiation would have been attempted with a view to having these agents restored. The growing hostility of the public banks, however, appears to have been more deeply seated, and the arguments which were to be so frequently repeated in future years began to be rehearsed. The fact that the provincials were private companies without public authorisation was the main line of attack. The Royal Bank also objected that the Glasgow banking companies had been set up without 'depositing a fund or stock of cash for the security of such as shall come to be possessed of their notes'. It was felt that this might be 'attended with great inconvenience to the country' which would 'greatly affect proper credits in general'.[14] Probably the provincial bankers felt that, so long as they had sufficient for their daily needs, they needed no such fund as their liability to the general public was unlimited, and in the event of closure or non-payment of notes all the assets of the partners could be attached for the bank's debts – a fact which they advertised when setting up these concerns. This was regarded as a great strength, unlike the public banks where the liability of partners was limited to their subscribed capital, making reserves all the more necessary. Certainly, any irresponsibility on the part of the provincial bankers, in terms of their note issues, could have a dramatic effect on the other banks but the possibility cannot be ignored that the public banks were jealous of the success achieved by the Glasgow bankers in particular, and therefore the objections to provincial banking expressed by the Edinburgh banks were perhaps only formalised criticisms which concealed a more basic hostility.

Any objections to the constitutions of the provincial banking companies could have been raised at their inception but no such reservations were made at the time. On the contrary, the public banks had actively encouraged these three new concerns. The change of heart occurred in late 1751. Unfortunately, none of the records of the Glasgow banks for that year are extant so that it is impossible to say whether they were making inroads into the Edinburgh banks' business or if the fear expressed by the public banks about the increasing paper circulation of the country reflected the realities of the situation. If the latter was the case and there was a danger of an excessive issue of paper credit drawing inflation and speculation in its wake, then the motive of the public banks, in dissociating themselves from all the provincial note issues and cutting themselves off from all possible connections with them both in Edinburgh and elsewhere, was perfectly understandable. The capacity to foresee a difficult situation and then to evade it was one which was to stand them in good stead at later dates.

This still does not explain either the initial warm reception given to the new banking companies or why there was a change of attitude in 1751. It seems likely, therefore, that the Ship and Arms Banks were expanding their business and, concomitantly, their note issues into areas which the public banks regarded as their own preserve. The removal of Edinburgh agents meant that holders of provincial notes could only obtain specie or other notes for them in Glasgow. This had the effect of keeping the notes in circulation for a longer period, thereby increasing the profitability of the issues.

The initial hostilities of 1751 were only the beginning of a long series which lasted for twenty years. In 1753 the Aberdeen bank succumbed to pressure from the public banks which had gathered together £1,400 of Aberdeen notes and presented them for payment in specie.[15] The Aberdeen partners decided that, faced with such hostility, they could not profitably prosecute their trade and retired from the banking business. The Glasgow men were made of sterner stuff. After 1751 their notes appear to have lost all currency in Edinburgh[16] but by 1756 they had crept back into that city and in June of that year the public banks issued an ultimatum to 57 Edinburgh merchants containing five articles. This document demanded that the merchants would not in any way do business with the Glasgow banking companies and more particularly that they would not 'keep any correspondence with any of the Glasgow Banks or with any other person or persons for their behoof'.[17] The five merchants who refused to agree to these articles had their credits with the public banks withdrawn.

The response of the Glasgow bankers to this escalation of hostilities was to try and negotiate terms of peace. They proposed that they should be allowed 'to bank to the extent of £120,000' and that they should confine their activities to the counties of Ayr, Renfrew, Argyle, Lanark and Stirling.[18] Total advances by the Ship Bank at that time amounted to £67,000.[19] If the Arms Bank was of a similar size, then the total advances of the two banks would be about £130,000 which, considering the smallness of capital and deposits, was largely based on the issue of notes. Total advances of the Bank of Scotland at this time were £169,000.[20] In fact what the Glasgow banks were advocating was the *status quo* with the single exception that they would not do any business in Edinburgh and the East. The joint committee of the public banks who were handling these negotiations thought that these terms were much too generous and did not even bother to take them before their respective boards.[21]

The directors of the public banks, however, began to find that the current of public opinion was running against them and that charges of monopoly had been levied. Their joint committee then hastened to propose to the boards of directors that negotiations should be re-opened, and two bases for agreement were proposed. The first of these suggested that the Glasgow banks should give up business and in return the public banks would open a joint agency in that city. The second ventured that the Glasgow banks should limit their sphere of operations to Glasgow, Paisley and Port Glasgow and confine their credit within a ceiling of £50,000. This latter suggestion was impractical as it would involve the Glasgow men in disclosing their accounts to the view of the Edinburgh bankers. Even so the Bank of Scotland rejected it because it would involve a recognition of the Glasgow companies as banks – something which they had been anxious to avoid. In any case neither of the proposals was likely to find favour with the Glasgow bankers. Six weeks later the joint committee decided that it would be good for their public image if they at least listened to the proposals of the Glasgow men,[22] yet it does not appear that they had any intention of compromising. By February, 1757 any hope of agreement was at an end and the public banks 'turned their thoughts on what measures would tend most to make these gentlemen weary of the Banking trade'.[23]

The ultimatum which the Edinburgh banks had issued in 1756 proved impossible to enforce. At least two of the Edinburgh private bankers preferred to maintain their Glasgow connections rather than continue their credits from the public banks. These firms were Wm. Cumming, and Fairholme and Malcolm.[24] This is some indication of the growing economic power which the Glasgow men wielded as a result of their increasing involvement in the tobacco trade. The purpose of the ultimatum, i.e. to keep Glasgow notes and bills out of Edinburgh, had been defeated and it was quietly laid aside. This left a strain on the relationship between the two public banks who now had no formal agreement between them against engaging in business with the men from the West. Twenty years of mistrust between the public banks had not been entirely removed by the agreement of 1751. Nevertheless, the committee hoped that the directors of both banks would 'bona fide keep it in their Eye to pursue such Measures as may prevent the Growth or success of Rival Companies, or any undue Extention of Paper Credit'.[25] This was the first overt admission that the Edinburgh men were worried about the success achieved by their Glasgow counterparts.

In the next stage of the battle the public banks re-joined their forces and appointed a Glasgow agent in May, 1757.[26] His function was twofold. He was appointed to carry on the normal business of a bank office but he was also to spare no effort in picking up Glasgow notes from the circle, replacing them with Edinburgh notes and presenting the Glasgow notes for payment in specie. It was thereby hoped to embarrass the Glasgow banking companies and thus force them to close their doors. The man appointed to this 'ungracious office'[27] was Archibald Trotter, a former partner in the private Edinburgh bank which then belonged to the Coutts brothers. The methods which the Glasgow bankers used to stall Trotter have been well documented. Often they paid their notes in sixpences which were counted slowly, 'accidentally' dropped and counted again. Sometimes the teller was called away, 'leaving the porter to blunder with great alacrity'. In one period of thirty-four business days Trotter managed to get payment for only £2,893. In January, 1759 he took out a protest against the Arms Bank for non-payment. They pleaded in defence of their tardy payment that Trotter had acted *in male fide*. The case was eventually settled out of court in 1763 after the Arms Bank had exhausted its delaying tactics.[28]

Trotter's activities certainly embarrassed the Glasgow banking companies, but they were not lacking in imaginative responses. In order to pay specie for their notes they paid a premium for gold and silver which they bought in Edinburgh. In 1759 the directors of the Royal Bank wrote to the Arms Bank complaining of this practice and claiming that it was 'harmful to the country'.[29] The letter was hardly necessary as the remedy was in the hands of the Royal and their friends at the 'Old Bank'. In 1761 the directors of the Royal concluded that the interest-free advances made by them to Trotter to enable him to pick up Glasgow notes 'could not tend to the profit of this bank'.[30] They decided to discontinue the practice. Trotter's agency, however, was not terminated immediately. He was still in business in 1763.

The lack of success achieved by the public banks in trying to remove their contemporaries from the banking scene was marked not only by the survival of the Ship and Arms Banks but by the arrival on November 3rd, 1761 of a third Glasgow Bank – the Thistle Banking Company (Maxwell, Ritchie and Company).

2. The 1760s – Further Formations

The birth of the Thistle Bank in 1761 heralded the arrival over the next eight years of a whole series of provincial banking companies. Most of them, like the Dundee Banking Company, were

> sensible of the great inconveniency which the merchants and manufacturers of this part of the country lie under by reason of their distance from Edinburgh, and the difficulty of procuring loans and negotiating cash accounts with the Banks there established.[31]

Clearly there was an unsatisfied demand in the provinces for banking services. The provincial bank formations between 1747 and 1772 are set out in Table 1.

Table 1

Provincial Banking Company Formations 1747–1772

		Date of opening	No. of partners at founding	Remarks
1.	Banking Co. at Aberdeen	1747	4	Closed 1753
2.	Ship Bank, Glasgow	1750	6	Dunlop, Houston & Co.
3.	Arms Bank, Glasgow	1750	31	Cochrane, Murdoch & Co.
4.	Thistle Bank, Glasgow	1761	6	Maxwell, Ritchie & Co.
5.	David Watson	c.1763	1	Private Bank, Glasgow
6.	Dundee Banking Co.	1763	36	Geo. Dempster & Co.
7.	Macadam & Co., Ayr.	1763	15	Joined No.13 in 1771
8.	Perth United Banking Co.	1766	87	Junction of 5 quasi-banks
9.	Johnston, Lawson & Co., Dumfries	1766	19	Joined No.13 in 1771
10.	Aberdeen Banking Co.	1767	109	
11.	General Bank of Perth	1767	43	Closed 1772
12.	Glasgow Merchant Banking Co.	1769	48	
13.	Douglas, Heron and Co., Ayr	1769	136	Failed 1772

In several cases the lack of interest shown in the regions of Scotland by the Edinburgh banks, despite a growing demand for bank credit, led directly to the formation of provincial banking companies. Certainly the public banks awarded a few credits in provincial areas and had appointed agents, often jointly, in some towns to provide and retire notes for these account holders. In Dumfries, Hugh Lawson, one of the founding partners of Johnston, Lawson and Co., had been employed by the Royal Bank to service its cash accounts in the south of Scotland.[32] His subsequent active participation in the new banking company there must be seen in the light of his realisation both of the potential profits of banking and of the unsatisfied demand for credit in his area. In Aberdeen the public banks had withdrawn their agent in 1764 only to reinstate him when they heard of the plan to open a provincial banking company in that city in 1766.[33] It was then too late to forestall the formation of the Aberdeen Banking Co. Had the public banks been prepared to provide full banking facilities in these towns, then new banking companies would have been rendered unnecessary although they might still have been formed. Doubtless the public banks would have preferred to repeat the Edinburgh pattern of banking in provincial towns as they had tried to do in Glasgow, but the manner in which the Glasgow banking companies had evolved had set a different pattern of banking which they were powerless to control. Aside from the questions of business competition, the public banks were genuinely concerned about the potentially destabilising effects of unrestricted note issues without adequate capital backing and the consequences for the Scottish balance of payments. Seemingly for this reason they were unwilling to extend their business any further.

Disregard for some areas of commercial life was not, however, confined to the Edinburgh banks. In and around Perth and Glasgow the small traders sometimes felt themselves to be poorly, if at all, served by the local merchant oligarchies who controlled the existing banking companies. Consequently the Perth men formed the General Bank in 1767 and the Glasgow men founded the Merchant Banking Company in 1769. This pattern of two or three local banks in a town was repeated elsewhere in later years. Apparently the first flushes of dynamism displayed by new banking companies seldom lasted more than a few years as bankers came to realise that the sure way to survival was the road of caution if not conservatism. This inevitably left some unsatisfied demand for services but the system was always sufficiently flexible to permit the formation of new banks to serve these requirements. The public banks' attitudes to the provincials, and that of the provincials to the new formations in the same areas, must both be seen in these terms. Existing banks were always afraid that new arrivals would be destructive of prosperity and stability.

The hostility of the public banks towards the Glasgow companies and to other new arrivals continued unabated. In February, 1762 several private Edinburgh banks were threatened that their cash accounts would be withdrawn unless they ceased to act as agents for the Glasgow banking companies. It appears that the latter had once again been employing the Edinburgh private bankers to supply them with Edinburgh notes and specie. Such was the shortage that a premium was paid for coin.[34] In the following year the proprietors of the Thistle Bank wrote 'in a most haughty and menacing strain' to the public banks complaining about the activities of Trotter. They received a reply 'in a very few words' stating that Trotter was employed 'to receive in payment the notes of the Bank of Scotland, Royal Bank notes or specie for such Glasgow bills or notes as came into his hands on their account'. A second letter in the same vein was thought to deserve 'no answer'. Several weeks later the Edinburgh banks received a warning from Alexanders, the private bankers, that the Thistle Bank was about to make demands on one or both banks for payment of their notes in specie.[35] This is the first indication that the initiative in this bankers' war was with Glasgow. The Edinburgh men agreed to take the benefit of the option clause in their notes and delay specie payments for six months to those who made large demands for coin.

The shortage of specie was particularly acute in the period 1761–5 but it was by no means a novel situation. Specie was never in abundant supply. The lack of coin forced many firms in trade and manufacturing to issue 'Birmingham buttons' and notes of small denomination as substitutes for coin. Notes for 1/– and 5/– were the most common. These notes often contained the option clause which was frequently invoked. In 1764 a writer in the *Scots Magazine* estimated that there were 14 note issuers in Scotland in addition to the public banks; the editor reckoned that there were twice that number.[36] Some commentators, including the Edinburgh banks, saw the development of small note issues and the use of the option clause as the cause rather than the result of the shortage of specie. Others were less dogmatic. One writer in the *Scots Magazine* was sufficiently acute to notice that the option clause was in fact designed to keep specie in the country, although he did admit that it was also designed to keep it in bank chests for as long as possible rather than in circulation.[37] Argument about whether uncontrolled note issues caused the specie shortage or vice versa were specious. In fact both arguments contained an element of truth. There seems little doubt that the issue of notes did contribute to an inflationary situation which had the effect of driving out specie and raising the inland exchange rate against London. This made it increasingly profitable for people to sell London bills in Edinburgh, at a premium, and ship the specie obtained thereby to London where it was sold for bills. The bills thus obtained were then sent to Edinburgh where the process began again. Specie became a commodity. The note issue, however, was not the only cause of the adverse balance of payments. Henry Hamilton thought that in 1762 'the underlying weakness of the Scots banking system was its attempt to build an extensive credit system on an inadequate cash basis',[38] but in that year there were only three note-issuing provincial banks, all in Glasgow, in addition to the Edinburgh public banks and a number of small note issues by firms other than bankers. Regrettably figures are not available to illustrate the total note issues in the difficult 1762–65 period but it seems unlikely that note issues were the major cause of the adverse exchange rate.

A number of other factors were at work which caused the balance of payments deficit. Sir James Steuart identified several of them. These included the importation of grain in years of poor harvests, the refunding of English loans for speculative purposes as the Seven Years War came to an end, payments drawn by expatriates for consumption and speculation in London and the payment to the London Exchequer of additional war taxes. This problem was further compounded by the removal of some 'industrious' people to serve in the armed forces, the absence of troops normally stationed in Scotland and 'the cutting off of several beneficial articles of commerce'.[39] Faced with all of these contributory causes to the problem, the role of the note issues and the option clause must be regarded as a small one. Nevertheless, it was a disturbing and disruptive element in the commercial world. As voluntary agreement to ban the clause was not possible because of the bad feelings amongst the banks it was decided, independently by the bankers in Edinburgh and Glasgow, that legislation should be sought to put an end to it and to the issue of bank notes of small denomination. True to form, the public banks interpreted this to include an end to the provincial bankers.

They thought that they should be

> the First Movers in an Application to Parliament agreeing to prohibit the optional clause and desiring some restraint may be laid upon the present undue and unbounded Circulation of Paper and for that purpose that no Company but such as were established by Publick Authority should be permitted to issue notes under the value of Ten pounds sterling.[40]

When the delegates who were to be sent to London to campaign for this legislation were briefed, they were told that they were to press for a monopoly of banking for the public banks and for the extinction of the provincial companies. If that could not be achieved, then they were to press for the restrictions of note issues by these companies to notes of £10 and over.

This alternative was important because, if accepted, it entailed the recognition of the provincials as banks. The delegates were also to secure an end to the option clause. The price which they were prepared to offer the Government was that so long as their 'Exclusive Privilege' should exist they would pay a fixed sum annually to the 'Trustees for Improving Fisheries and Manufactures'.[41] In short, it seemed that Mercantilist views prevailed at the public banks.

There seems to have been considerable support in the country for a duopoly system of the public banks. At meetings of heritors and commissioners of supply in Aberdeen, Edinburgh, West Lothian, Roxburgh, Haddington, Selkirk, Dumfries, Inverness, Elgin and Fife, resolutions were passed to the effect that provincial bank notes would be refused in payments. In practice, however, these resolutions proved to be of little effect because businessmen had to accept the notes that were offered to them or risk losing custom. This seems to have been very much a matter of country versus town where the landowning heritors and commissioners who, almost certainly, had connections with Edinburgh banks found themselves in a conflict of interests with the town-based merchant class who formed their own banks to provide for their monetary needs which had been largely ignored by the Edinburgh bankers. The only county which declared itself to be in favour of provincial bank notes, but without the option clause, was Renfrew.[42] Doubtless the fact that Sir James Maxwell of Pollok, Bt., a partner in the Thistle Bank, was chairman of this meeting had something to do with its outcome.

In a memorandum to Baron Mure, one of the Barons of Exchequer and a partner in the 'aristocratic' Thistle Bank of Glasgow, from the Lord Privy Seal, the proprietors of that bank, it was said, 'distinguished themselves by being the first movers of leaving out the optional clause, and sent a memorial containing their reasons in support of that measure to every Member of Parliament for this country'.[43] Their price for so doing was to be letters patent from the King which they hoped would place them on a legal basis with power to sue and be sued as a business entity. Such letters would of course be a substitute for a charter. It is interesting to note that the Thistle Bank and the public banks both claimed credit for having been the prime movers in the attempt to abolish the option clause. Clearly a very marked form of one-upmanship. Unfortunately, the truth of the matter is not known, as the Thistle Bank memorandum was undated. It is unlikely that the formation of plans by the public banks and the Thistle were separated by more than a few weeks.

There was considerable opposition amongst the Scottish M.P.s to the extension of exclusive privileges to the public banks. One of those opposed was George Dempster of Dunnichen, M.P. for the Fife Burghs. He was a founding partner of the Dundee Banking Co. in 1763 to which he gave his name, and of the Perth United Banking Co. in 1766. The M.P.s were generally agreed that the option clause together with notes under £1 must go and that all bank notes should be protestable for non-payment in the same manner as bills of exchange. (A court process of 1753 involving the Banking Company at Aberdeen had declared bank notes to be not protestable by summary diligence so that anyone holding a bank note which the issuer had refused to pay had to undergo a complicated legal process to obtain payment. Summary diligence greatly simplified the procedure.)

The provincial banking companies were not without their friends in high places. The Lord Privy Seal, who was a close friend of Baron Mure of the Thistle Bank, replied to the demands of the public banks by stating as a matter of principle,

> That the Trade of Banking is a matter not of Public favour but of Right to every subject in common so no Difference exists between Established Banks and Private Bankers except the formers being corporated.[44]

This was quite different from England where the six-partner rule operated – a rule which was extended to Ireland in 1783. It was the first expression of government support for free entry into banking. In the previous month Provost Ingram, a partner in the Arms Bank, had written to the Lord Privy Seal asking him to use his influence

> to promote a continuance of banks here, and, also, that they may be put on an equal footing with the Banks at Edinburgh.[45]

The Glasgow banking companies had not been slow to press for legislation. The above-mentioned letter from Ingram to the Lord Privy Seal had been accompanied by a 'memorial' which contained a draft bill which, if passed, would have abolished the option clause and made all bank notes protestable by summary diligence. No mention was made of bank notes of small denominations.

In March, 1764 the Bank of Scotland agreed to a bill which would have abolished option clauses and all notes under £1. The bill also provided for summary diligence on bank notes.[46] This concession amounted to a severe defeat for the public banks, so the claim by the historian of the Royal Bank that the Act, when it was eventually passed in 1765, did so 'through the insistence of the two Edinburgh Banks',[47] is only partially true.

Parliament was prorogued on April 19th, 1764 with the result that there was not time to bring in the bill. It next met on January 10th, 1765 and the early months of that year saw renewed activity amongst those in whose interest it was to have the bill passed. The three Glasgow banks met regularly to discuss it, but although there were minor points of disagreement over the causes of Scotland's monetary troubles, they were generally agreed that the option clause should be banned, that notes should be protestable by summary diligence and that small notes should be dispensed with. There was much debate over whether they should make a recommendation in their memorial on the minimum value of notes. It was eventually decided to leave that question to the Scottish M.P.s.[48] In a letter to the Dundee Banking Co. dated February 21st 1765, Dempster stated that at a meeting of the Scottish members agreement had been reached on a bill which included the option clause and summary diligence provisions but which set the minimum note value at 5/–.[49] This was probably a bluff. It was known that the Scots bankers favoured £1 as the smallest denomination of note whilst English interests favoured the £5 note. The Scots M.P.s probably felt that if they asked for 5/– notes, then the English interests would settle for £1. In the outcome the Act of 5 George III c.49 set £1 as the smallest value of a Scottish bank note.

The Act when it was passed was regarded as something of a victory for the provincial banking companies because it gave their notes a firmer legal standing. Although the struggle for legal recognition had been achieved, the struggle for 'de facto' recognition had not yet been accomplished.

When it came into operation the Act caused the banking system to contract. Five shilling notes had formed a large part of the total issue. For example they had constituted 17 per cent of the circulation of the Dundee Banking Co.[50] Early in 1765 the directors of that bank had thought it prudent, in view of the impending legislation, to cut back their circulation. Consequently no new cash accounts were awarded.[51] In Perth, where six very small quasi-bankers had issued notes, five of them joined forces to form the Perth United Banking Co. Most importantly the private, non-bankers' issues, most of which had been very small notes, disappeared.

The Act was a milestone in the history of Scottish banking. Certainly it permitted freedom of issue which was a potentially destabilising factor, but it ensured that banks had to pay their notes on demand. It was this aspect of note issues which ensured their increasing popularity with customers, and it was not long before the system began, once more, to expand. The events of the next seven years, although traumatic, established a system of banking which became the envy of the world.

3. The Note Exchange

The notes of banks provided a convenient medium of exchange for customers and indeed for anyone who came into possession of them. They were not subject to the disadvantages of a gold coinage, i.e. clipping, and the Act of 1765 ensured

C

that note holders could secure, on demand, 'lawful money of Great Britain' for their notes. In practice, however, most of the notes returned to a bank were applied in the reduction of debtor balances rather than in the withdrawal of specie from the reserves. Banks always tried to dissuade customers from withdrawing specie or from purchasing bills on Edinburgh and London with their own notes because these practices reduced the circulation and the profits.

By 1765 many of the initial difficulties which had developed with the early growth of the system had been overcome, but one major problem remained. A bank was only obliged to pay specie for its notes at its head office. There was no way in which a provincial banking company could be made to pay specie or bills for its notes in another provincial city or in Edinburgh. A bank, based in the Capital, if it had taken provincial notes in the course of business, had to go to the expense and risk of sending them to their place of issue for payment. A provincial banker was similarly burdened if he accepted the notes of another provincial banking company or of one of the public banks. The consequence of this was that banks did not generally take the notes of others in the course of business. Although most provincial bank notes had a purely local circulation in and around their place of issue, non-acceptance by other banks was a serious inconvenience for merchants who sold goods over a wide area and who were offered the notes of several companies in payments. This problem became acute as the pace of business accelerated in the years under discussion. The exception to non-acceptance of other banks' notes was the arrangement which had existed between the Bank of Scotland and the Royal Bank since 1751.[52] These banks accepted each other's notes and exchanged them on a regular basis. The Dundee Banking Co. had made a trial of taking Edinburgh and Glasgow notes in 1764, but this practice was ended during the retrenchment caused by the withdrawal of small notes in 1765.[53]

Table 2 sets out the names, dates of opening and note circulations of provincial banks which were in existence in 1765, together with similar details of those founded between 1765 and 1772.

Between 1765 and 1770 several attempts usually on a bilateral basis were made to overcome the difficulties created by the non-acceptance of bank notes by other banks. Early in 1768 the Aberdeen and Perth United banking companies agreed to a mutual acceptance and exchange of notes[54] which had the effect of encouraging the use of notes rather than specie by those merchants who traded between Perth and Aberdeen. The note exchange was effected in Edinburgh by the agents of these companies. The ledgers of the Perth United show that the notes of the Dundee Banking Co. were accepted and exchanged at irregular intervals, seemingly by direct remittance between the two towns.[55] Nevertheless, a start had been made. Unfortunately, nothing is known about the situation in Glasgow where, by 1769, four banking companies had been founded. It seems likely, however, that some accommodation had been reached, at least amongst the three older companies who had developed a close relationship during the 'option clause' period in the early 1760s.[56] By 1768 some provincial banking companies had made a positive start towards following the example set by the public banks in accepting the notes of neighbouring banks. There remained, however, a good deal of mistrust between companies which were, geographically, further apart. In one particular case this mistrust was well founded.

Table 2
Scottish Provincial Banking Companies 1765–1772
Note Issuers

		Opened	Amount	Date of Figure
1.	Ship Bank, Glasgow	1750	£ 65,000	1761
2.	Arms Bank, Glasgow	1750	200,000	contemporary estimate[2]
3.	Thistle Bank, Glasgow	1761	64,000	1763
4.	G. Dempster & Co., Dundee	1763	32,000	1768
5.	J. Macadam & Co., Ayr	1763	15,000	estimated
6.	Perth United Banking Co.	1766	44,000	1768
7.	Johnston, Lawson & Co., Dumfries	1766	15,000	estimated
8.	Aberdeen Banking Co.	1767	43,000	1768
9.	General Bank of Perth	1767	10,000	estimated
10.	Douglas, Heron & Co., Ayr	1769	200,000	1772
11.	Merchant Bank of Glasgow	1769	25,000	estimated

Notes   1. Estimates are based on the size of other balance sheet figures or on notes retired by neighbouring banks.
         2. The estimate for the Arms Bank was probably based on notes printed rather than actually issued.
         3. The Glasgow private bank of David Watson did not issue notes.
Sources   Sederunt books, general ledgers, balance books and letters of banks.

The 'aristocratic' Thistle Bank of Glasgow, in order to increase its own circulation, employed agents, on a commission basis, to 'pick up' the notes of others from the circle and replace them with Thistle notes. This was achieved by approaching shopkeepers and merchants who held notes and effecting an exchange, possibly with some slight monetary advantage as an incentive. The circulation was further augmented by risk banking, i.e. by discounting long-dated bills which would normally be declined by a bank. Undoubtedly, some of the problems arose as a result of over-zealous agents who, without the knowledge of their head office, and because they were being paid by commission, were anxious to do as much business as possible even if it meant taking risks. Equally there can be no doubt of the later complicity of head offices who were keen to force their circulation and embarrass their competitors.

The British Linen Co., which had begun to assume a banking function, also engaged in 'note picking' of this nature. A compromise was reached between this company and the Aberdeen Banking Co. in 1768 whereby the former agreed to withdraw all its agents from the counties of Aberdeen, Banff and Kincardine. Each agreed not to molest the other's circulation.

The best documented record of such early bank wars in the provinces is that concerning the Aberdeen Banking Co. and the Thistle Bank. In the years 1767–8 the latter appointed agents in the northern counties which the Aberdeen Banking

Co., although a new arrival on the banking scene, was concerned to establish as its own, exclusive territory. The Thistle Bank collected Aberdeen notes and demanded specie in return for them. These demands caused the Aberdeen directors to retaliate in like manner. In addition to regular agents in the northern counties they also appointed note pickers in Edinburgh, Glasgow, Brechin, Montrose, Stirling, Falkirk, Ayr, Kilmarnock, Dumfries, Hawick and Kelso.[57] They decided that they would 'persevere in the present measures against the Thistle Bank till they withdraw their agents here'. Always at pains to establish their purity of motive, they claimed that they had 'no wanton inclination' to distress the Thistle Bank and that they were 'desirous upon reasonable terms to live in harmony with all their neighbours'. They were determined to adhere to this resolution even 'if they should throw away all their profits'.[58] In December 1769, however, the Aberdeen and Thistle banks agreed to submit their dispute to arbitration. The arbiters were Lord Gardenstone for the Aberdeen Banking Co. and Baron Mure of Caldwell for the Thistle Bank, both of whom were partners in their respective concerns. The discussion dragged on until August 1770, by which time several proposals of the arbiters had been rejected. By then, however, both sides had been exhausted by the hostilities and the Aberdeen directors stated to the Thistle Bank cashier that their conduct in future would be 'entirely regulated' by his.[59] The Aberdeen Banking Co. minutes made little reference to the Thistle Bank thereafter.

Some indication of the scale of the dispute was given in the *Glasgow Chronicle* of 1769. It was reported that

> the Bank of Aberdeen made a demand on the Thistle Bank of Glasgow for £41,000 stg.; which was immediately paid in gold and silver specie.[60]

The necessity imposed upon a bank of making provision for paying specie on this scale placed an enormous strain on its resources. At its annual balance in February, 1768 the Aberdeen Banking Co's. ratio of specie to demand liabilities was 61.2 per cent; in 1769 it was 46.3 per cent. In the latter year profit and loss account carried a debit balance of £962.[61]

The public banks in Edinburgh tried to remain aloof from this bank war. They still regarded the provincial banking companies as a group of upstart merchants who had no right to engage in banking. Nevertheless, they did become involved on the periphery of the fight. The Thistle Bank, in order to pay demands for specie, collected the notes of the Royal Bank and Bank of Scotland and presented them for payment in gold and silver. This hostile action did not provoke any retaliatory measure from the public banks, who seemed content to pay their notes and let the provincials continue to fight amongst themselves. Although the war between the Aberdeen Banking Co. and the Thistle was probably the most vicious, all the provincial companies were involved at some time either on the offensive or defensive.

Credit for the first real attempt to settle the conflict must go to the most maligned of the early Scottish banks – Messrs. Douglas, Heron and Co. (the Ayr

Bank). When this concern opened for business in November, 1769 its directors wrote to all the Scottish banks assuring them that it was their intention 'to hurt as little as possible any bank or banking company in Scotland'. They intended 'receiving payment of notes offered to them which are issued by any company of whose credit they have a good opinion'. In particular, they requested that other banks would accept their notes in payment and exchange at stated periods. The request met with a positive, if cautious, response from some of the provincial companies. The Perth United, Aberdeen, Dundee, Glasgow Ship and Glasgow Arms all agreed to accept Ayr notes in payments and to exchange them and each other's regularly in Edinburgh over a trial period.[62] The British Linen Co. later joined this arrangement. The response from the public banks, on the other hand, was entirely different. The Royal Bank replied that,

from a principle of living at peace with everybody in the banking trade and to prevent all suspicions of taking up notes for unfriendly purposes, they do not receive in payment any notes but these of the Bank of Scotland.[63]

They promised to retire any of their notes which were taken by Douglas, Heron and Co. and hoped for a 'good understanding' between the two concerns. The Bank of Scotland, in keeping with its agreement with the Royal, replied in a similar vein.

The choice of Edinburgh as the location of the exchange was significant in that it reaffirmed the role of Edinburgh as the commercial capital of Scotland even from the point of view of the provincial bankers who might have been expected to see Glasgow in this capacity. Furthermore, it provided a firm foundation of experience on which to build when the exchange became general in 1771. The exchange was to be carried out weekly by the Edinburgh agents of the companies involved because this was undoubtedly a far cheaper and more efficient method than each bank remitting parcels of notes to several different banks and receiving the same in return. Unfortunately, no details of the volume of business done or the manner of settlement have survived.

For a few months the exchange worked well but by May of 1770 Douglas, Heron and Co. were suspected of note picking. The main accuser was the ever sensitive Aberdeen Banking Co., which declined to exchange its notes from Douglas, Heron and Co. at Edinburgh from June of that year.[64] A note war of varying degrees of intensity ensued between Aberdeen and Ayr but the note exchange continued to operate although, for the moment, not to grow.

In May, 1771 the public banks decided to break with tradition and accept the notes of the provincial banking companies in payments. This, of course, involved an extension of the note exchange. The fact that a number of the provincial bankers had already been exchanging their notes in Edinburgh encouraged the directors of the Royal Bank and Bank of Scotland to think that they would continue to do so in an exchange which embraced all the Scottish banks and banking companies.

Several reasons may be given for this radical change of policy on the part of the Edinburgh banks. Customer demand was probably the most important. In a joint letter to the Aberdeen Banking Co. they claimed that the measure 'was adopted at the general desire of the Merchants and Traders about Edinburgh'.[65] This 'general desire' was not just that the traders' inconvenience of non-acceptance would be overcome but, more particularly, that the note issues of the provincial banks would be controlled if they were required to retire their notes regularly. An anonymous writer in the *Scots Magazine* of 1770 advocated just this line of action. As a lover of his country, he could not help deploring 'the pestiferous itch that has infected men to deal in banking', and his remedy for stable growth was the acceptance by the public banks of the notes of provincial companies. This, he claimed, would have the effect of keeping Edinburgh notes in circulation and confining the issues of the provincial banks within proper limit.[66]

In addition to a wish to satisfy their customers, the public banks were also motivated by a desire to bolster their falling profits. The Bank of Scotland complained that

> the business of banking is now very different from what it was formerly and that it is very difficult to keep the company's notes in circulation with profits owing to the late erection of many new banking companies.[67]

The Royal Bank were aware that their 'first and most obvious improvement' should be 'the extension of their circulation'.[68]

The factor which enabled the public banks to change their policy so dramatically was the infusion of new men into their courts in the years 1770 and 1771. This was particularly true of the Bank of Scotland which admitted a number of Edinburgh private bankers to the directorate.[69] These men stood to gain both from the increase in public bank circulation which would result and from the contribution of provincial banking companies to the exchange. As private bankers they were often the agents of these concerns and would represent them at the exchange for which they would be paid commission.

The public banks took pains to befriend the provincials and to assure them of their purity of motive. Gradually, over the months from May to August 1771, all provincial banking companies were informed that their notes would be taken by the public banks and that they would be expected to change them once per week in Edinburgh. The Bank of Scotland and Royal Bank agreed to a form of letter to be sent to the provincial companies which stated,

> as nothing is meant by this measure hostile against them it is hoped the consequent transactions will be carried on in the most amicable manner.[70]

Declarations of good intent were backed up with more material attractions. In letters to the Dundee and Glasgow bankers the Bank of Scotland informed them that if at any time they

> shall have occasion for the assistance of the Bank of Scotland in the way of discounts the Directors will accommodate them as far as they can with any degree of convenience, and in general do everything in their power to preserve a good understanding between the two societies.[71]

As subsequent events in 1772 proved, both of the public banks were prepared to help the provincial companies out of their difficulties, and by being prepared, in this way, to act as lenders of last resort, hoped to increase their own prestige and control of the banking system.

Two decades of hostility or at least mistrust had made some of the provincial banks wary of the embrace of the public banks. The ever cautious Aberdeen Banking Co. resisted all overtures, maintaining that it was merely a 'neighbourhood' bank and could not agree to an exchange of notes at Edinburgh 'without acting in contradiction to the very spirit of their institution'. The fact that they had done so in 1770 was quietly forgotten. They agreed to pay their notes at Aberdeen as the law required them to do but hoped that the public banks would 'continue to decline receiving the notes of this Company as formerly'. The other reason for staying out of the exchange was that the practice of note picking by the agents of other banks continued unabated,

> a practice which . . . will defeat every measure that can be proposed either for establishing banking on a proper footing or for promoting that harmony that ought to subsist among all banking societies.[72]

A further reason for non-participation in the exchange and for discouraging other banks from accepting their notes was that the Aberdeen directors believed that such a line of action would give a free rein to their note circulation. If other banks refused to accept Aberdeen notes and this had no adverse effect on their own customers' desire to take them, then these notes would tend to stay in circulation longer, thereby increasing the profitability of the note issue and maintaining the amount of business that could be done. A company which took part in the note exchange on the other hand, was required to tailor its business to the amount of notes which it could keep in the circle. In 1774 the cashier of the recently founded Hunters and Co., bankers in Ayr, regretted

> the unlucky resolution of the Edinburgh Banks to take in our notes, by which they do us too much honour . . . This has for two months past kept us both bare and busy, by exchanging every Monday at Edinburgh with the 3 banks there, and prevents us from discounting so freely as we have done.[73]

The note exchange was thus an effective check on excessive issues of notes by participating banks.

The Dundee and Perth United companies were of a similar mind to their friends in Aberdeen. They resisted the embrace of the public banks, who then resorted to a period of 'rough wooing' which showed that the public banks were determined to enforce the exchange if necessary. The tellers of the Royal Bank and Bank of Scotland were sent north to demand payment for notes of the provincial banks and on 18th September, 1771 they demanded payment for £5,400 of Dundee notes. The following day they demanded £15,300 from Perth.[74] These figures represented approximately 18 per cent and 30 per cent respectively of these companies' total note issues.[75] Their cashiers wrote to their friends in

Aberdeen to inform them of what had happened, whereupon the Aberdeen directors, fearful that they might be presented with a similar demand, decided to join the exchange 'so far as to make a tryall'.[76] The Perth United and Dundee companies were similarly impressed by the advantages of exchanging their notes regularly in Edinburgh and joined the exchange. The reason for the willingness of some provincial companies to exchange with one another in Edinburgh but to reject a similar measure with the public banks lies in their expectation of the scale of the exchange. They feared that there was a greater tendency for their notes to find their way to Edinburgh and to the public banks than to other provincial towns – hence their initial resistance to the general exchange.

In June, 1772 the Bank of Scotland decided not to accept any more Aberdeen notes in payment. The reason for this is not clear but it may be that the Aberdeen Banking Company was suspected of infirmity and the Bank of Scotland was merely playing safe in view of the impending crisis.[77] The Royal Bank followed suit. Neither concern accepted Aberdeen notes again until February, 1774. On that occasion the Aberdeen directors rehearsed all the old arguments and declined to rejoin the exchange.[78] They continued to retire their notes as they were required by law to do but this was achieved by the occasional remittance of parcels of notes to Aberdeen and the return of sight bills on Edinburgh in exchange. It was not until the Royal Bank became Edinburgh agent for the Aberdeen Banking Co. in 1782 that the northern bank again took up membership of the exchange.[79] When a branch of the Bank of Scotland opened in Aberdeen in 1780 a local exchange of notes was agreed upon.

But the Aberdeen Banking Company was an exception. In general the provincial banking companies settled down to live in peaceful coexistence with the public banks, and when new banking companies were formed in the next half century, often one of their first actions was to apply for admission to the note exchange. The bankers accepted that although the exchange might be a short-run limitation on their business, the long-run benefits were greater. As the public enjoyed greater confidence in the note issues and the practice of note picking ceased, bank notes came to replace specie in circulation to such an extent that banks were able to operate on fractional specie reserves which were often only 2 or 3 per cent of demand liabilities. Therefore the note exchange was a permissive factor in business expansion.

The effect of the note exchange as a control on the over-issue of notes was attested by the witnesses of the 1826 Parliamentary Committee on Promissory Notes in Scotland and Ireland. Alexander Blair, Secretary to the British Linen Co., thought that it was 'impossible that there should be an over issue of our notes under the system of note exchanges which exists at present'.[80] Other witnesses were of the same opinion.

The note exchange played an important part in developing the stability which was such an important feature of the Scottish banking system. It was not, however, an infallible guarantee of safe practice. Messrs. Douglas, Heron and Co. in 1771 found that their notes were being returned upon them quickly from the exchange, and rather than tailor their business to the amount of notes which they could effectively keep in the circle they resorted to 'the practice of drawing bills of exchange upon London' to pay for their returned notes and other debts. The number and value of these bills increased until when the bank failed in June, 1772 their amount exceeded £600,000.[81] The note exchange acted as an indicator of a bank's business capacity. Those who ignored it did so at their peril.

4. The Ayr Bank

In December, 1768 the Bank of Scotland decided to 'put some limitation to the transaction on cash accounts' because of the increased demand for specie and bills on London. They were concerned to protect the exchange rate and to ensure that the specie-exporting events of 1761–5 did not recur. Accordingly, all cash accounts over £1,000 were restricted to that sum, and in May, 1769 it was decided that the maximum advance on cash accounts would be £500. Cash acounts rather than bills were singled out for this treatment, 'it being the intention of the directors to encourage hereafter the practice of discounting bills'.[82] The Royal Bank took similar measures. Nevertheless by July, 1769 both banks had stopped buying London bills and discounting inland bills,[83] moves which were designed to deflate the economy and prevent the exchange rate rising beyond the specie export points.[84]

This period of retrenchment frustrated considerable demand for credit and gave rise to the formation of Messrs. Douglas, Heron and Co. (the Ayr Bank). This concern opened for business in Ayr on 6th November, 1769 and branches were opened in Dumfries and Edinburgh within a few days. The size of this organisation in terms of capital (£150,000) and numbers of partners (140) and the fact that it opened a branch in Edinburgh left no one in any doubt that its main intention was to rival the public banks.

In 1769 there were already banking companies in Ayr and Dumfries and the choice of these sites as the head office and branch of the new concern is worthy of some consideration. John McAdam and Co. had been founded at Ayr in 1763 and Johnston, Lawson and Co. at Dumfries in 1766. Neither of these banking companies appears to have been large or to have had extensive business. The Ayr and Dumfries areas were essentially agricultural. Dumfries was an important market in the cattle trade with England and both towns to some small extent indulged in the tobacco trade with America. It seems likely that there was considerable scope for the provision of banking services in the south-west corner of Scotland, and the agricultural improvements movement which was getting under way at this time created a further demand for bank credit which was almost certainly larger than could safely be supplied by either of the existing banking companies in that area. The advent of Douglas, Heron and Co. therefore was a logical extension of the financial system in Ayrshire and Galloway and the opening of a branch in Edinburgh doubtless gave added fluidity to the settlement of debts.

The basis of Douglas, Heron's credit was land. In this respect it was different from many of the other provincial banking companies which had been founded principally on mercantile credit. Although all of the provincial banking companies included some landowners amongst their partners, none of them could match the landed wealth of the partners of Douglas, Heron and Co. which was said to equal some £3–4 millions.

Much of the land which was the basis of the company's credit was owned by the Douglas family. The Dukes of Queensberry and Buccleuch and Archibald Douglas of Douglas were all major shareholders; indeed the only major branch of the Douglas family not involved was that headed by the Duke of Hamilton. It was this branch of the family which had just lost the famous 'Douglas Case' to Archibald Douglas of Douglas so that its omission is not surprising. The other family which was heavily engaged in the bank was the Fergusons. This family seems to have been a satellite of the Douglas family and, although not nearly so wealthy, several members became deeply committed in the Ayr Bank. The roll of subscribers to the contract of co-partnery is an impressive list of the major landowners, and many of the minor ones, in South-West Scotland. Henry Hamilton thought that

> This lends substance to the view that agricultural improvements were being held in check by lack of working capital and that the chartered banks were doing little to help.[85]

This opinion is reinforced by the fact that 'some of the directors received credits before their shares had been paid up'.[86]

The motto adopted by the bank was 'Pro Bono Publico'. The proprietors thought that banking, 'when carried on on proper principles, is of great public utility, particularly to the commerce, manufactures, and agriculture of a country', with the result that they founded their bank on a 'solid, creditable and respectable footing'.[87] They felt that 'The utility and advantage of a bank of this kind to the country is too obvious to require any commentary'.[88] It seems likely that they felt the action of the public banks in protecting the exchange rate by deflating the economy whilst inhibiting imports would also limit finance for export industries and that therefore such action was counter-productive. They believed that 'too extensive credits could not be afforded to the Country, if unquestionable security was given to the bank'.[89]

The nominal capital of the bank was £150,000 of which £96,000 was subscribed when it opened for business. Twenty per cent was paid up at that date but further calls appear to have followed fairly rapidly. In May, 1772 it was found necessary to increase the nominal capital by £50,000[90] and the paid up capital in June 1772 was £130,000.[91]

From the outset the bank was guilty of overtrading. In addition to the branches at Dumfries and Edinburgh, agencies were established at Glasgow, Inverness, Kelso, Montrose, Campbeltown and other places[92] so that there was an agency or branch in every region of the country. Their main function was to circulate the notes of the bank and they did so with great enthusiasm. At one stage it was estimated that the notes of the Ayr Bank constituted two thirds of the total Scottish note issue, as the agents indulged in picking up the notes of other banks and placing Douglas, Heron notes in the circle in place of those removed. There was a particularly vituperative note war of this nature between the Ayr Bank and the Aberdeen Banking Company which was not settled until the latter joined the Edinburgh note exchange in September, 1771. The excess of notes thus issued 'would perpetually return upon the Company to be exchanged for other value', with the result that they would be 'perpetually contracting debts somewhere for answering the demands upon them'.[93] A vast London debt was built up both to meet repayments of notes and to pay bills.

The practice of drawing and redrawing bills on London was soon resorted to by the Ayr Bank. It was estimated that the money thus raised cost eight per cent per annum, whilst the bank received only five per cent on its advances. When the bank stopped payment in 1772 there were upwards of £600,000 of debts due in London in addition to £200,000 of notes in circulation and £300,000 of private loans to the company.[94]

The advances made by the company were

> placed so injudiciously, that they became in fact permanent loans of money; and the stream which by this means once issued from the company, being in reality never replenished, the company lost the command of their funds.[95]

The advances made to the proprietors allowed many of them to borrow what they had just paid in capital instalments. 'Such payment . . . only put into one coffer what had the moment before been taken out of another'.[96] The writers of *The Precipitation and Fall* complained not so much about 'the extent of our operations, so much as the partiality of them; not the greatness of the debt, so much as the fewness of the debtors'. It appeared to them that 'The great and cumbersome debtors of the Company, were the managers themselves'.[97]

Subsequent writers tried to be more explicit. Glover in *The Substance of the Evidence* maintained that the 'Liberalism' of Douglas, Heron and Co. 'consisted in financing speculation in West Indian property, building extravagance for the penurious nobility of Scotland and, in general every kind of social pretension which needed capital for its fulfilment'.[98] This type of finance was clearly at variance with their declared objectives. Much of the material written about the Ayr Bank was highly tendentious but there can be no doubt that a good deal of the credit which the bank was providing was converted into long-term loans which was bad banking because the notes which were issued when loans were first made came back for payment long before the loan was repaid. This imposed upon the bank the necessity of either finding specie or bills to pay them, and from an early date they chose the latter method. Consequently, they borrowed heavily in London to finance these bills. In March, 1771 the Edinburgh directors sent a deputation to London seeking relief. In a letter to the deputation the directors who remained in Edinburgh wrote that we are at this moment sitting here in a very disagreeable agitation of spirits, without any Edinburgh paper to assist us, no gold in the house, people waiting in the office for change, who have repeatedly called, and as often been denied, unless they would take draughts on London.[99]

That crisis was overcome by a remission of specie from Dumfries but it was a situation which must have recurred. Early in 1772 the Bank of Scotland loaned £10,000 in gold to Douglas, Heron for fifty days. Two weeks later a further loan of £5,000 in specie and bills was made and this figure was augmented one week later on 15th April, 1772 by £7,000.

Much of the trouble experienced by the Ayr Bank stemmed from mismanagement which was, in turn, caused by the inexperience of the directors. In a letter to the Duke of Queensberry in 1773 Alexander Ferguson, one of the directors at Edinburgh admitted that he

had not knowledge or experience sufficient to enable him to judge, what was the extent of credit that in prudence we ought to have given the country upon our then in paid capital.

He thought his fellow directors were equally ignorant and felt that he and they had opened their banking business 'without any experience to enable us to conduct ourselves properly'.[100] They took no account of the reflux of notes, while the establishment of a separate and almost wholly autonomous directorate at each of the three offices hindered effective management.

Whilst the directors pleaded ignorance as an excuse, some of the other partners, writing some years later in *The Precipitation and Fall*, accused them of criminal negligence and implied that there had been criminal intent:

we cannot, with justice, or propriety, confine the charge against the Managers of the Company to mere imprudence, ignorance or speculative errors.

If those established rules of conduct had been observed, even with a moderate degree of fidelity the Company's affairs could not have been plunged into such distress and ruin.[101]

Certainly there is much to be answered in the allegations made by the proprietors, but some of their charges were either highly contentious or sheer nonsense. One of the items with which they charged the directors was that when a directors' meeting at one of the branches was inquorate it often occurred that a director from another branch was invited to make up a quorum. This, they maintained, was unconstitutional but section eight of the contract provided for just such a situation.

In May, 1771 a general meeting enacted a bye-law whereby the consent of all three boards was required before a new cash account could be granted. This was apparently ignored on several occasions. The excuse was made by the Ayr directors that this was done because of the agreement entered into with the proprietors of John McAdam and Co. when that bank was taken over in 1771. They maintained that the contract obliged them to make advances to customers of the McAdam Bank. There were similar alleged irregularities when the Dumfries bank of Johnston, Lawson and Co. was taken over in the later months of 1771.

Both the proprietors of John McAdam and Co. and of Johnston, Lawson and Co. were made to sign undertakings that they would not undertake any banking enterprises in Galloway, Ayr, Kirkcudbright or Dumfries unless it was with Douglas, Heron and Co. This clause in the contracts suggests that Douglas, Heron was interested in creating a monopoly of banking services in the South-West. The price paid for Johnston, Lawson and Co. was £7,350 and for John McAdam and Co. £18,000. This latter figure was equivalent to twelve years' purchase.

When the collapse of Douglas, Heron and Co. occurred in June, 1772 it was not altogether unexpected. In December, 1771 the Bank of Scotland had proposed that the Ayr Bank should have its cash credit cut back to £5,000 and insisted that it register its contract with the Court of Session. The Royal Bank saw no reason for this credit reduction but agreed to the demand for the registration of the contract and throughout the early months of 1772 the Ayr Bank sought frequent loans of specie from other bankers.

The failure of Neale, James, Fordyce and Downe in London on June 10th, 1772 set off a wave of failure throughout the United Kingdom. There had been commercial crises before but this was the first which involved the banks to any extent. In the two weeks following the first London failure several Edinburgh-based private bankers stopped payment. This put Douglas, Heron and Co. under increased pressure, as a run on them for specie in exchange for notes began, following the circulation of rumours. They attempted to restore confidence by placing a notice in the papers offering a reward of £100 for information leading to the conviction of the 'person or persons who have been concerned in raising such an infamous report'.[102] At the same time they were applying to the public banks for further loans. They assured these banks that they had sufficient funds to cover their engagements to the London houses which had failed. They requested a loan in London bills and asked that 'the banks will allow £10,000 for the notes in the hands of each to lie at interest and take the balance at the daily exchange in their favour in London bills for four or six months'.[103] This was refused. At the same time the Duke of Queensberry had applied to the Bank of England for help. This too was turned down. A further round of failure on June 24th caused the Ayr Bank to close its doors on June 25th and a notice of suspension was inserted in the newspapers. It assured the holders of notes that the Ayr Bank was established on a solid foundation and that it would pay 5 per cent interest on its notes after 26th June. This was strictly illegal in terms of the 1765 Bank Act but the alternative was a general bankruptcy in terms of the Bankruptcy Act which had been passed only the previous month. Such a course of action would have caused more problems than it solved. Most people were content to hold their Ayr Bank notes, secure in the knowledge that the Duke of Queensberry alone could pay all the obligations of the bank several times over. The immediate problem was liquidity.

Several London traders and merchants, amongst whom there were very few Scots, opened a subscription to indemnify the Bank of England against loss if it would discount Douglas, Heron's bills, while notices began to appear in the papers informing readers that the country's leading nobles and gentry would accept the notes of Douglas, Heron and Co. in payment. Many of these men, like the Duke of Argyll, had no direct connection with the Bank and it appeared that the Ayr Bank was indeed founded upon a 'solid, respectable and creditable footing' even if it was not very credible. But directors, when given warning of their precarious situation in the early months of 1771, had made little attempt to extricate themselves from the situation, indeed they got deeper into trouble. The problems of the bank were so well appreciated that a London writer was able to compose the obituary of the Bank several days before it expired.[104]

The effects of the closure of Douglas, Heron and Company on the Scottish economy are difficult to assess. This is partly because of the blame which attaches to other bankers and traders who were also guilty of feeding the inflationary pressures, although not to the same extent. Numerous Edinburgh private banks stopped payment, as did the Glasgow Merchant Banking Company. This concern and a few others reopened after a few months' closure. Many did not. The credit-worthiness of other banks was underwritten by public subscription and the only other provincial bank to close permanently in this year was the General Bank of Perth, though it is not known exactly when it closed or if it had anything to do with the Ayr Bank crash.

A trade and industrial depression followed the 1772 crisis and work was suspended for a time on the New Town in Edinburgh and on the Monkland and the Forth and Clyde Canals. Tax yields fell. The responsibility of the Ayr Bank for all this could be long debated. When the Bank had opened in 1769 the Scottish economy was on the crest of a trade boom and a slump was bound to follow, considering that there was no systematic control of the money supply and banks were able to feed the speculation. Within two years of 1772 the economy was showing signs of a revival of business activity and by 1775 the recovery was well under way. In the long run the crash seems to have had few really damaging consequences.

Even in the short run those who were not directly concerned do not seem to have been unduly perturbed. In July, 1772 a 'Friend to the Public Credit' wrote to the papers stating that he was

> happy to find that the cloud which has now been gathering for a good many years; and threatening the credit of the country, has at last broke without doing much damage in a national way.

He was convinced that 'what had happened of late must have been foreseen by every man of judgement'.[105] If men of judgement had foreseen the crash, then they would have extricated themselves from the situation and escaped unharmed.

The people who lost most in the crisis were the partners in the bank. 'By August, 1775 only 112 out of 226 remained solvent.' The partners ultimately had to pay £663,397.[106] This amounted to £2,200 per £500 share, although some dividends were returned on solvent shares in the early 19th century. These returns were (as far as known): 1807 £60, 1811 £18, 1816 £20. Blocks of debts due to the bank were auctioned by public roups in the 1790s but many debts remained unsold, though some of these were still thought to be good. The debts owed by

Messrs. Garbet and Gascoigne, who had been involved in the large Carron Iron Company, proved particularly difficult to collect. In 1811 attempts were still being made to bring Gascoigne's money home from Russia.[107]

The calls on partners' shares caused considerable distress and bankruptcy. It has been estimated that £750,000 of property changed hands,[108] which constituted an active market in land. In 1780 Wm. Fairlie wrote home from Calcutta that

> Many of our India gentlemen are now bringing home their money for the purchase of lands which they imagine must be sold at a very low purchase. Mr. Ferguson is now sending home a few thousand pounds for that purpose.[109]

The group of people who made most from the crisis were the lawyers, who handled the fifty years of litigation which followed 1772. In many cases these men bought land which came onto the market as a result of bankruptcies. They were later to be noted for their agricultural improvements whilst being more prudent than the previous owners of their land.

When the Bank had closed its doors in June, 1772 it was hoped to reopen in three months' time and to resume a banking business, but it never did. In the meantime the proprietors had to find cash with which to meet their obligations. In July the Duke of Buccleuch was successful in persuading the public banks to take Douglas, Heron notes up to £120,000 provided suitable terms of repayment could be arranged.[110] This obviated the need to draw any more bills on London. Further attempts to raise cash on personal and then on heritable property proved to be inadequately productive and resort was then made to the sale of annuities, which was approved at a general meeting on November 2nd, 1772. These raised £450,000 as the rate payable on them was equivalent to between 12 and 15 per cent. Much of the money thus raised was mismanaged and one partner received a loan of £2,500 to enable him to pay a protested bill. Some £6,000 of the money was never accounted for.

The annuities were, however, a temporary expedient. They were redeemable. In 1774 the proprietors presented a bill to Parliament which, when passed, enabled them to convert the annuities into bonds which bore interest at 5 per cent. The money raised by the bonds was to be used to re-purchase the annuities and money realised from the Bank's assests was, in turn, to be used for re-purchasing the bonds.[111] Between 1772 and 1774 the 'Bank' was merely a front to service the annuities.

The Bank had begun to pay the interest on its notes in October, 1772 at Edinburgh and Dumfries, and to repay the notes themselves at Ayr, and things appeared to be moving quite smoothly or, at least, so the proprietors were given to believe. The November, 1772 general meeting was adjourned until January, 1773 but on December 21st preceding the directors entered a notice in the papers to the effect that 'the present situation of the company's affairs does not make such meeting necessary, they adjourn the same till further notice'.[112]

The extent to which the affairs of the bank were being run by a small clique is revealed in the correspondence of George Home who was later appointed to be 'factor and manager' of the Company's affairs. In a letter to his brother dated March 22nd, 1773 he revealed that although it was known to only five or six persons, it had been decided to wind up the company. He offered to his brother, who was in need of funds for his estate, help in securing for him, on heritable security, the deposit of £20,000 which the Court of Session held with the Ayr Bank as this would now come on the open market when the Bank closed. No other bank would accept the money as a deposit.[113]

A general meeting of the Bank on August 12th, 1773 resolved that the Bank should give up business, i.e. the annuities, and George Home was then appointed factor and manager.[114] In all these moves the three Douglas men, Queensberry, Buccleuch and Archibald Douglas of Douglas, figured prominently. These were the men who had the most to lose.

Throughout the winding up of Douglas, Heron and Co's. affairs the creditors maintained confidence in the ultimate ability of the Company to pay its debts. The public ultimately lost nothing in the debacle, but if the Bank had been managed properly the proprietors would have been equally fortunate.

The Ayr Bank was an attempt to provide banking services for the Scottish public which had been poorly, if at all, served by the public banks and which had been inadequately served in some areas by the existing provincial banks. Its main spheres of business were in the South and West of Scotland but its branch in Edinburgh actively competed with the public banks. The success it achieved in advancing credits and circulating its notes was remarkable. It has been estimated that at one stage its total liabilities formed 40 per cent of the total liabilities of all Scottish banks.[115] It numbered Carron Company amongst its borrowers and the Court of Session amongst its depositors. The reason for its success in attracting business is to be found in its liberality. It took no thought for the exchanges, as did the public banks which were trying to protect Scotland's specie supply by contracting credit. Furthermore it was prepared to accept customers' deposits at interest before the public banks developed this facility as a regular part of their services.

The Ayr Bank was an aberration from the trend of banking development, as the landholdings of the partners made it seem more like a John Law-type land bank than a Scottish provincial banking company. The ambition of the directors was not matched by their knowledge of banking principles and the failure proved to be a useful lesson to Scottish banks, many of whom had been caught up in the speculative fever. The Merchant Bank of Glasgow was forced to close its doors for a time and the other Glasgow banking companies swallowed their pride and asked the public banks for loans to tide them over the difficult period.[116] The crisis might have been much worse if the Edinburgh banks had not been prepared to act as lender of last resort in this instance.

The closure of the Ayr Bank left Scottish bankers straitened but wiser. The Bank Act of 1765, the formation of the note exchange and the salutary experience of 1772 had laid the foundations on which succeeding generations built a system which, in its day, was unique.

NOTES

1. Appendix A, Ship Bank Balance Sheets
2. Sir James Steuart, ed. A. S. Skinner, 1966, pp. 483–4
3. R.B.S., D.M.B. 6/10/1749 and N. L. S. Saltoun MSS., Banking papers. Memo *re* Aberdeen Bank
4. R.B.S., D.M.B. 3/11/1749
5. B.S., D.M.B., 6/7/1749 and 20/10/1749
6. N. Munro, 1928, p. 111
7. R.B.S., D.M.B., 23/11/1750
8. B.S., Miscellaneous Documents Edinburgh, Minute of the Two Banks Committee, 1/1/1752
9. B.S., D.M.B., 2/1/1752
10. D. Hume, ed. Rotwein, 1955, pp. 71–2
11. R.B.S., D.M.B., 27/7/1751
12. B.S., D.M.B., 2/1/1752
13. See Appendix A, Ship Bank Balance Sheets. Cash accounts drawn £38,000 – assume £50,000 authorised; bills discounted £9,000. Assume similar figures for Arms Bank, 1752
14. R.B.S., D.M.B., 27/7/1751
15. J. S. Fleming, 1877, Appendix B
16. *Scots Magazine*, January, 1752
17. B.S., D.M.B., 3/6/1756
18. *Ibid.*, 18/10/1756
19. S.R.A., TD 161/1, Ship Bank Balance Ledger
20. S.G. Checkland, 1975, Table 34
21. B.S. D.M.B., 18/10/1756
22. *Ibid.*, 18/10/1756
23. *Ibid.*, 3/2/1757
24. B.S., Miscellaneous Documents, Edinburgh Minutes of Two Banks Committee, 1756–7
25. *Ibid.*, 15/6/1757
26. R.B.S., D.M.B., 7/4/1757
27. Sir Wm. Forbes, 1860, p. 5n
28. *Ibid.*, p. 6n. See Morison's *Dictionary of Decisions*, p. 14607
29. R.B.S., D.M.B., 19/10/1759
30. *Ibid.*, 6/3/1761
31. C. W. Boase, 1867, P. xvii
32. R.B.S., D.M.B., 18/11/1765
33. B.S., D.M.B., 5/7/1764 and 11/6/1766
34. Ibid., 10/2/1762
35. Ibid., 15/12/1763, 22/12/1763 and 31/1/1764
36. *Scots Magazine*, 1764, p. 595
37. *Ibid.*, p. 89
38. H. Hamilton, 'Scotland's Balance of Payments Problem in 1762', in *Economic History Review*, 1952–3, p. 349
39. Sir James Steuart, 1966, p. 506
40. B.S., D.M.B., 30/12/1763
41. *Ibid.*, 6/1/1764
42. *Scots Magazine*, 1763–4
43. Mure of Caldwell, Part 2, vol. 1, 1883, p. 234
44. B.S., D.M.B., 1/2/1764
45. Mure of Caldwell, Part 2, vol. 1, 1883, pp. 208–9
46. 5 George III Ch. 49
47. Munro, 1928, p. 128
48. Mure of Caldwell, 1883 Part 2, vol. 2, p. 4
49. Boase, 1867, p.5
50. *Ibid.*, Balance Sheet 1765
51. Dundee Banking Co. Minute Book, 21/2/1765
52. R.B.S., D.M.B., 27/7/1751
53. Dundee Banking Co., D.M.B., 30/7/1764 and 24/8/1765
54. Aberdeen Banking Co., Letter Book, 30/1/1768
55. Perth United Banking Co., General Ledgers, 1768, 1769

56. Mure of Caldwell, 1885, part 2, vol. 2, p. 3
57. R. S. Rait, 1930, pp. 155–7
58. Aberdeen Banking Co., Agents' Letter Book, 12/7/1768
59. *Ibid.*, D.M.B., 17/8/1770
60. *Scots Magazine*, 1770, p. 333
61. Aberdeen Banking Co., Balance Books, 1768, 1769
62. *Ibid.*, D.M.B., 5/1/1770
63. R.B.S., D.M.B., 16/11/1769
64. Aberdeen Banking Co., D.M.B., 11/6/1770
65. *Ibid.*, D.M.B., 13/9/1770
66. *Scots Magazine*, 1770, pp. 353–4
67. B.S., D.M.B., 9/12/1771
68. R.B.S., D.M.B., 4/12/1771
69. N. Munro, 1928, pp. 398–415 and C. Malcolm, *The Bank of Scotland*, n.d., pp. 68–9 and 293–302
70. B.S., Edinburgh Miscellaneous Documents, Bundle 539
71. *Ibid.*, D.M.B., 10/7/1771
72. Aberdeen Banking Co., D.M.B. 14/8/1771
73. R. S. Rait, 1930, p. 176
74. Aberdeen Banking Co., D.M.B., 20/9/1771 and 24/9/1771
75. C. W. Boase, 1867, and Perth United Banking Co., General Ledger, 1771
76. Aberdeen Banking Co., D.M.B., 24/9/1771
77. *Ibid.*, D.M.B., 5/6/1772
78. *Ibid.*, D.M.B., 25/2/1774
79. R.B.S., D.M.B., 17/6/1782
80. P. P. Promissory Notes Committee, 1826, Evidence of Alex. Blair, p. 48
81. A. Smith, 1970, p. 413
82. B.S., D.M.B., 14/12/1768 and 24/5/1769
83. Aberdeen Banking Co., D.M.B., 24/7/1769
84. Anon., 'The Royal Bank and The London-Edinburgh Exchange Rate in the Eighteenth Century', in *Three Banks Review*, June, 1958, No. 38
85. H. Hamilton, 1963, p. 318
86. *Ibid.*
87. *Scots Magazine*, 1772, p. 304, extracts from the contract of the Ayr Bank
88. *Ibid.*, 1769, pp. 668–9
89. N.L.S., Fettercairn MSS., Second deposit Box. 54, Letter Alex. Ferguson to Duke of Queensberry, April, 1773
90. *Scots Magazine*, 1772, p. 304, extracts from contract
91. Anon., *The Precipitation and Fall of Messrs. Douglas, Heron and Co. late Bankers in Ayr*, 1778, p. 86
92. A. W. Kerr, 1926
93. *The Precipitation and Fall*, p. 18
94. *Ibid.*, p. 86
95. *Ibid.*, p. 19
96. A. Smith, 1970, p. 413
97. *The Precipitation and Fall*, pp. 27, 49
98. C. H. Wilson, 1941, p. 171
99. *The Precipitation and Fall*, App. 5, p. 56
100. N.L.S., Fettercairn MSS., Ferguson Letter
101. *The Precipitation and Fall*, p. 20
102. *Scots Magazine*, 1772, p. 313
103. R.B.S., D.M.B., 24/6/1772
104. *Scots Magazine*, 1772, p. 313
105. *Glasgow Journal*, 9/7/1772
106. Kerr, 1926, p. 93
107. Home of Wedderburn MSS., S.R.O. GD267/4/20, Letters 1788–1816
108. H. Hamilton, 1963, p. 325
109. Pollok-Morris MSS., Letter William Fairlie to Patrick Clark 23/8/1780
110. B.S., D.M.B., July, 1772
111. 14 George III, ch. 21

112. *Edinburgh Advertiser*, 21/12/1772
113. Home of Wedderburn MSS., GD 267/12/8
114. *Ibid.*, GD267/4/20
115. S. G. Checkland, 1975, Table 7. At the same time other provincial banking companies formed 25 per cent, public banks 21 per cent and private bankers 14 per cent of the system.
116. R.B.S., D.M.B., 30/6/1772

2

The Expanding System, 1772–1793

AFTER 1772 the economy went into depression but it was not long before bank advances began to rise toward their former levels, suggesting that recovery was on the way. In the case of the Aberdeen Banking Company they increased from year to year without interruption. Those of the Dundee Banking Company had regained their pre-1772 levels by 1773, though the Perth United Banking Company did not manage this until 1776.[1] The Merchant Bank of Glasgow was able to re-open its doors as early as October, 1772.[2]

1. The System Expands

At the end of 1772 there were eight provincial banking companies in Scotland. A further thirteen were formed in the next twenty years. Table 3 sets out the formations and closures in the period between 1772 and 1793.

The most notable feature in Table 3 is the relatively small scale of the enterprises in terms of numbers of partners although most were larger than their English counterparts – the country banks. There was no attempt to repeat the Ayr Bank type of experiment. Only the Perth Banking Company was of any size and it was really a re-formation of the Perth United whose initial contract period of 21 years had expired.

The failure of the Ayr Bank created an hiatus in the provision of banking services in the towns of Ayr and Dumfries but it was not long before the gap was filled. In January, 1773 a plan was already afoot to form a new banking company in Ayr. Three members of the Hunter family were partners, the most active of whom was James Hunter, merchant in Ayr, who had been an employee of the Ayr Bank. His son-in-law Wm. Wood, Junior, was the fourth partner. Another member of the family was a secret partner for a time. He was also called James Hunter and was a member of the Edinburgh private bank of Sir Wm. Forbes, James Hunter and Co., but when the connection was leaked he withdrew for fear that his participation would prejudice his other business interests. Nevertheless, he proved to be a useful source of advice and information to his relations in Ayr.

It was not only the local men who recognised the need for banking services. Provost Cochrane of the Glasgow Arms Bank had asked James Hunter to be agent for that bank in Ayr, and when rebuffed, put pressure on Hunter's friends not to participate in the new concern.[3] Nevertheless, the plans for the bank went ahead

Table 3

Scottish Provincial Banking Companies 1772–1793

		Year of opening		Remarks
a)	*Banks in existence at end of 1772*			
	Note Issuers			
1.	Ship Bank, Glasgow	1750		re-organised 1775–6
2.	Arms Bank, Glasgow	1750		failed 1793
3.	Thistle Bank, Glasgow	1761		
4.	Dundee Banking Co.	1763		
5.	Perth United Banking Co.	1766		1787 re-formed as No.16
6.	Aberdeen Banking Co.	1767		
7.	Merchant Bank of Glasgow	1769		closed temporarily 1772
	Private Banks			
8.	D. Watson, Glasgow	c.1763		became J. & R. Watson c.1793

		Year of opening	No. of partners	Remarks
b)	*Banks formed 1773–1793*			
	Note Issuers			
9.	Hunters & Co., Ayr	1773	4	
10.	Stirling Banking Co.	1777	8	
11.	Paisley Banking Co.	1783	9	
12.	Merchant Bank of Stirling	1784	7	
13.	Greenock Banking Co.	1785	4	
14.	Falkirk Banking Co.	1787	11	
15.	Campbell, Thomson & Co., Stirling	1787	c.4	
16.	Perth Banking Co.	1787	99	re-formation of No.5
17.	Paisley Union Banking Co.	1788	10	
18.	Commercial Bank of Aberdeen	1788	16	
19.	Leith Banking Co.	1792	18	
20.	Dundee Commercial Banking Co.	1792	10	
	Private Banks			
21.	A., G. and A. Thomson, Glasgow	1785	3	failed 1793

Table 4

Regional Patterns: No. of Banking Companies

	1772	1793
Glasgow and South-West	5	8
Edinburgh and South-East	–	1
Tayside/Fife	2	3
Central	–	4
North-East/Highlands	1	2
	8	18

and it was opened on 1st October, 1773. The paid-in capital was only £5,000 which made it a very small-scale affair, and its management was cautious, having learned valuable lessons from the crisis of the previous year. No cash accounts were to be awarded, in the light of 'the present state of the Credit of this Country' for there was a fear that these advances might be used to pay off debts due to Douglas, Heron and Co. As a general principle, it was laid down that 'the truest maxim in Banking is to extend Engagements as powers increase and not to expect additional powers from extending engagements'.[4] This was an accurate summary of the main lesson to be learned from the collapse of the Ayr Bank.

In August, 1773 the projectors of Hunters and Co. heard of a plan to set up a new bank in Dumfries which they regarded as their own area of business and attempted to get Hugh Lawson to take a share in their bank and to be their agent.[5] Lawson had founded the Dumfries Bank in 1766 but had not taken shares in the Ayr Bank when it took over Johnston, Lawson and Co. in 1771. Nothing came of this and the provision of banking services was left to the Bank of Scotland which set up a branch in that town in 1774.

In 1775, the business community of Glasgow and the West 'ran into its first great commercial storm when the War of American Independence left [them] with no obvious staple'.[6] The tobacco merchants did not take long to develop other business interests but the outbreak of the war caused some dislocation in the banking sector. The Ship Bank (Dunlop, Houston and Co.) closed its doors. The circumstances of this event are not known, but it seems that with the collapse of the tobacco trade its raison d'être vanished. There is no suggestion that it failed.

In the early months of 1775, the Royal Bank made a determined bid to capture some of the Glasgow banking business. They employed Dugald Campbell of Campbeltown to attempt to oust the Thistle Bank from the business of financing the warehousing of West Indies sugar before its re-export to Ireland. This venture was unsuccessful but it suggests that the Glasgow bankers were weakened by the outbreak of war and were therefore vulnerable to this type of assault.[7] In September, 1775 the Royal offered a loan of £50,000 to the Arms and Thistle Banks. Wm. Simpson, their teller, was sent to offer the loan at 5 per cent, or 4 per cent if the higher rate was refused. The outcome was not recorded but it is interesting to speculate that at a time when the Bank of Scotland had begun to open branches in other provincial areas the Royal Bank was trying to establish a strong position within the Glasgow business community. Its attempts to do so were, for the moment, unsuccessful.

Early in 1776, the Ship Bank was re-organised. The firm was Moores, Carrick and Co. which soon afterwards became Carrick, Brown and Co. The managing partner was Robert (Robin) Carrick, who had been an employee of the old Ship Bank. The other principal partner was John Brown. Carrick and Brown had been in partnership since 1761 as muslin manufacturers and they had bought substantial tracts of land in the city as an investment. The formation of this bank was important in two particular respects for it reflected the shifting economic power in the city from the tobacco trade to textile manufacturing which formed the basis of the industrial revolution. Secondly the company was opened initially in the old Ship Bank office in the Bridgegate, off the Saltmarket, then the centre of economic activity. But it soon moved into a new office in Glassford Street. Carrick and Brown had foreseen the westward growth of the city and had invested in land in the new building areas. To encourage this they moved their bank into the new town.[8]

The year 1776 saw the publication of Adam Smith's *Wealth of Nations*. At that time he calculated the whole circulation of Scotland to be £2m. of which he thought gold and silver coins formed 25 per cent. The remaining £1.5m. he claimed consisted of banknotes. These figures have been challenged by Professor S. G. Checkland who found that total note circulations in 1772 were only £864,000.[9] Although the circulation of coin in Scotland had decreased by half since 1707, Smith considered that Scotland's

> real riches and prosperity do not appear to have suffered any. Its agriculture, manufactures and trade, on the contrary, the annual produce of its land and labour, have evidently been augmented.[10]

The period of the industrial revolution was not far distant and this quotation shows that some indicators had already taken an upward turn.

The second of the new banking company formations in this period took place in Stirling in 1777. Stirling had a very mixed economy. There was an important malting and distilling industry and a market for agricultural produce. The town was also of growing importance in the manufacture of coarse woollens, much of which was exported. There were eight partners in the new banking company and the nominal capital was £30,000.[11]

The upsurge of economic activity during the 1780s coincided with the end of the American War of Independence and heralded the arrival of the industrial revolution. The few balance sheet figures which are available for this period and which are reproduced in Appendix A are testimony to this spurt in growth. For example total advances of the Perth United Banking Co. increased from £28,000 in 1775 to £64,000 in 1784. Between 1783 and 1792 eleven new enterprises were begun, most of which were located in the larger burghs.

In 1783 the Paisley Banking Co. was begun by a group of nine men who were mostly merchants in the Paisley and Glasgow area. The town of Paisley was an important centre of the textile industry where silk gauze and later muslins were the staple products.

A second banking company was formed there in 1788 when a group of ten landowners and merchants set up the Paisley Union Banking Co. The leading partner was George Houston of Johnstone. His business interests included cotton spinning and coal mining.

The duplication of banking services was extended to Stirling in 1784 when a group of merchants established the Merchant Bank of Stirling. There was a further formation in 1787 when Campbell, Thomson, and Co. was founded. Neither of these companies was of any size.

In 1785 the Greenock Banking Co. opened for business. There were four partners, two of whom were landowners and merchants; the others were merchants. Greenock was an important port, the main trading areas being the Highlands and Islands, Ireland and the Americas.

The Falkirk Banking Co. was founded in 1787 by a group of eleven men, most of whom were merchants in Falkirk. The town was at that time the largest cattle market in Scotland and there were also sizeable malting and distilling industries.

The year 1787 also saw the opening of the Perth Banking Co., but this was merely a re-formation of the Perth United Banking Co. whose original 21-year contract had expired. A new contract was drawn up, new partners were admitted and the old note issue was withdrawn and replaced by a new issue. All cash account loans had to be re-negotiated.

Aberdeen was blessed with a second banking company in 1788. The Commercial Banking Co. of Aberdeen was a breakaway organisation from the Aberdeen Banking Co, and similarly the Dundee Commercial Banking Co. was formed in 1792 by a group of men who had formerly been partners and customers of the Dundee Banking Co. Seemingly there was a tendency for companies, once well established, to become rather conservative in their lending practices. It was, however, always open to dissatisfied customers to break away and form a rival company.

The Leith Banking Co. was opened in 1792 by a group of eighteen men. Again most of them were merchants, Leith being an important trading and fishing port.

All of the above-mentioned companies issued their own notes. In 1785, however, there was founded a private, i.e. non-issuing, bank in Glasgow. The firm was A., G. and A. Thomson (father and two sons), all of whom had been involved in the Paisley Banking Co.

Some of these formations occurred in towns which already had banks. Glasgow, Aberdeen, Dundee, Stirling and Paisley all acquired additions to their existing provision of bank offices. The reason for this duplication in some towns must be sought in the size of the banks formed. Many of them were very small indeed. In a time of high demand for bank credits small banks soon reached the limit of their ability to lend or developed cautious lending policies. The unsatisfied demand which remained gave rise to other banking companies, and the proprietors of second and third banking companies in some towns were not only attracted into the business by the prospect of satisfying their own credit needs cheaply but also by the profits to be derived from extending their services to other businesses in the area.

Some of these banking companies, once established, found that the volume of business they could do might be enhanced if they set up branches in other areas. The public banks, especially the Bank of Scotland and the British Linen Company (which had assumed its new role by this time), set the example of branch networks. The provincials followed suit although none managed to establish more than a regional network. The pattern of branch formations will be discussed in Chapter 9.

This was also the period in which a number of the provincial banks began to accept interest-bearing deposits on a regular basis, although the Glasgow banks had done this almost since their inception. Such deposits enabled the banks to expand their assets and therefore to meet the demand for advances.

The setting up of branches and the taking of deposits were factors of the same general movement of increasing business activity. At a meeting in March, 1791 the directors of the Dundee Banking Co. resolved that,

> as the circulation of the Bank has considerably diminished, and probably owing to the number of Branches from other Banks which have opened in this and the neighbouring towns, it is expedient of this Company to establish Branches in other towns.

> The Bank to take in money on deposit, in sums not less than fifty pounds, and to make partial repayments in sums not less than ten pounds, and to allow interest at four per cent. if it is to remain six months, or three per cent. if it is to be payable on demand.[12]

In order to extend their services into surrounding areas, they adopted the expedient of accepting deposits rather than extending their capital. This general position was, in a sense, imposed upon them by the open entry and competitive nature of the banking industry because the branch system increased competition amongst the banks and forced them to provide a wider, and cheaper, range of services for their customers.

The year 1790 saw one of a series of proposals in Parliament which posed a threat to the profitability of the provincial banking companies. In that year the Bank of England sponsored a bill which, if passed, would have imposed a tax on bills of exchange, and it was assumed that this legislation would include banknotes. The interests of the provincial banks were defended by George Dempster of Dunnichen, who had been M.P. for the Fife Burghs from 1762 until 1790. Dempster wrote to Henry Dundas, the 'uncrowned King of Scotland' and Governor of the Bank of Scotland, expressing his concern that the proposed measure would be very damaging to the provincial banking companies. He maintained that 'many small banks are infinitely preferable to one or a few great ones the advantages of which are very much confined to the places where they are established'.[13] Dundas's reply to this line of argument has not survived. Nevertheless, such was the general opposition that the proposal was dropped.

The measure was no more popular in England where the banking system had developed along lines rather different from those of Scotland. The six-partner law determined that the country banks in England were, on average, smaller than their Scottish counterparts. More importantly, Acts of 1775 and 1777 had forbidden the issue of banknotes under £5. The Bank of England confined its operations to London, and the lack of a 'big-bank' influence in the provinces rendered the country banks freer in their operations. By 1793, it has been estimated, there were 280 country banks in England.[14]

One of these banks was the Exchange Bank in Newcastle (Surtees, Burdon and Co.) which had been founded in 1768. In 1788 the partners of that concern, together with two others, set up a branch in Berwick-upon-Tweed.[15] This was an English bank operating in a quasi-Scottish town in England. Although it will be mentioned from time to time, it will be excluded from the statistical tables.

2. Competition and Co-operation – The Public Banks

The new regime at the Bank of Scotland which had been responsible for the setting up of the note exchange in 1771 took another step forward in 1774 when it was decided that 'it would be not only for the interest of the Bank, but also of advantage to the country' if branches were set up in Dumfries and Kelso.[16] The policy of branching which had last been abandoned in 1733 was re-adopted. The Bank of Scotland was once again prepared to provide a range of banking services for customers in provincial areas.

The branches at Dumfries and Kelso were followed by openings at Ayr, Kilmarnock (1775), Stirling (1776), Aberdeen (1780), Paisley, Dunfermline (1781), Huntly, Elgin (1782), Perth, Montrose (1784), Kirkcaldy, Cupar, Wigtown (1785), Kirkcudbright (1790), Tain (1791), St. Andrews and Greenock (1792).

In order to support expansion of this magnitude, the paid-up capital of the bank was increased by stages from £80,000 in 1772 to £600,000 in 1793.[17] Several Acts of Parliament were required to achieve these extensions which progressed rapidly over the period. All this was done with a view to supplant the provincial banking companies. The public bank view of the provincials was expressed by George Home of Wedderburn who had been appointed to wind up the affairs of Douglas, Heron and Co:

> They are under no Controul. They have no object in view but their own particular interests and the publick are entirely unacquainted with the nature and extent of their transactions and the real situation of their affairs, they are also ignorant of the Capital upon which they carry on their trade.

He was of the opinion that the public banks were quite the opposite:

> It would have been much for the General Interest if the Capitals of the two Edinburgh Banks had been such as that the Directors could have with prudence extended their circulation so as to render the establishment of Provincial Banks unnecessary or unprofitable.[18]

He believed, however, that all was not lost and that by increasing their capital the public banks could still compete with the provincials and, as they were such superior institutions, check what he thought to be the excessive circulation of the irregulars and prevent the establishment of new ones, but his hopes were ill-founded. Both the public banks and the provincials increased their number of offices in the period up to 1793.

The Bank of Scotland's branches were sometimes first to offer banking services in towns where local initiatives came a little later. This was so in Stirling and Paisley. In other towns branches were set up where there was already a provincial bank as in Ayr, Aberdeen, Perth and Greenock. In the remaining towns the Bank of Scotland branch did not meet with opposition from local formations, at least in the 1774 to 1793 period.

In most of the towns where the Bank of Scotland set up branches it was first in the field. In other places, however, the British Linen Company had established offices. An exact definition of the nature of the business and the function of the agent at these offices of the British Linen Co. is extremely difficult to establish. Chapter 9 will deal with some of the definitional problems of branches and agencies but the British Linen Co. is a peculiar case because of the progressive nature of its changeover from linen trading and finance to general banking. The metamorphosis began in the 1760s, continued in the 1770s and was probably complete by the late 1780s. Some of the offices survived the transition and assumed banking functions, for example Inverness, Dumfries and Montrose, but others which may be assumed to have a purely banking function were added in the 1770s and 1780s, for example Forres (1771), Dunbar (1773), Hawick (1782), Langholm (1783), Duns (1784), Wigtown (1785) and Jedburgh (1788), and a sub-branch of Head Office was opened at Leith in 1792. Only at Leith was there a direct confrontation with a provincial bank, namely the Leith Banking Co. In Wigtown and Montrose, the British Linen Co. and the Bank of Scotland competed for business.

Neither the Bank of Scotland nor the British Linen Co. were able to foresee clearly the extent of the upsurge in demand for bank credit in the 1780s which called so many provincial banking companies into existence. Nevertheless, both companies had made and continued to make a considerable effort to provide for the credit requirements of provincial areas by means of branch networks. But they could not altogether overcome parochialism. Merchants in many towns preferred to provide for their own bank credit requirements by the formation of banking companies, for two reasons. The profits from local banking stayed in the area and were not carried off to Edinburgh. Secondly, local banking was likely to be more flexible, particularly in time of crisis although it was likely to be more vulnerable, if the crisis was severe, than the branch of a public bank. The latter could only establish a dominance over the banking services of a town if its agent was a man either of substantial economic power or of some personal magnetism. David 'King' Staig, the Bank of Scotland's agent at Dumfries was such a man; he was powerful both politically and economically and no significant local initiative rose to challenge him and the position of his bank in that corner of the country.

It seems likely that in some towns the opening of branches by Edinburgh banks thwarted the formation of local banks. In 1788 a plan was afoot to establish a bank in Dunbar in which the Earl of Lauderdale[19] was involved, but in that year the British Linen Company upgraded its office there to branch status and in 1790 appointed Messrs. Middlemass and Hay, two of the new bank's projectors, to be joint agents.[20] The Dunbar bank project was dropped.

In at least one case the reverse process occurred. In 1784 the British Linen Co. appointed James Gammell to be their agent in Greenock. The following year Gammell and three others formed the Greenock Banking Company with Gammell as managing partner, and the British Linen office closed.

One of the consequences of the spread of the Bank of Scotland and the British Linen Co. into provincial areas was the setting up of local note exchanges. When the Bank of Scotland opened in Aberdeen in 1780, it quickly came to an agreement with the Aberdeen Banking Co. to exchange notes without recourse to

Edinburgh. From 1789 the provision which had been made in Aberdeen was extended to other companies.[21] It seems that the concession was intended primarily for the British Linen Co., although it was also grudgingly offered to the provincial banks. The effect of the local note exchanges was to oblige the banks to retire their notes even more promptly than before, it no longer being necessary to send all the 'strange' notes to Edinburgh.

While the Bank of Scotland and the British Linen Co. extended their interests in provincial areas by setting up branches, the Royal Bank took a somewhat different line of action.

The Royal Bank founded only one branch – at Glasgow in 1783. The Bank of Scotland and the Royal appear to have established some agreement on spheres of interest, with the Royal in Glasgow and the Bank of Scotland in other provincial areas. It was a number of years before the 'Old Bank' opened an office in Glasgow. The Royal Bank branch was an immediate success. This may have been due to

> The establishment having been made at a time when the demands for money, that is for accommodation, were very great, and when the funds of the Glasgow Banks, seldom sufficient to satisfy such demands were more limited than usual by the great sum of Glasgow money then vested in Government Stocks . . .[22]

Investments in the public funds were popular at that time as a rise in price was expected with the approaching end of the American War. The Glasgow men were not alone in this speculation. Sir Wm. Forbes and the other partners in his Edinburgh private bank 'added considerably' to their private fortunes as a result of these investments.[23] It may have been that the money thus repatriated when profits were taken was instrumental in financing the upsurge in economic activity which then took place.

Robert Scott Moncrieff and David Dale, appointed joint agents at the new branch, took full advantage of the demand for accommodation. In the first year their directors awarded cash credits, recommended by Moncrieff and Dale, to the value of £25,600.[24] In less than half a century 'this Glasgow branch would be doing more business than any other individual office in Scotland, or out of London'.[25]

The Royal also sought to extend its influence in the provinces by becoming Edinburgh correspondent for some of the provincial banking companies in place of the private bankers who had traditionally filled this role. The first request for these services came in June, 1782 from the Perth United Banking Co. and when this met with a favourable response the news spread rapidly and the Merchant Bank of Glasgow, Aberdeen Banking Co. and Paisley Banking Co. all negotiated similar agreements. The Royal was to transact all Edinburgh business of these banks and to allow interest on their deposits up to fixed limits at 3 per cent while, in times of difficulty the Royal was prepared to make advances up to fixed limits at 5 per cent interest:[26]

> The Royal assured each of its new associates that, this measure has been well digested and is meant to be permanent and lasting. Indeed the beneficial consequences that in all probability both societies will reap from the connection will ensure the continuance of it.[27]

By assuming this role the Royal was in a good position to know the business of the provincial bankers, and by being prepared to offer loans in times of stress it had adopted a central bank type function as lender of last resort. This, together with the Bank of Scotland's branch extensions, tightened the influence which the public banks were able to exert over the provincial banking system.

When the testing time came in 1793, the Royal found that it was not equal to the task and relinquished the agreements after giving due notice.[28] Sir Wm. Forbes, Jas. Hunter and Co. resumed their agreements for the Aberdeen and Perth Banks.[29]

3. 1793 – The Crisis

The outbreak of war with revolutionary France in February, 1793 caused a run on the banks. In the rush for liquidity two Glasgow banks failed. There can be no doubt that these had been supporting a large volume of speculative transactions. They were the Arms Bank and the private bank of A., G. and A. Thomson. The Merchant Bank of Glasgow was also in difficulty and closed for a time.

By April, 1793 the situation in the West had become critical. James Fraser of the Bank of Scotland wrote to Henry Dundas:

> In Glasgow and its Neighbourhood, Manufactures and Trade have suffered a dreadful reverse. From the most flourishing condition they are plunged into the Depth of Distress. The private Banking Companies early began to withdraw from the Support of Credit, and now do nothing. The Royal Bank Branch there may be reckoned the only source of their supplies. What the Bank of Scotland could spare, after supporting its own numerous Branches, it has contributed as an Auxiliary, to a considerable Amount but all that both the Banks can afford is not sufficient to prevent universal Bankruptcy in Glasgow and the Neighbouring Towns if some more effectual Aid cannot be procured. That aid can come from Government alone.[30]

Eventually government acted. It authorised the issue of £5m. of Exchequer bills against which borrowers could deposit their trade goods in security and the crisis evaporated. Firms in Glasgow applied for £319,730 of the bills, which was the largest amount of any city apart from London.[31] Nevertheless, the help was too late to save the two banking companies.

The Arms Bank (Cochrane, Murdoch and Co.), the more important of the two casualties, had been opened in 1750 and had 31 partners. By 1793 the firm was Murdoch, Robertson and Co. with the partners reduced to four. Sir Wm. Forbes thought that 'their business had much declined'[32] from what it had once been. The failure occurred on 14th March but all debts were subsequently paid in full.

The Merchant Bank of Glasgow was apparently in the same declining condition as the Arms Bank. It may be speculated that the Royal Bank branch had made inroads into the business of these two concerns. This company, however, was able to recover and continue trading.

The firm of Andrew, George and Andrew Thomson failed for about £47,000 on 5th November, 1793. Andrew Thomson was the father of the other two partners. He owned the estate of Faskin and had been a partner in the Ship Bank from 1776.

In 1783, he and his son George were founding partners in the Paisley Bank where the younger son Andrew was apprenticed to the business. In 1785, however, they set up on their own and began the bank which was known by the firm name of A., G. and A. Thomson. It does not appear that this concern issued notes.

Another brother, John Thomson, was a partner in the Glasgow Buildings Company which was responsible for building part of the 'New Town an ambitious and important scheme, but one of doubtful profit for the original sponsors'.[33] The Thomson bank made an advance of £20,000 to this venture. It is also possible that the Thomsons were borrowing from their own bank to develop the coal mining business on the Faskin estate. This was bad banking because the advances could not be easily liquidated even if the security was good in the long term. In 1794 six plots of land in the George Square–George Street area of the city were disponed to John McCaul 'for behoof of the creditors of A., G. and A. Thomson'.[34] The sequestration was recalled in July, 1794 when the Thomsons found security for their debts but they never again engaged in banking.[35]

The two failures were both relatively small companies. Neither of them had widespread repercussions on the economy. The most devastating failure in this crisis was that of James Dunlop of Garnkirk who had many business interests including a partnership in the Greenock Banking Co. but whose major interest was in coal.[36] At the time of his failure Dunlop owed £9,100 to the Royal Bank and £25,387 to the Greenock Banking Co. As Dunlop was the latter's Glasgow agent the Royal tried to make the other partners liable for the £9,100 but the case went to the House of Lords in 1797 where the Royal's pleas were rejected.[37] Nevertheless, despite this difficulty the Greenock Banking Co. was able to re-order its finances, admit new partners and continue banking.

The public banks were asked to act as lender of last resort by some of the provincial bankers who found themselves in trouble. The Royal Bank advanced £12,500 in good security to the Arms Bank on condition that the Arms received further aid from the Bank of Scotland.[38] But when the Thomson Bank had applied to the public banks for £42,000 in November, 1793 all help was refused.[39] Apparently the public banks had second thoughts about acting as lender of last resort. The details of the negotiations have not been recorded but the reason for the refusal possibly lies in the fact that the public banks were having their own problems. Wm. Ramsay, a director of the Royal, believed that by June, 1793 the Royal's affairs were in a 'desperate condition'.[40] Ramsay had lost his nerve and the Royal recovered fairly well from the crisis but the problems it was undoubtedly having and the nervous condition of at least this director precluded the possibility of their extending any further help to the provincial banks at this time.

The public banks escaped from the crisis relatively unscathed. James Mansefield, a director of the Bank of Scotland, claimed that their circulation was 'not diminished at all' but that of the banking companies certainly was. Indeed the public banks rather 'augmented their accommodation to the country'.[41] Mansefield, who was also a private banker, probably overstated his case but in general his statement was correct.

The experience of 1772 and 1775 had been repeated. The provincial bankers had over-extended themselves and were forced to retrench or to ask the public banks for help. It was not only Glasgow that was affected. In Dundee the discounting of bills was curtailed and the capital of the Dundee Banking Co. had to be increased.[42] The Perth Banking Co. decided to restrict its discounts 'until the company's affairs are on an easier footing' and cash account limits were cut by 25 per cent.[43] Clearly many of the provincial bankers had forgotten the lesson of 1772.

Although the public banks had learned to live in peaceful co-existence with the provincials, they had not grown to like them. An anonymous writer in *The Bee* thought he could discern the undercurrents of the situation. He believed that

> the unlimited right of setting up Private i.e. Provincial Banks, their multiplicity in consequence of this right, the obscure character, and doubtful credit of some of the Bankers, afford a favourable opportunity for the directors of the Chartered Banks to offer themselves as Doctors to this Political Malady. Amputation will you may believe be their prescription, and thus leave the patient who only had a sore limb, without any limb at all.

He suggested that provincial banking companies should be regulated and not suppressed.[44] His views on this subject coincided with those expressed by George Dempster in a letter to Henry Dundas; it is possible that the author of the letter to *The Bee* was indeed Dempster, who believed that the names of all partners in banking companies should be registered and that banks and banking companies should pay specie for their notes at their branches and not just at their head offices.[45] The first of these measures was designed to make legal proceedings easier, the second to ensure perfect convertibility of the note issue. No move was made in this direction by the public banks. They were aware that the apparent advantages to the public of the provincial banking companies prior to 1793 'was so great that any application to the Legislature' for control of them 'would have been little listened to'.[46] They decided to tolerate the provincial banking companies which were at the height of their power in the 1790 to 1815 period. In 1802 their demand liabilities were 43.7 per cent of the total banking sector and advances were 49.1 per cent.[47] Total liabilities were 37 per cent of the system.

If the public banks were not prepared to do anything about the provincial banking companies, the customers of the latter certainly were. A number of them, disgruntled at the action of the Glasgow banks in the crisis of 1793, decided to form a joint-stock bank on the public bank model. It was intended that this Royal Bank of Glasgow should be incorporated by Act of Parliament and that it should have limited liability and freely transferable shares. The scheme was planned by a committee which included Dugald Bannatyne, Alex. Warrand, James Stirling, James McLehose, James Montieth, George McIntosh and Kirkman Finlay, who were some of the foremost merchants and manufacturers of their time. Sir John Sinclair of Ulbster was one of the original promoters. Despite an impressive list of subscribers the scheme came to nothing. Jas. Buchanan thought that the opposition of the public banks was the reason why the idea failed,[48] but this is doubtful. A letter from James Stirling, later to be one of the committee members and a customer of the Bank of Scotland, to Henry Dundas, Governor of that bank, made it clear that Dundas had the scheme in his mind as early as February, 1793.[49] The fact that Gilbert Hamilton, agent for Carron Company and Glasgow correspondent of the Bank of Scotland, occupied the chair at the planning committee meetings suggests that the 'Old Bank' was not adverse to the proposed formation. The Royal Bank may have been more hostile as the new concern would have been in direct competition with the Royal's branch.

The Royal Bank of Glasgow was stillborn. Instead the situation in Glasgow and elsewhere continued as it had developed over the previous 20 years but the system had been extended by new formations and by opening branches. The public banks had moved into direct competition with the provincials by their branch policy and, most importantly for the future development of banking, the practice of deposit-taking which enabled the banks to extend their advances even further had become widespread.

NOTES

1. Bank Balance Sheets – see Appendix A
2. *Glasgow Journal*, 8/10/1772
3. Hunter-Blair MSS., Jas. Hunter, Ayr to Jas. Hunter, Edinburgh, 14/8/1773
4. R. S. Rait, 1930, pp. 170–175
5. Hunter-Blair MSS., Jas. Hunter, Ayr to Jas. Hunter, Edinburgh 12/8/1773
6. T. C. Smout, 1972, p. 359
7. R.B., D.M.B., 1/3/1775 and 20/12/1775
8. Anon, *Old Glasgow Houses of the Old Glasgow Gentry* 2nd ed., n.d. quotes John Brown's journal, p. 160; and Rait, 1930, pp. 39–40
9. S. G. Checkland, 1975, p. 236
10. A. Smith, 1970, p. 395
11. J. C. Gibson, 1930, pp. 10–14
12. C. W. Boase, 1867, 1791
13. Melville Castle MSS., S.R.O. GD51/18/3, Dempster to Melville, 28/1/1791
14. L. S. Pressnell, 1956, p. 11, Table 1[3]
15. M. Phillips, 1894, p. 385
16. B.S., D.M.B., 27/7/1774
17. C. A. Malcolm, *The Bank of Scotland* n.d., p. 283
18. B.S., Melville MSS., Paper 1, Observations by George Home
19. B.S., Melville MSS., Paper 51, list of banks in Scotland
20. C. A. Malcolm, 1950, p. 181
21. B.L., D.M.B., 14/5/1789
22. B. S., Glasgow Thistle Bank Papers, Box 1, Bundle 7
23. Sir Wm. Forbes, 1860, p. 55
24. D. McNaughtan, The Royal Bank of Scotland 1780–1800, unpublished Dissertation, University of Strathclyde, 1972, p. 27
25. N. Munro, 1928, p. 150
26. R.B., D.M.B., 4/6/1782, 12/6/1782, 17/6/1782. See also D. McNaughtan, 1972, p. 22
27. R.B., D.M.B., 17/6/1782
28. Perth Banking Co., D.M.B. 22/3/1793
29. *Ibid.*, 5/6/1793 and Fettercairn MSS., Box 43, Jas. Jopp to Sir Wm. Forbes, 25/6/1793 and 14/9/1793
30. B.S., Melville MSS., Paper 62, Jas. Fraser to Henry Dundas, 27/4/1793
31. C. W. Boase, 1867, p. 179

32. Forbes, 1860, p. 77
33. J. R. Kellett, 1961, p. 219
34. G. G. Thomson, 1903, pp. 9–10
35. *Glasgow Mercury*, 28/7/1794
36. B. F. Duckham, 1970, p. 180
37. Murray Collection, Glasgow University Library, MU23 B19, notes by James Buchanan
38. D. McNaughtan, 1972, p. 21
39. Steel Maitland MSS., S.R.O. GD/193/1/1, Diary of Wm. Ramsay, 30/10/1793
40. *Ibid.*, 10/6/1793
41. P.P. Report from the Committee on the Circulating Paper, the Specie and the Current Coin of Ireland and also on the Exchange, 1804, evidence of James Mansfield
42. C. W. Boase, 1867, 1793
43. Perth Banking Co., D.M.B., 13/5/1793 and 21/3/1793
44. *The Bee*, January, 1782, p. 199
45. Melville MSS., S.R.O., GD51/18/3. George Dempster to Henry Dundas, 28/1/1791
46. B.S., Melville MSS., Paper 68, Memorandum to Dundas, 7/2/1794
47. S. G. Checkland 1975, Table 8. Total liabilities of the public banks were 54 per cent and those of the private banks were 9 per cent
48. Murray Collection, G.U.L. MU23 B19, Notes by Jas. Buchanan
49. B.S., Melville MSS., Paper 60, Jas. Stirling to Henry Dundas, 25/2/1793

3

Growth in the War Years, 1793–1810

1. The 1797 Suspension

THE war against France continued throughout the 1790s, and in the early weeks of 1797 there were rumours that the French were ready to invade Britain. These caused farmers and others to make a run on the banks for specie and on Monday, February 20th the banks of Northumberland, Sunderland and Durham did not open for business. The panic spread rapidly throughout the country and heavy demands for specie were made upon an already depleted reserve at the Bank of England. On Friday 24th the Governor of the Bank of England had an interview with Pitt and two days later an Order in Council was issued relieving the Bank of the obligation to pay its notes in specie.[1] Many country banks had already suspended payments to await the response of Parliament to the crisis. The suspension, which was intended as a temporary measure, continued until 1821 despite the fact that the Bank's reserve improved substantially during the two years following the Order in Council.

In Scotland the run on the banks began on Monday, 20th February. The demand for specie lasted for the whole of that week and the first two days of the next. Early on Wednesday, 1st March news reached Edinburgh of the Bank's suspension of cash payments and the response of the Edinburgh bankers was immediate. 'All ceremony or etiquette of public or private banks was now out of the question.' A meeting of bankers was held in the counting house of Sir Wm. Forbes, James Hunter and Co. but was soon adjourned to the head office of the Bank of Scotland where it was decided to follow the example of the Bank of England and suspend specie payments (see Appendix B). A public meeting was held at two o'clock that afternoon at which 'a resolution was instantly and unanimously entered into by those present to give every countenance and support to the Edinburgh banks'. A handbill was circulated in the city, a copy of which is in Appendix B, and the provincial banking companies were informed of what had taken place. The immediate effect of the suspension was uproar, but 'it was remarkable . . . after the first surprise and alarm was over, how quietly the country submitted . . . to transact all business by means of bank notes, for which the issuers give no specie as formerly'.[2]

In the provinces the directors of the Perth Banking Company decided to follow suit but they continued to give specie in small sums to selected manufacturers and shopkeepers; but this practice was soon discontinued when it was found that even these small amounts of coin were being picked up and hoarded. In any case the bank's image became tarnished as it was accused of partiality in the issue of specie.[3] In Glasgow the bankers followed the Edinburgh example and suspended cash payments. At a public meeting the merchants and manufacturers of the city declared that they were prepared to accept the inconvertible note in payments[4] and business went on much as before. In April Henry Dundas wrote from London to Sir Wm. Forbes to express his hope that 'the Circulation and Credit of Scotland is going on without any interruption'.[5] Forbes replied that things were now tranquil and voiced his conviction that 'there never was at any time more Silver in Scotland than at present but solely owing to its being hoarded up'.[6]

Government acted quickly to relieve the distress likely to be occasioned by the shortage of coin. Spanish dollars stamped with a likeness of George III were issued to circulate at 4/9d. and an Act was rapidly passed which suspended the Acts of 1775 and 1777. Under it English banks were enabled to issue notes under £5 in value.[7] This permission was later restricted to notes of £1 and over.[8] In Scotland, where £1 notes had always been an important part of the circulating medium, people resorted to tearing them into quarters, for use as 5/– notes.

An Act[9] passed on 27th March, 1797 gave permission to Scottish banks for notes under £1 in value to be issued and extensive use was made of this facility. The Dundee Banking Company by 1799 (February 20th) had issued notes to the value of £65,408–10/–. Of these, £12,762–10/– were in 5/– notes, i.e. 20 per cent of the total issue. Of the remainder £46,491 were in £1 notes, i.e. 71 per cent. Therefore 91 per cent of the total issue was in notes under £5.[10] The right to issue 5/– notes was extended to the Carron Iron Company by a further act of 1797.[11] Most banks availed themselves of this right despite the fact that it was a temporary measure. The authority for this issue of small notes was extended by a series of Acts[12] until 1799, when it was provided that the right of Scottish banks to issue notes under £1 in value would extend to 1st December 1800, 'and from thence to the end of the next Parliament and no longer'.[13] The reason for withdrawing the very small notes is not immediately clear. It seems likely, however, that the hoards of silver which had been concealed during the 1797 crisis came to be disgorged as confidence returned, thereby obviating the need for 5/– notes. When a similar shortage of coin occurred in 1803, following the renewal of hostilities, the government refused permission to issue 5/– notes.[14] The issue of Spanish dollars was thought to be sufficient for all needs.

It is interesting to compare the treatments accorded to Scotland and England. Scotland's note issue had been settled by the Act of 1765 which stated that £1 notes must be the smallest denomination. If the limit had been set at £5, as it was in England, then it is arguable that much of Scotland's economic growth would have been stultified for want of an adequate supply of a circulating medium. In England the need for settling the note issue question did not arise until 1775 when notes were payable 'under certain terms and restrictions',[15] especially in parts of Yorkshire where notes for 1/– and 1/6d. had produced 'the most iniquitous consequences'.[16] An Act of that year[17] settled that £1 should be the smallest denomination of note and that notes should be payable on demand. Two years later, however, this limit was raised to £5 so that no £1 notes could be issued in England between 1778 and the suspension of 1797. The Act of 1777[18] was a temporary measure but was made permanent in 1787.[19]

The reason for treating England differently from Scotland is not apparent as the debate on the 1777 Act is, unfortunately, not recorded in the *Parliamentary History*. The preamble to the Act, however, stated that the earlier legislation had produced 'very salutary effects'. Consequently it was thought to be a good idea to extend the benefits. It remains possible that the ideas of Adam Smith influenced the government. Smith's *Wealth of Nations*, published in 1776, expressed the view that 'it were better, perhaps, that no bank notes were issued in any part of the kingdom for a smaller sum than five pounds'.[20] This may help to explain why England was so treated, but leaves open the question, why was the Scottish note issue not similarly limited? There was certainly some pressure from Scotland against the proposal to include Scottish notes in the proposed Act and this may have been sufficient to persuade the government to change its intentions.[21]

The effects of the 1797 suspension in Scotland were less marked than they were in England. The use of £1 notes had already, to a great extent, replaced the use of gold coins and the suspension did nothing to change this once the initial panic had died down. 'The demand for gold, though legal, was met because it was so small.' Henry Monteith, a Glasgow manufacturer, later recalled that the Glasgow banks were always able to supply him either with gold or Bank of England notes for his trips to England during the suspension period.[22] Only the Bank of England was relieved of the obligation to pay in gold or silver.

The year 1798 saw the disappearance of two small banking companies. The Merchant Banking Co. of Glasgow, which had been weakened by the crisis of 1793, retired from business and the debts were sold by public roup.[23] Similarly the Stirling banking company of Campbell, Thomson and Co. retired in this year. Nothing is known of the state of its business.

As the war continued the Government's demands for finance grew more pressing. Pitt introduced a tax on income in 1799 and it was also suggested that a duty should be imposed on banknotes. As the country was at war it would have been 'unpatriotic' to oppose this measure. Consequently a duty of 2d. was imposed on small notes with no duties on larger notes.[24] Apart from the drain on profits the administration of this duty created other problems, especially for the provincial bankers. When the proposal was first mooted the public banks, possibly through the influence of Henry Dundas, were quick to secure for themselves the advantage of being allowed to compound the duty but this privilege was not extended to the provincial companies. As a result, the provincial bankers had to renew their note issues when the stamping took place, whereas the public banks were spared this expense. Robert Bogle, a London merchant of Glasgow origin, thought that the public banks had 'suspiciously obtained undue and unreasonable advantage'.[25]

In June, 1799 Wm. McDowall, M.P. for Glasgow, wrote to the Thistle Bank suggesting that a deputation representing the Scottish provincial banking companies be sent to London in order to secure the same privileges 'as had been awarded to the Chartered Banks'. The Leith Banking Company wrote to the Thistle Bank on 8th July, 1799 informing them that they, in conjunction with the British Linen Co. and Sir Wm. Forbes, James Hunter and Co. had sent a petition to the Lords Commissioners of the Treasury. The letter suggested that the Thistle Bank do the same and Archibald Graham, their cashier, lost no time in the matter; a draft petition was drawn up the same day. Hunters and Co. of Ayr had also been corresponding with the Ship Bank at Glasgow[26] and the Aberdeen Banking Co. wrote to their M.P. asking him to secure the same privileges for them.[27] This correspondence underlines the serious lack of a central organisation for taking concerted action on behalf of the non-public banks to protect their interests.

The provincial banking companies together with the Forbes Bank and the British Linen Co. had influential support for their point of view from the Duke of Atholl and Lords Kinnoull, Hay, Galloway and Strange.[28] All this, however, was as nothing when measured against the persuasive influence of the 'uncrowned King of Scotland'. Henry Dundas, Governor of the Bank of Scotland, had access to Pitt. Although, in a letter to the Duke of Atholl, he disclaimed any partiality in the matter it seems likely that he pressed Pitt to favour the public banks. In the letter he referred to the Ayr Bank collapse in which he personally had lost money, although he maintained that he was not hostile to the provincial banking companies and conceded that they did some good for the economy but they could not consider themselves to be on a par with the public banks. The provincial banks, he wrote, 'with few exceptions, . . . have either, when exposed to a pressure, crumbled down altogether, or rested for their safety upon the protection of the established banks'.[29] The provincial companies failed to gain the privilege of being allowed to compound the duty which had been accorded to the public banks.

The same disregard for the wishes of the provincial bankers was again exhibited in 1804 when an Act was passed which prohibited the re-issuing of £20 notes once they had been returned to a bank. The exceptions to this limitation were the public banks and the British Linen Co.[30] Only when the Bank Note Forgery Act was passed in 1801 were the views of the provincial banks taken into consideration,[31] although the evidence does not indicate the nature of their views. Generally the Edinburgh bankers were able to pull the strings of Government, essentially because of Henry Dundas's place in Parliament. The provincial banking companies were unable or unwilling to form a joint lobby, and even if they had it is very doubtful if they could have countered the power of Dundas. The economic and political position of the public banks condemned the provincials to second-class citizenship.

2. Expansion in the 1800s

Between 1802 and 1810 there were twelve provincial banking company formations in Scotland, all of which were note issuers. Five of these were located in the larger burghs and seven were in the lesser ones. The details of the formations are set out in Table 5 and the regional pattern in 1793 and 1810 in Table 6.

Table 5

Scottish Provincial Banking Companies 1793–1810

a)	Banks in existence at end of 1793	Year of opening	Remarks
	Note Issuers		
1.	Ship Bank, Glasgow	1750	
2.	Thistle Bank, Glasgow	1761	
3.	Dundee Banking Co.	1763	
4.	Aberdeen Banking Co.	1767	
5.	Merchant Bank of Glasgow	1769	Retired 1798
6.	Hunters and Co., Ayr	1773	
7.	Stirling Banking Co.	1777	
8.	Paisley Banking Co.	1783	
9.	Merchant Bank of Stirling	1784	Failed 1805
10.	Greenock Banking Co.	1785	
11.	Falkirk Banking Co.	1787	
12.	Campbell, Thomson and Co., Stirling	1787	Retired 1798
13.	Perth Banking Co.	1787	
14.	Paisley Union Banking Co.	1788	
15.	Commercial Banking Co. of Aberdeen	1788	
16.	Leith Banking Co.	1792	
17.	Dundee Commercial Banking Co.	1792	Re-formed as No.21 in 1802
	Private Banks		
18.	J. & R. Watson, Glasgow	c.1763	

b)	Banks formed 1794–1810	Year of opening	No. of partners	Remarks
	Note Issuers			
19.	Fife Banking Co., Cupar	1802	47	
20.	Cupar Banking Co.	1802	3	
21.	Dundee New Bank	1802	7	Re-formation of No. 17
22.	Kilmarnock Banking Co.	1802	6	
23.	Renfrewshire Banking Co., Greenock	1802	9	
24.	Falkirk Union Banking Co.	1803	14	
25.	Dumfries Commercial Bank	1804	3	Failed 1808
26.	Galloway Banking Co., Castle Douglas	1806	4	
27.	Dundee Union Banking Co.	1809	85	
28.	Glasgow Banking Co.	1809	17	
29.	Perth Union Banking Co.	1810	c.80	
30.	East Lothian Banking Co.	1810	56	

Table 6

Regional Patterns: No. of Banking Companies

	1793	1810
Glasgow and South-West	8	11
Edinburgh and South-East	1	2
Tayside/Fife	3	7
Central	4	3
North-East/Highlands	2	2
	18	25

Table 6 clearly marks out the South-West and Tayside/Fife as the growth areas. The reasons for this spate of bank formations are clear. One of the effects of the war was to drive up the price of wheat. Producers strove to increase their output and to improve their lands. This created a demand for credit, and in areas where the supply did not meet the demand new banks were set up. But this generalisation does not apply to all the formations at this time; it will be necessary to say something about each of the new banks in turn. Each new concern had certain characteristics which were peculiar to it. There is no common theme other than the price level, which will be used to illustrate the trend of new formations.

The Fife Banking Company, with 47 partners, was set up in Cupar in 1802. Very little is known about its business. Almost certainly its principal interest was in agriculture, but the branches which it established at Kirriemuir and Kirkcaldy[32] suggest that it was also engaged in financing textiles and coal.

The Cupar Bank opened about the same time as the Fife Banking Company. Its partners were only three in number – a farmer, a grocer and a tobacconist.[33] Possibly these three men had been excluded from participation in the Fife Banking Co. and decided to set up on their own. Robert Scott Moncrieff, agent for the Royal Bank in Glasgow, had been brought up in Fife. He was convinced that no one in the Cupar area had 'either money or sense to conduct a Bank'.[34] Later events proved him right The Cupar Bank numbered the Balgonie Iron Company amongst its customers,[35] but the bulk of its business probably came from the small traders and shopkeepers in Cupar.

The Dundee New Bank was formed in 1802 to take over and continue the business of the Dundee Commercial Banking Company, which had been in business since 1792 and whose numbers had been depleted by the death or withdrawal of partners.[36] Of the original partners, only John Baxter, textile manufacturer, and James Scott, cashier, joined the new concern. The new partners were George, 7th Baron Kinnaird, who was a partner in the London bank of Ransom, Morland and Co. and whose family seat was at Inchture near Dundee. Wm. Morland, another partner of that firm, also joined the New Bank. The other additions to the partnership were James and William Bell who had tanning and sugar refining interests in Dundee and London; and James Duff, a Dundee merchant, who became manager of the Bank.[37] This was the first occasion on which English interests had participated directly in the formation of a Scottish provincial banking company. The restructuring of the partnership was thought to have been necessary because 'the trade of the town demanded for its accommodation enlarged resources'.[38]

The Kilmarnock Banking Company was also founded in 1802. A year earlier the Bank of Scotland had decided to withdraw some of its branches because they were unprofitable. The Kilmarnock branch was one of those axed.[39] The withdrawal of that town's only bank office was not viewed with equanimity by those with vested interests. An attempt was made to get the Royal Bank to step in,[40] but when this request was refused the Kilmarnock men decided to set up on their own. John Parker of Barleith, who had been agent for the Bank of Scotland, appears to have been the prime mover. This was very much an agriculturally based bank: five of the six partners were estate owners.[41]

The Renfrewshire Banking Company in Greenock was the fifth formation of 1802. Some of the founding partners of this bank were customers of the Royal Bank's Glasgow branch. Amongst them were Alexander Speirs of Elderslie and John Hamilton (of Hamilton, Gardner and Co.).[42] The reasons for this breakaway have not been recorded but it is likely that a desire to participate in the profits of banking was a major reason. The bank was formed in competition with the Greenock Banking Co. and branches of the Bank of Scotland and British Linen Co. The correspondence of the British Linen agent with his head office suggests that there was considerable unsatisfied demand for discounts,[43] so that there was an opportunity for another bank. The Refrewshire Banking Company opened branches at Rothesay, Inveraray and Campbeltown, providing finance for the fisheries, distilleries, kelp production, cattle trade and the West Indies trade.[44]

The Treaty of Amiens bringing peace with France was signed in March 1802, by which time the bank formations of that year had either opened or were about to do so. The peace and harvest conditions combined to depress agricultural prices, and although war broke out again in April, 1803 agricultural prices did not rise until 1805.

The downward movement of prices put a damper on the enthusiasm of bank promoters. There was only one formation in 1803 – the Falkirk Union Banking Co. Its partners were involved in farming and distilling and the business reflected a similar pattern.[45] This bank overcame the difficulties of the year of its founding, but when agricultural prices took a downturn on the conclusion of hostilities in 1815 it failed and was sequestrated.

The Dumfries Commercial Banking Company was begun in 1804. The partners were James Gracie, a former accountant in the Bank of Scotland, his son William who was a writer, and James McNeil, a baker.[46] Nothing is known about this concern other than that it failed in 1808 with a deficiency of 10/– per £1.

In 1805 there occurred the failure of the Merchant Bank of Stirling (Belch and Co.). Sometime before this event Andrew and John Belch

> had a fictitious bankruptcy in contemplation, preparatory to which almost the whole floating capital had been put under Andrew Belch's power and influence, with the evident intention of individual appropriation.

In the event Andrew Belch absconded to London with £13,957 in notes and bills. When caught he pretended that he was not a partner in the company. This ruse proved unsuccessful but the criminality did not stop there. The Belch brothers had £5,000 of the bank's notes which they planned to distribute amongst their friends, which could later be entered as claims against the bank.[47] The estates of the partners yielded only 14/9d per £1. This was the first failure of a Scottish bank in which the public lost money.

Agricultural prices had begun to rise again in 1805 and in the following year the Galloway Banking Company was opened. Kirkcudbrightshire and Wigtownshire were agricultural areas with a profitable livestock and arable base but the industrial revolution did not pass them by. The industrial development which took place there was largely instigated by two men – James Murray of Cally and Sir Wm. Douglas of Castle Douglas. The latter was the promoter and principal partner of the Galloway Banking Company. Starting about 1785, he developed a wide range of economic interests which included

> two cotton spinning mills, woollen and carpet mills, tanneries, breweries, domestic spinning and hand loom weaving; the construction of turnpike roads, canals and harbours, and the creation of a country bank.

The banking company was 'an important means of mobilising capital and providing credit to landowners, farmers and merchants in southwest Scotland'.[48] It is interesting to note that it was almost the last of Douglas's enterprises. The reason for this may have been that branches of the Bank of Scotland and the British Linen Co. existed in the area. In addition the Paisley Union Bank maintained agencies in Newton Douglas (Newton Stewart), Dumfries, Kirkcudbright, Castle Douglas and Gatehouse.[49] The unifying link between these branches seems to have been that they were all in areas where the cotton industry had begun to develop. The Paisley Union, however, found some of these agencies to be unprofitable and began to withdraw them in the late 1790s. James Hannay, who had been a bank agent at Castle Douglas, became a partner in the Galloway Banking Co. It is arguable that Douglas did not set up his own bank until the demand for banking services created by his and other enterprises outgrew the capabilities of existing bank branches to supply it, so it remains possible that the bank was the culmination of his master plan for industrial development in the area and that the long-term success of his ventures depended upon financial independence which could only be achieved by erecting a bank as part of the business empire.

The Dundee Union Banking Company was opened on 22nd February, 1809. There were 85 partners. The Perth Banking Company in 1787, the Fife Banking Company in 1802 and this new bank in Dundee were the only co-partneries of any size which had been formed since the crisis of 1772. The balance sheets of the existing Dundee banks suggest that the new concern made inroads into their business.[50] This impression is confirmed by the fact that the Bank of Scotland withdrew its Dundee branch in 1810.[51] The new bank had probably been responsible for this closure but it did not capture all of the business. The British Linen Co. was quick to open a branch following the Bank of Scotland's withdrawal.[52]

The proprietors of the Dundee New Bank, founded in 1802 and re-formed in 1805–6, might have been expected to be the dynamic force in Dundee banking but this was not the case: the Dundee Union was formed to satisfy the unfulfilled demand for credit. The Dundee New Bank men, rather than concentrate their resources in the east, diversified their banking interests and were instrumental in forming the Glasgow Banking Company in 1809.

The Glasgow Post Office Directory for 1809 listed nineteen banks, branches and agencies in the city. Of these, nine were merely provincial bank correspondences for the collection of notes and bills. A further four were the branches of provincial banking companies and three were the branches of the public banks. The remaining three were Glasgow's indigenous banks: the Ship, the Thistle and the new Glasgow Banking Company. In addition to those enumerated above, the private banking firm of J. & R. Watson discounted bills but did not issue notes. Therefore before the formation of the Glasgow Banking Company in 1809 there were ten organisations all discounting bills in the city. In total the amount of commercial paper discounted by the banks and banking companies in Glasgow in 1809 was somewhere in the region of £3m.[53] It was into this fiercely competitive situation that the Glasgow Banking Company was born.

The initiative which resulted in the opening of the new concern came from a wide variety of people. Of the seventeen partners, four were also members of the firm of Ransom, Morland and Co. bankers, London. Of these men, three were partners in the Dundee New Bank. A further two partners of the Dundee concern joined the new Glasgow bank. These were John Baxter the textile manufacturer and Wm. Roberts, banker. James Dennistoun of Golfhill in Glasgow was the major partner. He held ten of the forty shares. John Tennent, brewer of Glasgow, also joined the company. Others included Walter Fergus, textile manufacturer, Kirkcaldy; John Grundy, woollen manufacturer, Bury; and John McGregor, merchant, Liverpool.[54] This was only the second time that an English connection was significant amongst the shareholders of a Scottish provincial bank.

The Perth Union Banking Company was formed in 1810. Very little is known about this concern. It should be seen as part of a general movement of bank formations brought about by increased demand for banking services caused by the war conditions which prevailed at that time. It may be possible that this concern concentrated on agricultural finance while the Perth Banking Co. focused its activities in the industrial sector, but it is impossible to be definite.

The East Lothian Banking Company which was founded in Dunbar in 1810 was another such concern. The partners, who were mainly tenant farmers, were aware of

> the singular utility and advantage of having a Banking Company in the County of East Lothian for promoting Trade, Manufacture, Agriculture and Industry and facilitating every branch of Commerce.[55]

By far the most important industry in East Lothian was agriculture. Not only was that county 'the most fruitful province in North Britain'[56] and 'the most fertile and finest farming land'[57] that Cobbett had ever seen, but war conditions had acted as an incentive to even greater efforts. Large numbers of troops had been stationed in the county and this influx of population had acted as a spur to the economy:

> the cattle and victual consumed by the troops was the means of farmers, traders and merchants attaining to moderate wealth, and no wonder they sang with zest,
> 'Bonapartes a freend o'mine
> I sell my wheat at ninety nine'.[58]

The prime mover of this bank was Christopher Middlemass. He had been agent for the British Linen Co. in Dunbar until 1808, when he had been dismissed for negligence following a robbery.

These twelve banking companies were the new arrivals in the 1797–1810 period. All to some extent owed their formation to the prosperity created by wartime conditions. To this list might be added the Berwick Bank. The Exchange Bank of Newcastle failed in 1803 and this also entailed the closure of its semi-autonomous Berwick branch. The hiatus was filled very soon thereafter by a new formation, the Berwick Bank (Mowbray and Co.). This was really an offshoot of the Darlington Bank (Richardson, Mowbray and Co.).[59]

The response of the public banks to these new formations was almost wholly hostile. In 1802 they resolved not to take the notes of any more provincial banking companies which might be established.[60] In some cases this action was thought to be well justified because some of the new formations resorted to note picking in order to force their circulations; the Renfrewshire and Galloway banks were the main culprits in this respect. The impact of the new formations was particularly felt in the West where Scott Moncrieff of the Royal thought that

All these wine merchants and grocers setting up their Shabby Banks whose sole object is to get their notes forced in the circle are a disgrace to the country.[61]

He advocated that they should not be allowed to issue notes to a greater extent than their paid-up capital and he was well aware that the public banks' decision to refuse the notes worked in favour of the new banks because the notes tended to stay in circulation longer. He suspected that 'the two Chartered Banks will be obliged in self defence to take in these new Bankers' Notes',[62] as indeed they eventually were.

In 1802 the Bank of Scotland decided to set up a branch in Glasgow. Consequently Gilbert Hamilton who was agent for the Carron Company and who had corresponded with the Bank of Scotland for a number of years was appointed to be agent. Scott Moncrieff welcomed this addition to the provision of banking services in the West. This was some indication that the existing banks, including the Royal, were unable to satisfy all the demand for credit. Moncrieff felt able to promise Hamilton 'plenty of business' but his prime interest, rather than to satisfy the demand for credit, was to 'demolish all the West Country Banks'.[63] Moncrieff was clearly not very fond of his neighbours.

The period from 1797 to 1810 was a period of rapid development of Scottish banking both in terms of the extension of the number of units and the amount of business conducted. It saw the failure of two banks and in neither case were the partners able to pay their debts in full, thus involving the public in losses.

Although the wartime situation created an environment suitable for business expansion it also created the necessity for increased taxation to pay for the war effort. Consequently a tax was imposed on banknotes in 1800. This duty was raised in 1805 to cover all banknotes, not just those of smaller denominations, and in 1808 all banks were required to purchase a licence authorising them to issue notes, the cost of which was £20 per annum. The provincial banking companies grew in numbers but this type of growth often reflected the inability or unwillingness of existing enterprises to grow in size and to provide for the increased demands for their services. The difficulties associated with restructuring a bank may account for this. Most new banking companies quickly established a level of business which was allowed to expand at a rate much slower than the growth of demand. The total system, however, whether measured in terms of banks or branches, does seem to have grown in line with customers' requirements.

3. 1810 – The Birth of a New Breed

The suspension of cash payments by the Bank of England in 1797 led to the depreciation of the pound sterling on the foreign exchanges. The extent of this fall in the value of money was, at first, very small but by 1809 the problem had become more acute.

The economist, David Ricardo, wrote a number of letters to the *Morning Chronicle* which he followed up with a series of pamphlets. The debate which he stimulated led to the appointment of a Select Committee which became known as the Bullion Committee whose function was to determine the causes of the depreciated currency. After their investigation they concluded that the over-issue of notes was the major cause of the adverse exchanges and recommended that the Bank of England should resume cash payments for its notes within two years.

The directors of the Bank rejected the report. They believed that the value of the note issue depended on its backing, and as their note issue was secured by government securities or good trade bills, they held that the notes were not depreciated. Rather, they contended that the problem of adverse exchanges was caused by an appreciation in the price of gold caused by scarcity. Parliament sided with the Bank of England and the report was rejected. The note issue remained inconvertible.

The impact of this debate on the Scottish banks was negligible. They had managed to stabilise the exchange with London in the late 18th century, and the bulk of Scottish foreign exchange dealings were conducted in that market. Therefore there was little that the Scots could do to stabilise the foreign exchanges without re-orienting their whole payments mechanism. In any case the Scottish banks operated with the minimum of gold reserves and were therefore largely spared the expense of paying the inflated price for gold.

It is interesting to note that although the Bank of England rejected the Bullion Committee's concept of the quantity theory of money, the Scottish public banks had worked in accordance with that theory in the 1760s and 1770s. In order to protect the exchanges, they had tried to reduce the amount of money in circulation[64] but this theory had been challenged by the real bills doctrine espoused by Adam Smith. This will be considered in more detail in Chapter 6.

In Scotland the year 1810 was significant because it witnessed the formation of the Commercial Banking Company of Scotland. This was an Edinburgh-based bank with a nominal capital of £3m. of which £450,000 was paid at the outset. It met with decided hostility from the public banks. The directors of the Bank of Scotland complained that

> Till now no private Banker or Banking Company have assumed the Name of a Bank or Banking Company of Scotland but have described themselves by a Firm either of Individual Names or of the particular place where they chiefly carry on their business.[65]

It was a new phenomenon on the banking scene whose scale and base in Edinburgh marked it as a rival to the public banks. Henry Cockburn, one of the shareholders, later wrote of it in just these terms. He criticised the public bankers:

> No men were more devoid of public spirit, and even the proper spirit of their trade than our old Edinburgh bankers. Respectable men they were; but without talent, general knowledge or any liberal objects, they were conspicuous sycophants of existing power . . . A demand for a Bank founded on a more liberal principle was the natural result of this state of things . . .[66]

Certainly Cockburn's work had a polemical element, causing him to overstate his criticisms, but the public banks did tend, to a considerable degree, to concentrate their resources in government securities rather than advances to customers.[67] The Commercial Banking Company of Scotland was designed to be more liberal with its credit.

The short-term effects of the formation of the Commercial Banking Co. of Scotland on the provincial banking companies were negligible. Within ten years the Commercial had become Edinburgh agent for the Perth Union Banking Co. and had opened branches in competition with other provincial banks at Crieff, Aberdeen, Glasgow and Banff. The importance of the Commercial for the future of the provincial companies lay in the precedent which it set in that it paved the way for the formation of other large-scale joint-stock banks which proved to be the death knell for the provincial banking companies.

NOTES

1. F. W. Fetter, 1965, p. 21
2. Sir Wm. Forbes, 1860, pp. 82–5
3. Perth Banking Company, D.M.B., 2/3/1797 and 14/3/1797
4. B.S., Glasgow Archives, Thistle Bank Papers, Resolutions of 1797
5. Fettercairn MSS., N.L.S. Acc. 4796 Second Deposit, Box 15 f43, Dundas to Forbes, 21/4/1797
6. Melville MSS., S.R.O. GD51/5/238, Forbes to Dundas, 24/4/1797
7. 37 George III ch. 32
8. 39 George III ch. 9
9. 37 George III ch. 40

10. C. W. Boase, 1867, 1799
11. 37 George III ch. 62. Professor R. H. Campbell informs me that this right was exercised but the notes had a purely local circulation
12. 37 George III ch. 137
13. 38 George III ch. 2
14. B.S., Glasgow Archives, Thistle Bank Papers, Royal Bank (Wm. Simpson) to Thistle Bank, 9/8/1803
15. 15 George III ch. 51, preamble
16. *The Parliamentary History of England*, 1814, vol. 18, pp. 574–5
17. 15 George III ch. 51
18. 17 George III ch. 30
19. 27 George III ch. 16
20. A. Smith, 1970, p. 422
21. Aberdeen Banking Co., D.M.B. 20/3/1775
22. W. Graham, 1886, pp. 123–4
23. *Glasgow Advertiser*, 26/2/1798
24. 39 George III ch. 107
25. B.S., Glasgow Archives, Thistle Bank Papers, Box 1/19/19, Robert Bogle to Thistle Bank, 29/6/1799
26. *Ibid.*, Box 1/19/–
27. Melville MSS., N.L.S. 1058 f62, Aberdeen Banking Co. to Alex Allardyce M.P. 27/6/1799
28. B.S., Glasgow Archives, Thistle Bank Papers, Box 1/19/19, Robert Bogle to Thistle Bank, 29/6/1799
29. *Ibid.*, Box 1/19/18, Dundas to Atholl, 30/6/1799
30. Wm. Glen, 1807, p. 53n
31. Fettercairn MSS., N.L.S. Acc. 4796, Second deposit, Box 11 f27, Robert Dundas to Sir Wm. Forbes
32. Inland Revenue (Scotland) S.R.O. IRS/1/1, Returns of Banking Companies in Scotland
33. B.L., D.M.B., 15/3/1802
34. R.B.S., Scott Moncrieff letters, R.S.M. to Wm. Simpson, 5/3/1802
35. Balgonie Iron Company, Sederunt Book, S.R.O. CS96/203
36. Boase, 1867, p. 223
37. R.B.S., Dundee Archives, 2/1/4a, Dundee New Bank Minute Book. Unfortunately the Kinnaird MSS. contain nothing about the families involvement in banking
38. Boase, 1867, p. 222
39. B.S., D.M.B. 7/10/1801
40. R. B. Scott Moncrieff letters, RSM to Wm. Simpson, 4/12/1801
41. Pollock-Morris MSS., Kilmarnock Banking Company Contract
42. Crichton-Maitland MSS., Speirs bank pass books, and Scott Moncrieff letters, RSM to Wm. Simpson, 18/1/1802
43. B.L., D.M.B., 1802
44. Parliamentary Papers, Report of the Select Committee on Promissory Notes in Scotland and Ireland, 1826, evidence of Roger Ayton
45. Falkirk Union Banking Co., Sequestration Sederunt Book, S.R.O. CS96/869, Depositions of partners
46. B.S., Edinburgh Archives, miscellaneous documents
47. Merchant Banking Co. of Stirling, Sequestration Sederunt Book, S.R.O. CS96/2349–52
48. I. Donnachie and I. Macleod, 1974, pp. 86–7
49. B.S., Glasgow, Paisley Union Bank, Journal 1795–6
50. C. W. Boase, 1867 Balance Sheets
51. B.S., D.M.B., 6/8/1810
52. B.L., D.M.B., 3/9/1810
53. See Chapter 6
54. B.S., Glasgow, Glasgow Banking Co., D.M.B. 1809–1843
55. E.L.B., D.M.B., S.R.O. B18/18/14
56. *Old Statistical Account*, 1793, vol. 5, p. 475
57. Cobbett, *Tour in Scotland*, pp. 89–90, quoted in J. A. Symon, 1959, p. 169
58. J. Martine, 1896, vol. 2, p. 106
59. M. Phillips, 1894, pp. 310, 385
60. Boase, 1867, p. 222

61. Anon., 'The Glasgow Financial Scene: Early 19th Century', in *Three Banks Review*, No.45, 1960
62. R. B. Scott Moncrieff letters, R.S.M. to Wm. Simpson, 3/2/1802 and 26/8/1802
63. *Ibid.*, 23/4/1802 and 1/5/1802
64. See above, Chapter 1
65. B.S., D.M.B., 1/12/1810
66. H. Cockburn, *Memorials of His Own Times*, 1856, quoted in *Our Bank: The Story of the Commercial Bank of Scotland Limited*, 1941, p. 13
67. S. G. Checkland, 1975, Table 8

4

The Beginnings of Decline, 1810–1825

THE period between 1810 and 1825 was one of change for the provincial banking companies. The total number of companies continued to expand up to 1815 but thereafter numbers began to fall as the post-war deflation began. In the early 1820s many banking companies found themselves in difficulties – some because of the fall in agricultural prices and others because of speculation in trade. Furthermore the forces which were to lead to the eventual eclipse of the banking companies began to be felt. These were the declining importance of the note issue and increased competition from public and joint-stock banks.

1. The Continuing War

Table 7 sets out the pattern of bank formations and closures amongst the provincial banking companies between 1810 and 1825 together with the number of continuing firms. Table 8 sets out the regional pattern.

The years 1810–1811 saw severe commercial distress. Speculation and a shortage of specie combined to produce a slump in business activity which was only partially relieved by a government issue of special loans to merchants and manufacturers.

There were no failures amongst the Scottish bankers, but it is clear that some were in extreme difficulty. In November, 1810 the Cupar Banking Co. tried to sell out to the new Commercial Bank. It was intended that the Fife men should become shareholders in the Commercial and that their business should be continued as a branch of the Edinburgh bank.[1] The directors of the Commercial, however, felt that the time was not right to open a branch in Cupar and the deal fell through. Early the following year the Cupar Banking Company closed its doors; although there was no sequestration of the company and all public debts were paid, the partners lost money in the winding up.[2] In 1815 the estate of John Ferguson, one of the partners, was sequestrated[3] but it is impossible to determine the extent to which the bank closure caused this failure.

These challenging conditions continued into the following year. High prices and increased difficulties in conducting trade with the Continent and America caused a number of business failures but again the Scottish banks escaped disaster. In November, 1812 the Greenock Banking Co. tried to reduce its commitments. It offered its Isle of Man business to the British Linen Co.[4] and in

Table 7

Scottish Provincial Banking Companies 1810–1825

a)	*Banks in existence at the end of 1810* *Note Issuers*	*Year of opening*	*Remarks*
1.	Ship Bank, Glasgow	1750	
2.	Thistle Bank, Glasgow	1761	
3.	Dundee Banking Co.	1763	
4.	Aberdeen Banking Co.	1767	
5.	Hunters and Co., Ayr	1773	
6.	Stirling Banking Co.	1777	
7.	Paisley Banking Co.	1783	
8.	Greenock Banking Co.	1785	
9.	Falkirk Banking Co.	1787	
10.	Perth Banking Co.	1787	
11.	Paisley Union Banking Co.	1788	
12.	Commercial Banking Co. of Aberdeen	1788	
13.	Leith Banking Co.	1792	
14.	Fife Banking Co., Cupar	1802	Failed 1825
15.	Cupar Banking Co.	1802	Retired 1811
16.	Dundee New Bank	1802	
17.	Kilmarnock Banking Co.	1802	Joined No.5 1821
18.	Renfrewshire Banking Co., Greenock	1802	
19.	Falkirk Union Banking Co.	1803	Failed 1816
20.	Galloway Banking Co., Castle Douglas	1806	Retired 1821
21.	Dundee Union Banking Co.	1809	
22.	Glasgow Banking Co.	1809	
23.	Perth Union Banking Co.	1810	
24.	East Lothian Banking Co.	1810	Failed 1822
	Private Banks		
25.	J. & R. Watson, Glasgow	c.1763	

b)	*Banks formed 1811–1825* *Note Issuers*	*Year of opening*	*No. of partners*	*Remarks*
26.	Caithness Banking Co.	1812	3	Joined C.B.S. 1825
27.	Montrose Banking Co.	1814	82	
28.	John Maberly and Co.	1818	1	
29.	Shetland Banking Co., Lerwick	1821	4	
30.	Arbroath Banking Co.	1825	113	
31.	Dundee Commercial Banking Co.	1825	198	

Table 8

Regional Patterns: No. of Banking Companies

	1810	*1825*
Glasgow and South-West	11	9
Edinburgh and South-East	2	1
Tayside/Fife	7	8
Central	3	2
North East/Highlands/Islands	2	4
	25	24

F

April, 1813 it tried to sell out to the Bank of Scotland.[5] Although agreement was reached on this takeover, the Greenock men withdrew in July. The Greenock Banking Co. re-ordered its finances and admitted new partners to continue the business. James Gammell who had been principal partner since 1785 retired.[6]

Elsewhere in Scotland different criteria determined the nature of economic activity. In the North economic change was made manifest in the clearances. In some areas, notably Caithness, attempts were made to provide employment for the dispossessed crofters. The fishing industry was perhaps the most common alternative, but some people found employment in textile and kelp production. It was into this situation that the Caithness Banking Company was born. It was formed at Wick in 1812. Almost nothing is known about this bank. It issued notes, but their circulation was confined to the northern counties, and it did not even correspond with an Edinburgh agent.[7] Nevertheless its formation in 1812 is testimony to the fact that Scotland did not have a unified economy subject to the same forces of expansion and contraction. Certainly the clearances had begun by this time.

In 1813 the provincial banking companies entered upon one of their periodic confrontations with the government. Disagreement arose over a proposed re-interpretation of the 1808 Stamp Duties Act. The Stamp Office intended that banknotes should not be re-issued without being re-stamped and that on the death or retiral of a partner the whole note issue should be renewed and therefore re-stamped. This was a serious problem for the English country banks but, if implemented, it would have been disastrous for the Scottish provincials whose partnerships were on average larger than their English counterparts and were consequently more liable to have to renew the issue. Hunters and Co. of Ayr complained that this proposal 'would cut them up by the root and render provincial banking in Scotland impracticable'. The public banks were exempt from the threat because of their public authority status and the privilege of compounding for the duty. But it was felt that all provincial banking companies

> would be under the necessity of discontinuing their circulating business, at once withdrawing from the support of the Merchant, Manufacturer and Agriculturalist that circulation probably amounting to a million and a half sterling.[8]

Opposition to the proposal arose in an *ad hoc* manner but soon consolidated so that a group of bankers appointed a legal agent, Mundell, in London to represent their interests.[9] The Government were convinced by the argument which said that the ruin which would be induced by their proposal would reduce the revenue by several times the amount that it was hoped the measure would produce. Consequently a compromise was eventually effected in 1815 by a simple increase in the amounts of the duty. Although the government and its officers were sometimes prepared to legislate or interpret legislation in particularly severe ways because of poor advice, it must be acknowledged that they were usually willing to see the error of their ways once these had been pointed out.

The French armies withdrew from Russia in 1812 and were defeated at the battle of Leipzig in October, 1813. The consequence was that the ports of Russia and North Germany were re-opened for trade. This fact was almost certainly crucial to the considerations which preceded the formation of the Montrose Banking Company in May, 1814. Montrose depended upon Baltic timber for its shipbuilding and cabinetmaking trades, while the linen, cotton and fishing industries were also important to the town. The Bank of Scotland and the British Linen Co. both maintained branches there. The former was withdrawn in 1818, possibly because competition from the new bank made its position untenable. This was an age of intense parochialism. A new provincial banking company which opened in competition with a branch of a public bank could be expected to attract custom more easily because of local loyalty, kinship and its initial liberality.

The war finally came to an end in June, 1815. Although it was not realised at the time, the peace marked the end of the expansion in the numbers of provincial banking companies.

2. The Beginnings of Decline in the Aftermath of War

In the period between 1815 and 1825 more provincial banking companies closed than opened, i.e. four opened and six closed.

On 18th October, 1816 the Falkirk Union Banking Co. was sequestrated. Its loans had been principally to 'men possessing large farms, store farmers also, jobbers in cattle'.[10] The harvest of that year was poor, but prices were higher as a result. The partners in the Falkirk Union were principally farmers and distillers, some of whom made the mistake of becoming their own bank's best customers. There was a deficiency of 10/6 per £1.[11]

The business failures in Glasgow during 1816 brought to light the embezzlement at the Royal Bank, Glasgow by the agent John More.[12] This event caused a crisis of confidence among the Royal's customers, many of whom took their business to other Glasgow bankers, principally the Glasgow Banking Company. (See Balance Sheets in Appendix A.) This gave that company the opportunity to extend its co-partnery and therefore its capital. The new partners, of whom at least some must have been former Royal Bank customers, were among the most important of the Glasgow merchants and included Henry Monteith, James Buchanan, Robert Dalglish, James Ewing, Robert Findlay, James Oswald, and Colin Campbell.[13] The admission of these men to the co-partnery strengthened the base of the Glasgow Banking Company.

Other banks were not so well placed during the crisis of 1816. The directors of the Montrose Banking Company were obliged to tell their staff that they

> cannot take it upon them to renew their engagements but to leave it to the next General Meeting to say whether they are to be continued or not as they are of the opinion that the expense of the establishment must be lessened.[14]

The General Meeting of that year agreed to renew the contracts but the salary of the accountant was reduced from £200 to £150 and that of the cashier from £300 to £200.[15]

Business conditions were little better in the early month of 1817. George Kinnear, an Edinburgh private banker and director of the Bank of Scotland, wrote to the Montrose Banking Co. to complain that there was

> certainly at present a difficulty in employing money in the Discount of good Bills as formerly . . . A number of people selling out of the 3 per cents. satisfied with the present prices have rendered Deposit Money very plenty.[16]

The high price of consols had depressed the yields and convinced the public banks that they were no longer able to allow 4 per cent interest on deposits. Consequently, they announced that deposits would in future bear interest at 3 per cent,[17] although the Royal was at times prepared to negotiate rates of interest with customers.[18] Very little is known about the provincial banking companies' response to this move, which created a novel situation. The Perth Banking Co. decided to follow the rate downwards, then hesitated because the British Linen and Commercial Banks had not reduced their rates. Then, 'having taken under their consideration the present state of the Company's funds', they decided to reduce the rate but changed their minds two months later because they were afraid of losing customers to banks which maintained the old rate. Finally, a year after the question had first been raised, they decided that balances up to £1,500 would be allowed 4 per cent and sums over £1,500 would earn only 3 per cent.[19] This was the first time that interest rate changes had forced the Scottish banks and banking companies into this kind of competition.

There was a short trade boom which began in the later part of 1817 and continued throughout 1818. During the upturn a new type of bank emerged on the Scottish banking scene. This was the Exchange and Deposit Bank of John Maberly and Co. (see below, section 3).

In 1819 the depression returned, prices fell and trade slumped. In England particularly there was a further deflationary influence in the contractive policies of the banks in anticipation of the return to cash-payments following the passing of Peel's Act in 1819. The deflationary policies of the banks and the contraction of trade combined to prolong the depression until 1822. In April, 1822 the government decided to delay the abolition of notes under £5 in England, which had been part of the return to cash-payments package. The intention was to reflate the economy.

In Scotland the return to cash payments did not present the same problems as it did south of the border. There was no danger (for the present) that £1 notes would be abolished, nor was there any likelihood that the Scottish bankers would have to build up large stocks of gold. With the exception of a short period following the Bank of England suspension in 1797, they had always been prepared to pay specie for their notes. It was seldom requested.

The plan to resume cash payments had been decided upon following the report of a Parliamentary Committee but the voice of Scotland was almost wholly silent on this question. Only Ebenezer Gilchrist, manager of the British Linen Co., was invited to give evidence to the committee, and his testimony[20] was almost devoid of knowledge and comprehension. He had not lived in Scotland prior to 1797 and could not answer the questions put to him about that period. He thought that if the Bank reduced its note issues, then the Scots bankers would follow suit, although he did not appear to be aware of the reasons for this supposed reaction, but he was aware of the dangers of a deflationary policy. No provincial bankers gave evidence to the Committee.

It was the agricultural areas which suffered most at this time. There was 'a mediocre harvest in 1819, good harvests and falling prices in 1820 and 1821'.[21] Mowbray and Co. (the Berwick Bank) failed in 1820, but it was replaced – probably the following year – by Messrs. Batson, Berry and Co. who styled their firm the 'Tweed Bank'. John Langhorn was the only partner of the Berwick Bank who joined the new concern. Again this must really be considered to be an English bank whose only branch was at Alnwick in Northumberland.[22]

In Scotland two banks found it prudent to retire. The Galloway Banking Company withdrew from business in October, 1821. It had contracted a single bad debt of £55,000 as bills to that extent had been discounted to a firm of cattle drovers who were forced to sell when prices were low.[23] The company had also been making large loans to its partners: for example, James Hannay had borrowed £5,000.[24] The partners lost a large sum of money, but all public debts were paid in full.

The Kilmarnock Banking Company also retired in 1821. Its business was sold to Hunters and Co. of Ayr. The Kilmarnock partnership had been restructured in 1819 following some bad losses,[25] but had never really recovered and was forced to sell out in 1821. Again it was predominantly an agricultural bank. One of the partners, Robert Kent, who was described as 'Farrier and Banker', had absconded with some funds which merely compounded the already troubled state of this banking company.[26] Despite the fact that Hunters and Co. took over the business, the Commercial Bank seized the opportunity to set up a branch in that town and succeeded in capturing some of the trade.[27]

Although the 1819 to 1822 period was marked by depression, there were areas of the economy which were able to expand. In 1821 the Shetland Banking Company (Messrs. Hay and Ogilvy) was founded. Wm. Hay and Charles Ogilvy together with the latter's two sons were engaged in a wide range of economic activities in Shetland. As general merchants they dealt in a large number of commodities which included fruit, kelp, meal, cattle, coal, cloth and salt. The mainstay of their trade was fishing, including whales. They also manufactured fish-oil, built ships, operated a cooperage, carried passengers to the islands and acted as a sort of employment exchange for seamen.[28] Hay was also agent for the North British Insurance Company.[29] The banking side was a small concern which was used by the partners to finance their other interests.

In 1822 the East Lothian Banking Company closed its doors. This failure was caused by the disappearance of the cashier with the company's funds. The directors acknowledged that they were partly to blame for this. They admitted that

> Whether by fraud and embezzlement of the Cashier; by misfortunes or mismanagement or by all these causes combined, the affairs of the East Lothian Bank are in great disorder.[30]

The directors had certainly been negligent in their supervisory duties. The firm was wound up under a trust deed and the debts were paid in full, while the Edinburgh agent, Sir William Forbes, James Hunter and Co., put a loan of £110,000 to enable the trustees to pay off the public debts.[31] Borthwick, the cashier, escaped to America.

Between 1822 and 1825 the economy was reflated. The English small notes were reprieved and government stock was converted to lower rates of interest. In June, 1822 Bank Rate was reduced from 5 to 4 per cent. The effect of the lowering of Bank Rate can best be seen in the records of the Montrose Banking Co. In July, 1822 Messrs. Barclay, Bevan, Tritton and Co. who were London correspondents for a number of provincial companies for whom they held large balances announced that, because of the fall in Bank Rate, they were about to reduce the rate of interest on deposits from 4 to 3 per cent. The Edinburgh and Dundee banks and banking companies also announced that interest allowed to depositors would in future be at the rate of 3 per cent and discounts would be charged at 4 per cent. The Montrose Banking Company had no real alternative but to follow suit.[32] This is an early example of how a change in Bank Rate affected rates of interest throughout the country.

The reflation of the economy brought two new banking companies into being – the Arbroath Banking Co. and the Dundee Commercial Banking Co., which was the second firm of that name.

> The establishment of the Arbroath Banking Company, took place from the idea of the merchants and residenters there wishing to secure part of the profit of the banking business to themselves, which they were in the habit of giving to branches of other establishments from other quarters.[33]

The Dundee Union and Montrose banking companies both maintained branches in Arbroath.

The Dundee Commercial Banking Company was established 'on the usual pretence of there being a deficiency of banking accommodation in the town'. In fact two of the promoters were the teller and accountant of the Dundee New Bank and a large portion of that company's customers became shareholders in the new concern.[34]

Despite the air of optimism in the economy, 1825 saw the closure of two banks. The Caithness Banking Company was taken over by the Commercial Bank in July of that year. The fact that no consideration was paid for goodwill[35] suggests that it was in poor condition, but none of its records have survived so that it is impossible to do anything other than speculate about its affairs.

The closure of the Fife Banking Co. in December, 1825 was a similar occurrence to that of the East Lothian Banking Co. three years earlier. The cashier had been dishonest and attempted to abscond but, unlike Borthwick, he was apprehended. The balance sheet of 1823 showed £6–7,000 in the funds, but in fact these had already been sold. A trust was formed, with the help of the British Linen Co. and the new National Bank of Scotland, to wind up the company's affairs. When an 'immense deficiency'[36] was discovered the British Linen withdrew, having discovered the 'extent of their obligations and of the sum required to give effectual aid and relief'.[37] This left the National to carry out the trust deed on its own. It did so because a sequestration 'at a time when the public mind was in such an alarmed state, might produce evils of the greatest magnitude'.[38] By that time the boom was coming to an end.

The year 1825 was also marked by the formation of two other banks in Scotland. Both were large-scale joint-stock banks (see introduction). The National Bank of Scotland was opened in March of that year. Its base was in Edinburgh and it opened a series of branches within months. It was similar in many ways to the Commercial Banking Co. of Scotland. The Aberdeen Town and County Bank, the second formation, had 470 partners, which marks it as being in a different class from the provincial banking companies already in existence. These were the first of a wave of joint-stock bank formations which, together with public bank expansion, ultimately swept the provincial banking companies out of existence.

By that time the banking companies had begun to decline as a proportion of the total system. In 1825 they constituted 24 per cent of total liabilities.[39]

3. John Maberly and Co.

John Maberly and his son William, who became secretary of the General Post Office, acquired Broadford Linen Factory at Aberdeen in 1811[40] where the products were coarse linen and sailcloth.[41] The manufactory at first transacted its banking business with the Bank of Scotland branch in Aberdeen but when the bank agent, John Thomson, requested some collateral security for the discounts it was refused. The transactions consisted of bills drawn by the factory manager on John Maberly in London. The amount of these bills current at one time varied between £6,000 and £12,000, and when further security was requested the account was removed to the Aberdeen Banking Co. and from there to the Commercial Bank branch, both of which also eventually demanded collateral. In 1816 the account was moved back to the Bank of Scotland when an agreement was reached that the bills would be discounted if endorsed by a third person.[42] Probably some of the bills involved were accommodation bills – hence the call for extra security.

In 1817 Stephen Maberly, who was a nephew of John Maberly and agent for his uncle in Aberdeen, began to issue notes of hand to his workers in payment of wages. Although some shopkeepers accepted them they were refused by the banks. In 1818 Stephen Maberly asked for admission to the note exchange but was refused. Clearly his note-issuing business was an incipient banking concern.

A few weeks later the banks in Edinburgh learned that John Maberly, M.P., was the principal partner in the factory run by Stephen Maberly,

and that this concern was without any previous communication, taking measures to enroach on the business of the Banking Establishments particularly that of the Bank of Scotland by altering the usual course of the London Exchange on Bills continued for a number of years past to the entire satisfaction of the Country; and was actually advertising to sell drafts on London at a par of Twenty days date, in place of Fifty days which was the established rate at Aberdeen.[43]

Since 1782 the banks in Edinburgh had been in the practice of drawing bills on London at 40 days and buying bills at 20 days, although in Aberdeen the drawing rate was 50 days.[44] The activities of Maberly posed a serious threat to this long-established custom and consequently to the profits of the existing banks.

Maberly's new banking concern was known by the name of the Exchange and Deposit Bank and branches were quickly established in Glasgow, Edinburgh, Dundee and Montrose.[45] The bills drawn on London were provided for by funds remitted from Scotland which had been obtained by agents of Maberly from the banks in exchange for their notes.

The Maberly notes which, after 1818, were issued in name of John Maberly and Co., were payable only in London[46] and because of this the other banks and banking companies refused to accept them from their customers,[47] preferring instead to close ranks and attempt to exclude Maberly from all banking business:

> It appeared that the 'bank' was set up, not to discount bills . . . the usual occupation of bankers – not to grant cash accounts – not to afford the public any one accommodation, but that of receiving their bank notes, and giving them his bills upon London at 20 days par, or receiving their money in deposit, on conditions of being repaid by a bill on London, when called for.[48]

It paid 4 per cent on deposits at a time when other banks paid only 3 per cent and Maberly was also prepared to invest his customers' money in the funds for which he charged only the normal broker's commission of 1/8 per cent.[49]

The early experience as a customer which Maberly had of bank charges for drawing bills on London led him to nurture ambitions on a grand scale. His business in Aberdeen had been forced to pay 50 days' interest for bills on London but he was aware that the public revenues were remitted by the public banks and private bankers to London by means of bills drawn at 60 days instead of 40 days charged to Edinburgh business customers. By 1819 Maberly had made overtures to the Treasury regarding the remittance of the public revenues from Scotland in which he offered 'to remit to any amount to London, by Bills at 20 days sight'. The Commissioners consequently felt that they could 'no longer feel themselves justified in permitting the Revenue . . . to be remitted as at present by Bills at 60 days'. Not wishing to be thought dishonourable or precipitate, the Commissioners requested that the existing remitters should scale down their charges.[50]

Faced with this ultimatum, the Edinburgh banks capitulated. At a meeting attended by the Bank of Scotland, Royal Bank, Commercial Bank, British Linen Co. and Sir Wm. Forbes and Co.,

> it was resolved that though they adopted the measure with reluctance it was absolutely necessary to alter the mode adopted by a new establishment very harrassing to the Banks of this and many other parts of Scotland.

It was decided to buy London bills from the public at par and to draw on London at 20 days[51] and the provincial banking companies followed suit. The revenue was in future to be remitted at 30 days' date, but Maberly was to have no part in it.

The Commissioners found Maberly's suggestion acceptable but preferred their established connections even if they were more expensive.

The bankers had been forced into adopting these measures. For those who remitted public revenue it involved some loss of income, i.e. 10 days' interest, but probably, on balance, no loss on ordinary business because the margin between buying and selling London bills remained the same, i.e. 20 days. The problem was more acute, however, for the provincial banking companies who had been accustomed to charging 5 or 10 days more than the Edinburgh banks for bills drawn on London. Maberly of course operated in the major provincial areas, which forced the banking companies to follow his rates. Consequently their margin on London drafts was cut from 25 or 30 days to 20 days. Although figures are not available, it is arguable that this had a significant effect on the profits of the provincial banking companies.

The banks and banking companies were decidedly upset by Maberly's activities, which were described as 'very harrassing'[52] and 'annoying'.[53] His insistence on remitting notes to Edinburgh in halves 'for security' was doubly distressing to the banks there. Nevertheless, the bankers were not without some effective responses. Maberly 'was not considered within the circle of the note exchange'[54] and the short-term effect of this was of course to keep his notes in circulation, but the longer-term effect was probably to reduce the willingness of the general public to use them. More imaginatively perhaps, they planned on 'drowning the miller by giving him more than he reckoned or hoped for'.[55] W. Graham, a late 19th century historian, revealed that Maberly's plan depended upon the banks paying in London bills for their notes which he had obtained by selling bills on London to his customers. This scheme had the effect of 'practically, though at second hand, placing on the other banks the burden of granting drafts to the public at ten days' while Maberly kept the profits. Initially the bankers paid their notes to Maberly in Bank of England notes rather than bills because the greater risk and expense of remittance to London was less favourable to his scheme.[56] When Maberly decided to reduce the par of exchange even further, to ten days, the bankers determined on even stronger measures. They decided to pay for their notes, held by Maberly in gold. Graham claimed that

> Shortly Maberly's coffers were full of unremunerative metal from which there was no relief save by expensive carriage to London. The banks continued this defence, or conspiracy as it might be better called, until their disturbers were compelled to curtail their business being unable to purchase London paper wherewith to retire the numerous drafts they had granted.[57]

The textile business was sold out but the banking side struggled on until it succumbed in the pressure of 1832. It was wound up under an English fiat of bankruptcy. The liabilities were £149,000 and the assets realised £77,000. The dividend was only 4/5d per £1.[58]

John Maberly and Co. was a fringe bank. But, unfortunately, virtually nothing is known about its customers or the volume of its business. There was no deposition with the sequestration papers, which show that money was being lent on mortgages over property in Birmingham and elsewhere,[59] but these papers are so lacking in detail as to make it impossible to say where Maberly and Co. drew its resources from.

The activities of John Maberly and Co. had administered a considerable shock to the established practices of Scottish bankers and the effect of Maberly's business was to close the ranks of the banks and banking companies. The Bank of Scotland was heard to concede that 'the various Banking Establishments all over Scotland . . . have been instituted to the great benefit of the public'.[60] This acknowledgement came rather late – for the days of the provincial banking companies were almost over.

NOTES

1. C.B.S., D.M.B., 20/11/1810
2. B.S. Edinburgh, Miscellaneous Documents
3. S.R.O. CS96/683. John Ferguson's sequestration
4. B.L., D.M.B., 9/11/1812
5. B.S., D.M.B., 12/4/1813 and 26/7/1813
6. J. Buchanan, 1884, p. 29
7. A. W. Kerr, 1926, p. 134
8. Melville MSS., S.R.O., GD51/296/1–2
9. S.R.O. CS311–2132, Box 207, G. Kinnear to Montrose Banking Co., 7/11/1815
10. P.P., Select Committee on Promissory Notes . . . 1826, evidence of Thomas Kinnear, p. 138
11. S.R.O., CS96/988, Falkirk Union Banking Co. sequestration
12. S. G. Checkland, 1975, p. 297
13. B.S., Glasgow, Miscellaneous Papers
14. Montrose Banking Co., D.M.B., 7/2/1816
15. *Ibid.*, 5/6/1816
16. S.R.O., CS311/2142 Box 207, Letter George Kinnear to Montrose Banking Co., 21/5/1817
17. B.S., D.M.B., 21/7/1817
18. R.B.S., D.M.B., 18/2/1818
19. Perth Banking Co., D.M.B., 29/7/1817, 19/8/1817, 1/10/1817 and 4/8/1818
20. P.P. Resumption Committee evidence 1819, pp. 214–216 and Lords Committee pp. 143–5
21. L. S. Pressnell, 1956, p. 474
22. M. Phillips, 1894, p. 162
23. P.P. Select Committee on Promissory Notes . . . 1826, evidence of John Commelin, p. 173; and C. Malcolm, *The Bank of Scotland in Dumfries*, n.d.
24. S. Francis, 1961, p. 142
25. Pollock-Morris MSS., Jas. Fairlie's Letter Book, 22/3/1819
26. S.R.O., CS96/848, Robert Kent's sequestration
27. C.B.S., D.M.B., 1/3/1821, 17/5/1821
28. N.L.S., Acc. 3250, Hay of Hayfield MSS., Boxes 27–110
29. *Ibid.*, Box 41, Letter Wm. Hay to N.B. Ins. Co., 23/6/1842
30. S.R.O. GD1/265/1, Minutes of General Meeting, 4/5/1822
31. S.R.O. Register of Deeds vol. 229, Bond of Relief, 8/8/1822
32. Montrose Banking Co., D.M.B. 9/7/1822, 10/7/1822, 2/8/1822
33. P.P. Select Committee on Promissory Notes . . . 1826 evidence of Hugh Watt, p. 187; and *Arbroath Guide*, 1924–5
34. C. W. Boase, 1867, p. 334
35. C.B.S., D.M.B., 24/6/1825
36. B.S., Edinburgh, B.L. Papers
37. C. Malcolm, 1950, p. 101
38. N.B.S., D.M.B., 7/12/1826
39. S. G. Checkland, 1975, Table 14

40. B. Lenman and E. Gauldie, Sources of Capital for Industrial Growth in East Central Scotland, unpublished article
41. C.B.S., D.M.B., 16/5/1823
42. B.S., Melville MSS., Paper 151, Memo re John Maberly and Co.
43. *Ibid.*
44. *Caledonian Mercury*, 8/7/1819
45. P.P. Select Committee on Promissory Notes . . . 1826, evidence of John Maberly, p. 171
46. *Ibid.*, evidence of James Hadden, p. 274
47. B.S., Edinburgh, Montrose Banking Co., D.M.B., 6/10/1819
48. *Caledonian Mercury*, 8/7/1819
49. C.B.S., D.M.B., 18/12/1818
50. B.S., Melville MSS., paper 152, M. Pemberton to Bank of Scotland, 5/4/1819
51. S.R.O. CS311/2142, Box 207, Letter Geo. Kinnear to Montrose Banking Co. 2/7/1819
52. *Ibid.*
53. C.B.S., D.M.B., 18/12/1818
54. P.P. Select Committee on Promissory Notes . . . 1826, evidence of Alex. Blair, p. 50
55. W. Graham, 1886, p. 144
56. C.B.S., D.M.B., 18/12/1818
57. Graham, 1886, p. 144
58. *Ibid.*, pp. 143–4
59. P.R.O. B/3/3641–2, Maberly Sequestration Papers
60. B.S., Melville MSS., paper 151, p. 17, Memo re Maberly, 2/4/1819

5

The Eclipse and End, 1825–1864

THE years between 1825 and 1864 saw the total disappearance of the provincial banking companies and their replacement by joint-stock banks. The period began with a government attack on the small notes which was successfully fought off, but increased competition especially from the new joint-stock banks undermined the ability of the provincial banking companies to continue in business.

1. The 1826 Reports

Between 1822 and 1825 the economy expanded, primarily owing to the opening up of trade with South America, and the promotion of joint-stock companies was on a scale previously unknown. Many of these companies were of a highly speculative nature and in December, 1825 the bubble burst. 'There was no parliamentary enquiry after this crisis, because there was but little difference of opinion as to the causes'.[1] The small notes and the country banks were blamed. Consequently an Act was passed which prohibited any new issue of notes under £5 in England and Wales.[2] Some members of Lord Liverpool's government felt that if small notes were a danger in England they would be such in Scotland also.

There was good historical precedent for advocating that £5 should be the smallest denomination of banknotes. Adam Smith had suggested it 50 years previously.[3] In February, 1826 it became known that legislation, similar to that for England, was planned for Scotland.

The result was a deluge of petitions from all over Scotland and the North of England from banks, landowners, town councils, industrialists and other business-men in support of the status quo. One of the moving spirits behind the protest was Sir Walter Scott. Writing under the pen name of Malachi Malagrowther, he sent a series of letters to the editor of the *Edinburgh Weekly Journal* in defence of the Scots pound note, urging Scotsmen to petition parliament to drop the proposed legislation.

Scott based his polemic on the clause of the 1707 Treaty of Union which guaranteed that all legislation affecting the northern kingdom should be 'for the evident utility of the subjects within Scotland'.[4] He believed that Scotland was a country which had been converted

> from a poor, miserable and barren country, into one, where, if Nature had done less, Art and Industry have done more, than in perhaps any country in Europe, England herself not excepted.[5]

The banks, he alleged, had played a major role in this development. He appealed to Scots pride to defend the right of Scots banks to issue one pound notes. 'There are no Scotchmen so humble that they have not a share in a national insult, so lowly that they will not suffer from a national wrong.'[6] He played upon the seeming needlessness of the proposed legislation, stating that to ban small notes in Scotland because they might be a potential source of danger was 'very like the receipt of Sheepface in the farce who kills his master's sheep to prevent their dying'.[7] Nor were the letters short on facts, for Scott was well aware of the success achieved by Scots banks, particularly in comparison with their English counterparts. 'We are well, our pulse and complexion prove it – let those who are sick take physic'.[8]

Scott's letters were attacked in the English press. One writer who styled himself E. B. Waverley published a series of letters in reply. But this pseudo-Waverley was himself attacked and Scott defended in an article in *Blackwood's Edinburgh Magazine*. Malagrowther had

> sounded the long forgotten trumpet of chivalry and addressed the Scottish people not as heartless misers but as the descendants of the martial and the high minded. He spoke of public matters in the obsolete [i.e. venerable] language of a patriot and a statesman.[9]

Clearly emotion played an important part in this campaign. F. W. Fetter attributed the authorship of this article to David Robinson,[10] a freelance author of articles on economics. Important support for Scott's position also came from Thomas Joplin whose famous essay on banking was first published in 1822 and went through its fifth edition in 1826. Joplin set out the failure pattern of English banking and went on to state that

> the Scotch banks never fail, nor is any danger ever apprehended from them, and . . . in consequence, Banking is carried on in that kingdom to an extent unknown, and, of course, with advantages totally unfelt in our own.[11]

Joplin was instrumental in securing legislation in 1826 which permitted joint-stock banks in England and Wales. Scott may have taken much of his information from Joplin's essay.

Scott's motives in writing the Malagrowther letters were, almost certainly, not entirely disinterested. He and his publishers were two of the casualties of the commercial crisis.[12] Both were already insolvent and Scott's affairs were wound up by trustees. He was well aware that any contraction of credit by the Scottish bankers necessitated by the withdrawal of small notes would render his chances of extricating himself from his embarrassments ineffectual and a general deflation in the economy would make his position even more difficult. It is possible that Scott's authorship of the letters under an ill-disguised *nom-de-plume* was designed to curry favour with the banks who were his principal creditors.

The most important of the bankers who resisted the proposals was George Kinnear. He was a director of the Bank of Scotland and a private banker in Edinburgh. He wrote to his correspondents advising them that the government would 'adhere to their theories unless the country make so resolute a stand as to deter them'. Bankers were asked to tell their customers what the consequences of the removal of small notes would be, i.e. that the cash credit system would have to be severely curtailed.[13]

The effects of Scott's polemic and Kinnear's advice were startling. 'Men of all parties; who had never agreed on any one subject before, were united in this' defence of small notes.[14] James Gibson Craig, an Edinburgh lawyer, when asked what the opinion of the people of Scotland was with regard to the proposed change in currency replied, 'the opinion is universal against any change of the system'.[15] In the Lords, Scott found support from Melville, Rosebery, Aberdeen, Lauderdale and Caernarvon. The last of these expressed his amazement that 'the House should be called upon to alter the currency of Scotland, when no human being had complained that that currency did not work well in practice'.[16] The Earl of Liverpool asked for a Select Committee on the question but Earl Grosvenor, however, thought that the enquiry could be of no service and that Scott had 'excited fears in the minds of ministers'.[17] In the Commons the debate showed a similar pattern. Keith Douglas thought that 'Parliament ought to show some deference for the petitions which were coming up from all parts of Scotland'.[18] Mr. Abercromby thought that the Scots people wanted change but he was accused by W. Dundas of being out of touch, which he undoubtedly was. Mr. Maberly, who had a vested interest, thought that people in Scotland would dislike a gold currency but still maintained that the system should be changed.[19] The opinion of Parliament was essentially in favour of the status quo, but Liverpool's suggestion that there should be committees of inquiry into the Scottish and Irish systems was accepted.

The Commons and Lords Committtees sat from March to May 1826, taking evidence from Scots and Irish bankers and businessmen and from the governor and directors of the Bank of England. The evidence from the Scottish witnesses supported in large measure what Joplin and Scott had said in their essays. In fact the form of the questions asked by the Committee members seems to have been prompted by these writings. The evidence of the Scots bankers in defence of the one pound note was unequivocal. John Commelin, agent for the British Linen Co. at Dumfries, thought that 'the system of cash credits could not be supported unless by an issue of small notes'.[20] Hugh Watt, cashier of the Arbroath Banking Company, and one of Scotland's most experienced bankers, assured the Committee that if small notes were done away with, then the profits of the banking trade would be diminished and the banks would be unable to pay interest on deposits with the result that the beneficial effects of small savings would vanish.[21] Roger Aytoun, manager of the Renfrewshire Banking Company, thought that the removal of small notes would cause his company to withdraw its distant branches with disastrous consequences for the west coast herring fisheries which depended heavily on cash accounts and small notes because the people engaged in that trade 'have generally expended their stock in trade in erecting stores, and in the purchase of vessels necessary for carrying it on: their capital is expended'.[22] Andrew Coventry, Professor of Agriculture at Edinburgh University, was afraid of the effects upon farmers if credit was curtailed as a result of the withdrawal of the small notes.[23] James Gibson Craig alleged that the work of the Parliamentary trustees for new roads in Scotland would be hampered by the withdrawal of credit as most of them depended for short-term credit on cash account facilities provided by the banks.[24] Kirkman Finlay, a leading Glasgow merchant, when asked if he thought that bank services had been conducive to the prosperity of Scotland in the past thirty years, replied 'I think that it is one of the ingredients, and perhaps I should say the principal ingredient, of the prosperity of the country'.[25]

Only John Gladstone, merchant in Liverpool, whose early commercial experience had been in Leith, sounded a note of caution. He was convinced that the mode of banking in Scotland

> has led to an extension of business there, that has employed those issues, and that has produced consequences in its results both inconvenient and injurious.[26]

He did not say what those consequences were, nor was he asked.

The Scots bankers were generally united in defence of the system. Alexander Blair, Secretary of the British Linen Co., argued that an over-issue of notes was impossible because of the system of note exchanges which was in operation.[27] Even in the crisis of 1825 only one man had 'applied' for gold and that was John Maberly, the maverick of the Scottish banking scene. Maberly thought that a run for gold on the Scottish banks would force them to close in 48 hours.[28]

In this he was undoubtedly correct because the banks operated on very small specie reserves, but he failed to acknowledge the stability which the Scottish system had shown in the recent crisis. Samuel Thornton, a director of the Bank of England, alleged that the safety of the Scots note issue rested 'principally on its reliance on the English supply of a metallic currency',[29] but Jeremiah Harman, also a director of the Bank, confessed that the Scots bankers had made no demands for gold upon the Bank during the recent crisis. Roger Aytoun of the Renfrewshire Banking Co. insisted that 'a great deal more gold and silver has been sent to London than drawn from it; we never have had occasion to get gold from London'.[30] Nevertheless, although these specific statements were true, it remained a fact that London was the Scottish bankers' traditional source of supply for gold and there was a fairly steady, if small, flow of specie from London to the Scottish bankers. It must not be overlooked, however, that there was a similar flow of specie southwards from banks and in the pockets of travellers. The amounts involved were likely to be small compared with the demands from the English provinces. The main point at issue, however, remained unchallenged. No Scottish banker had been forced to go to the Bank of England for gold during the crisis of 1825–6.

The overwhelming mass of evidence in support of the Scots system of banking was such that before long it became clear that the concern of the Committees was not how they might change that system, but how they might maintain it and yet confine the Scots notes within Scotland. Several Scottish banking companies had kept branches in the North of England and the notes of these companies had served as an important part of the circulating medium in the northern counties for many years – a state of affairs which was maintained by English merchants and manufacturers who supported the Scots in their campaign to keep small notes.

Gold had long ceased to be in any significant circulation in Scotland and consequently the banks had very small reserves of that metal. Silver and copper served the purpose of small change and most witnesses testified to the adequacy of their supply. Kirkman Finlay, when asked if there was any circulation of gold at present in Glasgow, replied, 'So small that it may be called none at all'.[31] This was a situation which was to the benefit of the banks for they made a handsome, but by this time decreasing, profit from their note issues.[32] Whatever the advantages of the note issue to the banks it cannot be denied that it was a system in which the public confided their trust.

Despite the impression given by the witnesses to the Committees that all was well, a few of the banking companies were, in fact, in some trouble during the 1825–6 crisis. The fate of the Fife Banking Company has already been mentioned. The Stirling Banking Company was also in difficulty, although it did not succumb until July 1826, by which time the reports of the Parliamentary Committees had already been written. The company had been in trouble in 1824 when it was found that the cashier had been making unauthorised advances and had accumulated a large number of past-due bills. John Thomson, one of the partners, thought that the company could have recovered from this difficulty if the commercial crisis had not come when it did.[33] The major customers of the company were grain dealers, maltsters and distillers,[34] many of whom became bankrupt in the crisis, thus precipitating the failure of the banking company whose debts were paid in full. No other failures occurred amongst the provincial banking companies, but many were in difficulty, while others found it prudent to cut back their lending or to decline new business. The Perth Banking Co. refused new cash account applications – "the state of the times not rendering it expedient".[35] The Glasgow Banking Co. found it necessary to transfer money from capital account to reserves,[36] while the Montrose Banking Co. was forced to borrow money from the Bank of Scotland.[37] All of these companies survived the 1825–6 crisis. Only the Fife and Stirling Banking Companies failed and their problems were much more deep-seated than simple liquidity problems associated with the commercial crisis.

In England there were sixty country bank failures in the harvest year 1825–6.[38] This fact, compared with the Scottish experience, impressed the members of the Select Committees. Although not entirely convinced by the assurances of witnesses, the Commons commissioners felt that Scottish banking was

> a system admirably calculated, in their opinion, to economise the use of Capital, to excite and cherish a spirit of useful Enterprise, and even to promote the moral habits of the people, by the direct inducements which it holds out to the maintenance of a character for industry, integrity and prudence.[39]

The Lords Committee concurred and the Bank of England agreed with the conclusions. John B. Richards, Governor of the Bank, believed that 'so long as the currency of Scotland is kept within its own limits it cannot affect the general circulation of England'.[40] To this end an Act was passed which prohibited the issue of Scottish notes under £5 in England after 5th April, 1829.[41] Sir Walter Scott had been vindicated and Scotland kept her small notes.

One of the outcomes of the enquiries was an Act which had the effect of giving legal recognition to the banking companies.[42] Until then the law had been uncertain as to the constitution of these concerns. The new legislation confirmed case law and enabled them to sue and be sued in the name of their cashier or manager. Any judgement against such an officer was to be effectual against the whole partnership or co-partnery. Annual returns were required from the company stating its name, the names and addresses of the partners, the name of the cashier or manager and the location of branches but this Act did not receive the publicity it might have been given. Several months after its passing the Montrose Banking Co. directors confessed themselves to be 'unaware that this Act had passed into law' and were consequently 'ignorant of its provisions'.[43] In fact the 'greater number of the banks in Scotland . . . failed to make the Statutory returns'.[44] Kinnear advised his correspondents that they were not compelled to comply with the Act[45] but this was wrong. When some of the Fife Banking Co. actions before the Court of Session were suspended because of non-compliance with the Act,[46] and others were threatened that the penalty clause would be invoked, the bankers were sufficiently impressed that compliance was necessary. The initial hostility to the new legislation was caused by the requirements which called for disclosure of the names of partners. The banking companies, particularly the co-partneries, had often tended to be secretive about their membership – there was always a suspicion about what government might do with the information. Nor were the bankers very impressed by the benefits of the new Act. The practice of suing and being sued in the name of the cashier or manager was one which the courts had long recognised. The Act merely gave legal recognition to a well-established custom.

2. The Joint–Stock Takeover

In England the Bank Charter Act of 1826 repealed the statute of 1708 which had forbidden English banks, save the Bank of England, from having more than six partners. This removal of the restraint on joint-stock banking in England took place largely because of the activities of Thomas Joplin who had campaigned since 1822 for an end to the restrictive legislation which embodied the six-partner law. Joplin believed that joint-stock banks were likely to be more secure institutions than the country banks, simply because their large numbers of partners provided an extended responsibility for the banks' debts. The legislation of 1826 allowed for the formation of joint-stock banks in England outwith a 65-mile radius of London but in 1833 even this restriction was removed, the only condition remaining being that banks within that radius could not issue notes. Such banks, of course, were unlimited in their liability, as were their Scottish predecessors.

Joplin had been highly impressed by the freedom from failure of the Scottish

G

banking companies, particularly the larger co-partneries, a fact which he used to illustrate his claims about the benefits of large banks in comparison with the six-partner banks.[47] The idea of large-scale banking caught on relatively slowly in England,[48] but by the mid 1830s there was a steady flow of formations.

In Scotland there had never been any limitation on the number of partners who could form a banking company and the nature of the organisations which grew up in consequence has been discussed above.[49] In the 1830s in Scotland a wave of large-scale joint-stock banks came into being. This development had been anticipated in the formation of the Commercial Bank in 1810, and the National Bank and the Aberdeen Town and County Bank, both in 1825, but the real period of growth was in the 1830s. These new concerns initiated dynamic programmes of branch extensions and competed actively both with the public banks and with the provincial banking companies. The latter, unable to meet this competition, succumbed and many were taken over while others failed. Table 9 sets out the experience of the banking companies between 1826 and 1864.

Table 9
Scottish Provincial Banking Companies 1826–1864

		Year of opening	Remarks
a)	*Banks in existence at end of 1825*		
	Note Issuers		
1.	Ship Bank, Glasgow	1750	Amalgamated with No. 17, 1836
2.	Thistle Bank, Glasgow	1761	To U.B.S. 1836
3.	Dundee Banking Co.	1763	To R.B.S. 1864
4.	Aberdeen Banking Co.	1767	To U.B.S. 1849
5.	Hunters and Co., Ayr	1773	To U.B.S. 1843
6.	Stirling Banking Co.	1777	Failed 1826
7.	Paisley Banking Co.	1783	To B.L. Co. 1837
8.	Greenock Banking Co.	1785	To. W.B.S. 1843
9.	Falkirk Banking Co.	1785	Retired 1826
10.	Perth Banking Co.	1787	To U.B.S. 1857
11.	Paisley Union Banking Co.	1788	To U.B.S. 1838
12.	Commercial Banking Co. of Aberdeen	1788	To N.B.S. 1833
13.	Leith Banking Co.	1792	Failed 1842
14.	Dundee New Bank	1802	To Dundee Banking Co. 1838
15.	Refrewshire Banking Co., Greenock	1802	Failed 1842
16.	Dundee Union Banking Co.	1809	To W.B.S. 1844
17.	Glasgow Banking Co.	1809	Amalgamated with No.1 1836
18.	Perth Union Banking Co.	1810	To N.B.S. 1836
19.	Montrose Banking Co.	1814	To N.B.S. 1829
20.	John Maberly and Co.	1818	Failed 1832
21.	Shetland Banking Co.	1821	Failed 1842
22.	Arbroath Banking Co.	1825	To C.B.S. 1844
23.	Dundee Commercial Banking Co.	1825	Retired 1838
	Private Banks		
24.	J. & R. Watson, Glasgow	c.1763	Failed 1832

		Year of opening	No. of partners	Remarks
b)	*Banks formed in 1826–1864*			
	Note Issuers			
25.	Glasgow and Ship Bank	1836	28	Merger of Nos. 1 & 17 To U.B.S. 1843

Table 10 sets out the pattern of takeovers, mergers, retirals and failures in chronological form.

Table 10

Scottish Provincial Banking Companies 1826–1864:
Takeovers, Mergers, Retirals & Failures

a) *Takeovers*

Montrose Banking Co.	1829	to	N.B.S.
Commercial Banking Co. of Aberdeen	1833	to	N.B.S.
Thistle Bank, Glasgow	1836	to	U.B.S.
Perth Union Banking co.	1836	to	N.B.S.
Paisley Banking Co.	1837	to	B.L.
Paisley Union Banking Co.	1838	to	U.B.S.
Dundee New Bank	1838	to	Dundee Bkg. Co.
Hunters and Co., Ayr	1843	to	U.B.S.
Greenock Banking Co.	1843	to	W.B.S.
Glasgow and Ship Bank	1843	to	U.B.S.
Dundee Union Banking Co.	1844	to	W.B.S.
Arbroath Banking Co.	1844	to	C.B.S.

b) *Mergers*

Ship Bank, Glasgow Bank	1836	Glasgow and Ship Bank

c) *Retirals*

Falkirk Banking Co.	1826
Dundee Commercial Banking Co.	1838

d) *Failures*

Stirling Banking Co.	1826
John Maberly and Co.	1832
J. & R. Watson, Glasgow	1832
Leith Banking Co.	1842
Renfrewshire Banking Co.	1842
Shetland Banking Co.	1842

There were six failures in the 1826 to 1844 period. Two of these – the Stirling Banking Co. and John Maberly and Co. – have already been mentioned (see Chapters 4 and 5). The old Glasgow private banking house of J. & R. Watson failed in 1832 at a time when the economy was expanding. The firm had been making advances on mortgages. One loan on the security of a factory in Clydebank was for £20,000[50] and another firm, Watson and Lennox, had borrowed £24,000.[51] Neither of these loans was sound. The bank seemingly also lost money in a weaving factory at Finnieston, which it had acquired several years before and which it operated on its own account. One of the mainstays of the banking business lay in the correspondences with a number of provincial companies for whom Watson's collected bills and notes, but the number of these accounts decreased in the 1820s as a result of failures and mergers and the stability of

Watson's business was further undermined by a robbery in 1830 in which heavy losses were incurred. This combination of ill-fortune and bad banking combined to cause the failure in June, 1832.[52]

Despite a decade of speculation and rapid economic growth interspersed with commercial crises, there were no further failures amongst the provincial banking companies until 1842. In that year there were three – the Renfrewshire, Shetland and Leith banking companies. The Royal Bank had been Edinburgh agents for both the Renfrewshire and Shetland companies and was instrumental in bringing both to a close. As early as 1839 the Royal had complained to the Renfrewshire that the note exchanges had been running consistently against them and that the balance due to the Royal on their account was too high. Threats that the Royal would cut them short unless they curtailed their business met with half-hearted responses. There was always the excuse that they were trying to restrict their business, but demands for credit for the fitting out of ships and for the import of Irish grain in winter could not properly be refused and this situation continued throughout 1840. The Royal tried to insist that the bills discounted by the Renfrewshire should be endorsed to and collected by the Royal. By this time the debt amounted to £39,000 which was largely covered by personal securities, Royal Bank stock and deposited bills. Later in that year the Royal resorted to the re-discounting of Renfrewshire bills. When the commercial crisis came in 1842 the Royal Bank's Greenock branch made losses and the account with the Renfrewshire deteriorated even further; in March the Royal Bank directors ordered all transactions to cease on the account. One week later, on 30th March, the Renfrewshire closed its doors.[53] The obituary in the *Greenock Advertiser* recognised that the company had been 'without that wealthy backing . . . which once was its own lot' and claimed that

> The fact of its limited capital was so well known that but for the confidence reposed in the character of the manager the public would have ceased to deal with it long ago; and even as it was, it is understood that many of its former customers have long ceased to do business with it.[54]

The dividends amounted to 9/3d on liabilities of £225,600.

The experience of the Shetland Banking Company in its failure was very similar, although in its organisation this company was in a way unique. It had ceased to issue its own notes in 1825, preferring instead to use those of the Royal Bank with whom it negotiated a substantial credit. The affairs of the bank were heavily involved with the mercantile side of the partners' business, Messrs. Hay and Ogilvy, so when the bankruptcy occurred the trading business owed £31,284 to the banking side at a time when deposits were only £28,000.[55] The total debts of the banking company were £65,783.[56] Hay attributed the failure to 'a continued series of bad crops and bad fishings in the islands'. In 1840 they had prepared 30,000 barrels for herring but had only filled 2,500[57] and the situation continued to deteriorate until 1842, when the account with the Royal had become so bad that in June of that year further drafts were refused.[58] The whole banking and mercantile business collapsed. As a study in failure the Shetland Banking Company is an excellent example of a banking business being conducted in an irregular manner with all considerations of good banking practice being sub-ordinated to the needs of one, rather speculative mercantile concern. A first dividend of 5/– per £1 was paid on the estate but the official returns suggest that the sequestration was never completed.[59]

The role of the Royal Bank in these two failures requires some comment. The directors of the Royal tried hard to accommodate their provincial customers, although at all times attempts were made to cover these advances, usually by the deposit of discounted bills. The actions of these two provincial companies were irresponsible. While Renfrewshire tried to force a larger circulation than its deposits and capital would bear, the Shetland's activities were less than honest. That the Royal should keep these accounts for so long was a tribute to its business loyalties. But that both failures resulted in losses to the public suggests that the Royal should have closed the accounts long before it did.

The Leith Banking Company was the third failure of 1842, although the reasons for its failure are not clear. This company was in the habit of setting up a tent at Highland shows and trysts in which it conducted banking business. There were branches at Callander, Dalkeith and Galashiels, which suggests that the Company was involved in financing agricultural products and woollens, in addition to the business at Leith which would include fish and overseas trade. Total debts were £124,000 and the total dividends were 13/4d. per £1.[60]

The Tweed Bank in Berwick (which was really an English country bank) also failed in December, 1841.[61] The partners had been involved in the whaling trade where they lost money, much of which they had borrowed from the bank.[62] Total debts were £276,500 and the dividends amounted to 10/2d. per £1.[63]

The most important feature of this period, however, was not the failures of the banking companies but rather the arrival of the joint-stock banks and the takeover, by them, of most of the remaining provincial banking companies. Table 11 sets out a full list of joint-stock bank formations between 1810 and 1844. Both the Commercial Bank and the National Bank were awarded Royal Charters in 1831, but without the benefit of limited liability which this status usually conferred. (Some of the new formations styled themselves 'banking companies' while others used the more convenient 'bank'. The latter style will be used throughout for the sake of uniformity and to prevent confusion with the provincial banking companies.)

By the early 1830s the development of a new scale of industrial enterprise, particularly in the iron industry, but reflected elsewhere, created difficulties for the banking companies, particularly the small partnerships. The scale of finance required by some of the new businesses was larger than that which many of the banks could safely provide. J. W. Gilbart, a contemporary banker, advised that

> A small banker should not attempt to take large accounts. Banks, otherwise well administered, have been ruined by one large account.[64]

The growth of the joint-stock banks must be seen against the background of a general growth in size of business units. Gilbart thought that 'It was probably in consequence of the greater strength of the new banks that the old ones found it expedient to discontinue business'.[65] The trend towards the disappearance of banking companies and their replacement by joint-stock banks was apparent in 1835, that is, even before the takeover movement had really begun. In that year John Thompson of the Royal Bank thought that it did 'not require a spirit of prophecy to foretell that the Country Banks must gradually quit the field'.[66]

Table 11

Joint-Stock Banks 1810–1844

	Name	Date of opening	Remarks
1.	Commercial Bank of Scotland	1810	
2.	National Bank of Scotland	1825	
3.	Aberdeen Town and County Bank	1825	
4.	Glasgow Union Bank	1830	Union Bank of Scotland from 1843
5.	Ayrshire Bank	1830	
6.	Western Bank of Scotland	1832	
7.	Central Bank of Scotland	1834	
8.	North of Scotland Bank	1836	
9.	Caledonian Bank	1838	
10.	Clydesdale Bank	1838	
11.	Eastern Bank of Scotland	1838	
12.	Edinburgh and Leith Bank	1838	To No.19 1844
13.	Southern Bank of Scotland	1838	To No.12 1842
14.	City of Glasgow Bank	1839	
15.	Paisley Commercial Bank	1839	To No.6 1844
16.	Glasgow Joint-stock Bank	1840	To No.19 1844
17.	Greenock Union Bank	1840	To No.10 1843
18.	Glasgow Bank	1843	To No.6 1844
19.	Edinburgh and Glasgow Bank	1844	

Some provincials were apprehensive at the arrivals of the joint-stocks but felt that all was not lost. John Scott, cashier of the Paisley Union Banking Co., believed that the setting up of a branch of the Western Bank of Scotland in Paisley would 'to a certain extent injure the Paisley business of the old establishments but on the other hand it may perhaps enable us to get rid of a bad customer or two'.[67]

Most of the provincial companies conducted an orderly, if hasty, retreat; few resisted the onward march of the joint-stocks and several companies spent some time in the 1830s and early 1840s actively offering their business, on terms, to another bank. The Dundee Union Banking Co. tried to sell out to the Royal in 1833,[68] and to the Commercial[69] in 1838, before it joined the Western in 1844. The Renfrewshire Banking Co. approached the Royal in 1833[70] and the National in 1836[71] with a view to disposing of its business. The Aberdeen Banking Co. approached the National in 1844 but with no result.[72] These were a few of the abortive attempts at withdrawing from business. Other companies met with early success in their efforts to sell-out (see Table 9 above).

The joint-stock banks were not always the passive recipients of the provincial banking companies' business. Some of them, notably the Glasgow Union Bank, actively sought to take over the provincials. An offer was made in 1836 for the business of Scotland's oldest provincial banking company, the Glasgow Ship. This probably came from the Glasgow Union, but the Ship proprietors preferred to merge their interests with another banking company rather than a joint-stock. Consequently a union was effected with the Glasgow Banking Co. in July, 1836.[73] This was a merger and not a takeover. The new concern was called the Glasgow and Ship Bank Company and it was a 'private firm of the old type'.[74] Nevertheless this apparent preference for a co-partnery type of organisation rather than a joint-stock form concealed the intention of the Glasgow Banking Co. to become 'an open or public Bank'.[75] The plan to convert the Glasgow and Ship into a joint-stock bank was discussed regularly but hesitation followed upon delay and in 1840 the excuse was made that the discussions before Parliament rendered a decision on the matter ill-advised.[76] In May, 1843 it was decided that the time was ripe to bring a new contract into operation, increase the capital and throw the stock open to the public, provided that 'the Bank's affairs should, at the approaching balance, be placed on a simple, correct and intelligible footing'.[77] To this end a circular was issued to partners calling for further discussions, for the business of the bank was, at this time, unstable. Deposits were being lost at an alarming rate; some of the funds were 'locked up in an irregular, inconvenient and comparatively unproductive way', and one of the tellers had defrauded the bank of a sum of money.[78] It was not a very attractive package with which to go public. Consequently when an offer was made for the business by the Glasgow Union Bank in 1843 it was accepted with alacrity. The Glasgow and Ship partners declared that this was the best way to carry out their long-discussed plan of becoming a joint-stock bank[79] but, in truth, a union with another bank was very necessary if it was to be saved from recurring liquidity crises caused by the outflow of deposits.

The Glasgow and Ship Bank Co. had been founded in 1836 to meet the challenge of the joint-stock banks, and although some members of this concern were aware that the most effective way to meet the challenge would be to convert their co-partnery into a joint-stock company, there were dissident elements amongst the shareholders. The delays caused by this element effectively prevented progress, and the merging of the interests of the Glasgow and Ship Bank into the Glasgow Union Bank, which now changed its name into the Union Bank of Scotland, marked the end of the banking companies in Glasgow. The Thistle had already joined the Union Bank in 1836.

The experience of the banks and banking companies in Dundee provides a good example of the tensions which developed in the 1830s. The Bank of Scotland had withdrawn its branch there in 1810 because

> it did not pay and the reason that it did not pay was that the local banks ruined its business by their local connection and competition.[80]

In 1833, however, the branch was re-opened and the National also opened an office. The British Linen Co. had been represented there since 1811. These banks competed actively with the four local banking companies.[81]

In 1833 the Royal Bank tried to join the Dundee banking fraternity by taking over the business of the Dundee Union Banking Co. but the offer was rejected as inadequate. The following year the Royal did succeed in becoming Edinburgh agent for the Dundee Union, but a similar bid for the Dundee Banking Co's. agency was unsuccessful.[82] In 1833 the Dundee Union again asked the Royal to open a branch in Dundee which would take over their business. It was intended that the Dundee Union partners should become shareholders in the Royal. David Milne, cashier of the Dundee Union, held the opinion that

> it would be better if the great Metropolitan Banks were alone to supply the circulating medium and that the best way of securing to these bodies the undisputed possession of the field is to encourage the Country capitalists to become partners of the Great Banks, rather than of the Country Establishments.[83]

Once again, however, the Royal remained unconvinced of the advisability of this connection and the plan was dropped. In 1836 the Royal set up a Dundee branch without a local connection and the Dundee Union eventually joined the Western Bank of Scotland in 1844.

By 1838 the banking companies in Dundee had become 'the subject of much conversation' because of

> the small Banking Capital employed, the very high rate of interest paid on deposits, these taken in connection with the immense amount of Promissory Notes payable on demand, of Bills discounted current and past due and the sums due in Cash Accounts, without as far as known to us any tangible reserve funds in Government Securities to meet periodic panics.[84]

This criticism was basically true. Certainly the reserves of the Dundee banking companies were, proportionally, much less than those held by the public banks. The Dundee New Bank in 1838 held cash and call money of £20,000 against demand liabilities of £158,000; there were no investments in government securities. The Dundee Banking Co. held cash, call money and investments in the Funds of £24,000 against demand liabilities of £445,000, which was not a very safe position to be in during a period of frequently recurring commercial crises. The Dundee Banking Co. had doubtful debts of £82,000 which subsequently raised £55,000 and a paid-up capital of only £29,000.[85] Despite its weak position it was able to take over the business of the Dundee New Bank in 1838 and in so doing acquired the services of its manager C. W. Boase,[86] who was highly regarded as a professional banker. Boase put the joint business on an even keel by building up large balances of call money in Edinburgh and London, and the co-partnery continued until 1864.

The fourth banking company, the Dundee Commercial, was also in some difficulty. Seemingly the whole capital of £50,000 and a further £20,000 had been lost.[87] The business was hastily sold to the equally hastily erected Eastern Bank of Scotland. In fact the Eastern was merely a rescue operation for the Dundee Commercial in which the staff retained their positions.[88]

The experience of the Dundee banking companies amply illustrates the position in which most of the provincial bankers found themselves. Their businesses had become unprofitable because they were losing deposits and their note circulations were decreasing. It remains to be considered why this was the case.

The most obvious cause of the decline of the provincial banking companies was, quite simply, the growth of the joint-stock banks which attracted business away from the provincials. The new banks were often preferred to the smaller companies because their large proprietary offered greater security to customers.[89] Of course some of the new joint-stocks were either poorly managed or failed to become profitably established. Their fate is recorded in Table 11. But generally they presented a much more stable facade to the public than did the majority of the provincials. Although there appears to have been an enormous increase in total bank deposits in the 1830s, the profits of many banks diminished because deposits, both old and new, tended to be spread over a larger number of banks and banking companies. The National Bank directors were aware that

> The great competition which now exists amongst the numerous banks in Scotland has had the effect . . . of reducing the profits of Banks in operation.[90]

There had always been competition between the various banking offices but it had never before been so widespread or so deeply felt.

Although the provincial banking companies were the most badly hurt, the public banks also felt the strain.[91] The Bank of Scotland in particular had its profits squeezed. It attributed the fluctuations and general decrease in profits between 1814 and 1840 to four causes. The note circulation which had formerly been the major source of profit had decreased due to the increased competition for business and the growing use of cheques. Secondly the yields on government securities had fallen by more than one per cent. Thirdly the par of exchange on London had been reduced from 50 days to 5 days. Lastly commission on bills and on letters of credit had been reduced while stamp duties on notes had been increased.[92] All of these factors, but particularly the first, affected the provincial banking companies in more or less degree.

One possible solution was to inaugurate a system of commission charges on all accounts, like those operated by the English banks, but the high level of inter-bank competition rendered the necessary agreement on this impossible. The alternative solution, given that the note circulations could not easily be expanded, was to try to attract more deposits. But then the loss of circulation had to be more than doubly matched by increases in deposits if profit levels were to be maintained because the profit margin on deposits was only 1½ or 2 per cent whereas it was about 4 per cent on notes. It was clearly beyond the capabilities of the economy to generate deposits at this rate. The provincial banking companies had reached a critical level of vulnerability to which they could only respond by taking the easy way out. The Edinburgh private banks also disappeared in this period. Only the largest and the stongest banks could survive in this highly competitive market.

Apart from the major factors outlined above there were a number of underlying pressures which further served to weaken the stability of the provincial bankers. Between 1836 and 1842 there were a number of very poor harvests and fishing seasons. The textile industries enjoyed mixed fortunes. Booms led to excess capacity, and the resultant slumps in 1837 and 1842 undermined the financial integrity of the banks and banking companies which had been financing the expansion. The iron industry enjoyed better fortunes, especially in Scotland, but the scale of finance required by this industry was far greater than could be safely provided by the provincial banking companies. Generally the period between 1836 and 1842 was one of instability in the economy. The development of the international economy tended to worsen the effects of trade slumps.

The attitude of Parliament also contributed to the feelings of insecurity amongst bankers generally. The period leading up to 1844 witnessed the famous debate between the Banking and Currency Schools of thought. The Banking School argued that banking should be left entirely free of government control with the important proviso that note issues should be freely convertible. The Currency School countered that the Bank of England had a duty 'to preserve the value of the currency by varying issues of Bank notes so as to maintain equality between the market and mint prices of gold'.[93] The Currency School won the argument; the effects of this will be discussed below. The debate had taken place over a number of years and it had been obvious to the interested parties from an early date that there was a danger of some restriction being placed on the rights of bankers to issue notes. The uncertainty which this created undermined the confidence of many bankers and must be considered a contributory cause of the disappearance of some of the provincial banking companies.

The rise of the joint-stock banks both in England and Scotland created secondary difficulties for the provincials. The new banks enticed the staff of the provincials into their employment by offers of higher salaries. This was a serious problem for all bankers in an age when trained staff were in very short supply. More will be said of this in Chapter 8 but it must be included amongst the lesser causes of the decline of the provincials.

Very few of the provincial banking companies attempted to survive by adapting their organisation to the new situation in which they found themselves. They had become too small. In 1838 Robert Bell of the Royal Bank, Glasgow staff asked the directors for a rise in salary on the grounds that he was supporting the agent 'by giving him more time to go into the proposals of parties wishing business with us on a scale which the limited capitals of the Local Banks cannot admit of'.[94] The provincial banking companies had become largely irrelevant to the age. In 1843 the Greenock Banking Co., the last of the partnerships,[95] joined the Western Bank of Scotland, and by the end of 1844 only three banking companies remained – all of them co-partneries. These were the Perth, Dundee and Aberdeen Banking Companies.

3. The Remainder Succumb

By 1844 the government were clearly determined to do something to control the supply of money. The Bank Charter Act of that year[96] prohibited the formation of any new note-issuing banks in England. If two banks merged, their right to issue was to be forfeited. Already existing issues were to be confined to the average of the twelve weeks preceding 27th April, 1844. The issue of the Bank of England was also limited, in this case to a fiduciary issue of £14m. plus a further issue equivalent to the gold and silver reserve. The effect of this legislation was to tie the major part of the supply of paper money to gold.

Once again Scotland was given separate treatment. The Scottish Bank Act of 1845[97] prohibited the formation of any new banks of issue. Existing issues were to be limited to the average of their issues in the year preceding 1st May, 1845. This authorised circulation could be exceeded provided that the excess be covered by specie (at least three quarters of which had to be gold) held in the bank's vaults. The total authorised circulation for Scotland was £3,087,209. The shares of the three remaining provincial banking companies were as follows:

Dundee Banking Co.	£33,451
Aberdeen Banking Co.	88,467
Perth Banking Co.	33,656

£155,574, i.e. 5 per cent of the total

Clearly the provincial banking companies had been eclipsed. They were no longer a potent force on the Scottish banking scene.

The legislation of 1845 was not generally welcomed by the Scottish bankers. Many of them saw it as a threat, although not so serious as that of 1826, and the directors of the Perth Banking Co. thought 'that any change in the Banking System of Scotland is quite uncalled for and must be injurious to the Community'. Consequently they called for widespread opposition to the proposals which they felt threatened to unsettle a system 'which has for upward of a century worked so well and proved so beneficial to this Country'. Opposition to the proposed legislation, however, was much less vociferous than it had been in 1826.

There were two reasons for this. Most importantly the right to issue small notes was not threatened, and of course the note issue was not so important to a bank's profitability as it had once been. Secondly, when the proposals for Scotland became known the bankers perceived that the legislation would do little real damage. After a year's operation of the new legislation the Perth directors conceded that 'no evil consequences have resulted from the new law, beyond the heavy expense which the keeping of large stocks of bullion entails upon banks'. They were quick to change their minds when the crisis of 1847 broke over them and the legislation of 1844 had to be suspended. They then came to view the legislation of 1844 and 1845 as 'unsound and injurious' and as having a 'mischievous tendency'. By 1848 they were even more convinced that their verdict of 1847 was the right one. The necessity of building up and maintaining large gold stocks

> prevented many of the Scotch Banks from rendering that assistance to trade and commerce which might have greatly mitigated the pressure. Besides the withdrawal of so much gold from the Bank

of England for storing so unnecessarily in the coffers of the Scotch Banks, tended greatly to increase the panic in London and the South Country and thus the operation of Sir Robert Peel's Act produced the very evils which it was intended to prevent.[98]

This was in marked contrast to the crisis of 1825–6, when the Scottish banks did not require to buy gold in London. There can be little doubt that this was a fair assessment of the workings of the Act. But the inflow of gold from California and Australia in the early 1850s meant that gold stocks could be built up fairly cheaply and note issues expanded. It did not, however, prevent a recurrence of the trade cycle which produced crisis again in 1857.

It is tempting to suggest that the three remaining provincial banking companies in Dundee, Perth and Aberdeen survived into this period because they had some factor in common. Certainly they were amongst the largest and the oldest of the banking companies, and size, at least, seems to have been important in the struggle for survival. Only the banking companies with substantial deposits survived into the late 1840s. The geographical location of these three companies might also be considered a reason for their continued existence after 1844. It may be argued that Perth was geographically isolated from the mainstream of economic development and that the dynamism of the late 18th century had not been sustained in the 19th. But this may not be said of Aberdeen and Dundee, which were heavily committed to the industrial revolution although somewhat distant from the main centre of activity in the West. Certainly the directors of the Perth Banking Co. claimed to be

happily exempted from the severe vicissitudes to which other localities are exposed. If we have not in prosperous times the same measure of busy excitement neither do we suffer the same deep depressions in seasons of general dullness. This steadiness enables us . . . to pursue the even tenor of our way . . .[99]

In Aberdeen, however, things were different. There was a very active industrial economy in the city. The Aberdeen Banking Co. had succeeded in converting itself into an even larger-scale bank in 1839 and there were 418 partners in 1844.[100] By that date, however, its affairs were in poor shape. An abortive attempt was made to sell the business to the National Bank.[101] In 1842 the directors had discovered that the cashier had been making advances without their knowledge, and although they were confident that many of these debts were good, their hopes proved to be ill-founded. By 1849 the amount of bad debts had mounted and the famous Banner Mill had come into the possession of the bank in default of an advance[102] but its business was badly depressed. At the general meeting of 1849 the directors tried to make an estimate of the losses 'that may be anticipated from certain large involvements into which the bank was drawn many years ago'.[103] Failure was imminent, but was averted by the intervention of the Union Bank. The latter offered an exchange of shares in return for which it took over the business of the Aberdeen Banking Co. The 35,000 shares were valued at 30/-, which was far below their book value of £2–4/-[104] but the partners were glad to get anything. They engaged in several years of recrimination and litigation against the directors.

At the same time the Union Bank made a bid for the business of the Perth Banking Co. which was rejected. However, the offer was renewed in 1857 and met with a favourable response. Although the Perth business had been increasing, profits had not and the directors believed that consolidation rather than competition amongst bankers was the best policy and was in the interests of their shareholders. Several of the joint-stock banks had lately set up Perth branches and the extension of branch banking generally was going on at a rapid rate. The directors felt that

> There was great danger that credit would be unduly inflated and which could only issue in a few years or probably in a much shorter period in losses and panic. [105]

The anticipated crisis broke within weeks of the agreement. The Perth Banking Co. shares at the time were priced at twice their par value.

A bid was also made, by the Union Bank, for the Dundee Banking Co. in 1857. This move was supported by the directors in Dundee but they needed 100 per cent approval from their shareholders to effect the merger. Seemingly two partners refused their assent and after some delay the Union Bank directors lost their tempers and withdrew the offer. [106] The Dundee Banking Co. eventually joined the Royal Bank in 1864. Seemingly with the development of the jute industry 'Dundee's trade now rested on a wider basis and the opportunities of a purely local institution were likely to dwindle'. [107] The Dundee Banking Co. was the last of the provincial banking companies. It had lasted 100 years and 6 months. That it did so was due as much to its good management and strong local connections as to any other factor.

The amalgamation movement which had swallowed the provincial banking companies between c.1830 and 1864 was not peculiar to them. The private banks in Edinburgh had also disappeared both by failure and takeover. Even the joint-stock banks themselves were not immune from this trend towards bigness, and by the end of 1864 twelve public and joint-stock banks were all that remained to constitute the Scottish banking system. In England, too, the number of country banks had decreased. From a peak of 783 in 1810 the official statistics showed that the number of country banks declined to 311 in 1842. Thereafter the number fell even further as the power of the joint-stock banks increased. Although the English country banks did not entirely die out until 1953, they had ceased to be an important part of the English banking system by the 1890s.

The effect of the removal of the provincial banking companies was to leave Scotland with a banking system appropriate to the needs of a rapidly growing economy. The age when the banking companies filled those needs had passed but the result was also, to some extent, to depersonalise the banking business. The banking companies had been essentially local organisations with considerable common identities of personnel and interests between partners and customers. The growth of large-scale joint-stock banking tended to change this and country-wide branch networks with the consequent spread of professional management reduced the extent to which partners could dominate the lending activities of the bank. There were of course exceptions to this but it holds good as a general rule.

The joint-stock banking movement and the continued dynamism of the public banks in Scotland combined to render the provincial banking companies inefficient; the wide branch networks of the larger banks made inter-town transfers of money quicker and cheaper; there were economies of scale in administration costs and there was greater security to the public because of the large numbers of partners. The growth of these large-scale banks underlined a process of renewal and of growth in the economy. The smaller banks could not compete and the age of the Scottish provincial banking companies was at an end.

NOTES

1. A. Feaveryear, 1963, p. 194
2. 7 George IV ch. 6
3. A. Smith, 1970, p. 422
4. Malachi Malagrowther (Sir Walter Scott), 1826, 1st letter, p. 41
5. *Ibid.*, p. 22
6. *Ibid.*, 2nd letter, p. 5
7. *Ibid.*, p. 41
8. *Ibid.*, 1st letter p. 28
9. *Blackwood's Edinburgh Magazine*, vol. 19, 1826, p. 597
10. F. W. Fetter, *Scottish Journal of Political Economy*, vol. 7, 1960, p. 217f
11. T. Joplin, 1827, p. 16
12. E. Quayle, 1968, *passim*
13. S.R.O. CS311/2142 Box 207, Geo. Kinnear to Montrose Banking Co., 10/3/1826
14. Parliamentary Debates, Lords 27/2/1826, Earl of Rosebery
15. P.P., Report from the Lords Committee on Promissory Notes . . ., 1826, evidence of J. G. Craig, p. 271
16. Parliamentary Debates, Lords 17/3/1826, Earl of Caernarvon
17. *Ibid.*, Earl of Grosvenor
18. *Ibid.*, Commons, 16/3/1826, Keith Douglas
19. *Ibid.*, 14/3/1826, Abercromby, Dundas, Maberly
20. P.P. Report from Select Committee on Promissory Notes . . ., 1826, evidence of John Commelin, p. 179
21. *Ibid.*, Hugh Watt, p. 187
22. *Ibid.*, Roger Aytoun, p. 191
23. *Ibid.*, Lords, Andrew Coventry, p. 161
24. *Ibid.*, Commons, J. G. Craig, p. 265
25. *Ibid.*, Kirkman Finlay, p. 69
26. *Ibid.*, John Gladstone, p. 226
27. *Ibid.*, Alex. Blair, p. 48
28. *Ibid.*, Lords, John Maberly, p. 179
29. *Ibid.*, Commons, Samuel Thornton, p. 285
30. *Ibid.*, Lords, Roger Aytoun, p. 127
31. *Ibid.*, Commons, Kirkman Finlay, p. 57
32. See S. G. Checkland, 1975, p. 193
33. S.R.O. CS96/2346, Stirling Banking Co., Sederunt Book, 1826
34. B.S., Edinburgh, Miscellaneous documents, B. S. Stirling to Alex. Blair, 4/12/1832
35. Perth Banking Co., D.M.B., 13/3/1826
36. Glasgow Banking Co., D.M.B., 12/9/1826
37. S.R.O. CS311/2142 Box 207, Montrose Banking Co. to Kinnear, 6/3/1826
38. L. S. Pressnell, 1956, p. 488
39. P.P., Report from the Select Committee on Promissory Notes, 1826, p. 12
40. *Ibid.*, Lords, p. 189
41. 9 George IV ch. 65

42. 7 George IV ch. 67
43. S.R.O. CS311/2142 Box 207, Montrose Banking Co. to Kinnear, 10/12/1826
44. *Ibid.*, Low and Rutherford W.S. to Montrose Banking Co., 7/12/1826
45. *Ibid.*, Kinnear to Montrose Banking Co., 11/12/1826
46. *Ibid.*, 15/12/1826
47. Joplin, 1827
48. S. E. Thomas, 1934
49. See Introduction
50. S.R.O., CS96/450, J. & R. Watson sequestration minutes, 29/10/1832
51. *Ibid.*, 29/6/1832. It is not known what the security was nor if the principals were related
52. *Ibid.*, 29/10/1832
53. R.B.S., D.M.B., 17/4/1839, 24/4/1839, 15/4/1840, 9/9/1840, 23/10/1832
54. *Greenock Advertiser*, 1/4/1842
55. N.L.S., Hay of Hayfield MSS., Accession 3250, Box 78, f1, Hay's examination
56. S.R.O. CS283/4, Sequestration Returns, 1843
57. N.L.S., Hay of Hayfield MSS., Box 41 f1, Letter Wm. Hay to National Provincial Bank of England, 14/2/1843
58. *Ibid.*, Hay to Sir Wm. Forbes and Co., 8/7/1842
59. S.R.O., CS285/52 and CS283. Sequestration processes and returns
60. J. Buchanan (Glasguensis) 1884, p. 37
61. D. Hardcastle Jnr., 1843, p. 451
62. M. Phillips, 1894, p. 162
63. *Bankers Magazine*, 1849, p. 779
64. J. W. Gilbart, 1849, vol. 1, p. 36
65. *Ibid.*, vol. 2, p. 547
66. R.B.S., D.M.B., 4/11/1835
67. Houston of Johnstone MSS., Bundle 17, John Scott to Ludovic Houston, 31/7/1832
68. R.B.S., D.M.B., 15/5/1833
69. C.B.S., D.M.B., 25/1/1838
70. R.B.S., D.M.B., 5/6/1833
71. N.B.S., D.M.B., 23/6/1836
72. N.B.S., D.M.B., 11/1/1844
73. B.S., Glasgow Banking Co., D.M.B., 28/7/1836
74. R. S. Rait, 1930, p. 210
75. *Ibid.*, p. 108
76. Glasgow and Ship Banking Co., D.M.B., 15/1/1840
77. *Ibid.*, 3/5/1843
78. B.S., Glasgow, Report of Committee of Management of the Glasgow and Ship Bank Co., 30/7/1841
79. Glasgow and Ship Bank Co., D.M.B., 9/11/1843
80. P.P., Report from the Select Committee on Promissory Notes . . . 1826, evidence of Thos. Kinnear, p. 138
81. The Dundee Banking Co., Dundee New Banking Co., Dundee Union Banking Co. and Dundee Commercial Banking Co.
82. R.B.S., D.M.B., 30/7/1834, 6/8/1834
83. *Ibid.*, 4/11/1835
84. *Ibid.*, 18/7/1838
85. C. W. Boase, 1867
86. J. T. Ward, 1968
87. C. W. Boase, 1867, p. 403
88. S.R.O., IRS 1/12, 1840; and J. M. Reid, 1938, p. 320
89. W. H. Logan, 1844, p. 174
90. N.B.S., D.M.B., 1/12/1842
91. T. R. Gourvish, 1969
92. Anon., No title. On Banking Profits, 1840, B.S.
93. Pressnell, 1956, p. 208. For a further analysis see F. W. Fetter, 1965
94. R.B.S., D.M.B., 23/5/1838
95. *Greenock Advertiser*, 3/11/1843
96. 7 and 8 Victoria ch. 32
97. 8 and 9 Victoria ch. 38

98. Perth Banking Co., D.M.B., 8/7/1844, 13/7/1846, 12/7/1847 and 10/7/1848
99. *Ibid.*, 9/7/1849
100. *Bankers Magazine* 1844, August
101. N.B.S., D.M.B., 11/1/1844
102. Rait, *op. cit.*, p. 262
103. B.S., Edinburgh, miscellaneous documents, Aberdeen Banking Co. reports
104. U.B.S., D.M.B. 1/6/1849 and Rait *op. cit.*, p. 163
105. Perth Banking Co., D.M.B. 13/7/1857
106. B.S., Glasgow Archives, Union Bank papers, 1857
107. Reid, 1938, p. 130

Part Two
THE BUSINESS AND ITS ORGANISATION

6

The Business

1. The Balance Sheets

THE provincial banking companies developed the practice of constructing annual, and sometimes quarterly, balance sheets from the outset. The earliest available is that for the Ship Bank, Glasgow in 1752.[1] The Aberdeen Banking Co. even produced weekly abstracts of balances from 1768. In this way they were somewhat ahead of their time. Professor Pollard, speaking of the industrial revolution period, has suggested of businesses generally that 'Balances are struck, not at regular intervals, as checks and controls, but at the end of books, to save transfers to new folios'.[2] The Scottish provincial banking companies did not follow this general rule, in fact some of the contracts of these concerns stipulated that annual balances were obligatory.[3]

The balance sheet of a business organisation is the basic statement of its affairs which presents 'a still picture of the position . . . at a stated single moment in time'.[4] This static characteristic is its major limitation. Banking was, and to a lesser extent remains, a seasonal business where advances and consequently note issues were at their highest during the payments seasons, i.e. at Martinmas and Whit. These were the busy times of the year. Consequently the bankers preferred to balance their books when there was less pressure of business. Generally the months of February, June and September were favoured. This failure to follow the calendar year introduces a distortion into the balance sheets which must be borne in mind when the figures are being used for analysis. The Aberdeen Banking Company balance books suggest that the difference in total advances between the high and low points of the business year averaged about 20 per cent.[5] To remove this difficulty it would be necessary to produce, say, monthly balance sheets and to average them, which is of course impossible.

A further limitation on the use of these accounts lies in the fact that they seldom included branch figures. Agents in the branches were usually allowed to receive deposits and discount bills and for this they received a supply of the company's notes (see Chapter 9). The figures for branches which usually appeared in the 'companies' balance sheets were the deposits (seldom differentiated from head office deposits) and the balance due by the agent. This latter figure was not necessarily the amount of bills discounted by him although it may be taken to approximate to that figure. Occasionally the balance against the branches was taken as advances to agents net of deposits at branches. Where possible the exact nature of the balance has been stated in the Appendix but extreme care must be taken in using these figures. Only in the cases of the Dundee Banking Co. and the Dundee New Bank is it possible to determine the exact extent of the branch business.

A minor reservation about the use of balance sheets lies in the practices of banking companies regarding bills of exchange. These were discounted or rather 'bought', but as there was a considerable demand for London paper they were also sold to customers who required bills to make payments in the Capital. Consequently the amount appearing on the balance sheet might bear no relation to the amount acually discounted with the result that total credit for a bank's customers might be understated in the balance sheet. The qualification 'might' is important here because it seems that the practice of selling bills of exchange in this way was not universal. Many bankers instead preferred to draw on their London agents, selling the draft rather than trade bills to their customers. On *a priori* grounds it seems likely that the draft on a London agent was the commoner practice because the amount required could be obtained by simple inscription, whereas it would be more difficult to marry a number of trade bills to a customer's particular requirements. The evidence of the few remaining bill books is insufficient to be definite about this, but the references to London bills in the minute books suggest that the draft on London was the preferred mode of procedure, certainly after 1790. With most of the available balance sheets it is impossible to be certain about which practice was preferred or if both were used. The possibility that bills of exchange were being sold must therefore be kept in mind in assessing the total amount of credit.

A balance sheet is not specifically designed to convey information. 'It is rather a by-product of the system of double-entry accounting'[6] which merely confirms that the books have been balanced. It need not say anything about the quality of the balances but despite this inadequacy and the reservations expressed above it is sometimes the only point at which contact can be made between the observer and the business unit. Its value therefore is considerable; a series enables inter-bank comparisons to be made and sometimes even aggregates for the whole system to be calculated.

A balance sheet is also of interest for the historian of accounting. The banking companies constructed balance sheets so that profits could be determined and dividends declared. As has been suggested above, this was not a common practice amongst businesses generally. There is also evidence to show that attempts were made to rank assets in order of their liquidity.[7]

2. Capital and its Rewards

The historian of English bank accounting claimed that even in the 1820s the banks displayed no awareness of the importance of showing capital as a separate account in their books.[8] In businesses generally it is widely accepted that 'the notion of capital as a permanent, autonomous factor was virtually unknown'.[9]

The evidence from the records of the Scottish provincial banking companies both supports and contradicts these generalisations.

The treatment of capital may be divided into two general approaches which match the separation of the banking companies into partnerships and co-partneries. The latter tended to have a much more formal method of capital accounting than the former.

The Glasgow Ship Bank was one of the partnerships whose treatment of capital was rather informal. In 1785 the paid-up capital amounted to £31,500 which was divided into nine shares of £3,500. Thereafter it is only at the occasional re-ordering of the partnership on the death or admission of a partner that the formal paid-in capital can be determined. The reason for this is that the partners' share accounts were treated almost like current accounts where interest was credited to them at the rate of 5 per cent and profits were added unless the partner chose to take cash. Deposits and withdrawals could be made seemingly at will by the partners. In 1817 Robin Carrick, the senior partner, paid in £2,623 but withdrew £8,815 the following year[10] and when he died in 1821 his share account amounted to £47,695–8/–. The removal of this sum reduced the total paid capital of the firm to £44,163–19–3.[11]

The last balance sheet of the first Dundee Commercial Banking Co., a partnership bank, in 1801 revealed paid-up capital of £2,000 and profits for the year of £499. In May the following year the business was re-formed as the Dundee New Bank with an almost entirely new proprietary. The capital of the new concern was to be £58,000 divided into 29 shares of £2,000 each,[12] but when the first balance sheet of the concern was produced after seven months' business no money had yet been paid on account of capital. The company had in fact operated for a time without any paid-in capital. This state of affairs was soon changed, however, and the balance sheet for 1803 showed that 10 per cent of the nominal capital had been called in. Thereafter the balance sheets showed paid-in capital and accumulated profits as separate accounts although it is impossible to say if this reflected the company's accounting practice as these balance sheets were presented, from the original books, by the company's historian and sometime manager at a much later date. Nevertheless, the situation in the early stages of the company's existence reflects how casual the treatment of capital could be.

The co-partneries as befits larger organisations, treated their capital accounts much more formally and paid-up capital was kept strictly separate from all other accounts. The records of the Dundee, Perth United and Aberdeen Banking Companies prove that this was the case. Article 3 of the Dundee Banking Co. contract expressly stated that no partner had the power to withdraw any part of his capital.[13] The Aberdeen Banking Co. had a rather unusual way of displaying its capital account. The entry on the liabilities side of the balance sheet was the nominal capital while the uncalled capital was included as an asset. Nevertheless, the balance was the same as if paid-in capital alone had been displayed in the balance sheet.

Although this basic difference existed between the approaches of the partnerships and co-partneries to capital accounting, certainly in the 18th century, the partnerships generally came to adopt the more formal approach in the 19th century. Where capital was appreciated as 'a permanent, autonomous factor' its nature was always simple. There was only one type of share and at no time did the banking companies issue preference shares or debentures.

The capital of the banking companies could be augmented in two ways: either by further calls, or by additions from profits. The contract of the companies usually stipulated what the nominal amount of capital was to be and a portion of this, sometimes only about 10 per cent, was called up at the outset. This was certainly the case with the Dundee Banking Co. but the Perth United called 25 per cent at the beginning, the East Lothian 35 per cent and the Aberdeen Banking Co. 30 per cent.[14] As the business of these companies increased, so the capital was enlarged up to the limit set by the contract. This was achieved either by making further calls on the partners or by transferring money from the profit and loss or reserve accounts. It was usually the practice to pay no dividends on capital for the first few years of business in order to let the balances in either or both of these accounts accumulate.

A number of banking companies included clauses in their contracts whereby if a certain percentage of the capital was lost in the course of business, then the company could be closed. In the 1826 contract of the Dundee Banking Company the limit was set at 10 per cent. A year ealier the new Dundee Commercial Banking Company had stipulated that if one fifteenth of the capital was lost, then closure would follow. The contract of the Perth Banking Co. in 1808 gave power to one third of the partners to insist on closure should 5 per cent of the stock be lost.[15] These were relatively small trigger mechanisms but in most cases there was no need for them and in the case where there was a need (the Dundee Commercial) the directors kept the shareholders ignorant of the true state of affairs until a takeover had been arranged.

Unfortunately very little can be said about bad debts. Those incurred by the Perth Banking Co. between 1787 and 1808 amounted to only a few hundred pounds but other companies were not so successful. The practice in the Montrose Banking Co. was to write off bad debts against profits in the years in which they were incurred[16] and it seems likely that this was the general procedure.

Some companies began to keep reserve accounts in the late 18th century into which they paid undivided profits and, as has been said, most companies made no distribution of profits in the first few years of business in order to allow a reserve fund to accumulate. But it was not until 1844 that the Perth Banking Co. opened a reserve account specifically to meet losses on discounts. The 19th century practice of other companies in this respect is not known but the English country banks were late in developing reserve accounts.[17]

The average paid capital of the banking companies *c*.1810 was £31,000, the range being from the Galloway Banking Co's. £8,000 to the Glasgow Banking Co's. £100,000. Comparable figures for the English country banks are not available but it has been estimated that the average starting capital in England was in the region of £10,000.[18]

The limit to the capital account set by the contract was of course a notional figure. As there was no limit to the liability of the shareholders it became evident in 1788 that

> it was possible to regard the provision of a certain amount of capital as merely providing for the original contribution of the partners and not as the subscription of a certain defined amount of the stock.[19]

This discovery arose out of the winding up of the Ayr Bank when calls were made on partners beyond the extent of the nominal capital specified in the contract. Although the principle of limited liability had been acknowledged by the Court of Session in the case of the Arran Fishing Co. in 1757,[20] there were no subsequent trials to affirm this case law. The constitutions of the public banks guaranteed them limited liability but the provincial bankers were, it would seem, averse to the principle. The four Glasgow companies founded between 1749 and 1769 all published advertisements in the newspapers to the effect that the partners were bound 'jointly and severally' for the payment of their notes,[21] that is, that the entire estates of each of the partners were liable for the debts of the firm. The publication of these advertisements must be seen as a public relations exercise designed to convince the public that it was quite safe to accept and hold the notes of these companies. Confidence was established in this way especially if the partners were well known and respected in the community.

The role of capital in the practice of banking is a difficult one to determine because of the nature of the business. Bankers issue notes and accept deposits which enable them to expand their advances and, therefore, notes and deposits should properly be considered as current, or demand, liabilities. Like trade credit in a manufacturing concern they form part of the working capital.

The information available on the returns to capital is very fragmentary. It is also somewhat biased, as there are few figures for the companies which failed. Nevertheless it is necessary to make use of what is available. A further limitation on the usefulness of the figures lies in the fact that some banking companies paid interest on capital. This practice was not very widespread.

Profitability may be considered in two main ways. Firstly, gross and net profit may be studied from the point of view of the firm as a business unit, and secondly dividends and yields may be scrutinised from the point of view of the shareholders. The figures which have come to light are set out in Tables 12 to 17. Where possible, comparisons have been made with English country banks, the Bank of England, the Bank of Scotland, and, in Table 17, with government securities.

Table 12 sets out net profit as a percentage of paid capital for seven banking companies. This ratio is generally thought to be a good indicator of the performance of a business unit, but in this industry and at this period it does have limitations. The reservation about notes and deposits as part of the capital structure have already been mentioned. The Commercial Banking Co. of Aberdeen and the Dundee New Bank were both partnerships with small paid capitals. That of the latter amounted to £5,200 in 1807 but demand liabilities were

£330,000.[22] This fact explains why its profit ratio was so high in the early years. The decline on this ratio in later years was caused by an increase in paid capital as much as by decreases in business profits. The same may be said of the Commercial Banking Co. of Aberdeen, although its capital increase came entirely from profits. The partnerships in particular seem to have inclined to the view that large sums of paid capital were unnecessary because the law stipulated that the liability of the partners was unlimited. This, rather than a large paid capital, was felt to be sufficient security for depositors and note holders. The experience of the co-partneries gives a better indication of the trends in the industry because their capital structure tended to be more rigid. The Perth Banking Co. figures in particular reflect the trend towards lower profits from the 1830s.

Table 13 shows net profit as a percentage of capital employed, i.e. net profit plus reserves; this is perhaps a more satisfactory indicator of profitability than Table 12, as some banking companies built up reserves from undistributed profits which, because they remained as a liability to the company, should properly be considered to be part of the paid-up capital. A comparison of the Commercial Banking Co. of Aberdeen figures in Table 12, column (1) and 13, column (3) is very illuminating in this respect. The results in the latter Tables are more modest than in the former. Again, in Table 13 the decline of profits in the 1830s is particularly noticeable.[23] The Dundee Banking Co. alone escaped this trend. At a time when note issues, which had been the major source of profit, were either stagnating or declining the Company was able to increase the deposit side of its business, thus maintaining, and even for a time increasing, its profit levels. Partly it was able to do so because it took over the business of the Dundee New Bank. The respite, however, lasted only until 1864.

It was possible to provide comparable figures of net profit as a percentage of capital employed for two English country banks.[24] It is, however, impossible to say how typical the Banbury and Bedford banks were of the English experience. Nevertheless, some interesting facts emerge. The highly profitable Banbury Bank had a small capital, and although the note issue fluctuated widely over the period for which there are figures, the trend was one of slow increase. Deposits on the other hand more than doubled between 1828 and 1845. The Bedford Bank vastly increased its capital from about 1830, thus driving down the profit ratio. Its deposits fluctuated widely but experienced no increase, and note issues declined. Rather curiously this bank kept very large sums of non-earning cash in reserve. Presumably if it had found an outlet for this money, then profits would have been much higher, taking them above the average Scottish performance. Higher charges were probably a causal factor of the seemingly greater profitability of the English banks, it being their practice to charge commissions on accounts which were not levied in Scotland. But for the reasons already mentioned above and because of the smallness of the sample it would be unwise to make too much of this evidence.

Table 14 sets out gross profit as a percentage of total liabilities. This is intended as rough guide to the comparative cost of funds to the Scottish economy as compared to the English. The most notable feature of this Table is again the higher ratio of the English banks. This fact, if general, would seem to be some justification for the viewpoint of those who praised Scottish banking methods, i.e. that the real cost of working capital to businessmen was less in Scotland than in England, but here again the verdict must be a qualified one because of the shortage of data.

Tables 15, 16 and 17 consider the second way of looking at profitability, i.e. from the point of view of the shareholder in terms of dividends.

Table 15 shows dividends as a percentage of paid capital and compares the provincial banking company performance with that of the Bank of England and the Bank of Scotland. Table 16 shows dividends plus additions to capital from profits as a percentage of paid-up capital although this does not include payments into reserve accounts. The results show that, on the whole, the provincial banking companies fared better than did the national banks of Scotland and England. Professor Cameron compared the Bank of Scotland and Dundee Banking Co. figures (which have here been presented anew) and concluded, albeit tentatively, that

> the sure way to survival in the Banking world of Scotland was to take the low road of relatively riskless investment. Of those who took the high road many did not survive, but those who did not only earned higher profits; they also had the satisfaction of contributing to the development of the national economy.[25]

He characterised the Bank of Scotland as a 'riskless investor' because in most years its investments in the funds were greater than total advances to customers, whereas the Dundee Banking Co. on the other hand concentrated its resources on advances. The evidence available for testing this hypothesis futher is rather sketchy. Briefly, the Commercial Banking Co. of Aberdeen, the Dundee Banking Co. and the Perth Banking Co. may be defined as risk bankers, i.e. customers' advances were their major earning assets. Many of the provincial banking companies did invest in the funds and even in foreign securities but these resources were usually regarded as a reserve for sale in emergencies. The figures of Tables 15 and 16 seem to confirm Professor Cameron's conclusions.

Details on yields, that is, dividends in relation to market price of shares, are very rare. Those available are set out in Table 17. They suggest that the yields on bank shares were generally higher than those on British government securities. Any further conclusions or speculations would be wholly unsupported by evidence.

On the whole the provincial banking companies made good profits before the 1830s, but anticipated profit was not the only reason why people were moved to invest in these concerns. Partners were often the first customers and the assurance of a good supply of credit was a great attraction to many potential shareholders. More will be said of this and other motives for investment in Chapter 7. The profit decline in the late 1820s and 1830s was matched by a decline in the numbers of partners in banking companies as replacements became difficult to find for partners who had retired or died. Prospective banking shareholders placed their funds with joint-stock banks.

Table 12

Net Profit as a percentage of Paid Capital: Annual Average by Decade per cent

Period	(1) Commercial Banking Co. of Aberdeen	(2) Dundee New Bank	(3) Dundee Commercial Banking Co. No.1	(4) East Lothian Banking Co.	(5) Paisley Union Banking Co.	(6) Perth Banking Co.	(7) Hunters and Co., Ayr
1751–60							
1761–70							
1771–80							
1781–90	3.5						
1791–1800	14.0		21.0			12.8	
1801–10	38.8	70.9				10.0	
1811–20	35.3	22.8		5.9		15.6	
1821–30	40.0	25.2			15.2	10.7	
1831–40	13.7	13.3			21.3	12.4	21.5
1841–50						11.0	20.0
1851–60						8.3	
1861–70						8.6	
Overall Average	29.0	27.2	21.0	5.9	17.7	11.2	21.0

Notes 1 Bank of Scotland, Edinburgh Archives, Miscellaneous Papers (1789–1833)
2 C. W. Boase, *Century of Banking in Dundee*, 2nd ed., Edinburgh 1867 (1807–1838)
3 *Ibid.*, (1792–1801)
4 East Lothian Banking Co., Sederunt Book, S.R.O. B18/18/14 (1811–1814)
5 Paisley Union Banking Co. Journal, Bank of Scotland, Glasgow Archives (1821–1837)
6 Perth Banking Co. General Ledgers, Bank of Scotland, Glasgow Archives (1788–1856)
7 R. S. Rait, *History of the Union Bank of Scotland*, Glasgow 1930 (1831, 1836, 1841)

Table 13

Net Profit as a percentage of Capital Employed, i.e. Paid Capital plus Reserves[1]

Annual Averages by Decade per cent

Period	(1) English Country Banks[2] Banbury	(2) Bedford	(3) Commercial Banking Co. of Aberdeen	(4) Dundee[3] Banking Co.	(5) Dundee New Bank	(6) Ship[4] Bank, Glasgow	(7) Glasgow[5] Bank	(8) Montrose[6] Bank	(9) Paisley Union Bank	(10) Perth[7] United Banking Co.	(11) Perth Banking Co.
1751–60				25.3		19.9					
1761–70				12.8							
1771–80			3.3	15.3							
1781–90			8.7	8.5						8.0	
1791–1800				17.9		12.7			13.3	13.9	
1801–10		19.5[9]	10.1	10.6	58.3	14.7					
1811–20		24.8	4.6	13.0	17.8	11.4			7.2		
1821–30	38.6[8]	7.2	6.9	19.4	19.8	16.1	9.8	6.4			9.8
1831–40	46.8	3.9	2.4	13.5	9.8	8.1		7.6	13.7		6.5
1841–50	63.1	3.0		14.9							5.4
1851–60				11.0							
1861–70											
Overall Average	49.9	12.6	7.0	14.7	21.5	14.4	9.8	7.1	11.4	10.2	7.5

Notes

1 Sources and end dates as for Table 12
2 L. S. Pressnell, *Country Banking in the Industrial Revolution*, Oxford, 1956
3 C. W. Boase, *Century of Banking in Dundee*, 2nd ed., Edinburgh, 1867 (1764–1864)
4 Ship Bank, Balance Ledger and Journal, Bank of Scotland, Glasgow Archives (1752–1761, 1796–1836)
5 Boase, *op. cit.* (1810–1819)
6 Montrose Bank Sederunt Book, Bank of Scotland, Head Office Archives (1815–1828)
7 Perth United Banking Co., General Ledger, Bank of Scotland, Head Office Archives (1771–1786)
8 1828–1845
9 1801–1845

Table 14
Gross Profit as a percentage of Total Assets: Annual Average by Decade per cent

Period	(1) English Banks Banbury	(2) English Banks Bedford	(3) Dundee Banking Co.	(4) Dundee Commercial Banking No. 1	(5) Dundee New Bank	(6) Glasgow Bank	(7) Perth United Banking Co.
1751–60							
1761–70			3.0				
1771–80			3.7				2.5
1781–90			4.0				3.3
1791–1800			2.8	2.1			
1801–10		3.0	2.0		2.4		
1811–20		3.5	1.5		1.8	3.1	
1821–30	2.9	2.6	1.3		1.7		
1831–40	3.2	2.2	1.5		2.1		
1841–50	4.0	2.0	1.9				
1851–60			2.1				
1861–70			2.2				
Overall Averages	3.4	2.9	2.4	2.1	1.9	3.1	2.8

Notes   Sources and end dates as for Tables 12 and 13

Table 15

Dividends as a percentage of Paid Capital: Annual Averages by Decade per cent

Period	(1) Bank of England	(2) Bank of[2] Scotland	(3) Aberdeen[3] Banking Co.	(4) Commercial Bank of Aberdeen	(5) Dundee Banking Co.	(6) Dundee New Bank	(7) Dundee[4] Union Bank	(8) Dundee[5] Commercial Bank No. 2	(9) Montrose Bank	(10) Perth Banking Co.
1751–60	4.6	6.8								
1761–70	5.0	5.9			19.6					
1771–80	5.5	8.2	13.7		15.2					
1781–90	6.3	7.3	8.3		12.2					
1791–1800	7.0	6.6		2.8	5.5					10.0
1801–10	9.5	10.2		2.9	6.7	33.0				10.6
1811–20	10.0	8.8		6.9	9.4		8.6		5.6	15.4
1821–30	8.4	6.7		3.5	12.2	17.1	8.4			9.8
1831–40	7.8	6.4		4.2	9.0	0.9	8.3	8.9		8.8
1841–50	7.5	7.5			8.1		8.0			6.9
1851–60	8.8	8.8			11.8					5.0
1861–70	9.6				11.7					6.1
Overall Averages	7.5	7.5	11.0	4.3	10.7	10.0	8.4	8.9	5.6	9.2

Notes

Sources and end dates as for Tables 12 and 13

1 Sir J. Clapham, *The bank of England*, 2 vols. Cambridge, 1944
2 C. W. Boase, *Century of Banking in Dundee*, 2nd ed. Edinburgh, 1867 (1764–1864)
3 Aberdeen Banking Co., Balance Books, Bank of Scotland Aberdeen Archives
4 Boase, *op. cit.* (1811–1843)
5 *Ibid.* (1828–1837)
6 (1815–1822)

Table 16

Dividends and Additions to Capital from Profits as a percentage of Paid Capital:
Annual Averages by Decade per cent

Period	(1) Bank of Scotland	(2) Commercial Bank of Aberdeen	(3) Dundee Banking Co.	(4) Dundee New Bank	(5) Perth Banking Co.
1751–60	9.2				
1761–70	8.4		23.3		
1771–80	8.2		15.2		
1781–90	7.3	3.5	14.7		10.0
1791–1800	6.6	9.2	8.4		10.6
1801–10	10.2	11.0	6.7	97.2	15.4
1811–20	8.8	6.3	9.4	17.2	9.8
1821–30	6.7	8.8	16.8	21.3	8.8
1831–40	6.4	3.8	9.0	16.2	10.8
1841–50	7.5		8.1		5.0
1851–60	8.8		11.8		6.1
1861–70			11.7		
Overall Average	7.9	8.3	12.0	28.6	9.7

Notes   Sources and end dates for Tables 12–15

Table 17

Yields, i.e. Dividends per Share as a percentage of Share Prices

Period	(1) British[1] Government Securities	(2) French[1] 5% Rentes	(3) French[1] 3% Rentes	(4) Aberdeen Banking Co.	(5) Arbroath Banking Co.	(6) Dundee Banking Co.	(7) Dundee Union Bank	(8) Montrose Bank
1813	4.9	7.9		4.0				4.5
1815	4.5	7.5						5.3
1818	3.9	7.2						6.4
1820	4.4	6.7						6.5
1822	3.8	5.6		4.0				
1840	3.4	4.5	3.9	3.9	5.5	6.7	5.3	

Notes   1   S. Homer, *A History of Interest Rates*, New Brunswick, 1963

Although profits were good in all but the concluding years of the life-cycle of the banking companies, they do not appear to have been so high as those of the English country banks. This situation, however, had a corollary. The smaller gross profit to total assets ratio for Scotland suggests, if the sources are typical, that the Scots were paying less for their credit than the English. Two reasons may be adduced for this. Firstly there was a greater degree of competition amongst bankers in Scotland, especially in towns where there was a branch of one of the public banks. Competition tended to keep charges low. Secondly the fact that many of the banking companies were substantial partnerships and co-partneries whose largest customers were often the partners themselves meant that there was no incentive to institute higher charges.

3. Cash Accounts

One of the major ways in which the banking companies advanced money to their customers was by means of the cash account. The origins of this type of advance in the late 1720s was discussed in the introduction. Cash accounts (sometimes referred to as cash credits) were engagements 'to lend money when it is wanted'.[26] The borrower's obligation was drawn up in a bond signed by him and two or three of his friends who thereby guaranteed the advance. It was essentially a personal bond – no other formal security being required. A copy of one of these bonds is included in Appendix C. Some specific examples of advances of this type will be given in Part Three. This section is primarily concerned with the manner in which these accounts were granted and operated.

Cash accounts were awarded by the directors of the banking companies and not by the salaried staffs, and this was often made specific in the contracts which set out the duties of the directors. Even cash accounts which were operated on at the branches were awarded after application had been made to the directors at head office. A recommendation was usually required from the branch agent in these cases. Once the credit had been authorised the bond was drawn up and signed, whereupon transactions on the account could begin.

The bonds and accounts were regularly checked by the directors. The Aberdeen Banking Co. instituted quarterly reviews[27] but other companies found that annual or half-yearly checks were sufficient. If a bond was found to be deficient in any way, as a result of either the death or bankruptcy of a party, then orders were issued that a new signatory should be found, and if this proved impossible, then the account was closed. If it was found that the account was inactive, then the account holder was instructed to have more transactions or suffer it to be withdrawn. As a result of one of these periodic purges in 1820 Henry Houldsworth, the textile manufacturer, had his cash credit with the Paisley Union Banking Co. terminated.[28] Most bonds included a clause which gave to the banking company the right to revoke the credit (see Appendix C), but it seems that this right was seldom exercised other than for the reasons already mentioned.

The cash account and other advances were useful means of circulating the notes of the banking companies and hence were the basis of their profitability. The East Lothian Banking Co. demanded

> That all persons privileged with such credits shall be diligent in promoting the interest of the . . . Company by circulating their notes and therein improving every opportunity to the welfare of the Bank which the peculiar situation and trade of every such person may afford.

Consequently it was laid down that all account holders 'shall operate annually on the same four times at least to the extent of the credit otherwise it will be withdrawn'.[29] The Dundee New Bank was even more severe with its customers and demanded that cash accounts should be drawn to the amount of the credit at least six times per year.[30] Other companies were less specific, merely requiring the customers to have frequent operations on their accounts and ensuring that the credits should not become dead loans.

Certainly profit maximisation was the major reason for the banks insisting on the rapid turnover of cash credits, but another reason may have been the desire to have an inflow of coin and the notes of other banks, as balances were reduced, with which to pay note exchange obligations – so the regulation on cash accounts has implications for liquidity. It also has implications for bad-debt control, for bankers 'read' the movements in their customers' accounts for guidance on credit-worthiness.

Some companies set limits on the size of the cash accounts which they would award. In 1766 the Perth United set an upper limit of £500 on its accounts.[31] Twenty years later the Perth Banking Co. set the limit at £1,500[32] and it does not appear that this limit was ever raised. The average of the first hundred cash accounts awarded by the Perth Banking Co. was £525. The smallest were in the £100–150 range while the largest were on the limit of £1,500.[33] It is impossible to give supporting evidence on this matter for the banking companies as a whole, but the few examples which have survived suggest that the Perth Banking Co. was fairly typical of the other companies, with the exception of those in Glasgow whose accounts tended to be somewhat larger, certainly in the 19th century.

Customers were usually required to confine their accounts to one bank. This limitation was designed so that a banker could be more certain of the total obligations and therefore the credit-worthiness of his customers. In 1790 several customers of the Dundee Banking Co. were awarded credits at the new Dundee branch of the Paisley Banking Co. Amongst these was John Baxter, the famous textile manufacturer. When the Dundee Banking Co. directors heard of this they took steps to ensure that customers confined their banking business to one company. Nevertheless examples can be found, principally amongst people with large business interests, of businessmen with two or more cash accounts in different banks. In 1783 Alexander Garden of Troup had accounts with the Bank of Scotland, Sir Wm. Forbes, James Hunter and Co., and the Aberdeen Banking Co.[34] In 1803 James Dennistoun, West India merchant, had accounts at the Thistle Bank and the Glasgow branch of the Royal Bank.[35] Although these exceptions can be found, it is true to say that the general rule was that a customer should confine his business, certainly his borrowing, to one bank. This rule hardened as banking practices became more formalised in the 19th century.

An early abuse of the cash account system was perpetrated in Aberdeen where customers of the banking company adopted the practice of drawing money in the morning, trading with it and paying their cash balance back in the afternoon. The effect of this was to give them free credit because interest was only calculated on the balance at the end of the day. When the Aberdeen directors realised what was happening it was a simple matter for them to put an end to this malpractice by threatening withdrawal of the facilities if they continued to be abused.[36]

It rapidly became customary to allow account holders to accumulate credit balances on their cash accounts for which interest was allowed at the rate of 1 per cent below lending rate (which was 5 per cent for most of the industrial revolution period). The acceptance of deposits in this way was a great convenience for customers whose cash requirements were often seasonal, for deposits of this type could be drawn at will in any amount that was needed. More will be said of deposits below but it is important to recognise that the cash account was not merely a credit device; indeed the deposit balances on cash accounts at the Thistle Bank far exceeded the overdrawn balances, at least between 1783 and 1792.[37]

The security required for an advance on a cash account was the personal worth of the borrower and usually two of his friends or business acquaintances who were prepared to sign his bond. Frequently the essentially personal nature of the obligation concealed a more tangible security. It often occurred that a guarantor (more accurately called a cautioner in Scotland) was a landowner or a shareholder in the bank, in which case these assets became attachable if the debt became bad because the whole heritable and moveable estate of a signatory was liable in cases of default. In order that a credit should be granted, the directors of the bank had to be convinced of the credit-worthiness of the principal and/or his backers. Cash credits could easily be obtained by those people who came from the same class as the bankers, i.e. the 'merchant class' because business communities were sufficiently small and close-knit for a banker to have a very shrewd opinion of the credit-worthiness of the other members of the same social grouping. Aspiring entrants to this group had a slightly more difficult time in obtaining credit facilities. It was always possible for a group of them to form a banking company of their own and this opportunity was sometimes taken, as is evidenced by the formation of second and third banks in some towns. Alternatively they could seek the patronage or forge a business link with a member of the merchant or landed classes who would then become their passport to a cash account or to discount facilities by guaranteeing their credit. The records of the Aberdeen Banking Co. show for example that Lord Gardenstone was prepared to sign the cash credit bonds of several of the merchants and manufacturers who settled in his planned village of Laurencekirk.[38] The minutes of this and other banks which have survived show that cash account applications were very seldom refused. Any aspiring trader or manufacturer who could get one or two good names on his bond was assured of having his application passed. Such was the close nature of business and family relationships that acceptable guarantors were not hard to find. In cases

J

where the applicant was of small substance or was not well known the number of signatures required for the bond was increased. Bonds with five or six names were not uncommon. In his evidence to the Parliamentary Committee of 1826 a former employee of the Perth Banking Co. was able to boast that cash credits

> were granted to small farmers who required assistance in stocking their farms, or perhaps carrying on a small cattle trade; they were granted to shopkeepers, principally commencing business, such as drapers or haberdashers, and to tradesmen commencing any business where he required a little money to purchase stock with, as perhaps his own savings did not amount to a sum sufficient to enable him to lay in that stock, the bank granted him an account for £100, £200 or £300 as they thought his business was extended enough to require.[39]

This witness overstated his case, as many of the credits awarded by this bank were given to partners and others well established in business, but his statement was essentially true as many credits were given to people just starting in business. The extension of credit facilities to the lower levels of the business community gave the widest possible circulation to the notes of the issuing banker.

A great advantage of cash credit facilities from the customer's point of view was that accounts were awarded without limit of time and did not require to be periodically renewed. They provided the customer with a flexible instrument of credit which could be drawn and repaid at will but this factor, viewed from the banker's standpoint, was not advantageous. He saw them as being inflexible, and at times of crisis when the banker wanted to contract credit the customer was often in need of credit and if he had not already done so he could draw out cash to the extent of his bond. To thwart this possibility the Perth Banking Co. in the crisis of 1793 reduced the ceiling on authorised credits by 25 per cent,[40] although there is evidence to suggest that other banking companies followed this example. But some limited their restrictive measures on cash accounts to moral suasion and concentrated their contractive activities on discounts.

It has been mentioned already that cash accounts were not intended to be permanent loans, but rather to be actively operated credits. The careful operator, however, could both satisfy his bank's note-circulating requirements and supply himself with a long-term loan. The example of the Stanley Cotton Co. account with the Perth United Banking Co. between 1785 and 1787 may illustrate this point. The account was opened on 4th July, 1785. The upper limit was £1,000. Table 18 sets out the balances at the end of each calendar month, together with the total amounts of deposits and withdrawals per month. Figures in brackets represent the number of transactions. This account seemingly satisfied the bank's requirements for cash credits that they should be operated upon frequently (thus helping to circulate the bank's notes), but only in November, 1786 did the monthly balance fall below £700 and in most months the outstanding balance was even larger. In this way the proprietors of the Stanley Mill used their cash account to provide themselves not only with a source of circulating capital but also with a long-term loan. This type of illustration could be repeated many times over. It must be borne in mind that this is only the cash account; there were probably also discounts on behalf of the Cotton Company, but the volume of these unfortunately cannot be determined. This example should in large measure explain why cash accounts were popular with customers. A further reason is to be found in the manner of charging interest on these accounts.

Table 18

Stanley Cotton Co. in account with Perth United Banking Co.[41]

Cash Account Transactions 1785–1787

		Deposits	*Withdrawals*	*Balance*
1785	July		600 (10)	600 av.
	Aug	270 (1)	500 (6)	835
	Sept	730 (2)	772 (16)	870
	Oct	662 (4)	565 (12)	877
	Nov	100 (1)	320 (9)	780
	Dec	150 (2)	120 (4)	1,000
1786	Jan	360 (2)	105 (5)	970
	Feb	150 (1)	335 (5)	715
	March	545 (2)	515 (8)	900
	Apr	—	130 (4)	870
	May	50 (1)	50 (3)	1,000
	June	—	—	1,000
	July	680 (3)	420 (15)	740
	Aug	—	260 (9)	1,000
	Sept	45 (1)	85 (1)	1,040
	Oct	460 (1)	420 (8)	1,000
	Nov	865 (2)	250 (2)	385
	Dec	—	605 (9)	990
1787	Jan	640 (3)	415 (4)	765
	Feb	—	185 (6)	950
	March	550 (4)	600 (6)	1,000
	Apr	505 (1)	505 (6)	1,000
	May	1,030 (2)	30 (1)	—
				Bank closed

Interest was charged on the balances actually outstanding on the account and was calculated on a daily basis which meant that the customer paid only for the credit which he used. In effect cash accounts could be cheaper than bill discounts because the latter cost the customer interest on the whole bill whether he needed all of the cash or not. Here again the cash account was a flexible and economical instrument of credit from the customer's point of view. This point was made by several of the witnesses to the 1826 Promissory Notes Committee.

The Usury Laws limited the rate of interest which could be charged for credit to 5 per cent, and this rate prevailed throughout the 18th century and up to 1822 when it was reduced to 4 per cent. The rate was raised to its former level in the crisis of 1825 and in the remainder of the life-cycle of the banking companies it fluctuated between 4 and 5 per cent, depending on whether credit was easy or difficult. The repeal of the Usury Laws in 1833 did not result in an upward movement of interest rates. No commission was charged on these accounts.

Generally all banks and banking companies charged the same rates, and of course the Edinburgh banks usually determined what that rate should be. There were a few cases of provincial bankers charging different, usually higher, rates than the Edinburgh banks but these occurrences where short-lived. In December, 1840 the Edinburgh bankers agreed on new rates of interest on deposits and advances but these were resisted by the Glasgow bankers, led by the joint-stock Glasgow Union Bank, who claimed that 'the rate at Glasgow is practically determined by the value of money in Lancashire and Yorkshire'.[42] This fact was eventually acknowledged by the Edinburgh men who agreed to keep the rates at 5 per cent on advances and 3½ per cent on deposits. This was the first occasion that the provinces had succeeded in holding out against Edinburgh, but by that time there was only one provincial banking company left in Glasgow and it played a minor role in the debate.

Despite their cheapness, cash accounts were not the major earning assets of the banking companies, certainly after about 1780. Some figures for the Perth United Banking Co. illustrate this trend.

Table 19
Perth United Banking Co.[43]
Income from advances (Gross)

	1770–71	1780–81
Bills discounted	£ 184	£ 304
Inland Bills	423	900
Bills of Exchange	216	95
Total Bills	823	1,299
Obligations Receivable	128	102
Cash Accounts	1,481	1,093
	£ 2,432	£ 2,444

Professor Cameron's claim of Scottish Banking, generally, that

> Bills of exchange, the staple assets of many contemporary banks in other countries, were the least important earning assets of the Scottish Banks. Of greater importance were loans on personal or heritable bonds . . . The largest volume of lending however, took place by means of loans on cash account

is untrue of the banking companies for most of the period in which they were in operation. His assertion that 'Cash accounts remained an important lending device of the Scottish banks until at least the second quarter of the nineteenth century'[44] has more validity, although the measure of 'important' varied from bank to bank. The cash accounts of the Dundee Banking Co. declined as a proportion of total advances between 1825 and 1864, while those of the Perth Banking Co. increased both in volume and as a proportion of advances.[45] The different experiences of these companies may be attributable to the varying types of business conducted by them. The Perth Banking Company seems to have been more concerned with the finance of agriculture, where the cash account was more appropriate, than the Dundee Banking Company whose customers were, predominantly, industrialists.

Although it is important to analyse the nature of total advances from the bankers' point of view, too much should not be made of the distinctions if the customer's credit requirements are the major criteria. It is arguable that cash accounts and discounts were complementary parts of the provision of credit rather than alternatives to one another; while the cash credit was traditionally used to finance wage payments and small running expenses, the discount provided finance for production and sales. This is of course a simplification but it is a view advanced by one of the earliest writers on the subject and consequently must be given some credence.[46] Bank borrowers usually had both a cash account and discount facilities. Both were important parts of the credit mechanism and had distinctive roles.

4. Bills

There were three types of bill which the banks and banking companies would discount. Firstly local bills, usually termed 'bills discounted', were payable in the town in which the bank operated. Secondly 'inland bills' were payable in other Scottish towns and payment was obtained by sending them to agents or other banks in the towns on which they were drawn who collected the sums due in return for a small commission or a reciprocal arrangement. Thirdly 'bills of exchange' were foreign bills but in addition 'bills drawn in Scotland and payable in England are accounted foreign bills'.[47] Most 'bills of exchange' were in fact drawn on London.

Despite the division of bills into three different categories, the generic term *bills of exchange* will be used to describe all types of bills. Again specific examples of discounts will be largely confined to Part Three. Foreign bills were 'bought' rather than discounted. Such was the terminology used but in practice the effect was the same. A certain amount of the bills handled by the banking companies were in fact bills on London, i.e. foreign bills. These were sent to the London correspondents a few days before they were due. The correspondent then collected payment for them and credited his principal's account.

The importance of bills of exchange to the business world of the 18th and 19th centuries cannot be overstated. A contemporary perceived that

> Bills of exchange are universally acknowledged to be the most useful instruments of commerce; nor is it easy, in the present day, to conceive how an extensive trade could be carried on without them.[48]

A seller of goods drew up a bill of exchange which was accepted, i.e. signed across the face, as an acknowledgement of debt by the purchaser and returned to the seller. Bills were usually marked for payment at a stated future date – normally three months from the date of the transaction. This gave the purchaser time to sell the goods and collect payment for them which enabled him to pay the bill when the original seller presented it for payment. The bill of exchange, therefore, was an instrument of credit, as well as a document of debt, whether or not a banker was involved in the transactions. Bankers became party to the bill if the seller wished cash for it before the purchaser was due to pay. If this was the case the bill was taken to the banker who discounted it, that is, he gave cash for it less interest and charges. The banker then held the bill until it matured, whereupon he presented it for payment. Three days of grace were allowed for payment and if the bill was not paid it was then protested. The protest was a fairly simple legal process by which the holder of the bill attempted to procure payment for it.

Frequently the accepter of the bill was required to pay the amount due to a third party and not to the person who drew it up. This was particularly the case with foreign bills where it would have been physically impossible for the accepter to pay cash to the drawer because of the distances which separated them. In these cases the third party (the payee) was usually an agent or the banker of the drawer although sometimes his creditor.

Very often the local and inland bills which were discounted were not strictly bills of exchange but rather promissory notes. These took the form of i.o.u.'s in which the purchaser in a transaction drew up a note in which he promised to pay the value of the goods to the seller. Despite this basic difference between bills and promissory notes, namely that the drawer was the seller in the former case and the purchaser in the latter, 'the privileges . . . rules and decisions relative to the one may be held as applicable to the other, which will render it unnecessary to treat of them separately',[49] and, of course, banknotes were also promissory notes.

Bankers often preferred to lend against bills of exchange, as compared with making advances, because bills were a more flexible medium from the bankers' point of view. Certainly cash accounts were useful for circulating notes, but unlike discounts they could not be easily decreased in times of crisis when banks required to increase their liquidity. Discounts, on the other hand, were fixed-time loans. They matured and were paid in a number of ways – either in the bank's own notes, in the notes of other banks, in specie or in balances with agents, and in these ways liquidity was increased, new discounts could be refused and the balances thus amassed could be used to pay deposits if there was a run on the bank. A number of bills would mature each week, thus providing a useful flow of cash which provided the basis for the liquidity of the bank.

Rather than refuse discounts altogether when money was tight, it became common practice under such conditions to discount only short-dated bills. Normally bills at three months' date formed the majority of discounts but if a banking company wanted to be more certain of its liquidity, i.e. to have a faster flow of cash, it might consent to discount bills with only 30 or 60 days to run. Conversely in times when money was easy it often occurred that bills of 4 or 6 months were discounted. In this way the bankers had a choice of method in the rationing of discounts.

Throughout much of the industrial revolution bankers generally believed in the *real-bills* doctrine of Adam Smith. This stated that so long as all bills represented real commercial transactions and were drawn at short term or the term of the transaction, then banks could not issue notes to excess causing inflation and commercial crisis. A *real* transaction may be defined as one in which there was a transfer of the ownership of goods.

Some banking companies laid very great stress on this doctrine; for example the Dundee New Bank informed its agents that it was not the business of a bank

> to supply Capital to a Country but only to give activity to such as many be employed by others by discounting their bills for real transactions at short dates and therby keeping it in constant circulation.

It was a 'first principle' in sound banking only to discount bills which were drawn 'in the regular course of trade'.[50]

Similarly the directors of the East Lothian Banking Co. told their staff and branch agents that customers should only be allowed to discount bills 'to the extent necessary for the carrying on of their business in a regular and business like manner' and that bills should only be discounted for people 'who have the prospect in a short while to repay it without being obliged to touch their real property'.[51]

The function of these advice notes was to ensure that agents would not discount any *accommodation bills*. The latter were often called *wind bills* and the drawing of them was referred to as *kite-flying*. If a man wanted to have credit for speculative purposes he might draw a bill on another man, preferably at some distance, who would accept it to accommodate his friend. The first man would then take it to a bank for discount. In this way the bank increased the supply of money without any comparable increase in the supply of goods. Bankers, following the advice of Adam Smith, were usually keen to avoid discounting these accommodation bills, more especially as one such bill might give rise to a whole chain of dubious paper. In order to pay the bill the friend might draw a bill on the first man, this time for a higher amount (to cover interest etc.) which he would then discount, having first had it accepted, and this practice of drawing and re-drawing might continue for some time. The money might be used for speculation, consumption or for investment in some long-term project, but if the bank at some point in the chain refused further discounts, then the loan became doubtful because the project which it had been used to finance had not yielded the required proceeds.

The banker was always faced with the problem of how to recognise these bills when they were presented for discount. The only way he could tell was 'from the general character of the parties and the nature of their trade',[52] and to most banks and banking companies accommodation bills were anathema. Nevertheless it is clear that some were discounted. The Ayr Bank in particular was guilty of discounting them, but the fate of that concern was the main example which Smith used to demonstrate the inadvisability of this procedure. Following the publication of Smith's book there were a few cases which make it clear that some banks were prepared to countenance these bills. In 1815 the Dundee New Bank, then under new management, ordered that these types of bill should not be taken, as 'at present the Directors wish that description of bills to be declined'.[53] The clear implication of this is that they had previously been discounted in full knowledge of their status.

Bankers could accommodate their customers by letting their bills *lie-over* when they fell due, i.e. by not demanding payment when the bill matured. In 1761 fully 66 per cent of the bills discounted by the Ship Bank in Glasgow had been allowed to lie-over, that is, they were *past-due*.[54] Again in 1793 Henry Glassford requested the Thistle Bank to renew his bill to George Mackintosh and Co. 'once more for 6 months'.[55] In times of crisis bankers had little alternative to letting some bills lie-over, for if they insisted on payment they might precipitate a bankruptcy which would further damage their security. The shortage of evidence on discounts makes it impossible to tell how common these practices were, but it is worth recording these examples as a further indication of the flexibility of credit instruments.

The real-bills doctrine was widely supported, but it did have its detractors, amongst whom was Henry Thornton the London banker.[56] The doctrine was objected to on the grounds that a fresh bill of exchange is drawn at each stage of manufacture when goods are transferred from one producer to the next so that one set of goods may give rise to several bills of exchange, all of which may be current at the same time. it would 'only be the last holder of the goods who would have them, and be enabled to devote the proceeds to the payment of the last bill only'.[57] He would pay his acceptance and so, in theory, the money would in turn be used to pay all the bills which had arisen in the production of the goods. Trouble arises if the goods cannot be sold or if their market price falls – then several bills may be protested for non-payment. The security which the doctrine claimed exists in *real-bills* is therefore seen to be largely illusory.

The point must be made that bankers translated their fear of the potential abuses of accommodation bills into the formula of the real-bills doctrine but in fact there was nothing essentially fraudulent or dangerous about this type of credit. Indeed the cash-account system was a form of credit analogous to the accommodation bill in that credits were not tied to particular transfers of goods. But bankers, following Smith's advice and remembering the Ayr Bank collapse, were afraid that their credit might be abused. Although the real-bills doctrine has been seen to be largely fallacious and the cash credit system may be characterised as similar to accommodation bills, there were nevertheless good reasons for avoiding this type of paper.

If a trader persuaded ten of his friends to accommodate him with their names and he discounted the bills at his bank, it was his duty to provide funds to meet them at maturity. There was then really only one principal debtor and ten sureties. None of the ten made provision to meet the bill which they had accepted but all this time the bank would be under the impression that the reverse was the case. In this example there would be a much greater chance of disaster than if the bills were real. Although there was little essentially dangerous about accommodation bills, they were potentially a very hazardous undertaking. The real bills doctrine was therefore retained as a useful operating principle although discredited as an axiom.

The bill of exchange was an important instrument of trade and bank credit. In England, particularly in Lancashire, bills rather than bank notes formed the largest part of the circulating medium,[58] passing from hand to hand by simple endorsement. The extent to which the circulation of trade bills fulfilled a similar role in Scotland is a matter for debate. When Dr. Johnson and James Boswell visited the Highlands and Islands in 1772 they found that rents were often paid in drovers' bills, and in the early 18th century bills circulated freely in the north and helped to finance an active trade

> not only in such home products as Easdale slate, Morayshire grain and Findhorn salmon, but in coffee beans from Rotterdam, wines from Bordeaux and olives of the Mediterranean shore.[59]

By the 1830s, however, Hugh Watt, a banker with wide experience of business conditions in central and northern Scotland, was able to claim that the most important part of the banking business of Scotland consisted of the discounting of bills but, unlike England, 'Scotland has no bill circulation whatever'.[60] Seemingly the success achieved by the banks and banking companies in circulating their notes had rendered a bill circulation unnecessary. Nevertheless the matter was not so clear-cut as Watt suggested. The historian of Scotland's woollen industry discovered that by 1830, in the borders, the bill of exchange circulated 'as freely as money, often covered in endorsements'.[61] This conflicting evidence suggests that there were regional patterns of monetary experience. The borders certainly were never very well served by branches of banks and banking companies; nor did the counties of Roxburgh, Selkirk and Peebles generate banking companies of their own. Furthermore Gulvin claimed that bank credit did not begin to play an important role in the woollen industry until the 1820s.[62] Therefore if there was little bank credit going to the industry, then there would be small chance of circulating bank notes. Consequently bills of exchange were transferred by endorsement, thus providing a type of circulating medium which was not required in most other parts of the country.

The re-discounting of bills by banks was not an important activity. The practice of selling London bills for the convenience of customers has been mentioned above but this practice seems to have declined in favour of drawing bills on London agents. In any case this was a service to customers rather than a conscious re-discounting attempt to smooth the banker's cash flow. Nevertheless a few examples of this type of activity have survived. In 1774 the Aberdeen Banking Co. tried to sell London bills to banks in Dundee, Perth and Montrose but was unsuccessful because the banking companies in these places had no need for bills,[63] and in 1803 the Dundee New Bank sent £4,000 in bills to one of its partners in London with instructions to discount them and place the proceeds to its account with the London agent. The Montrose Banking Co. was forced to re-discount some bills in London in the crisis of 1826.[64] Generally, however, this type of business was frowned upon. Hugh Watt, onetime employee of the Perth, Arbroath and Huddersfield Banking Companies, claimed that it was the practice of Scottish bankers 'not to re-discount any bills'.[65] Re-discounting was regarded by some as a sign of weakness.

Although it was loath to sell bills which it had discounted itself, the Perth Banking Co., at least, was prepared to buy the bills of other banks. In 1834 the directors of that concern approved of its Bills Committee discounting London bills to the Manchester Bank provided that they were endorsed by that bank. The initial sum involved was £40,000 but further amounts were approved at later dates.[66] This is the only surviving example of this type of business being done.

Interest was charged on bills at the *legal rate*, usually 5 per cent, for most of the industrial revolution period. But bankers were also entitled 'to charge a reasonable sum by way of commission, on account of their remitting the bill for acceptance, and necessary expenses'.[67] The extent to which banks availed themselves of this entitlement is not widely known. Certainly in 1810 the Perth Banking Co. directors decided that the charge made for discounting bills was not sufficient 'to cover the expense attending the negotiating of them'.[68] It does not appear that extra charges were levied on local bills but those payable in Glasgow, Dundee, Stirling, Paisley and Greenock were charged an extra 10 days' interest. Bills drawn on other towns were charged similar rates. This charge could be a potential source of profit because several bills might be posted in the same packet, which would be a saving to the banker. The practice of charging commission in this way was probably fairly general and this was certainly the case with London bills, which have been discussed in Chapter 4.

In times of easy money bankers either reduced the rate of interest or increased the tenor of the bills which they were prepared to discount, or did both. In times of crisis the reverse was the case, within the interest rate ceiling imposed by the terms of the Usury Laws. In these ways the bankers sought to regulate and ration their advances.

5. Other Advances

Some banking companies were prepared to make advances on the security of heritable property. This was a favourite method of the public banks, but it was not popular with the provincial, which were more concerned to finance trade and industry. In any case their capital was seldom sufficient to support a number of long-term loans of this nature and only a few traces of this type of advance are to be found in the records of the provincial banking companies, particularly in the early years.

The Aberdeen Banking Co. balance sheets from 1768 to 1787 display a small but continuing interest in heritable bonds. In 1768 they totalled £8,000 in total advances of £48,000. In 1787 the figures were £4,000 and £158,000.[69] This company kept a record of all the entailed estates in Scotland so that it could not be deluded by an offer of security over land which had been entailed.

Hunters and Co. of Ayr also advanced money on what they described as 'Permanent Security' loans, but when crisis broke in 1778 they were forced to recall half of the money advanced in this way.[70]

These advances were probably fixed-term, lump sum loans. An Act of 1696 had made it illegal for heritable security to be pledged for debt to be incurred in the future, meaning cash accounts could not be awarded against the security of heritable property, only fixed sum advances could be made in this way. This restriction, however, was temporarily withdrawn by the Scottish Bankruptcy Act of 1793 (clause 12)[71] but was soon reimposed and was not finally withdrawn until 1856.

The Perth Banking Co. in the 1830s and 1850s made a few advances on heritable security, but these were never a very significant portion of the total advances. In October, 1856 they decided to lend money in this way to the extent of the funds in the reserve which had been set aside to meet losses on investments, and the following month they advanced £30,000 on the security of the Black-ruthven Estate.[72] These loans were usually for a number of years.

The banking company with the most active interest, so far as is known, in these securities was the Dundee Banking Co. Heritable bonds for a few hundred pounds began to appear in the balance sheets in the later years of the Napoleonic Wars but in the years which followed the peace they began to grow until 1823 when they took a sudden leap forward from £2,000 to £77,000. Thereafter they grew to rival discounts as an earning asset. There was clearly a very marked change of policy, but it is difficult to determine exactly why this happened. Possibly the glut of money and the generally low rates of interest encouraged this company to lend money on heritable bonds at 5 per cent. One of the loans made was on the security of the Island of Harris, but when the duty on imported barilla was abolished the kelp which was produced there became almost valueless and the banking company lost £15,000. Despite this these loans proved popular, and although they declined in volume in the late 1830s they increased again in the 1840s (see Appendix A).[73]

Nevertheless, despite the example of the Dundee Banking Co. heritable bonds were not in the mainstream of provincial banking practice.

Although the cash credit has been compared to the modern overdraft, the analogy is not quite perfect because the former required a signed bond. The first known example of an *overdraft* occurred in the records of the Perth Banking Co. when in 1829 Sir Neil Menzies, Bt., was allowed 'to overdraw his account to the extent of one thousand pounds', if necessary for 'temporary' accommodation.[74] No bond was required. From 1839 the term 'overdrawn accounts' appeared in the balance sheets of the Dundee Banking Co. and the manager of the company was later able to boast that 'Nothing was ever lost by thus accommodating respectable customers with occasional overdraughts for moderate amounts'.[75] The practice of the public banks in allowing customers to overdraw their accounts seems to have begun in the early 1830s.[76] This development probably arose out of a need for a more flexible system of short-term lending.

The Glasgow and Ship Banking Co. took a life insurance policy as security for an advance in 1842. Premiums on the policy were to be made via the bank or were to be intimated to it by the insurance company.[77] There is no indication of the volume of lending against this type of security nor of the number of advances of this kind.

6. Investments

There were two aspects to investments in government funds and bills or other securities. Firstly they were treated as a reserve which could be sold or pledged for an advance when money was short. Secondly they were a repository, often highly profitable, for surplus funds. These two functions were, of course, not entirely separate but they were sufficiently diverse to warrant separate consideration.

The market for these investments was in London and consequently purchases were made on behalf of the banking companies by their London correspondents. More will be said about this in Chapter 10.

Investments were made with 'surplus money in London when the sum comes to be large and is to be stationary'.[78] By rendering their surplus funds productive in this way the bankers were enabled

> to allow interest upon a vast number of small sums deposited with them, generally the savings of the industrious classes of the community, to the great and manifest advantage of the country.[79]

The alternative was to keep surplus funds in non-earning specie or on deposit with London or Edinburgh correspondents. But these men usually put a ceiling on the volume of deposits on which they were prepared to pay interest. Consequently investments in the funds and government bills became an important part of banking practice for many companies.

Investments in government securities were a popular form of reserve because a banker, if his position was illiquid, could borrow against them on better terms than on any other form of security.[80] Alternatively he could sell them although this action might entail a loss on the transaction. In this respect government bills were preferred to funds because they had fixed maturity dates and values and were therefore more marketable in time of crisis than the funds. Bank of England stock was also thought to be a good investment because it was 'readily convertible'.[81]

The development of formal reserve policies, with particular investments being tied to reserve accounts, was a slow one. There are only two examples on which to draw. In 1836 the Glasgow Banking Co. decided that £15,000 from its Dependancy Account should be invested in Bank of England stock[82] and in 1856 the Perth Banking Co. tied its reserve fund for losses on investments to a loan of £30,000 on a heritable bond.[83]

Some banking companies took a long time to develop investment policies. The Dundee Banking Co. placed no money in funds or government bills until 1803[84] and the Montrose Banking Co. boasted in 1824 that it had hitherto confined its business to banking 'without entering into any speculation in the public funds or shares'.[85] That was an error because in 1818 it had held the following stocks:[86]

£ 5,658	in	3½%	Annuities
9,423	in	5%	Navy Annuities
6,579	in	3%	Consols
£21,660			

Nevertheless by 1824 these had been sold and in 1826 the weakness of the company's position was revealed. In the crisis of that year it was forced to borrow £10,000 from the Bank of Scotland which, in order to make the loan, had to sell Consols. The Montrose Banking Co. was required to replace these in three months' time irrespective of the price, and in order to meet this obligation it made a time purchase of Consols at the same price the Bank of Scotland received for them. This account was continued until the debt was repaid in 1827 and the only cost to the Montrose Banking Co. was the interest and brokerage.[87]

Clearly the banks and banking companies which did not keep reserves were in very exposed positions in times of crisis. A problem arises, however, in determining at what level reserve policy stops and a profit-oriented investment policy begins. The point has sometimes been made mainly by polemicists, that investments like these deprived home-based trade and industry of funds. The truth of this matter may never be known. But two points are worth making. Firstly the investments to total assets ratio for the Ship Bank averaged about 24 per cent, and other liquid assets were not likely to have been large. Although no cash balance figures are known, similar figures for other companies suggest about 2 or 3 per cent. Therefore if this estimate is used for the Ship Bank, then total cash and investments were somewhere in the region of 26 per cent of total assets. Most other banking companies probably had smaller ratios. In modern banks the ratio has often been nearer 50 per cent, although there has been a downward trend in recent years. Secondly the point must again be made that virtually the only time customers were heard to complain of a shortage of bank credit was at the height of a commercial crisis.

There were really two aspects of investment policy. One was the reserve consideration, already mentioned, and the other was the need to find 'eligible investments' for money which would yield a satisfactory return and perhaps also appreciate in value. Many of the banking companies were not above speculating.

The practice of the banking companies may be illustrated by reference to the surviving records. It is not pretended that these examples are typical, for adequate data are lacking, but they do suggest some of the problems faced and the solutions found.

One of the best sources for the study of investment practice is the journal of the Ship Bank, 1785–1836.[88] The management of this concern was principally in the hands of one man from 1785 to 1821, Robin Carrick. The company's investment policy under Carrick's direction was both shrewd and successful. Funds were bought in large quantities when prices were low, for example in 1797, 1803, 1814, 1816 and 1820. When the Ship Bank had surplus cash and the funds were high, Carrick bought government bills, as in 1810, 1817 and 1818. Table 20 sets out the income from investments in government funds and bills and in banks' stocks. R. S. Rait provided some balance sheet totals[89] which make it possible to calculate investments as a percentage of total assets in several years. These are set out in Table 21.

Table 20

Ship Bank, Income from Investments in Government Funds and Bills
and Banks' Stocks

Year	(1) Funds and Bills	(2) Bank of England	(3) Scots Banks	(4) Total (1)(2)&(3)
1786	£ 1,952			1,952
1787	759			759
1788	90			90
1789/1795	0			0
1796	3,009			3,009
1797	7,049			7,049
1798	8,684		60	8,744
1799	8,573		60	8,633
1800	8,573		64	8,637
1801	8,573		64	8,637
1802	8,813		64	8,877
1803	10,169		64	10,233
1804	8,915		64	8,979
1805	10,110		64	10,174
1806	9,721		64	9,785
1807	9,332		64	9,396
1808	6,461		64	6,525
1809	4,862		64	4,926
1810	4,057		64	4,121
1811	4,016		75	4,091
1812	4,190		75	4,265
1813	3,678		75	3,753
1814	3,686		75	3,761
1815	4,217	400	75	4,692
1816	4,772	400	100	5,272
1817	7,303	1,100	100	8,503
1818	7,344	1,100	100	8,544
1819	8,228	1,100	100	9,428
1820	7,372	2,200	100	9,672
1821	8,845	3,590	100	12,535
1822	7,341	3,840	100	11,281
1823	11,663	3,792	100	15,542
1824	3,655	4,400	85	8,140
1825	3,925	1,840	85	5,850
1826	250	1,800	85	2,135
1827	300	1,600	85	1,985
1828	600	2,200	85	2,285
1829		2,400	85	2,485
1830		2,400	85	2,485
1831		2,400	85	2,485
1832		800	85	885
1833		2,400	672	3,072
1834	199	2,000	529	2,728
1835			529	529

Total income from Investments 1786–1835 = £254,128

Source   Ship Bank Journal, 1785–1836
Note   Figures for dividends on Scottish bank stocks based on C. Malcolm, *The Bank of Scotland*
         and R. Cameron, *Banking in the Early Stages of Industrialisation*

The extent of the Ship Bank's investments in negotiable securities is set out in Table 22. The sheer volume of these investments suggests that in this case the need for an adequate reserve was a secondary, but nevertheless still important, consideration to that of profit. The attraction of investments over advances is obvious, for in addition to the yield there was also the possibility of capital appreciation. Although the funds might also depreciate, the shrewd investor who bought when the price was low could be virtually certain of an eventual rise in price, thus generating a capital gain. He merely had to bide his time. When the Ship Bank's investment policy changed in 1823 following the death of Carrick, large amounts of securities were sold and the net profit realised on these sales was £21,963. The lack of Ship Bank minute books makes it impossible to say exactly what considerations inspired these disposals.

Table 21

Ship Bank, Investments as a Percentage of Total Assets

Year	(1) Investments	(2) Total Assets	(3) %
1799	£121,600	542,409	22.4
1820	230,113	848,477	27.1
1821	193,235	1,028,456	18.8
1822	269,272	991,487	27.1
1828	67,617	1,072,042	6.3

The records of the Perth Banking Company for the 1829 to 1857 period provide more certain grounds for assessing investment motives, although here again the experience of this company may not be regarded as typical because very little evidence for other companies exists but it does provide an indication of some of the problems faced by a bank having to make investment decisions from a provincial city.

From 1818 the London and Edinburgh correspondents of provincial banking companies began to limit the balances of their correspondents on which they would pay interest. These decisions were made from two motives. Firstly in times of easy money the bankers in Edinburgh and London found it difficult to employ funds profitably. Secondly, in times of crisis the money was liable to be withdrawn, thereby creating a liquidity problem. In the case of the Perth Banking Co. the limit enforced by Barclays, the London correspondents, was set at £50,000 in 1818 but this had been further reduced by stages to £5,000 in 1827. Forbes, Hunter and Co., the Edinburgh correspondents, imposed a ceiling of £15,000 in 1824.[90] The balance sheets are not available before 1830, but from other evidence in the minute book it seems that the company had to find alternative outlets for about £80,000 as a result of their correspondents' actions. This, of course, was in addition to any increase in deposits which the bank attracted.

Table 22
Ship Bank Investments 1786–1836 at cost

Year	(1) 3% Consols	(2) 3% Reduced	(3) 3% Deferred	(4) 4%	(5) Short Annuities	(6) Long Annuities	(7) 5% Navy	(8) Total Funds	(9) Govt. Bills	(10) Total Govt.	(11) Bank of England	(12) Scots Banks	(13) Total
1786	13525						2946	16471		16471			16471
1787	3381						7044	10425		10425			10425
1788	2276							2276		2276			2276
1789													
1790													
1791													
1792													
1793													
1794													
1795	6132			17792	11974	22253		28385	10838	39223			39223
1796	9359			17792	27706	38004		77129	5262	82391			82391
1797	39798			17792	22553	41972		127268		127268			127268
1798	39798	1058		17792	20103	41972		123173		123173		1200	124373
1799	40533			17792	18696	41972		120400		120400		1200	121600
1800	40533			17792	15014	41972		118993		118993		1200	120193
1801	40533			17792	12460	41972		115311		115311		1200	116511
1802	51469			17792	9535	41792		123693		123693		1200	124893
1803	61586	14878	839	17792	7628	48236		152866		152866		1200	154066
1804	61586	14878	839	17792	3768	48236		150959		150959		1200	150959
1805	61586	14878	839	17792	861	48236		147099		147099		1200	148299
1806	61586	14878	839	17792		48236		144192		144192		1200	145392
1807	61586	14878	839	17792		48236		143331		143331		1200	144531
1808	55274	14878	839	12662		48236		131889		131889		1200	133089
1809	36068			4180		45615	10222	88484		88484		1200	89684
1810	32491			4180		44667		92508	17155	109663		1200	110863
1811	37641			4180		45450		86498	17155	103653		1200	104853
1812	26161			4180		45450		75791	22200	97991		1200	99191
1813	26161			4180		45450		75791	3124	78915		1200	80115
1814	26161			4180		45450		75791	3500	79291		1200	80491

Year	(1) 3% Consols	(2) 3% Reduced	(3) 3% Deferred	(4) 4%	(5) Short Annuities	(6) Long Annuities	(7) 5% Navy	(8) Total Funds	(9) Govt. Bills	(10) Total Govt.	(11) Bank of England	(12) Scots Banks	(13) Total
1815	26161	18038		4180		45450	6000	99829	7134	106963	10305	1200	118468
1816	26161	18038		4180		45450	37110	130939	7134	138073	18819	1200	158092
1817	26161	18038		4180		45450	37110	130939	17524	148463	23156	1200	172819
1818	26161	8183		4180		45450		83974	61365	145339	23156	1200	169695
1819	26161	45338		4180		45450		121129	4874	126003	23156	1200	150359
1820	26161	45338		4180		45450		121129	35925	157054	71859	1200	230113
1821	12036	37963		4180		42616	12430	109225		109225	82810	1200	193235
1822		68983		17196		39670		125849	59413	185262	82810	1200	269272
1823				5000				5000	59413	64413	113120	1200	178733
1824	93776					23716		117492	12534	130026	30901	1200	162127
1825									12534	12534	54228	1200	67962
1826									12534	12534	22814	1200	36584
1827	16038							16038	12534	28572	43076	1200	72848
1828									12534	12534	53883	1200	67617
1829									12534	12534	53883	1200	67617
1830									12534	12534	53883	1200	67617
1831									12534	12534	53883	1200	67617
1832									12534	12534	35069	1200	48803
1833						6558		6558	12534	19092	45187	13487	77766
1834									12534	12534	45187	13487	71208
1835												13487	13487
1836											53281	13487	66768

Notes

1 The figures given for Government bills between 1825 and 1834 are estimates based on 1824 figure
2 Figures for long annuities between 1812 and 1820 are estimates but may be assumed correct to the nearest £1,000
3 All figures represent balances held at bank's annual balance on July 1st in each year

K

Professor Pressnell has argued that these decisions of the correspondents 'encouraged the shift of country money from London bankers to the bill brokers'.[91] There is no suggestion that this was the case with the Perth Banking Co., although it remains a possibility. Certainly this company chose a number of other avenues for investment some of which, although less liquid than short-notice deposits in the London money market, were nevertheless sufficiently marketable to ensure a degree of liquidity whilst providing a higher yield than call and short-term money. In 1824 the sum of £30,000 was invested in new 4 per cent annuities and £20,000 in French 5 per cent Rentes. In 1827 loans of £20,000 each were made to the Arbroath Banking Co. and the Glasgow Bank for one year at 4 per cent and 3½ per cent respectively.[92] The placement of these sums must be seen against a background of active investment and trading in the funds which had been bank policy since 1814. When the bank's contract was renewed in 1829 the reformed company bought the following investments from the old concern at market prices:[93]

3% Consols	£ 36,948
3½% Consols	10,000
4% New	85,500
Bank of England	13,300
Royal Bank	5,650
	£151,398

At the end of the first year of trading the new co-partnery showed investments in the public funds and other marketable securities to be valued at £134,143. Throughout the 1830 to 1857 period the yield on Consols and other government securities continued to decline, thus causing the bank to seek alternative outlets for its surplus money. The search for 'eligible' investments was the duty of the three-man bills committee whose minutes, if they kept any, have not survived. Nevertheless some idea of the committee's decisions and general investment policy can be gleaned from the directors' minutes of 1829–1857 and from the investment register of 1841–1857.

To some extent the necessity for an active investment policy was imposed by the state of bank competition in Perth. A branch of the Bank of Scotland had been opened in the 1780s, to be followed in 1807 by the British Linen Company, the Commercial Bank in 1835, the Royal Bank in 1855 and the Clydesdale Bank in 1856. The Perth Union Bank was opened in 1810 and was taken over by the National Bank in 1836. Lastly the joint-stock, Central Bank of Scotland was founded in 1834. All these concerns competed with the Perth Banking Company. It therefore seems unlikely that this bank could have found a business outlet for all of its resources, with the result that it was forced to invest in other areas. It may seem tempting at first sight to suggest that the withdrawal of funds from Perth and their subsequent investment elsewhere may have been instrumental in retarding industrial growth in the region. Growth proved disappointing in the 19th century after a promising start in the 18th. This, however, would be a superficial and almost certainly inaccurate assessment. The competition for business in Perth is unlikely to have been all for deposits. Given that the lending and deposit rates of the banks were the same, then all banks would have to be prepared to provide a full range of banking services. It is extremely unlikely that there was much, if any, unsatisfied demand for credit.

Perth Banking Co. money found outlets in American bonds, overseas banks, foreign bonds, re-discounts and special advances to customers as well as in the more conventional but seemingly less profitable avenues of government funds and British banks. All of these will be considered in turn.

In October, 1837 the directors decided to purchase £15,000 of Dutch 5 per cents and in December of that year a further £20,000 was invested in 2½ per cents. Short-dated London bills held by the bank were discounted in order to provide the cash for this last purchase. (It is impossible to say, however, if these bills were acquired in the normal course of business or if the bank had been placing money on the London discount market via brokers.) The Dutch 2½ per cents were yielding 4.75 per cent in 1837 whilst British 3 per cent Consols were yielding only 3.30 per cent.[94] The bank's motive in purchasing the Dutch stocks needs no further explanation. Nevertheless in 1838 the stock was sold and the bills committee was authorised to invest up to £100,000 in American stocks.[95]

The decision to invest in America can only be described as highly speculative. The financial system of the United States in 1838 was chaotic. The historian of American finance claimed that 'in the troubled period 1837–1845 foreign investors stopped buying American securities'.[96] But with prices low, yields were likely to be high, certainly in excess of 5 per cent, although just how high is not certain because the dates of purchase and the nominal values of the stocks were not revealed. The purchase of U.S. Bank stock is particularly difficult to explain as the charter of this concern expired in 1836 and, although it continued in business until 1841, its deposits were gradually dispersed to 'pet banks'. Perhaps it was expected that the federal government would pay off the capital but it never did. The whole investment in this stock was lost. Table 23 sets out the Perth Banking Co's. investments in American stocks as they stood in the books in 1841 and traces their progress thereafter.

Table 23

Perth Banking Company American Investments 1841[97]

Stock at 1841	Cost	Amount lost	Account closed
U.S. Bank	£30,670	£30,670	1857
New York State	19,674	624	1844
Louisiana State	10,089	2,869	1846
Pennsylvania State	10,035	599	1854
Ohio State	20,069	2,803	1848
	£90,537	£37,565	

These investments represented 36 per cent of total investments in negotiable securities and 17 per cent of total assets. Of the total investment in American stocks 41.5 per cent was lost, exclusive of unpaid dividends. Thereafter the company avoided all further investments in the American economy.

The fact that such obviously poor investments could be made says little for the company's appraisal techniques. Information about stocks thought to be suitable for purchase was obtained by the cashier who made occasional trips to London, Liverpool, Manchester and even Paris to meet bankers and investors from whom he obtained the necessary details. The Perth Banking Co. was not alone in making these investments: the period between 1837 and 1842 saw whole series of losses on foreign stocks. In 1842 James Capel, the stockbroker, informed the Royal Bank that 'the severe losses made in Spanish, Portuguese, South American and to which must be added North American, has given the Investors a great distaste for all Foreign Funds'.[98]

The failure of the Perth Banking Company's American investments caused the directors to seek alternative outlets for their funds. In 1841 the ill-fated Royal Bank of Australia announced that it would purchase the acceptances of Scottish banks at 15 months' date, giving in payment deposit notes or bills at 5 years' date at 5 per cent. The Perth Banking Co. decided to take up this offer to the extent of £30,000. By May, 1844 the company held £39,040 in this way. Most of these matured or were sold in 1847, but by 1849 strenuous efforts were being made to recover the remaining £5,000, and after protracted negotiations and litigation this was eventually accomplished in 1856.[99] An interesting event arose out of this investment. In 1843 the Perth Bank had £10,000 on deposit with Barclays in order to pay its acceptances to the Australian concern. Barclays refused to allow interest on this money with the result that it was placed, at call, with Overend, Gurney and Co. This is the first clear indication that the Perth Bank or any banking company was placing money with a discount house.

In 1854 the committee began to discount 6-month bills of the Oriental Bank Corporation accepted by 'Barings and others at 7½ per cent'. There is some evidence to show that these discounts were renewed as they fell due.[100] These investments proved to be satisfactory and there was no difficulty with payments. Nevertheless they were expensive in one sense. Two members of the Perth Banking Co. staff left to join the Oriental Bank.

An outlet for surplus funds was also sought in India. In July, 1856 the sum of £10,000 was invested via Gladstone, Wylie and Co. and the East India Company, but this money was called back to Britain in January 1857 because of a fall in Indian and a rise in British interest rates. By March of that year the situation was reversed and £15,000 in silver was sent by James Wylie and Co., on behalf of the Perth Bank, to Gladstone, Wylie and Co. in Calcutta who were to invest, at their discretion, in East India Government securities or in loans on security. The money was still there when the banking company was taken over in May, 1857.[101]

Although the directors did not buy any railway shares for behoof of the bank they were prepared to lend money to customers who wished to invest in the railways and the shares were usually taken in security. In 1845 Craigie, the cashier, went to London where he was advised by the merchants and bankers whom he met that loans on the security of railway stocks were a perfectly safe investment.[102] By that time the bank had already advanced £10,000 for one year at 5 per cent to Robert Allan of Edinburgh on the security of 178 Edinburgh and Glasgow Railway shares. The disposition in security permitted the bank to sell the shares if the price fell to 58. They then stood at 63. In 1845 Richard Dawson of Liverpool borrowed upwards of £30,000 on the security of Midland Counties Railway Stock. Neither Dawson nor Allan were regular customers of the bank.[103]

George, Thomas and John Buchanan, the proprietors of the Stanley mills in Perthshire, were regular customers. They borrowed £25,000 on bills in 1845 and railway stock was lodged in security.[104] In that same year J.M. Patton, J. Condie and W. Peddie, all of whom were sometime directors of the company, asked for a loan of from £50–£60,000 on their joint obligation, to be invested in 'sound dividend paying stocks' the vouchers of which were to be lodged in security. They agreed to meet any loss to the bank which it might incur in selling Bank of England stock to make the loan, provided that such a loss did not exceed half the profit on the investment. This loan was agreed to and in fact totalled £51,000, which was equivalent to slightly more than half of the bank's paid-up capital. When the stocks depreciated the borrowers tried to make out that they had acted in the best interests of the company which at the time of the loan 'had much anxiety about the Bank of England Stock and experienced at that dangerous season the greatest difficulty in finding any safe and remunerative investments'. No one was entirely convinced by this profession of purity of motive but there was a great deal of sympathy for these men, and when the bank was taken over in 1857 only Patton's portion had been paid and £34,000 remained outstanding.[105]

The directors also invested the bank's money in the more conventional types of security. By 1856 the yield on Consols had begun to improve and £23,563 was invested to yield 3½ per cent. In 1841 the bank held £168,984 (cost) in Bank of England stock. By May, 1847 the balance was down to £114,393, at which it remained for ten years.[106] In 1836 the bills committee had been authorised to buy Exchequer bills from time to time with spare cash.[107] The investment register (from 1841) shows no investments of this kind although it is possible that they were included in the bills book which is not extant.

Following the failure of the American investments the bills committee began to invest several thousand pounds in the shares of Scottish banks. The amounts involved by May, 1850 are set out in Table 24.

Table 24
Perth Banking Company Investments (at cost) in
Scottish Banks as at 31/5/1850[108]

British Linen	£ 5,162
Royal	16,739
Union	10,734
National	6,069
Commercial	3,934
	£42,638

This aspect of the investment policy was a little more successful than some of the others. Although small losses were made on Bank of Scotland stock sold in 1846, profits were made on National Bank and Commercial stocks sold in 1854 and the remaining bank stocks were held until the takeover in 1857. The prime reason for investing in the Scottish banks seems to have been for income rather than speculative gain. The yields on the bank stocks which figured in the investment register averaged 3.8 per cent in 1840. Unfortunately, no figures are available for the yields when the bank stocks were actually purchased. Clearly after their bitter American experience the directors were prepared to tolerate smaller returns on ostensibly safer investments. Higher yields could have been procured in French Rentes and other foreign bonds but the directors doubtless fought shy of further overseas government defaults.

It is often difficult to determine whether a particular investment was made with a view to steady income or speculative gain. The period between 1830 and 1860 was one of enormous change in the structure not only of the British but of the world economy. Faced with declining returns from traditional sources of profit, for example note issues and government securities, the bankers sought alternative sources of investment. The experience of the Perth Banking Company provides an interesting example of one company's attempts to place its funds without falling into the snare of over-concentration in one area, but criteria of success in this field are difficult to establish. Hindsight suggests that the American investments and some of the railway advances were unwise, but the directors, given the constantly changing situation in which they were working, could do little better than follow the policies of others who were better placed occupationally and geographically to make and follow objective investment decisions. Perth was isolated from the main financial centres, and although agents were maintained in these areas and the cashier made occasional fact-finding trips to them, this was not sufficient to ensure a perfect knowledge of the investment and money markets. A permanent physical presence was required to achieve that. Yet even those with that presence made mistakes in their investment policies. Therefore the question of whether geographical isolation from the centres of monetary activity was a limiting factor in the formation and execution of an investment policy must remain unanswered. That losses were made is an expected feature of any long-term investment programme, especially in times of rapid change and development.

The few figures for other banking companies revealed a similar diversity of interests. The two Paisley banking companies in the 1830s invested in a mixture of British, French and Dutch government securities, Scottish and Irish bank stocks and Bank of England stock.[109]

After the Napoleonic Wars the shares of the public banks became a popular investment with the banking companies. Although the yields on these shares were moderate, their purchase became fashionable because they could often be used as security for loans from the Edinburgh banks. In 1828 the Renfrewshire Banking Co. bought £12,000 of Royal Bank stock which it pledged as security for a loan of £10,000 one year later.[110] When the firm of J. & R. Watson failed in 1832 they held £6,510 in Royal Bank stock but it was pledged to that bank as security for a loan of £6,000.[111] Public bank stock might also be used as security for running credits. In 1823 Hunters and Co. of Ayr were awarded a credit of £10,202 by the British Linen on the security of their stock in that concern.[112] The holding of these stocks and their subsequent pledging as security became an important feature of Scottish banking particularly in the 1830s, as the Edinburgh private bankers disappeared and the public banks assumed the role of correspondents for the provincial banking companies. A block of public bank shares became a passport to a correspondence agreement with a public bank and therefore to a loan. This facility was vitally important in the 1830s and 1840s because many of the provincials lost deposits, and the loans which they obtained from the public banks helped them to overcome the resultant short-term liquidity and re-adjustment problems.

Profits on investments in negotiable securities could be substantial because apart from the yields it was possible to make a capital gain when the stocks were sold. Some companies were active speculators. The earliest examples of investment in negotiable securities were by the Glasgow bankers in the years of the American War.[113] In April, 1782 the Thistle Bank made a special dividend of £1,167 to its partners. This represented

> the neat profit that arose from the sale of Government Stock, subscribed for by the company on the first day of March last and sold on the nineteenth of the same month.

In 1786 an impressive £12,107 profit was divided amongst the partners as the surplus on the sale of all the company's government stock.[114] The Ship Bank had also been dabbling in the funds. After the war it invested £43,036[115] in the funds (possibly in 1784 when the average price of 3 per cent was 55½). These were sold in 1785 (average price 63), 1786 (74), and 1787 (73½).[116] Unfortunately it is not possible to say what profit was made on these sales. The only other profit figure available is one for the Perth Banking Co. in 1824 when profits of £13,437 were made on sales of government stocks,[117] and the money in this case was paid into surplus profit account. Clearly speculation in the funds could be a very profitable business indeed.

Whether as a speculative gamble or as a profitable repository for surplus money, investments in the funds and in government bills were often an important feature of the near-liquid reserves of the banking companies. The role of other liquid assets will be the subject of the next section.

7. Liquid Assets and Reserves

The most liquid of the assets of the banking companies took three forms – namely balances with correspondents in London and Edinburgh, the notes of other banks, and specie. Each of these will be considered in turn.

The nature of the relationship between banking companies and their correspondents in London and Edinburgh will be discussed in Chapter 10 but something must be said here about the balances involved which might be either on the assets or the liabilities side of the balance sheet. The agreements usually stipu-lated that the principal should have the right to overdraw his account up to a fixed limit but generally the banking companies preferred to keep correspondents' accounts in debit.

Balances in these accounts accumulated as the proceeds of discounted bills drawn on London or Edinburgh were paid into the correspondents' accounts in these cities and diminished as bills were drawn on them. Clearly this could be a rather seasonal business.

The London and Edinburgh accounts were the first line of defence if those with claims against the company refused to take banknotes and if there was insufficient specie to pay the debt. A bill on London or Edinburgh was usually an acceptable alternative. In times of crisis, as deposits were withdrawn, the accounts with the correspondents were quickly utilised, but it must be added that this was often to their displeasure, because they then had to liquidate their assets. From 1816 this factor gave rise to the general decline in the interest-bearing deposits which these men were prepared to hold for their provincial customers.

The mixed notes which often figure in the balance sheets were the notes of other banks and banking companies which had been taken in the course of business. These were unimportant as a reserve asset because they were exchanged at least once per week after the formation of the note exchange in 1771. The amount which appeared in the balance sheet would largely depend on whether the exchange took place before or after the balance was struck. Nevertheless, in times of pressure the amount of mixed notes taken between exchanges might prove to be a useful temporary relief from liquidity crisis.

The most discussed but often the least important reserve asset was specie balances. The banking companies do not appear to have kept a fixed proportion of specie to demand liabilities. Adam Smith postulated that banks should keep a sum equal to 25 per cent of the note issue in specie balances,[118] but it is not at all clear if he meant this to be a fixed rule or merely used that figure as an example. At any rate it gives some impression of Smith's order of thinking but it made no impression on the bankers. Cash balances were very small indeed, certainly by the 19th century, when holdings of specie were often so small as to preclude their being considered as reserves, for by that time they were no more than working balances. Table 25 sets out the specie to demand liabilities ratio for several provincial banking companies. The decreasing ratios in the late 18th century reflect a steadily increasing degree of public confidence in the note issues of the banking companies. This confidence grew to such an extent that in the 19th century the bankers were able to operate with fractional reserves.

A growth of public confidence, however, was not the only reason that the bankers were able to operate with such small balances, because customers were actively discouraged from asking their bankers for specie. There was perhaps an element of truth in the remark of an anonymous pamphleteer that

> Any southern fool who had the temerity to ask for a hundred sovereigns, might, if his nerves supported him through the cross examination at the bank counter, think himself in luck to be hunted only to the border.[119]

Table 25

Scottish Provincial Banking Companies:
Specie to Demand Liabilities Ratios (Annual Averages by Decade per cent

Dundee Banking Co.		Aberdeen Banking Co.		Perth United Banking Co.		Dundee New Bank		Greenock Banking Co.	
1764–70	9.1	1768–70	48.7	1767–70	18.2				
1771–80	13.0	1771–80	11.7	1771–80	18.2				
1781–90	16.6	1781–87	4.0	1781–87	12.6				
1791–1800	7.1								
1801–10	3.2					1806–10	0.6		
1811–20	1.3					1811–20	0.8	1814–20	0.9
1821–30	0.6					1821–30	1.0	1821–28	0.7
1831–40	0.5			*Perth Banking Co.*		1831–38	1.6		
1841–50	0.9			1831–40	1.4				
1851–60	2.1			1841–50	1.6				
1861–64	4.0			1851–57	3.4				

Sources

Dundee Banking Co. and Dundee New bank	Boase, 1867
Aberdeen Banking Co.	Balance Books
Perth United Banking Co.	General Ledgers
Perth Banking Co.	Minute Books and Circulation Books
Greenock Banking Co.	Balance Books

Specie was anathema to the bankers because it did not earn interest, it was nearly always in short supply and it had to be imported from England, at some expense, if there was any demand for it. Consequently they made strenuous efforts to economise on the use of it.

When specie was imported it often came from Newcastle rather than London because of the cheaper transportation costs. Cost of transport and insurance from London were probably in the region of 1½ per cent of the value of the shipment, but the Dundee Banking Co. discovered in 1767 that it was ³/₈ per cent cheaper to bring specie from Newcastle.[120] Other banks and banking companies, notably the British Linen Co. and the Ship Bank, had discovered that fact even earlier. Even as late as 1847 the Perth Banking Co. ordered gold from London and Newcastle.[121] There was also a market in gold amongst Scottish banks and banking companies. Some companies even established mutual specie aid arrangements. The provincials often obtained coin from their correspondents in Edinburgh although more often direct from the public banks, but there was also an active market in coin amongst the bankers in the provinces.

Specie balances began to increase after 1845 as bankers began to exceed their authorised issues and had to back the excess with gold and silver. This did not really pose any problems as the gold discoveries in California and Australia made supplies of that commodity abundant. It was nevertheless an unwelcome expense to have to build up supplies of specie.

Both because of public confidence and bankers' devices the banks and banking companies achieved a remarkable economy in the use of gold. Thomas Attwood thought that the Scots,

> by a system of union and combination which had been perfecting for one hundred years, had established . . . a kind of Moral Bank Restriction Act, which enabled them to pay 'worthless' debts and 'worthless' taxes in 'worthless rags' and prevented the possibility of their being suddenly called upon to pay such debts and such taxes in heavy gold.[122]

Attwood's view of the specie position of Scottish bankers, if rather jaundiced, was essentially correct, but he went on to concede that the system proved a paper circulation to be more satisfactory than gold. It was certainly a system which worked well in Scotland.

8. Banknotes

Without doubt the issuing of banknotes was the central element in the business of banking; they obviated the need for barter and lubricated the wheels of industry and commerce. As credit instruments they were a welcome response to the poverty of Scotland. Gold and silver coins were often in short supply due to the adverse balance of payments. Banknotes, therefore, fulfilled two needs. They provided a circulating medium and were the element in the equation which enabled the bankers to create credit.

Paper money made a substantial contribution to the development of the

Scottish economy but, as with advances, it must not be imagined that it was a feature of credit creation which had no upper limit. One of the earliest historians of Scottish banking noted that it was a

> mistake for a newly formed bank of issue, or its customers to imagine that it might go on discounting bills by means of notes . . . A bank of issue soon learns . . . that the parcels of its own notes which lie behind its counter are not a part of its assets . . . are not even in any sense banking funds – and that the portion of its notes in circulation belong to its liabilities. When these very elementary facts are mastered there is an end to all illusion as to what may, and may not, be done by the issue of notes.[123]

Bankers had always to be prepared to retire their notes on demand because convertibility was the essence of a successful note issue and confidence depended upon it. But as the Scottish system grew to maturity, and confidence increased, the tests of convertibility were seldom applied. People did not ask for specie in exchange for notes. The consequences of this development are apparent in the figures of Table 25. Bankers no longer had to maintain large stocks of coin, and customers who did not wish to hold notes were more often content to deposit their money at interest so that, in effect, the customer exchanged one bank liability for another. Similarly, when customers withdrew deposits they were usually paid in notes.

Notes were for long the main source of profit of the banking companies. Consequently they were issued whenever an opportunity presented itself, as when customers discounted bills, drew on cash accounts or, as has been mentioned above, withdrew deposits. In the formative years it was often the practice to 'push' notes by paying an agent a small commission to circulate them in the course of his business but this practice was largely stopped after the formation of the note exchange in 1771, although there is an example of the East Lothian Banking Co. paying an officer of the Excise a commission of $1/8$ per cent on notes circulated by him in 1810.[124] Generally banking companies gave bundles of notes to partners who were going to fairs, markets or on tour, with instructions to circulate the notes as widely as possible. They were not paid for their trouble. The more widely the notes were scattered, the longer they were likely to stay in circulation and the higher were the profits derived from the note issues.

The claim that the cash credit system could not be maintained without the privilege of issuing notes was one which was made by the Scottish bankers who were called to give evidence to the 1826 Parliamentary Committee on Promissory Notes. That the claim was accurate seems to have been confirmed by the management of the London and Westminster Bank. When that company was in process of being formed in the 1830s, its directors hoped that they would be able to offer a similar range of services to that provided by Scottish banks and banking companies. When they investigated the matter more closely, however, they discovered that the cash credit system could not be profitably operated without the benefit of a note issue[125] and as a London-based bank this was denied to them. The inability of this bank to operate a cash credit system indicates the central role which the note issue played in the Scottish banking system. No wonder it was defended with such energy in 1826.

By the 1840s, however, the note issue had decreased in importance. Customers had begun to use cheques to transfer money, with the result that the demand for notes decreased. This was of course a factor in the decreasing profitability of the banking companies in the 1830s and 1840s which has been discussed in Chapter 5.

Banknotes were not legal tender. This was decided in the case of Watson *v* Chalmers in 1756. Watson, an Edinburgh writer to the signet, was offered Glasgow banknotes in payment of a bill by Chalmers, a Leith merchant. Watson refused to accept the notes and Chalmers pled tender of payment by banknotes. The court turned down the plea and held that all payments must be in coin of the realm unless otherwise stipulated.[126] The law remained unchanged throughout the period under review.

From 1800 banknotes were subject to taxation for revenue purposes. The rate imposed was 2d per £1 note, and in 1805 this was raised to 3d per £1 and no note was allowed to circulate for more than three years without being re-stamped. This restriction proved both vexatious and difficult to operate and it was removed in 1808 when the duty was raised to 4d per £1. Guinea notes were taxed at 8d and £5 notes at 1/–. These rates remained in force until 1815 when they were again raised. Notes of £1 and £1–1/– were taxed at 5d and £5 notes at 1/3d with higher rates for other notes.[127] These rates remained in force until the late 19th century, but the administrative burden was partially removed in 1854 when the principle of commutation, which had previously been allowed to the public banks, was extended to all banks and banking companies. Before that date notes had to be sent to the stamp office in London for stamping – a lengthy and expensive process.

One of the other burdens which the bankers suffered as a result of their issuing notes was the attention of forgers. Despite the severe penalty – capital punishment – the problem was ever present. It became particularly acute in the years of the Napoleonic Wars when French prisoners practised note forgery on an extensive scale. In March of 1797 John Likely, cashier of the Paisley Union Banking Co., proposed that the banking companies should form an association for prosecuting forgers, and in July, 1799 Archibald Graham of the Thistle Bank proposed a wider association amongst bankers for prosecuting forgers 'and other objects affecting their common interests'.[128] Nothing came of these suggestions until 1819, when a 'bankers association against forgers' was formed. The intention was to pool the expenses of pursuing and prosecuting forgers. Twelve provincial companies joined, each of which paid an annual subscription of £20 which was later raised to £45 per annum, but the association closed in 1824, by which time £1,254 had been spent on its object.[129] The reasons for its closure are not clear but it remains possible that some members were slow to pay their dues or that others withdrew because they derived no direct benefit from it.

Bankers' attitudes to forgeries were never clear-cut. In 1803 the Paisley Banking Co. refused to pay some notes which had been forged. Scott Moncrieff of the Royal Bank was incensed by this and insisted that 'all respectable Banks pay their forgeries'.[130] In 1836, when the National Bank branch in Stirling took three forged notes of the Perth Banking Co., they presented them for payment, which was refused, and the cashier of the Perth Banking Co. maintained that it was not his practice to ask for payment of forged notes taken by his company. Consequently he would not pay forged Perth notes.[131] The law on this matter was quite clear and a banker was not obliged to pay value for forgeries committed against him. Moreover he was entitled when a forged note was presented to put a mark on it certifying that it was forged.[132]

9. Deposits

The practice of receiving deposits developed at different times in different areas. It is certainly significant that the banking companies which were first to accept deposits were in the main centre of economic activity – Glasgow.

The balance sheets of the Ship Bank in Appendix A show deposits on cash account from 1752 and there were also balances under 'Promissory Notes' which were negotiable interest-bearing receipts. The Thistle Bank, too, accepted deposits on cash accounts at least from 1769 but in neither of these cases were the deposits very large in relation to advances. Nevertheless the development was significant. The Glasgow banking companies had begun to mobilise the savings of people from Glasgow and the surrounding area and to lend them to other customers. Although these were small beginnings, the bank deposit habit caught on rapidly, and by 1786 total deposits at the Thistle Bank were £143,000 and by 1792 they were nearly £250,000[133] – 86 per cent of advances.

In other areas where, perhaps, there was less demand for credit the deposit-gathering practices of the banking companies were slower to develop. Deposits were accepted by the Perth United Banking Co. from 1768 and although they amounted to nearly £10,000 in 1770 they declined thereafter and were never more than a few hundred pounds in the remaining 17 years of the contract.[134] The Aberdeen Banking Co. began to accept deposits in 1770. Growth came in the 1780s when deposit balances grew from a few thousand pounds in the 1770s to £36,000 in the middle years of the 1780s, i.e. 23 per cent of advances. The Dundee Banking Co. did not begin to accept deposits on a regular basis until 1792. It was competition from other banks and banking companies which prompted the Dundee Banking Co. to accept deposits. The Dundee Commercial Banking Co., founded in 1792, accepted deposits from the outset.[135] Thereafter deposits were accepted in two forms – cash accounts and interest (deposit) receipts. Cash account holders who found themselves with a surplus of cash could deposit it in their account and interest was allowed and calculated on these sums on the daily balance. It was perfectly possible for an account to be in credit for a whole year but more often the account fluctuated between debit and credit. The amount of interest due to a customer for the periods when his account was in credit was deducted from the amount due by him for the times when he had been in debit. Interest was applied at the end of the financial year.

Deposit receipts (sometimes called interest receipts) were lump-sum lodgements which attracted interest at the same rate as deposits on cash accounts. For a period these were time deposits (usually three months) and were sometimes subject to minimum balance requirements. The Perth Banking Co. in 1792 was prepared to accept time balances of £200 and over but one year later the limit was reduced to £100 in response to customer demand. In 1796 the minimum time on deposit before interest was allowed was reduced to three weeks and in 1810 the minimum deposit value was reduced to £10. These trends continued ever downwards and the deposit receipt registers for the 1840s show deposits as small as £2.[136] There is little evidence on the practices of other companies in the 19th century but it is a safe assumption that they were similar to those of the Perth Banking Co.

The trend in these limits was paralleled by the English experience but the English country banks paid interest only on deposit receipts. In 1832 only one third of the deposits held by Stuckey's Bank bore interest. It was not until the joint-stock banks developed in England that interest was paid on current accounts.[137]

In 1810 the first savings bank was formed in Scotland at Ruthwell in Dumfriesshire and from there the movement spread rapidly throughout the rest of the country. In many cases the funds gathered by these concerns were deposited with the banks and banking companies where preferential terms were often given on these accounts. In 1815 the Perth Banking Co. decided to allow 5 per cent interest on deposits of savings banks. This was 1 per cent above the usual rate and was designed to enable the savings banks to pay higher rates of interest to their depositors. It was the hope of the Perth directors that this would encourage 'frugal and industrious habits amongst the labouring classes',[138] and in 1819 deposits were received from savings banks at Perth, Auchtermuchty, Dunkeld and Meigle and from the Dunkeld Carpenters Friendly Society.[139] The Shetland Banking Co. accepted deposits from the Shetland Savings Bank.[140] The balances on these accounts were not large – under £200 – and the banking companies made no profit on them. (Interest was allowed at 5 per cent, which was also the rate charged for advances.) The fact that many banks and banking companies accepted these deposits must be seen as an act of altruism and genuine concern that the virtues of thrift be encouraged in the labouring classes.

The banking companies also received temporary deposits from tax and customs and excise collectors but, unfortunately, few accounts remain. The remittance of the public revenue to London from Edinburgh was firmly in the hands of the public banks and two of the private bankers but the provincial banking companies were often the first holders of the money who remitted it to Edinburgh. In 1824 the Board of Excise asked its district collectors to approach all banks to see what terms they would offer for remitting the revenues to Edinburgh. The Perth Banking Co. offered the same terms as before, that is, by bill on Sir Wm. Forbes and Co. at eight days' date. The directors assured the Board that their company offered 'the most undoubted security for all their transactions'.[141] The question of security was an important one in an age when the provincial banking companies were still not well trusted by the public banks. In 1829 the Paisley Banking Co. undertook to remit revenues from Renfrewshire.

The Royal Bank directors who were a party to the agreement took 'special consideration of the circumstances that the Paisley Bank hold a large sum of Royal Bank Stock'.[142] Archibald Campbell was the collector of the Land Tax in Perthshire in the 1760s and his account with the Perth United Banking Co. showed weekly deposits of smallish sums and quarterly withdrawals of the whole balance.[143] The deposits of tax collectors were never a large part of banking company deposits, certainly in the 19th century when deposit-taking had developed as a regular part of the banker's service. In this respect the situation was different from that prevailing in England, where country banks held public money for longer periods and used it to finance business activities. In Scotland the revenues generally were quickly remitted to the public and private banks in Edinburgh and the provincial bankers had little opportunity to make use of them.

Occupational breakdowns of depositors have had to be abandoned because more than 50 per cent of depositors could not be identified, as they were seldom described in ledger pages other than by name. The one feature which did stand out about these ledgers was the large number of women who were depositors. In 1761 women held 14.4 per cent by value of the deposits on promissory notes in the Ship Bank.[144]

Professor Smout, in an article on the role of landowners in economic development, speculated that the banks and banking companies 'must have counted a vast number of landowners among their depositors'.[145] There is little evidence from the records of the provincial banking companies to support this contention. Certainly there were landowners who were depositors but, on balance, people from this group were borrowers. Professor Smout cited the example of George Dempster of Dunnichen, but Dempster had an overdrawn cash account with the Perth United of which he was a founding partner and he was also awarded a cash account for £500 with the Dundee Banking Co. of which he was also a founder member and to which he gave his name.[146] The amounts borrowed were greatly in excess of the capital paid in on his shareholdings. On the occasions when peers were mentioned in the records it was usually as borrowers either on their own account or as guarantors for loans to trusts. It must be remembered that outside Edinburgh and Glasgow the contribution made to economic growth by the banking companies in the 18th century was very largely on the basis of pure credit and not on the basis of deposit money channelled into advances. This of course does not disprove Professor Smout's theory that landowners' money was being channelled into industrial investment by financial intermediaries. Although the provincial banking companies do not appear to have been the recipients of the deposits of a 'vast number of landowners', it remains likely that the Edinburgh banks, both public and private, were.

Throughout the 18th century and into the 19th the interest allowed on deposits of all kinds was 4 per cent, i.e. 1 per cent below that charged on advances. Some companies, notably the Thistle Bank, were of the opinion that this was an insufficient margin to afford them an adequate profit. They were nevertheless aware that unilateral action on their part to change the rate would almost certainly lead to an outflow of deposits to banks which kept the old rates. In 1792 George Kinnear, their Edinburgh correspondent, advised against any action on rates but agreed that he should contact Scott-Moncrieff of the Royal Bank Glasgow branch 'to make up all differences'.[147] Graham of the Thistle Bank did not give up hope of action to reduce deposit rates but nothing came of his endeavours. The question arose again in 1804 but the public banks refused to countenance any change. As an alternative Graham suggested charging a commission on cash accounts but this suggestion, too, met with a negative response.[148] The changes which Graham had suggested were largely in line with the practice of English country banks where in 1793 the rates generally allowed for deposits were 3 and 3½ per cent and where commission was charged on cash accounts by the few banks which operated that system.[149]

It was not until 1822 that a wider margin between borrowing and deposit rates was opened. In that year interest rates were lowered to 3 per cent on deposits and 4 per cent on discounts but remained at 5 per cent on cash accounts[150] and in 1824 deposit rates were reduced to 2½ per cent.[151] Thereafter the rates fluctuated more often, with the margin between deposits and advances varying between 1½ and 2 per cent. In most cases the rates were set by the Edinburgh bankers and the provincial companies merely had to follow suit.

The Tables in Appendix A show clearly the trends in the deposit-taking of the provincial banking companies. Most were losing deposits in the 1830s at a time when total bank deposits were increasing. The joint-stock challenge was making itself felt. More than this, many depositors were encouraged to invest their money elsewhere, either directly in industry or in foreign government securities. It was this pressure to repay deposits that drove many of the banking companies to give up their business.

10. Other Balances

There were a number of other balances which appeared in the balance sheets. Of these, the balances of branches and agents will be discussed in Chapters 9 and 10. Of the remainder none were very important but they are worthy of a brief mention.

Many banking companies rented their accommodation but a number of them bought the house in which they conducted their business. The cost of these houses, together with their furnishings, was included in the balance sheets. The Perth Banking Co. in the 1790s constructed what was probably the first purpose-built banking house in Scotland. The cost of the new building was £1,300 plus £150 for the land, and it was ready for occupation in December, 1791. It was a substantial structure. The flat above the office, two cellars and part of the south garret were given to the cashier free of rent for his own use. The porter was given a ground-floor room and a basement room. The remainder of the building, save for the office, was let out at competitive rates and the directors were justifiably proud of their new building. In the leases they stipulated that

No possessor or tenant of any part of the building shall allow of any water or other things to be thrown from the windows, – that no poultry or any such animals be fed or kept in the garret story – and that the vents be frequently swept at least once in three months to prevent alarm or danger from fire.[152]

There is little to suggest that the banking companies made any allowances for depreciation on their property. In the 1850s the Dundee Banking Co. deducted £100 p.a. from its property account, but this is the only example that can be found of this type of accounting.[153]

The items paper and stamps frequently occurred in the balance sheets. The amounts involved were never large – usually under £200. The balances were the stocks of unprinted banknote paper and stamped bill paper. Both were more usually included under sundries.

NOTES

1. Ship Bank Balance Ledger, 1752–61
2. S. Pollard, 'Capital Accounting in the Industrial Revolution', in Crouzet, 1972, p. 124
3. E.g. Perth Banking Co. Contract in D.M.B., 16/1/1786
4. P. Bird, 1971, p. 3
5. Aberdeen Banking Co., Balance Books 1768–1787
6. M. Greener, 1968, p. 1
7. Aberdeen Banking Co., Balance Books 1768–1787
8. H. C. F. Holgate 1948, p. 13, cited by Pollard in Crouzet, 1972, p. 125
9. Crouzet, 1972, p. 35
10. *Ship Bank Journal*, 1785–1836
11. R. S. Rait, 1930, p. 55
12. C. W. Boase, 1867, p. 223
13. Dundee Banking Co., D.M.B., Contract
14. Boase, 1867; Perth United General Ledgers; East Lothian, D.M.B; Aberdeen Banking Co., Balance Books
15. Dundee Banking Co., Contract 1826, clause 19; Dundee Commercial Banking Co., Contract 1825, clause 26; Perth Banking Co., Contract 1808, clause 31
16. Perth Banking Co., D.M.B., 1787–1808; Montrose Banking Co., D.M.B., 1814–22
17. Pressnell, 1956, p. 229
18. *Ibid.*, 1956 pp. 226–7
19. J. R. Christie, 'Joint-stock Enterprise in Scotland before the Companies Acts', *Juridical Review*, vol. 21, 1909–10, p. 145
20. R. H. Campbell, 'The Law and the Joint Stock Company in Scotland', in P. L. Payne (ed), 1967
21. *Glasgow Courant*, 8/1/1750, 5/11/1750, 5/11/1761, 11/5/1769
22. Boase, 1867
23. For analysis of the causes of this decline see Chapter 5
24. L. S. Pressnell, 1956, Appendices 2 and 5
25. R. Cameron, 1967, p. 94
26. P.P. Select Committee on Promissory Notes . . . 1826, evidence of T. Kinnear, p. 115
27. Aberdeen Banking Co., D.M.B., 19/6/1771
28. Paisley Union Banking Co., D.M.B., 20/7/1820
29. S.R.O., B18/18/14, East Lothian Banking Co., D.M.B., 7/11/1811
30. Dundee New Bank, D.M.B., 13/8/1803
31. S.R.O., SC49/30/60, Perth United Banking Co., Contract, Article 11
32. Perth Banking Co., D.M.B., Contract, Article 8
33. *Ibid.*, 11/4/1787 – 6/11/1787
34. N.L.S., Fettercairn MSS., Accession 4796, 2nd deposit, Box 43, A. Garden to Sir Wm. Forbes, 7/10/1783
35. R.B.S., Scott-Moncrieff letters, 5/8/1803
36. Aberdeen Banking Co., D.M.B., 16/11/1770

L

37. Thistle Bank Account Ledgers 1783–6 and Balance Book, 1786–1792
38. Aberdeen Banking Co., Cash Account Bond Registers
39. P.P. Select Committee on Promissory Notes 1826, evidence of Hugh Watt, p. 189
40. Perth Banking Co., D.M.B., 21/3/1793
41. Perth United Banking Co., General Ledgers, 1785–1787
42. Anon., Pamphlet on Banking Profits, no title, 1840
43. Perth United Banking Co., General Ledgers
44. R. Cameron, 1967, pp. 75 and 77
45. Appendix A; and R. H. Campbell, 1971, p. 138
46. H. D. MacLeod, 1891, p. 160
47. *Ibid.*, p. 17
48. *Ibid.*, p. 51; and R. Thomson, 1825
49. *Ibid.*
50. Dundee New Bank, Private Letter Book, 12/1/1803 and 24/3/1804
51. East Lothian Banking Co., D.M.B., 10/2/1814
52. P.P. Select Committee on Promissory Notes . . . 1826, evidence of John Commelin, p. 172
53. Dundee New Bank, Private Letter Book, 16/10/1815
54. Ship Bank Balance Book, 1752–1761
55. Thistle Bank Papers, Box 1 bundle 14, H. Glassford to Thistle Bank, 21/11/1793
56. H. Thornton, 1802
57. Macleod, 1891
58. T. S. Ashton, 1945, and S. G. Checkland, 1954
59. A. R. B. Haldane, 1973, p. 48
60. H. Watt, 1833, pp. 11, 38
61. C. Gulvin, 1973, p. 62
62. *Ibid.*
63. Aberdeen Banking Co., D.M.B., 25/2/1774
64. Dundee New Bank, Letter Book, 19/3/1803; Montrose Banking Co., Letter Book, 1826
65. H. Watt, 1833, p. 55
66. Perth Banking Co., D.M.B., 13/11/1834
67. Thomson, 1825, p. 169
68. Perth Banking Co., D.M.B., 1/8/1810
69. Aberdeen Banking Co. Balance Books
70. R. S. Rait, 1930, p. 179
71. 33 Geo. III ch. 74. See Boase, 1867, p. 258
72. Perth Banking Co., D.M.B., 17/10/1856 and Investment Register
73. Boase, 1867
74. Perth Banking Co., D.M.B., 22/6/1829
75. Boase, 1867, p. 552
76. Checkland, 1975, pp. 385–6
77. Glasgow and Ship Banking Co., D.M.B., 13/12/1842
78. M. Phillips, 1894, p. 118, quoting letter of Thistle Bank to Davidson, Bland and Co., 8/1/1788
79. R.B.S., D.M.B., 19/8/1829
80. S. E. Thomas, 1934, p. 254
81. Perth Banking Co., D.M.B., 30/11/1847
82. Glasgow Banking Co., D.M.B., 22/1/1836
83. Perth Banking Co., D.M.B., 17/10/1856
84. Boase, 1867
85. S.R.O. CS311/2142, Box 207, Montrose Banking Co., Letter Book 13/12/1824
86. Montrose Banking Co., D.M.B., 28/12/1818
87. S.R.O. SC311/2142, Box 207, Montrose Banking Co., Letter Book 17/6/1826 and incoming letters 3/4/1826 and 28/3/1827
88. Ship Bank Journal, 1785–1836
89. Rait., 1930, Ch. 2
90. Perth Banking Co., D.M.B., 17/1/1818, 16/10/1823, 13/1/1824 and 3/4/1827
91. Pressnell, 1956, p. 88
92. Perth Banking Co., D.M.B., 31/8/1824, 29/10/1824, 29/5/1827, 15/6/1827
93. *Ibid.*, 24/4/1829
94. S. Homer, 1963, Tables 19, 28
95. Perth Banking Co., D.M.B., 6/6/1838

96. M. G. Myers, 1970, p. 119
97. Perth Banking Co., Investment Register 1841
98. R.B.S., D.M.B., 2/3/1842, quoted by S. G. Checkland in M. C. Reed, 1975, p. 49
99. Perth Banking Co., D.M.B., 20/7/1841 and Investment Register
100. *Ibid.*, 6/1/1854, 1/12/1855 and 23/5/1856
101. *Ibid.*, 30/7/1856, 23/1/1857, 27/3/1857 and Investment Register
102. *Ibid.*, 31/5/1845
103. *Ibid.*, 20/3/1843, 17/5/1845 and 31/5/1845
104. *Ibid.*, 19/8/1845
105. *Ibid.*, 14/11/1845, 17/10/1856 and Investment Register
106. Perth Banking Co., Investment Register
107. *Ibid.*, D.M.B., 29/11/1836
108. *Ibid.*, Investment Registers
109. Paisley Union Banking Co., D.M.B., 23/7/1832; and B.L., D.M.B., 31/10/1837
110. R.B.S., D.M.B., 3/12/1828. 26/11/1829
111. S.R.O., CS96/450, Sequestration Book of J. & R. Watson, 1832
112. B.L., D.M.B., 27/5/1833
113. See Chapter 2
114. Quoted in Rait, 1930, p. 124; and Thistle Bank Balance Ledger, 1786–92
115. Rait, 1930, p. 53
116. Homer, 1963, p. 161
117. Perth Banking Co., D.M.B., 9/7/1824
118. A. Smith, Skinner (ed) 1970, p. 399
119. Quoted in F. W. Fetter, 1965, p. 122
120. Dundee Banking Co., D.M.B., 17/8/1767
121. Perth Banking Co., D.M.B., 30/11/1847
122. T. A. H. Wood, 1828, p.116
123. R. Somers, 1873, pp. 100–1
124. S.R.O., B18/18/14, East Lothian Banking Co., D.M.B., 16/8/1810 and 17/6/1811
125. T. E. Gregory, 1936, vol. 1, pp. 26–7
126. W. Graham, 1886, p. 231
127. *Ibid.*, pp. 226–7
128. Thistle Bank Papers, Likely to Graham, March, 1797, Graham to Leith Banking Co., 16/7/1799
129. Pass Book of bankers' association for prosecuting forgers
130. R.B.S., Scott Moncrieff letters, R.S.M. to William Simpson, 23/2/1803
131. Perth Banking Co., D.M.B., 1/11/1836
132. Glen, 1807, p. 158, N.7. Borland v Thistle Bank, 1768
133. Thistle Bank Account Books, 1769–1772 and Balance Ledger, 1786–92
134. Perth United Banking Co., General Ledgers, 1769–1787
135. Boase, 1867
136. Perth Banking Co., D.M.B., 22/11/1792, 8/7/1793, 30/5/1796, 30/3/1810, and Deposit Receipt Register 1841–44, and Coupar Angus Branch, 1841–57
137. Pressnell, 1956, pp. 249–50 and 166
138. Perth Banking Co., D.M.B., 3/4/1815, 13/5/1853
139. Perth Banking Co., Branch Control Ledger, 1819
140. N.L.S., Hay of Hayfield MSS., ACC. 3250, Hay and Ogilvie day book, 1822–3
141. Perth Banking Co., D.M.B., 17/3/1824
142. R.B.S., D.M.B., 30/12/1829
143. Perth United Banking Co., General Ledger, 1768–9
144. Ship Bank Balance Ledger, 1752–61
145. T. C. Smout, 1964, p. 225
146. Perth United Banking Co., General Ledgers; and Boase 1867
147. Thistle Bank Papers, Thistle to Kinnear and Kinnear to Thistle, 1792
148. *Ibid.*, Memorial on Rates of Interest
149. Pressnell, 1956; pp. 253, 241
150. Montrose Banking Co., D.M.B., 10/7/1822 and 2/8/1822
151. B.L., D.M.B., 25/10/1824
152. Perth Banking Co., D.M.B., 20/12/1791
153. Boase, 1867

7

The Partners

1. The Pattern of Share Ownership

THE nominal value of shares in the provincial banking companies was usually £200, certainly in the co-partneries. But the full value was seldom called up at the outset (see Chapter 6). The partnership shares had larger nominal values, often £1,000, which was more usually fully paid when the company commenced business. There was a tendency over the years for the nominal value of shares to be reduced. This movement was particularly encouraged by the joint-stock banks, whose shares were often £10 or £20. The lower prices of these shares brought them within the price range of smaller investors and so extended the market for them which in turn, it was hoped, would enlarge the number of persons loyal to the bank.

A categorisation of the partners in the banking companies by profession would be of considerable interest, but there are some limitations on providing this, for by far the most common purchasers of shares were the 'merchants'. This designation included men with a wide variety of economic interests including trading, manufacturing, shipowning and plantation owning. They might also be land-owners, having purchased an estate with the profits of trade.[1] Similarly, those who appeared as landowners in the contracts of co-partnery may in fact have derived the main part of their income from trade or from the law. Yet despite these limitations the figures do give a broad indication of the patterns of share ownership, and these are given in Tables 26 to 32.

The Arms Bank was the first banking company to be founded on the extended co-partnery basis. The predominance of tobacco merchants was to be expected, and the inclusion of an excise collector is worthy of note.

Table 26
Arms Bank, Glasgow:
Occupational Distribution of Shareholders[2]

	No. of shareholders in 1750	Per cent
Merchants (mostly tobacco)	27	87
Small trades (tanner & weaver)	2	7
Professions (writer)	1	3
Others (excise collector)	1	3
	31	100

Table 27 reflects a tendency towards concentration of share ownership. In 1767 there were 142 partners in the Aberdeen Banking Co. and in 1788 only 124. Although numerically stable at 46, the merchants increased their holdings of stock by 10 per cent. The professional group, although reduced in numbers from 30 to 27, increased its share by 6 per cent to almost equal the landowners' share. The professionals included doctors, ministers and academics, but the bulk of this group consisted of writers (lawyers). Although a number of writers were proprietors from the outset, it is possible that this group was responsible for the growth of deposits in the 1780s. Certainly the cash account ledgers of some of the Glasgow banking companies show that writers were a significant source of deposits in the 1790 to 1830 period.

Table 27
Aberdeen Banking Company:
Occupational Distribution of Shareholders[3]

	Shares held in 1767	Per cent	No. of shareholders	Shares held in 1788	Per cent	No. of shareholders
Landowners	84	42	42	48	24	27
Merchants	59	30	46	79	40	46
Small trades	2	1	2	6	3	3
Professions	33	16	30	45	22	27
Others	22	11	22	22	11	21
	200	100	142	200	100	124

The General Bank of Perth was one of the 'merchant banking companies' which were established in a number of towns in opposition to already established banking companies. It seems to have consisted of the lesser merchants and tradesmen of the town.

Table 28
General Bank of Perth:
Occupational Distribution of Shareholders[4]

	No. of shareholders in 1767	Per cent
Landowners	4	9
Merchants	22	51
Manufacturers	1	2.5
Small trades	9	21
Professions	1	2.5
Others	6	14
	43	100

Unfortunately the amount of each partner's shareholding is not known.

The Glasgow Merchant Banking Co. was of the same genre as the General Bank of Perth. In fact there were a few partners common to both.

Table 29
Glasgow Merchant Banking Co:
Occupational Distribution of Shareholders[5]

	No. of shareholders in 1771	Per cent
Landowners	2	4
Merchants	40	84
Manufacturers	3	6
Small trades	1	2
Professions	1	2
Others	1	2
	48	100

The difference in Table 30 between 1787 and 1808 reflects changes in definition rather than in the pattern of share ownership in the Perth Banking Co. The decline in the shares of the merchant group was caused, primarily, by members of that group who re-defined themselves as manufacturers. In particular members of the Sandeman, Richardson and Caw families, who were the proprietors of the major textile manufacturing units in the area, had begun to call themselves manufacturers rather than merchants. Doubtless the latter group still contained people who would have been more accurately included in the former.

Table 30
Perth Banking Co:
Occupational Distribution of Shareholders[6]

	Shares held in 1787	Per cent	No. of shareholders	Shares held in 1808	Per cent	No. of shareholders
Landowners	6	2	1	26	6	7
Farmers	14	4	5	27	6	17
Merchants	270	79	72	249	57	93
Manufacturers	9	3	3	42	10	19
Small trades	24	7	11	53	12	29
Professions	11	3	5	33	7	13
Others	6	2	2	10	2	3
	340	100	99	440	100	181

Again it has not been possible to give a breakdown of the proportion of the shares held by each group in the Montrose Banking Co. but the large number of farmers amongst the shareholders is a good indication of the greater agricultural basis of this company compared with any of the others.

The Arbroath Banking Co. was amongst the last of the banking companies to be founded but the pattern of share ownership was really little different from those which had gone before. There was still a heavy predominance of merchants, although those who described themselves as manufacturers were of growing importance.

Table 31
Montrose Banking Co:
Occupational Distribution of Shareholders[7]

	No. of shareholders in 1814	Per cent
Farmers	26	31
Merchants	31	38
Manufacturers	1	1
Small trades	3	4
Professions	12	15
Others	9	11
	82	100

Table 32
Arbroath Banking Co:
Occupational Distribution of Shareholders[8]

	No. of shares held in 1825	Per cent	No. of shareholders
Landowners	13	8	6
Farmers	13	8	10
Merchants	64	37	32
Manufacturers	22	12	22
Small trades	7	4	7
Professions	13	8	13
Others	41	23	23
	173	100	113

It is easier to be more certain about the major business interests of the members of the partnerships because of the smaller numbers involved.

The first banking company to be formed was the Banking Co. at Aberdeen in 1747. The partnership was re-formed in 1749 following the resignation of two members, but the principal business interest of the partners was the hosiery trade.[9]

The six partners in the Ship Bank, founded in Glasgow in 1749, were principally involved in the tobacco trade. When the Ship joined the Glasgow Bank in 1836 there were four partners, all of whom were landowners and all of whom were described in the agreement as 'bankers in Glasgow'.[10]

The Thistle Bank, Glasgow opened in 1761. All six partners were landowners but five of them were also tobacco merchants,[11] including John Glassford, one of the greatest of the tobacco lords who had formerly been a partner in the Arms Bank. Wm. Mure of Caldwell, who shortly afterwards became a Baron of the Exchequer in Scotland, was also a partner.

The nine partners of the Paisley Banking Company of 1784 were five Paisley and three Glasgow merchants and a landowner. One of the Glasgow merchants, also a landowner, was Andrew Thomson of Faskin, who set up his own private bank in Glasgow the following year. By 1825 there were only five partners: two landowners, a London merchant and two Paisley bankers.[12]

A rival company, the Paisley Union Banking Co., was set up in 1788. There were ten partners, five of whom were landowners: three in Paisley, one in Glasgow and one in Bo'ness. These five also had extensive mining and trading interests. The other five were all merchants: four in Paisley and one in Glasgow.[13] John Cochrane, one of the Paisley merchants, was in partnership with Charles Tennant in a bleachfield at Eastwood near Paisley.[14] The leading partner, however, was George Houston of Johnstone, whose major interests were cotton spinning and coal mining. Both were carried out on his estate.[15]

A third Renfrewshire company was the Greenock Banking Co., founded in 1785. There were four partners: two landowners and two merchants. Three of the partners were James Dunlop of Garnkirk, Andrew Houston of Jordanhill and James McDowall, merchant in Glasgow. These three were the sons of founding partners of the Ship Bank. The fourth partner was James Gammell, merchant in Greenock. Dunlop, Houston and McDowall were involved in the West Indies trade and Dunlop was also heavily committed in coal mining and had interests in iron and glass. Gammell, who was the managing partner of the company, was a member of a firm of Newfoundland merchants.[16] By 1843 there were six partners, and of these two were bankers, three were landowners (one of whom was also a Liverpool merchant), and one was a shipbuilder in Greenock.[17]

The Kilmarnock Banking Co. was founded in 1802 and there were six partners. Five were landowners and one was a merchant.[18]

When the Falkirk Union Banking Co. failed in 1816 there were six partners. Three were landowners, one of whom was also a distiller. One was a writer, another was a distiller and the last was described as a resident in Falkirk.[19]

The Stirling Banking Co. failed in 1826. There were at that time seven partners. This was a very broadly based concern. The partners consisted of a landowner, a textile merchant, a wood merchant, a writer, a brewer, a carpet manufacturer and a resident in Stirling.[20] The more rigid definition of the occupations of the partners which can be given for this concern is probably a factor of the greater specialisations which were taking place by this time. As the scale of industry and trade grew, people were forced to specialise in particular areas. The era of the general merchant and the use of this term was approaching its end.

It has not been possible to give a breakdown of the occupations of the partners in all of the provincial banking companies. Nevertheless the examples which have been given are a good cross-section not only of the different types of banking company but of regional banking patterns. Generally it may be stated that the 'merchant' class predominated in most concerns. It is also worthy of note that, by the 19th century, a number of people described themselves as 'bankers'. Clearly banking was emerging as a profession in the provinces. This of course says nothing about people's motives for investing in banking companies, for which several reasons may be adduced. These were profit, provision of a circulating medium, easy credit and social considerations.

The returns to capital have already been discussed in Chapter 6. The figures produced there suggest that the dividends paid by the banking companies provided a consistently higher return than could be made in alternative forms of investment – government funds and public bank stocks – and in all cases were higher than the 'legal rate' of interest. It is unfortunately impossible to suggest how bank profits compared to profits in other industries or indeed to say much about the speculative element in some investments. Speculation was not generally a factor affecting the decision to invest in a provincial banking company because shares, once purchased, tended to be held for many years. Clearly the return to capital was an important consideration for most, if not all, investors.

Just as important for some shareholders was the easy availability of credit which membership of a banking company often guaranteed, for the partners were often their banks' own best customers. A few figures may illustrate this point. Of the first hundred cash accounts awarded by the Aberdeen Banking Co. in 1767–8, no fewer than 54 went to partners in the concern. These accounts, however, were 62 per cent by value of the authorised credit on this type of account.[21] When the first balance of the Paisley Union Banking Co. was struck in June, 1789 the partners had drawn £3,834 out of a total of £9,291 advanced on cash accounts, which was 41.3 per cent of the total.[22] Unfortunately, it is impossible to give similar figures for discounts. The second contract of the Perth Banking Co. began in 1808 and from then until the end of 1809 a total of 154 cash accounts were awarded. Of these, 77 valued at £49,300 and representing 68 per cent by value of the total went to partners of the company. Of the remaining 67 bonds, 30 valued at £9,050 and representing 13 per cent of the total included a partner as security on the bond. The contract of the company stated that partners' shares would be held as security for their obligations. These figures, then, show that 107 cash accounts valued at £58,350 and being 81 per cent of authorised advances of this kind were covered, in part at least, by shares. A further 19 bonds (£7,400, i.e. 10 per cent) included a landowner either as principal or security. Therefore 91 per cent of cash accounts awarded between 1808 and 1809 were covered, in whole or in part, by land or shares.[23] The message of these figures is clear. Potential customers, especially those requiring large advances, should be landowners, partners or be able to persuade one of these men to sign their bond. Apparently the Perth Banking Co. had become oligarchic in nature and restrictive in practice, thus opening the way for a new banking initiative in the city. This came in 1810 when the Perth Union Banking Company was formed.

The examples of partners obtaining credit could be augmented from the records of other companies. This type of credit was an important factor in Scottish economic development because partners in banking companies were usually the leading entrepreneurs in their areas, and if some sectors of the business community felt that they were being starved of funds, then they could either form their own company, which often happened, or they could go to the branches of the public banks which existed in most large towns.

Easy access to credit facilities could, of course, be abused. A writer in the *Scots Magazine* in 1763 accused the Glasgow tobacco merchants of getting special loans from their own banking companies which enabled them to hold back supplies from the market until prices rose, 'while those who are not partners cannot get a shilling more than their bank credit, unless they happen to be particular favourites'.[24] Credit facilities were and are always liable to this type of abuse, but this particular accusation seems to have been politically motivated, for the period between 1761 and 1765 was extremely difficult for the bankers (see Chapter 1) and the provincial banking companies appear to have responded more helpfully than the public banks. In May, 1762 John Campbell of Achmore, factor to the Earl of Breadalbane, having been refused further credit by the Royal Bank, approached two of the Glasgow companies, both of which offered him accommodation although he was unknown to them. He remarked that it seemed odd

> that they extended their credit to strangers and support their former customers . . . while a Royal and a Chartered company tells their old friends . . . to shift for themselves.[25]

Alleged abuses such as those suggested by the correspondent of the *Scots Magazine* are always difficult to prove. There is no real reason for supposing that the Glasgow banking companies were guilty as charged in 1763. Nevertheless, it remains possible, perhaps even likely, that there were malpractices of this kind at some stage in the careers of the provincial banking companies.

A third motive for investing in banking companies was the opportunity which this created to provide a circulating medium, which was certainly the case with the earliest formations. The quantity of gold, silver and copper coins in circulation was small; their quality was poor. 'In general, the efforts of entrepreneurs to fill the gaps in the currency sprang from the desire to meet the routine needs of business'.[26] Banknotes gave fluidity to commercial transactions and it is therefore arguable that they enable business expansion to take place in two ways. Firstly there was the credit factor and secondly the transactions factor. Paper money, certainly post-1765, gained growing acceptance because it obviated the need for weighing coins at every transaction.

The fourth motive to be considered relates to the social standing of partners. This factor was particularly important amongst the larger co-partneries and may be clearly seen in the records of the Perth United, Aberdeen and East Lothian Banking Companies. In these companies the prime movers included the provost, town clerk and burgh chamberlain. They also included the leading businessmen, churchmen and often the master and office bearers in the local masonic lodge. The foremost men in a town such as Dunbar might consist of a group of about twenty people. Bearing in mind the family and business relationships between these and the lesser lights, the impression is of very closely knit communities. Banking companies were usually begun by a group of the more important men who then solicited subscriptions from the remainder of the business community. To refuse might mean ostracism from society at every level, and membership was often 'sold' as patriotism which cemented business and social relationships.

Social factors always play an important part in business and the provincial banking companies were no exception. It must be suggested, however, that most people would be swayed by the economic arguments for membership. Social considerations, although important, must have come bottom of the list of motivating factors, but most banking companies were fully subscribed in a very short time.

Nevertheless the expectation of direct monetary returns, i.e. dividends, may not have been the major factor in determining the allocation of the partners' resources when they first invested in the banking companies. Investors were probably principally attracted by the possibility that their total economic activity would be enhanced by membership, for a ready supply of credit would enable them to expand their businesses.

2. Ownership and Control

The management structure of the banking companies was usually specified in the contracts signed by all the partners before the commencement of business. Such contracts were usually recorded in an official register of deeds, sometimes at the Court of Session, more often at the local Sheriff Court. A number, however, cannot be traced but it may be presumed that all companies had some sort of formal agreement.

The one known exception to this general rule was the Paisley Union Banking Co. There was a contract at the outset but it expired in 1830. At that time Ludovic Houston, one of the three partners, was on the continent and the other two wanted to continue the partnership but to admit new members, but they saw Houston's large debt to the company as an obstacle to this. The business was continued, therefore, on 'joint account and risque' without a contract. Houston came home in 1832 but did not pay off his obligations and the concern was further continued without a contract. This situation continued until the company was taken over by the Glasgow Union Bank in 1838.[27] Such a situation could exist only because the Paisley Union was a very small partnership; it could not possibly have existed in one of the co-partneries.

The partnership agreement or contract of co-partnery in Scots law had the advantage of continuity and was not rendered null by the withdrawal of a member. Anyone who wished to retire merely had to intimate this fact in the newspapers and by circular letter to the bank's correspondents,[28] whereupon he could sell his share and have nothing more to do with the business. Technically the contract was nullified by the death of a partner unless the contract stipulated otherwise[29] but the banking companies appear to have got round this limitation by making provision for the inheritance of shares.

Shares in the co-partneries were nominally freely transferable but in practice there were limitations on this. They could not be sold if the partner owed money to the company unless there was other security. The Dundee Banking Co. in 1826 granted the right to shareholders

> to sell and transfer the whole, or any of their shares, to any person or persons they please; provided such person or persons shall be approved of by the directors.[30]

The sting in the tail was common to most provincial banking companies, for the directors had the good name of the business to think of. They did not want undesirables as partners. Often contracts stated that shares were to be offered for sale to the directors in the first instance. Usually members were further prohibited from holding shares in other banks.

Ultimate authority in the banking companies rested with the shareholders at their annual meeting, although power structures were less well defined for the partnerships than for the co-partneries, for the smaller companies did not require such a formal organisation. Although the shareholders were nominally the source of all power, the reality was somewhat different and in practice shareholders' meetings were little more than rubber stamps on the intromissions of the directors.

The only known case of any power being wielded by shareholders or any attempt to criticise the directors being made occurred in the history of the Montrose Banking Co. Management of that concern was conducted by seven directors who were elected at the first meeting in 1814 and continued to be re-elected at every annual meeting at least up to 1822, there being only one change, in 1821. There was, however, some opposition to the directorate although it did not receive very much support from the other proprietors. James Clark, who was one of the prime movers and who had been proposed but rejected for the directorate, introduced a motion at every general meeting between 1815 and 1819, designed to give the proprietors more oversight and control of the bank's affairs. Eventually he sold his share, having given up the attempt to change the contract. Clark's opposition to the directors, although never well supported, was instrumental in ensuring a greater attention to business by the directors. In 1818 he complained that they had not given 'that regular attention' demanded by the contract. Five months of the preceding year had elapsed without any of their proceedings, if any, appearing on record but in the following year they met on average twice per month.[31] Thus, although the individual shareholder could not force his opinions on directors, he could at least ensure that they did what they were supposed to do.

The best run of minute books which has survived is that for the Perth Banking Co., 1787–1857. Generally the shareholders' meetings were quiescent. There was a provision in the contract that three of the thirteen directors should retire annually, but what happened in fact was that three retired but were usually re-elected the following year. The result was that the directorate was drawn from a pool of sixteen men and new men were admitted only when old men died or retired. In this way directorates were self-perpetuating. They were usually unpaid, but as they were often substantial borrowers it must be conceded that there were advantages in being a director and general meetings were conducted to say thank you to the directors.[32] This must be seen as a factor of the social control which the leading group in a town's community could exercise and which has been discussed above.[33] To criticise the directors would be to invite ostracism.

This assessment of the system, however, assumes that there were criticisms to make. In fact the directors declared regular dividends which kept the shareholders contented, and attendances at general meetings fell off sharply after the first few years of business. But even when there were grounds for complaint, or at least questions, the shareholders remained, it would seem, unmoved. In 1841 those who attended the general meeting of the Perth Banking Co. heard the directors' report refer to 'the best proofs of the bank's prosperity – the large sum of profits realised in the past year'.[34] In fact the profits then were the lowest since 1830, but the report was approved and no-one dissented.

The real power lay with the directors. In the partnerships, which were usually managed by all the partners acting in concert, it could occur that effective power rested with one man. Robin Carrick wielded such control over the Ship Bank that one observer was moved to comment, 'Robin Carrick was the Ship Bank'.[35] In the co-partneries, on the other hand, power rested with a board of directors. But even here it was always possible for one director to impose his ideas on the others by sheer force of personality. Christopher Middlemass of the East Lothian Banking Co. was such a man, for the minute book gives the impression that his word was law.

The directors of the East Lothian Banking Co. were charged with the 'ordering, directing and superintending of the management of the Company's business'.[36] Similarly the directors of the Perth Banking Co. were to order, direct and superintend the management and 'to give necessary instructions to the cashier and other officers' and were to meet weekly or oftener if required. At these meetings, or as often as they thought it necessary, they were to 'examine the Books of the Company and the Company's Cash'[37] and effective management of the Company's affairs was achieved by the committee system. The Aberdeen Banking Company also administered its business in this way.[38]

The types of committee formed by the Perth Banking Co. were analogous to those operated by the Bank of England.[39] A daily or 'ordinary' committee of four directors, two a quorum, was appointed annually, 'for advising the cashier about discounting bills and other matters of business that may occur betwixt the meetings of directors'. In October each year an inspection committee was appointed with the purpose of examining the annual balance of the books, otherwise the cash and cash books were examined weekly by another committee. In March each year all the cash account bonds were checked to see if there was any need for new securities from guarantors. These three committees were appointed by the directors from amongst their number at the meeting following the general meeting, but *ad hoc* committees were often appointed for such diverse purposes as superintending the building of a new office and examining the Company's business to see if there were any 'inconveniences', i.e. irregularities.

This committee system worked well and the minute book suggests that the directors were assiduous in their duties; directors' meetings had an average attendance of ten, out of a possible thirteen, members. Only in 1798 did the system show any weakness. In that year the cashier was found to have been discounting bills without the advice of the ordinary committee and the directors' response was immediate: they increased the cashier's required bond of fidelity from £2,000 to £3,000. Discount days were in future to be only Monday, Wednesday, and Friday, a common practice amongst banks, and bills offered for discount were to be in the office between 12 noon and 2 p.m. for inspection by the committee. Any bill refused was not to be presented again 'but to the whole committee', and a system of initialling bills was introduced to ensure that there could be no evasion of the regulations.[40] The speed with which the directors acted on this occasion, together with the sound business sense revealed in the above, suggests that the Perth Banking Company was very conscientiously managed.

Other banking companies were not so fortunate in their choice of directors. The East Lothian Banking Company collapsed in 1822 because the directors had failed to give that degree of attention to the business required of them by the contract. In fact they had probably allowed themselves to be rendered inactive by Middlemass, and their lack of application gave to the cashier the opportunity to embezzle large sums of money from the company.[41] A similar lack of attention to duty precipitated the collapse of the Stirling Banking Co. in 1826.[42] In the long run a system of management by committee could only work if the directors discharged their supervisory functions.

Very little is known about the style or quality of management in the partnership banking companies. Arguing *a posteriori*, the only failures amongst the banking companies which involved losses to the public occurred in the partnerships. This may simply have been because of smaller total resources but it is also possible that it indicates poor management. Not only did the partnership tend to have smaller financial resources, they also had less manpower and therefore could not develop a control system so easily as the co-partneries.

The question has sometimes been raised whether or not bankers are entre-preneurs.[43] Certainly in the Schumpeterian sense the provincial bankers played an important role in the development of Scottish banking and were responsible for some important innovations, the most important of which was deposit taking (see Chapter 6). At a simpler level, if the entrepreneur is defined as the man or men who make business decisions, then the bankers were entrepreneurs.

There is, however, another side to this question. Schumpeter believed that it was

> important for the functioning of the capitalist machine . . . that bankers should be independent agents. If they are to fulfil their function . . . they must first be independent of the entrepreneurs whose plans they are to sanction or to refuse.[44]

In the case of the Scottish provincial banking companies, and indeed in many other banking systems, Schumpeter's criterion was not met, for bank directors were usually also industrialists or traders who borrowed from their own banks. There was never any question of the banking companies as such attempting to exercise direct control over other business units but the inter-linkages at board level between banking and the other sectors ensured that maximum use was made of entrepreneurial talents. These men were therefore in positions where they could exercise the greatest leverage.[45] Although they were usually asked to leave the room while their own credit applications were discussed, the result was a foregone conclusion, i.e. their own financial aggrandisement, but as the major industrialists and employers in the area their continued existence and growth was of vital importance for the development of the local economy.

Day to day management of the bank office was in the hands of the chief officer, usually called the cashier. This man was often a partner in the company; he was never a director, and his role in the organisation will be discussed more fully in Chapter 8.

NOTES

1. T. M. Devine, in Ward and Wilson, 1971
2. S.R.A. B10/15/1606, Bond of Corroboration of Glasgow Arms Bank, 1750
3. Aberdeen Banking Co., Stock Transfer Journal 1767 and Letter Book 1767–1794
4. S.R.O. Register of Deeds, Mack 1770 1/207/22, Note payment Bond of General Bank of Perth
5. S.R.A., B10/15/7432, Bond of Corroboration of Glasgow Merchant Banking Co., 1771
6. Perth Banking Co., D.M.B., 1787 and Stock Ledgers, 1808
7. Montrose Banking Co., D.M.B., 3/2/1814
8. *Arbroath Guide*, 29/11/1924
9. B.S., Edinburgh, Miscellaneous Documents, Details on provincial banking companies
10. R. S. Rait, 1930, p. 210; and B.S., Glasgow, Glasgow and Ship Bank Contract, 1838
11. Rait, *op. cit.*, p. 121
12. J. Buchanan, (Glasquensis), 1884, pp. 24, 26
13. C. F. Freebairn, 1924, p. 110
14. N. Crathorne, 1973, p. 56
15. *Old Statistical Account*, vol. 7, pp. 63, 66, 79, 81
16. J. O. Mitchell, 1905; G. MacGregor, 1881, appendix; J. Buchanan, *op. cit.*, p. 27; and B. Duckham, vol. 1, 1970, p. 181
17. Buchanan, *op. cit.*, p. 31
18. Pollock-Morris MSS., Kilmarnock Banking Company Contract, 1802
19. S.R.O. CS96/869, Falkirk Union Banking Company sequestration 17/10/1816
20. S.R.O. CS96/2346, Stirling Banking Company sequestration 14/8/1826
21. Aberdeen Banking Co., Bond Register 1767–8
22. Paisley Union Banking Co., General Ledger 1788–9
23. Perth Banking Co., Bond Register 1808–9
24. *Scots Magazine*, 1763, p. 133
25. Campbell, Tullich, Rosyth MSS., Campbell of Achmore letters, 15/5/1762
26. L. S. Pressnell, 1956, p. 22
27. Paisley Union Banking Co., D.M.B., 22/7/1830, 23/7/1832 and 16/7/1838
28. R. Bell, *Dictionary of the Law of Scotland*, 1815, vol. 1, p. 207
29. *Ibid.*, p. 212
30. Dundee Banking Co., Contract of Co-partnery 1/8/1826
31. Montrose Banking Co., D.M.B., 1814–22, 3/6/1819, 4/6/1819
32. Perth Banking Co., D.M.B., 1786–1808, 1805–1830, 1828–1857
33. See Ch. 7, pt.1
34. Perth Banking Co., D.M.B., 12/7/1841
35. Mitchell, *op. cit.*, p. 167
36. East Lothian Banking Co., D.M.B., 25/10/1809
37. Perth Banking Co., Contract of Co-partnery 1787
38. Aberdeen Banking Co., D.M.B., 1767–1776
39. J. Clapham, 1946, vol. 1, pp. 109–110
40. Perth Banking Co., D.M.B., 2/5/1787, 14/10/1788, 4/11/1788, 3/11/1789, 5/1/1790 and 11/5/1798
41. S.L., CS Processes November–December, 1822, case 57
42. S.R.O., CS96/2346, pp. 525–528
43. R. Cameron, 1963, pp. 50–5
44. Schumpeter, quoted in R. Cameron, *op. cit.*
45. Cameron, *op. cit.*, p. 54

8

The Staff

1. Recruitment

THE numbers of staff employed by the banking companies varied from firm to firm but usually there was a cashier – occasionally called manager – an accountant, a teller, one or two clerks and a porter. A standard condition of employment was that staff members should have no other business interests, but in practice the cashiers often managed to combine their duties with an insurance agency; for example, James Watson of the Thistle Bank was an agent for the Sun Fire Office in 1833.[1] In the same year Roger Aytoun, cashier to the Renfrewshire Banking Co., was on the local management committee of the Scottish Widows Fund Life Assurance Co.[2] These men were, of course, management staff for the rule against secondary business interests tended to be more strictly enforced against other, more junior members of staff.

Any description of staff recruiting must include two different categories – seniors and juniors. Briefly, senior staff may be defined as including cashiers and accountants. Junior staff make up the remainder. The inclusion of tellers in the latter category may be objected to as this position was often filled by an older member of staff but the teller, unlike the cashier and accountant, had no role to play in management. For this reason, and others which will become apparent, tellers have been included as junior staff. All members of staff, whether senior or junior, were appointed by the directors, who also determined the salaries to be paid. In some cases salaries had to be approved by general meetings of the partners but in the cases observed the recommendation of the directors was never rejected.

For much of the industrial revolution period the banking companies found it extremely difficult to recruit senior staff because the mushrooming number of bank offices set up, especially from the 1780s, created a sellers' market for trained men. Cashiers and accountants were, almost never, appointed from within the company. There appears to have been some barrier to vertical movement into management within the firm. Consequently senior men usually had to be appointed from other companies. The reason for this refusal to promote from within was never made clear.

One of the manifestations of this pressure on the supply of trained staff was the comparatively young age at which appointments were made. The only known age at appointment is that of Wm. Borthwick who became cashier to the newly formed East Lothian Banking Co. at the age of 20 or 22.[3] At that age his practical experience was not likely to have been more than five or six years but, despite this, he was placed in charge of the daily running of the company. Although this is the only known example of the age of a cashier, the fact that some senior staff in other concerns achieved very long service suggests that appointments could come to very young men.

The most favoured recruiting ground was amongst the other banks and banking companies. In 1768 Alexander Simpson, who had been accountant at the Royal Bank in Edinburgh, was recruited into the Aberdeen Banking Co. to be its cashier.[4] The branches of public banks also proved to be a fruitful field for the provincial companies; for example, in 1814 David Hill, who had been on the staff of the Montrose branch of the British Linen Co., was appointed to be accountant in the new Montrose Banking Co.[5] He later rose to become cashier. Even when the joint-stock banks were formed they proved to be a useful source for the provincials although this was often a two-way process. Whilst the hunters were hunting, their stock was often poached. In 1841 the Perth Banking Co. recruited David Craigie to be their cashier. He had formerly been agent for the Edinburgh and Leith Banking Co. at Leith.[6]

Other provincial companies were perhaps the most fruitful areas for recruitment. James Austin, the first cashier for the Montrose Banking Co.,[7] had formerly been accountant in the Perth Union Banking Co., and the Paisley Union recruited their first cashier from the Stirling Banking Co. in 1788 and their accountant from the firm of Allan and Stewart, private bankers in Edinburgh.[8] Wm. Borthwick went from the Falkirk Union to the East Lothain Banking Co. in 1810.[9]

Senior staff were also recruited from the law and trade. George Aitken, writer in Cupar, became cashier to the Fife Banking Co. in 1802,[10] while Duncan Spottiswoode, merchant in Perth, was prepared to become cashier of the Perth Banking Co. in 1809 'as soon as he should by attendance on the General Business acquire a competent knowledge of the detail of it'.[11]

The partnership banking companies tended to have fewer staffing problems. Very often their senior staff were appointed from amongst the partners: Robin Carrick became cashier of the Ship Bank when he and others re-formed it in 1776. James Hunter and Wm. Wood became managers of Hunters and Co., Ayr when it opened in 1773; both were partners.[12]

Whereas senior staff in the partnerships were often partners from the outset and were in some cases the prime movers in the formation of the company, in the co-partneries the situation was rather different. In these concerns cashiers and, sometimes, accountants were asked to become partners after they had been appointed to their posts, and in these cases shares were often provided at preferential rates. In 1815 James Austin was offered several shares in the Montrose Banking Co. at par when the market price for a £100 share was £110.[13] In 1851 David Craigie, cashier of the Perth Banking Co., was offered 10 shares at par when the market price was £150 per £100 share.[14] The object of offering these favourable terms to staff was, of course, to bind their interests as closely to the company as possible, for a shareholding was thought to be an added incentive to members of staff to do well in their jobs. Furthermore it made leaving more difficult because the shares would have to be sold if the employee was going to join another bank. There was the further difficulty that the regulations governing the transfer of shares meant that an approved purchaser had to be found.

The recruitment of junior staff was much less of a problem as the training which banks and banking companies provided soon came to be recognised as a useful background for any commercial career. Recruits therefore were not hard to find.

Tellers were usually promoted from within the firm from amongst the clerical staff and clerks were recruited as apprentices and trained on the job. The Aberdeen Banking Co. seems to have been the first of the provincials to introduce formal indentured apprenticeships. This scheme was begun in 1770 and the period of indenture lasted four years. The Perth Banking Co. adopted a three-year scheme in 1790 when they found that their young men were leaving almost as soon as they had become useful in the job. The period of training was extended to four years in 1799. Young men were usually taken on at the age of 15 or 16.[15] Most banking companies operated similar types of arrangement.

Apprentices came from amongst the sons of the merchant and similar groups. Between 1793 and 1825 the Perth Banking Co. recruited apprentices from the families of teachers, a shipmaster, merchants, a master carpenter and a tax collector. Fathers of apprentices were often partners in the company.[16]

Two exceptional cases are worthy of special note. Robin Carrick entered the Ship Bank as an apprentice in 1753 at the age of 16. His father had been minister at Houston and tutor to Andrew Buchanan, one of the partners in the banking company. Five years later Carrick became accountant in the concern but he does not appear to have been bound by the stricture which prohibited bank staff from engaging in other business. In the 1760s he set up in business as a muslin manufacturer and by 1776 he was sufficiently wealthy to be the principal partner in the renewed Ship Bank.[17] When he died in 1821 his fortune was estimated at £500,000. This was held to be 'the biggest pile that a Glasgow man had as yet scraped together'.[18] Unfortunately it is impossible to separate his banking interest from his other business in an attempt to disaggregate his income. Nevertheless this is a good example of how someone from relatively humble origins could progress in the business world of the industrial revolution.

The other noteworthy example is that of Wm. McAlpine, who started his working life as a weaver. He joined the Paisley Union Banking Co. as a porter in 1788 and four years later rose to be clerk.[19] Doubtless job mobility of this nature brought social mobility in its wake.

The problems which did exist in recruiting and training new staff were both caused and exacerbated by the nature of the staff market. It was a very fluid situation. John Thomson began his banking career with the Stirling Banking Co. His subsequent career took him to Edinburgh, Perth and Aberdeen with the Bank of Scotland, and then Glasgow and back to Edinburgh with the Royal Bank.[20] Edinburgh and London were magnets for Scottish bank staff, and when the joint-stock banks (often founded on Scottish principles) began to be set up in England and Ireland there was a very considerable drain on the staffing resources of the banks and banking companies.[21] Within Scotland the emergence of joint-stock banks in the 1830s put a premium on trained staff. In 1844 David Craigie, cashier of the Perth Banking Co., was offered a job in the Glasgow Bank. Craigie told his directors about this offer and they increased his salary immediately by £150 p.a. Craigie stayed.[22] Occasionally staff were attracted away from banking. In 1789 James Millar, cashier of the Greenock Banking Co., left to become Professor of Mathematics at Glasgow University.[23]

The problem of staff departing for other posts became so serious for the Perth Banking Co. in the 1790s that they began to require six months' notice of an employee's departure,[24] which is yet another indication of the general problem of recruiting and keeping trained staff.

2. Work

Training for work in a bank took place in the office and this was generally true of industry and commerce:

> Since formal management training was so rare as to be negligible, and since formal education ended at an early age managers typically were trained by practical work in the firms.[25]

This generalisation certainly holds true of the provincial banking companies.

The chief officer of a banking company was the cashier, although in one or two cases a manager was also appointed.[26] The duties of the cashier were

> to ask, demand, receive, sue for, discharge and renounce, all and sundry Debts and sums of money due . . . also to Subscribe the Notes to be issued . . . and in general to subscribe and execute, sign, seal and deliver all Deeds and Obligations which by law and practice the Cashier of a Banking Company may do.

With the exception of the accountant he also had to exercise superintendence over the staff.[27] Robin Carrick of the Ship Bank was given to making surprise checks on the tellers' books when they were out to lunch.[28]

The cashier was subject to the general superintendence of the directors, particularly in the co-partneries. In many cases, however, the directors were rather lackadaisical about their duties, which gave the cashier a large measure of autonomy, a freedom which was sometimes abused. The cashier of the Fife Banking Co., for example, employed a substitute who did the work for a fraction of the salary.[29] Others like Borthwick of the East Lothian Banking Co. used the shortfall in directorial superintendence to embezzle money. Generally, however, the cashier, although subject to control by the directors, did enjoy a large degree of autonomy in the daily management of the office. In companies where the cashier was a partner he often enjoyed the right to discount bills without further advice. Carrick of the Ship Bank certainly enjoyed this right, but even in the multi-partnered East Lothian Banking Co. Wm. Borthwick was allowed to discount bills up to £400 on his own initiative when there was no doubt as to the stability of the customer.[30] In even more formally structured companies, like the Perth Banking Co., it appears that the cashier had no discounting rights.

The duties of the accountant were

> to State and Settle all Accounts, Constitute and Ascertain all Balances that are or shall be owing to the company by any person or persons by Cash Accounts or any other manner of way and to subscribe the said Stated Accounts in order to fix and ascertain a Balance and Charge Against the several persons that are or may be bound and engaged to Repay such balances.[31]

He was the chief book-keeper.

The accountant was, in most cases, independent of the cashier although his inferior in office. Both the accountant and cashier were individually responsible to the directors and served as effective checks on one another.[32]

The designation and duties of junior staff were often flexible. When Alexander McCulloch joined the Thistle Bank in 1789 his contract of employment outlined his duties as 'teller, clerk and assistant'.[33] Apprentices in the Perth Banking Co. were often employed as assistant tellers.[34] Where more than one teller was employed, the senior man usually held that position permanently but the others were more junior staff who undertook a period of telling duties as part of their training and when the office was busy.

Many companies suffered occasionally from dishonest staff, but in order to safeguard against this all members of staff were required to find security for their intromissions. This took the form of a bond signed by two or more cautioners, often the relatives of the employee, in which they undertook to pay to the company losses up to a fixed amount occasioned to the bank by the employee's shortcomings due to negligence or theft. A fixed amount was specified on the bond and in the case of Alexander McCulloch, teller in the Thistle Bank, this was set at £500. As teller, McCulloch's 'chief business was to pay silver and other specie for their notes as demanded. For this purpose he was entrusted with £500 in specie, which when paid away, was replaced by fresh supplies in exchange for the notes he had got in'.[35] In this way the £500 entrusted to McCulloch was matched to the full extent by his bond of fidelity. The security required was usually equivalent to the amount of risk involved. In 1808 the Perth Banking Co. set the requirements of staff fidelity bonds at £5,000 for the cashier, £1,500 for the accountant, £2,000 for the teller, £500 for the clerk and £200 for the porter.[36] Despite the security requirements the problem of absconding staff was not unknown in many banking companies. When a member of staff ran off the enquiry which followed usually revealed a situation where supervision had been inadequate.

Where a loss occurred as a result of negligence the member of staff usually had to pay the shortfall himself, but occasionally staff were permitted to write all or part of it off to profit and loss account. In 1833 the accountant in the Perth Banking Co. was allowed to write off 80 per cent of his losses. It was felt that to have allowed him the whole loss would have established 'a bad procedure'.[37]

The hours which staff were required to work varied greatly. In 1750 the Glasgow banking companies opened their offices from 'Ten to Twelve forenoon and from Three to Five o'clock afternoon excepting Saturday and that day from nine to eleven o'clock Forenoon'.[38] By 1808 these hours had become 10 a.m. to 1 p.m. and 2 p.m. to 3 p.m. on weekdays and from 10 a.m. till noon on Saturdays. Soon afterwards banking companies also began to open from 1 till 2 p.m.[39] In Dundee the practice seems to have been rather different. The Dundee banking companies opened on Saturday afternoons until 1826. In August that year they began to close at 12 noon on Saturdays, but when a customer complained there was a reversion to the old opening hours, whereupon the bank clerks organised a petition amongst the principal inhabitants and manufacturers. They obtained 140 signatures to the petition and the principle of a Saturday half-day was confirmed.[40] The staff, of course, had to work on beyond opening hours until their books were balanced, so it is impossible to generalise about working hours. Certainly there were times when a balance was quickly achieved. The situation was, with the exception of Saturday working, probably not very different from what it is to-day.

Staff were not allowed holidays other than statutory bank holidays. During the reign of George III there were ten bank holidays. In 1820 these were January 1, January 30 – King Charles' martyrdom, Mar. 31 – Good Friday, May 29 – King Charles restored, June 4 – King George III's birthday, August 12 – Prince of Wales's birthday, September 22 – King George III's Coronation, October 25 – King George III's accession, November 5 – Gunpowder Plot, and December 25.[41] This list says something about King George's opinion of the institution of the monarchy.

Staff, generally, were not subject to transfer to other offices. Agents in the branches employed their own staff. Nevertheless, there were a few examples of transfers being made. In 1812 Wm. Cowbrough was teller in the East Lothian Banking Co., having been recruited from the Falkirk Union Banking Co. He became accountant in that year and when the company's agent at Selkirk died suddenly in 1814 Cowbrough was sent to take his place.[42] This is the first known example of a staff transfer in the records of the provincial banking companies. In 1818 Robert Stewart, clerk in the Perth Banking Co., was sent to Inverness to help in the setting up of a new agency there.[43] Hugh Watt, also of the Perth Banking Co., was sent round the branches in 1820 to inspect their books and cash. This is the first suggestion of an inspector of branches, although the public banks had appointed inspectors several years earlier. Watt was later appointed to be Dunkeld agent[44] and in 1825 he became cashier of the Arbroath Banking Co. He later went south to become manager of the Huddersfield Banking Co. – an English joint-stock bank founded on Scottish principles.

3. Salaries

Table 33 sets out the average salaries for bank employees at 10-yearly intervals between 1770 and 1840. These figures are compiled and averaged from data fragments for a wide variety of banking companies. They have been rounded off to the nearest £5. In the 1830s and 1840s only a few figures were available – so their typicality is in doubt. These salaries could, of course, be augmented in a number of ways. The cashier was often provided with free accommodation, as was the porter who usually lived on the premises. Both were given free coal and candles or an allowance in lieu. Frequently some element of salary was made dependent on results. When the Montrose Banking Co. began in 1814 its senior staff were promised increases of £50 in the following year if the company was 'successful' in its first year,[45] but this could work both ways. When profits slumped in 1816 the salary of the cashier was reduced from £300 to £175 and that of the accountant from £200 to £150.[46] In some companies incentives took the form of profit-sharing; for example, the cashier of the Paisley Union Banking Co. received 2½ per cent of net profits each year.[47] The Dundee New Bank were more generous: their cashier received 5 per cent of net profits.[48]

Table 33
Scottish Provincial Banking Companies:
Staff Salaries 1770–1840

	Cashier	Accountant	Teller	Clerk	Apprentice	Porter
1770	£100	50	35	30	—	—
1780	130	—	—	35	—	15
1790	150	60	45	40	—	20
1800	200	90	80	45	—	20
1810	340	130	120	60	—	30
1820	350	180	—	90	—	—
1830	400	200	180	100	30	50
1840	500	—	—	—	—	—

The junior staff were less fortunate for it seems that it was not customary to pay apprentices until the 1820s. Clerks and tellers were luckier. Their salaries were at least the equivalent of that of a skilled workman. Porters' perquisites have already been mentioned. For security reasons either a porter or a junior clerk was often required to sleep on the premises, and sometimes he had company in this task. David Mitchell, porter for the Thistle Bank in 1819, was allowed £10 for 'two years maintenance of the dog'.[49]

There was a continuing upward trend in salaries throughout the period under review, even although money wages in other sectors declined in the second quarter of the nineteenth century. This may largely be attributed to the shortage of trained people, to the rapid rate of turnover and to inflationary tendencies in the economy. The latter were particularly severe in the first decade of the 19th century. In that period the Perth Banking Co. made frequent *ex gratia* payments to staff for their 'extra trouble'.[50] In fact this was probably a move, by the directors, to placate their staff without committing themselves to fixed higher salary levels. Doubtless other companies adopted similar measures. Higher salaries, in the long run, were unavoidable.

Salary increases were negotiated on an individual basis, although in the public banks there were cases of joint application, but there are no known attempts at collective bargaining amongst provincial bank staffs. Members of staff made application to the directors, who either granted or refused the request. Occasionally salary increases were decided by the general will of the shareholders at an annual business meeting but this general will was, of course, informed by the directors.

Members of staff were not impotent if their requests were refused, for they could take their labour elsewhere and frequently did. The bargaining position of staff was, in fact, fairly strong. When John Caw's apprenticeship with the Perth Banking Co. ended in 1823 he was offered a clerkship at a salary progressing in four years from £60, through £70 and £80, to £100 p.a. He refused. The offer was then raised by £10 p.a. in the first three years and this time he accepted.[51] Although applications for increases were usually couched in somewhat obsequious terms, they belied the real bargaining power which the member of staff possessed.

There was no retiral age for bank staff which was, of course, standard practice in the professions. Employees usually worked on until they died in harness. Ill health, however, often forced retiral and in these cases the directors felt disposed to make a financial provision. Their generosity was conditioned both by the length of service of the employee and the economic climate at the time. In 1841 Walter Miller retired as teller after 50 years' service with the Perth Banking Co. and was given a pension of about half his salary.[52] Unfortunately there is little other evidence of this sort of thing so that it is impossible to say what the general practice was. Pensions, it would seem, were not given as of right. They were *ex gratia* payments which frequently had to be 'earnestly solicited'.

NOTES

1. B.S., Glasgow, Thistle Bank Papers
2. Edinburgh Univ. Archives, Bk. 6 19², Life Insurance proposal 21/2/1833
3. *Caledonian Mercury*, 20/4/1822
4. R.B.S., D.M.B., 8/4/1768
5. Montrose Banking Co., D.M.B., 3/12/1814
6. Perth Banking Co., D.M.B., 15/2/1841
7. Montrose Banking Co. D.M.B., 11/1/1814
8. Rait, 1930, p. 186 and C. F. Freebairn, 1924, p. 111
9. S.R.O. CS96/987, Falkirk Union Banking Co. sequestration papers
10. Buchanan, 1884, p. 38
11. Perth Banking Co., D.M.B., 4/7/1809
12. Rait, 1930, p. 172
13. Montrose Banking Co., D.M.B., 18/7/1815
14. Aberdeen Banking Co., D.M.B., 15/6/1770 and 19/10/1770
15. Perth Banking Co., D.M.B., 21/10/1790, 14/2/1799 and 27/2/1847
16. *Ibid.*, 1793–1825
17. Rait, 1930, pp. 39–40
18. Mitchell, 1905, p. 170
19. Freebairn, 1924, p. 111
20. P.P. Select Committee on promissory notes . . . 1826, evidence of John Thomson, p. 144

21. Crouzet, 1972, p. 88
22. Perth Banking Co., D.M.B., 2/5/1844
23. Greenock Banking Co., Journal, 1786; and *Matriculation Album of The University of Glasgow*, 1728–1858, entry 3536
24. Perth Banking Co., D.M.B., 16/8/1796
25. Pollard, 1968, p. 147
26. Dundee New Bank, D.M.B., Contract draft 1802
27. S.R.O. Register of Deeds, Mack. vol. 290, f829, Factory and B18/18/14; East Lothian Banking Co., D.M.B., 24/11/1812
28. Senex, vol. 2, 1884, p. 234
29. Joplin, 6th ed., 1827, p. 134
30. East Lothian Banking Co., D.M.B., 31/5/1810
31. S.R.A., B10/15/6511, Commission and power by Arms Bank to James Struthers, 1757
32. Paisley Banking Co., Dundee branch letters, Jas. Fraser to Jas. Scott, 15/12/1791; and Montrose Banking Co., D.M.B., 3/2/1814
33. B.S., Glasgow, Thistle Bank Papers, Bundle 9/1, Contract of employment
34. Perth Banking Co., D.M.B., 20/4/1787
35. B.S., Glasgow, Thistle Bank Papers, Bundle 9/3, Submission in arbitration, 1792
36. Perth Banking Co., D.M.B., 15/2/1808, 24/3/1808
37. *Ibid.*, 11/6/1833
38. *Glasgow Courant*, 8/1/1750, 5/11/1750
39. Glasgow Post Office Directories
40. Boase, 1867, pp. 351–2
41. *Edinburgh Almanac*, 1820
42. East Lothian Banking Co., D.M.B., 31/12/1812 and 9/6/1814
43. Perth Banking Co., D.M.B, 21/9/1818
44. *Ibid.*, 29/8/1820, 10/11/1823
45. Montrose Banking Co., 3/2/1814
46. *Ibid.*, 5/6/1816
47. Paisley Union Banking Co., Journal 1795–6, and D.M.B., 13/7/1821
48. Dundee New Bank, D.M.B., regulation 3
49. Thistle Bank Papers, miscellaneous receipts
50. Perth Banking Co., D.M.B., 4/7/1809, 6/7/1809
51. *Ibid.*, 10/11/1823, 22/11/1823
52. *Ibid.*, 14/5/1841

9

The Branches

THE terminology used by the provincial bankers to describe their branches is extremely varied and, therefore, rather confusing. The words 'branch', 'sub-branch' and 'agency' might all be used to describe an office of a bank where business was conducted.

For the purpose of clarity a *branch* is 'any office, other than a head office, where banking business (i.e. lending and/or deposit taking) was carried out by someone, usually designated an *agent*, appointed for that purpose by the directors of a company on behalf of that company'. This rather general definition is necessary because of the changes which took place not only in the organisation and business in the period under consideration, but also because of the way in which bankers thought about them. For example, when the Dundee New Bank set up a branch at Brechin in 1802, it decided on a 'regular branch' rather than on 'an agency on commission'.[1] This distinction rested upon the manner in which the agent was paid. The style *agent* has often given rise to confusion, and in fact this term survived in use as a description of branch managers until 1946.[2] Some branches, certainly in the early years, were lending offices only and did not receive deposits.

1. Formation and Distribution

The Bank of Scotland had opened branches in several towns in 1696 but these had been withdrawn. A similar experiment in the 1730s was equally unsuccessful, and no further attempts at branches were made until 1774. The British Linen Co., formed in 1746, maintained a series of agents throughout the country who were 'concerned with the production of spun flax and woven yarn and the sale of parcels of linen sent from Edinburgh'.[3] As the Company developed banking functions in the late 1750s the agents began to circulate notes by making advances, and several of these offices continued in existence throughout the period under consideration.

The first provincial banking company to open branches was the Aberdeen Banking Co. By 1770 it had offices in Inverness, Huntly, Forres, Peterhead, Banff, Montrose and Fraserburgh.[4] There were also a number of agencies elsewhere but these were merely note-pickers which do not meet the definition of a branch.

The Bank of Scotland began to develop an extensive branch network from 1774 and the Royal set up an office in Glasgow in 1783. Given this lead and the early example of the Aberdeen Banking Co., some of the provincials were not slow to follow. Although eighteen of the provincials did not establish branches, the other twenty-seven did, with companies such as the Aberdeen Banking Co. and Renfrewshire Banking Co. reaching totals of six and five respectively in 1825. Table 34 sets out the extent of the branches of the banking companies in 1793, 1810 and 1825. Table 35 lists those concerns which had no branches.

Table 34
Scottish Provincial Banking Companies: Branches in 1793, 1810 and 1825

	1793	1810	1825
1) Aberdeen Banking Co., 1767–1849	Forres, Huntly, Inverness, Banff, Keith, Elgin (6)	Forres, Huntly, Peterhead, Banff, Keith, Elgin (6)	Fraserburgh, Huntly, Peterhead, Banff, Keith, Elgin (6)
2) Aberdeen Commercial Banking Co., 1788–1833	Arbroath (1)	None	None
3) Arbroath Banking Co., 1825–1844			Coupar Angus, Forfar (2)
4) Hunters & Co., Ayr, 1773–1843	Irvine, Maybole (2)	Irvine, Maybole (2)	Irvine, Maybole, Kilmarnock (3)
5) Caithness Banking Co., 1812–1825			Wick
6) Dundee Banking Co., 1763–1864	Arbroath, Brechin, Forfar, Kirkcaldy (4)	Arbroath, Forfar (2)	None
7) Dundee New Bank, 1802–1838		Arbroath, Forfar, Brechin (3)	Forfar (1)
8) Dundee Union Banking Co., 1809–1844		Not known	Arbroath, Forfar, Brechin, Montrose (4)
9) East Lothian Banking Co., 1810–1822		Selkirk, Haddington (2)	
10) Falkirk Banking Co., 1785–1826	Glasgow (1)	Glasgow (1)	Glasgow (1)
11) Falkirk Union Banking Co., 1803–1816		Glasgow (1)	
12) Fife Banking Co., 1802–1825		Kirriemuir, Kirkcaldy, Glasgow (3)	Kirriemuir, Kirkcaldy (2)
13) Galloway Banking Co., 1806–1821		Dumfries, Kirkcudbright (2)	

	1793	*1810*	*1825*
14) Glasgow Banking Co., 1809–1836		Kirkcaldy (1)	Kirkcaldy (1)
15) Greenock Banking Co., 1785–1843	Glasgow (1)	None	Glasgow, Port Glasgow, Rothesay(3)
16) Leith Banking Co., 1792–1842		Callander, Dalkeith, Galashiels, Langholm (4)	Callander, Dalkeith Galashiels, Langholm (4)
17) John Maberly & Co., 1818–1832			Glasgow, Edinburgh, Dundee, Montrose (4)
18) Montrose Banking Co., 1814–1829			Arbroath, Brechin (2)
19) Paisley Banking Co., 1783–1837	Glasgow, Dundee (2)	Glasgow (others not known)	Glasgow, Stranraer, Irvine, Alloa (4)
20) Paisley Union Banking Co., 1788–1838	Glasgow, Hamilton, Beith, Maybole, Greenock, Dumfries, Newton Douglas, Castle Douglas, Kirkcudbright, Gatehouse, Saltcoats, Carlisle, Alnwick (13)	Glasgow, Hamilton, Beith (3)	Glasgow Hamilton, Beith (3)
21) Perth Banking Co., 1787–1857	Dunkeld, Crieff, Auchtermuchty, Coupar Angus (4)	Dunkeld, Coupar Angus (2)	Dunkeld, Crieff, Coupar Angus, Inverness, Auchtermuchty (5)
22) Perth Union Banking Co., 1810–1836		Not known	Dunkeld, Alloa, Coupar Angus (3)
23) Renfrewshire Banking Co., 1802–1842		Glasgow, Rothesay, Inveraray, Cambeltown (4)	Glasgow, Rothesay, Inveraray, Cambeltown, Port Glasgow (5)
24) Stirling Banking Co., 1777–1826	Alloa (1)	Alloa (1)	Alloa, Kinross (2)

Notes   Companies with branches not encompassed by Table 34:
        1. Ayr Bank, 1769–72 – Dumfries, Edinburgh
        2. Perth United Banking Co., 1766–1787 – Dunkeld, Crieff, Auchtermuchty
        3. Glasgow and Ship Banking Co., 1836–1843 – Kirkcaldy and Glasgow Cross
Sources Minute books, directories, almanacks

Table 35
Scottish Provincial Banking Companies:
Companies without Branches

1.	Banking Co. of Aberdeen	1747–1753
2.	J. Macadam and Co., Ayr	1763–1771
3.	Cupar Banking Co.	1802–1811
4.	Johnston, Lawson and Co., Dumfries	1766–1771
5.	Dumfries Commercial Banking Co.	1804–1808
6.	Dundee Commercial Banking Co. No.1	1792–1802
7.	Dundee Commercial Banking Co. No.2	1825–1838
8.	Ship Bank, Glasgow	1749–1836
9.	Arms Bank, Glasgow	1750–1793
10.	Thistle Bank, Glasgow	1761–1836
11.	J. & R. Watson, Glasgow	c.1763–1832
12.	Merchant Banking Co. of Glasgow	1769–1798
13.	Thomsons, Glasgow	1785–1793
14.	Kilmarnock Banking Co.	1802–1821
15.	General Bank of Perth	1767–1772
16.	Shetland Banking Co.	1821–1842
17.	Merchant Banking Co. of Stirling	1784–1805
18.	Campbell, Thomson and Co., Stirling	1787–1798

Several reasons may be suggested for the emergence of branch systems. Of the companies which developed them, the most common pattern was to have several offices in satellite towns. This type of situation developed in Aberdeen, Arbroath, Ayr, Dundee, Dunbar, Cupar, Greenock, Montrose, Paisley, Perth and Stirling – in short in all the major burghs with the exception of Glasgow. The reasons for this pattern of development seem clear, for communications were easy between proximate towns, which helped bankers maintain their knowledge of business conditions and individual credit worthiness. Branches were of convenience to customers living in their vicinity and of advantage to bankers in that they promoted note circulations. The mainstay of the economy in towns with bank branches was likely to have been the same as in head office towns – usually agriculture and textiles. It must therefore be argued that branch offices were often a logical extension of head office business.

Sometimes the pattern of branches was dictated by the pattern of industrial location. The numerous branches of the Paisley Union Banking Co., formed in the years 1788–91, were set up in areas where a start had been made with the opening of water-powered cotton mills. These included Castle Douglas, Hamilton, Newton Stewart, Maybole and Oban,[5] but unfortunately it has proved impossible to discover any more direct link between these bank branches and industrial undertakings.

Occasionally branches were set up principally to service the business of a partner and only secondly to develop new business. The Greenock Banking Co. set up a Glasgow branch under its partner, James Dunlop, in 1785. His business interests were in coal, glass, iron and the West Indies trade[6] and when he failed in 1793 he owed more than £25,000 to the banking company.[7] Seemingly he had used bank money to finance his own business interests. The Glasgow Banking Co.

was formed in 1809 and had only one branch – in Kirkcaldy. It seems that the main reason for the location of this office was to provide services for the textile manufacturer Walter Fergus, one of the partners, who was the first agent.

With only one exception branches were in different towns from their head office. This was the Glasgow and Ship Banking Co. Its head office was in Virginia St., which was in keeping with the westward movement of the business community. But the old Glasgow Cross area had been left devoid of bank offices, for even the Glasgow Union Bank which had been founded in 1830 and set up its office near the Cross had moved westwards a few years later. The Glasgow and Ship Banking Co., seeing the need for an office in the old commerical centre of the city, set up an office in the Trongate in 1839.[8]

A number of the provincial banking companies established branches in Glasgow. In 1802 there were four of these: the Falkirk, the Renfrewshire and both Paisley banking companies. Glasgow was of course an important centre of Scotland's commercial life and was an attractive outlet for funds. In addition a number of banking companies maintained correspondents (usually also styled 'agents') whose job it was to collect bills for payment.

Rather paradoxically only one banking company, the ill-fated Ayr Bank, ever set up a branch in Edinburgh. Perhaps the experience of Douglas, Heron and Co. may well have served as a warning of what might happen if any of the provincials entered the Edinburgh arena. Certainly they would have incurred the wrath of the public banks and this alone may have been enough to deter them. The Glasgow and Ship Banking Co. had it in mind to open in Edinburgh in 1838 but that project, like many others devised by the directors, never came to fruition.[9]

Some places where business was conducted were not really bank offices at all. The Leith Banking Co. had a tent for this purpose at Highland shows and agricultural markets,[10] and the Perth Banking Co. sent a representative to the cattle market in Newburgh.[11]

Several banking companies ventured south to set up branches in England. The Paisley Union Banking Co. had offices in Carlisle, Alnwick, Penrith and Wigton (Cumberland) in 1796, but these were closed shortly afterwards.[12] 'Most of the private banks established before 1810 in the Carlisle area issued Scottish notes'.[13] For example the Workington Bank issued £1 notes of the Dundee New Bank.[14] A number of manufacturers in the North of England also paid Scottish notes to their workers. In 1811 Messrs. Elliot and Foster, cotton manufacturers in Carlisle, entered into an agreement with the East Lothian Banking Co. whereby that company's notes were paid out to their employees and this arrangement, of course, involved an element of credit. When the banking company closed in 1822 Elliot and Foster were sequestrated. In addition to cash of £10,000, their mill, valued at £12,000, was transferred to the bank's trustees.[15]

Such was the volume of business in Carlisle that a note exchange was set up in 1813 by the East Lothian Banking Co. and the British Linen Bank.[16] It is difficult to find a reason for the popularity of Scottish notes in the North of England, especially in the 1797 to 1826 period when English bankers were permitted to issue notes under £5 in value. Certainly the cash account facilities that accompanied the note issues were an attraction but it must also be considered that the Scottish bankers attracted this business because they had built up a reputation for trustworthiness and stability. Certainly when there was a threat to the small notes in 1826 the protests from Cumberland and Northumberland concentrated on the defence of the Scottish small notes and very little was said about English notes. Again, in 1828, when the issue of Scottish notes was prohibited in England there was a repetition of the protests of two years earlier.[17]

In 1824 the Leith Banking Co. decided to open a branch in England at Carlisle, but before they did so they took legal advice on the status of such business and were advised that this operation would be illegal in terms of the Act which prohibited English country banks from having more than six partners. They ignored this advice and opened their branch. No attempt was made to prosecute them under the Act[18] and when Scottish notes were banned from circulation in England the Leith directors overcame this by registering their Carlisle branch as an English bank.[19] This office was closed in 1836 when the agent left to become manager of the Carlisle City and District Banking Co.[20]

Only the Dundee Union Banking Co. opened a branch in London.[21] The date of this venture is not known but it was certainly trading in 1824. The agents – Chalmers and Guthrie – were paid a salary of £500 but unfortunately nothing further is known about the business. The Dundee Union also corresponded with Messrs. Glyn and Co.[22] No other banking company seems to have experimented with a London branch.

No fewer than 18 of the banking companies had no branches. Of these, eight were very small and short-lived affairs (i.e. under ten years). A further five lived and died before branch banking was common among the banking companies. Of the remaining six, one was a non-issuing private company, two were located in Glasgow, one in Dundee, one in Kilmarnock and one in Shetland.

The failure of the Kilmarnock and Shetland Banking Companies to branch out may be attributed to their lack of opportunity. There was really nowhere for them to go in their areas that was not already well served by other companies. The same might be said of the Dundee Commercial Banking Co. (No. 2), although it was a rather different case. It was a relatively large company both in terms of capital and shareholders and was therefore better able to compete. Perhaps its success in winning local business from the Dundee New Bank rendered a branch network unnecessary.

The two Glasgow companies without branches were the Ship and the Thistle. Indeed, with the exception of the Glasgow Banking Co., none of the Glasgow companies ever formed branches. The reason for this must lie in the fact that they found sufficient business to deploy their resources in Glasgow. This is not to suggest that their advances were always employed in Glasgow – far from it. The city was the commercial centre of the West of Scotland and controlled a wide variety of business throughout the region. The cash account ledgers which have survived bear witness to the fact that Glasgow bank credit financed businesses from Campbeltown in the West to Falkirk and Bo'ness in the East.

It has been suggested by Professor Cameron that

> Typically a bank would have three or four branches, usually in near-by satellite communities, but many banks also maintained branches in Glasgow.[23]

This generalisation is clearly unsatisfactory because, of 45 companies, 27 (i.e. 60 per cent) had branches. Only 17 of these conform to Professor Cameron's description, i.e. 38 per cent. of the overall total. A further 18 (i.e. 40 per cent) had no branches at all. Moreover Professor Cameron has in some cases confused correspondences for bill collections and note retiral facilities with branches. Clearly there was no typical Scottish bank or banking company in terms of branch banking.

2. The Business

For most of the period under review the primary purpose of branches was to put notes into circulation, which was achieved by remitting notes to the agents who then discounted bills for their customers.

The acceptance of deposits at branches was usually a later development. The Perth Banking Co., for example, did not permit its agents to take deposits until 1808.[24] In nearly every case where figures are available, branches were in net spending areas, that is, where advances exceeded deposits (see especially Dundee New Bank, Branch Balance Sheets in Appendix A). Therefore the concept of branch banking as a system in which branches were formed in saving areas, from which money was transferred to spending areas, is invalid in the case of the provincial banking companies. Such a view belongs to an era when the supply of money could not be so easily expanded, as was possible in the days of unrestricted note issues.

Most of the branch business consisted of note issuing by discounting and later of deposit taking. Cash accounts could be operated upon at branches, but these were awarded by the directors and remained the responsibility of head office. Discounts were made by the agents who were liable for any bad debts thus arising, and usually they were fully responsible, but in some cases their directors were prepared to make an allowance. In 1829 the Auchtermuchty agent of the Perth Banking Co. discounted a forged bill for £450 and the directors agreed to pay half this amount although 'not bound to do so'.[25] Other companies were more generous. The Alloa agent of the Stirling Banking Co. was liable for only one-third of the bad debts incurred by him.[26] Clearly the liability of agents was an encouragement to caution.

As the system of branch banking matured, the services provided by the agents increased. From 1816 the Perth Banking Co. began to permit agents to draw bills on the company's correspondents in Edinburgh and London and drafts under £1,000 were to be honoured without question by the correspondents, but those in excess of that amount were 'to be advised'. From 1841 agents were allowed to draw on head office and correspondents, and issue interest receipts and letters of credit without communication with head office.[27] All this was in keeping with the practice of other banks, for such was the degree of competition between banks that all services had to be matched.

The agents were allowed to provide these services only because the degree of supervision over their businesses had been increased. This has been mentioned in Chapter 8 but may be briefly re-stated. From the early 19th century branch inspections became an increasingly important element of business life and checks on branch books were usually made by a team of directors. John Baxter and Wm. Bell of the Dundee New Bank were nominated to inspect branch books and cash in 1803. They found things in order save for a small error in the bills at Forfar.[28] In the Perth Banking Co. this duty was delegated to a member of staff,[29] and in the East Lothian Banking Co. branch supervision was performed by the cashier who was also a partner.[30]

The inspection of branches was not systematic but was usually instigated after some incident had arisen to make it necessary. In one case the Dundee New Bank directors had discovered that agents had been taking deposits at 4 per cent and using the money to discount for their own account. This practice was ended and agents were warned that all transactions must be for behoof of the bank.[31] Similarly the East Lothian Banking Company's system of inspection was begun only after some irregularities at the Selkirk branch.[32]

During commercial crises the business at the branches was the first to be cut back. The reasons for this seem clear, for the quality of business was of paramount importance. Directors at head office were more likely to trust their own judgement not to discount doubtful bills but agents, it was felt, were more likely to make fundamental errors of this kind. Furthermore directors were more likely to have personal business ties with people in the head office area and were therefore more inclined to help them through a crisis. In 1803 the Forfar and Brechin agents of the Dundee New Bank were restricted to discounts of £500 per week each.[33] Cutbacks might also take the form of a return to 'normal' banking, i.e. to discounting only real bills. In 1815 the Montrose Banking Co. refused to countenance the discounting of accommodation bills.[34] Seemingly in times of easy money the normal restrictions on discounts had been relaxed. When the turn came in the trade cycle all the old standards were re-imposed. Bankers could also curtail credit by restricting the tenure of bills.

All of these restrictions were of course eventually imposed on head office business but the branches were the first to suffer, and when the going became really tough branches were closed. The Brechin branch of the Montrose Banking Co. was ended in 1816 and in 1827 the directors told their Arbroath agent that they would not stand in his way if a more favourable situation presented itself.[35] Thus it was the branches that were the first to be curtailed when trouble arose.

3. The Staff

The men selected to be branch agents were usually

tried men of business, who have proved, by the manner of conducting their own affairs, their capability of successfully transacting whatever may be confided to them.[36]

Many of the agents were writers. Wm. Craig, writer in Galashiels, was agent for the Leith Banking Co. and was popularly known as 'God's Lawyer' because he arbitrated in disputes between townsmen.[37] Bank directors were usually careful to pick only men of the highest integrity.

Agents were not restricted from engaging in other businesses. Hugh Watt, sometime employee of the Perth Banking Co., thought that the office of agent was accepted

> not altogether for the salary, but because it gives influence to the agent in the town; it promotes his own business if in trade; and, if a writer or attorney he makes it pay him as a notary and solicitor, when it may not do so as a bank agent.[38]

Agents were given no formal training save when necessity demanded it. When George Banks, agent for the East Lothian Banking Co., was found to have been discounting bills to excess he was invited to attend at Dunbar for a few days 'to receive instructions that he may be better able to conduct the company's business in a regular manner'.[39]

In the Angus area in particular there seems to have been considerable mobility of agents, with men moving from the service of one banking company to another, often for financial gain but sometimes as branches opened and closed. But there could also be remarkable continuity of service. Wm. Bett was appointed agent at Coupar Angus for the Perth Banking Co. in 1795. He was still there in 1857 when the Company was taken over and his appointment was continued by the Union Bank until he died in harness in May, 1861 at the age of 87 after 66 years service.[40]

New branches were usually set up on trial and were closed if the business failed to develop. The pay of agents was often tied to the amount of business conducted and it was usually left to be settled until after the branch had been in operation for a year. Agents were paid either by salary or commission but the former became the commoner method by the early 19th century. In 1795 the agents of the Dundee Banking Company were paid commissions of ¼ per cent on bills discounted, they guaranteeing the amount; ³/₈ per cent on London bills, they guaranteeing one half, and 1/10th per cent of all interest they received on cash accounts or paid on deposits.[41] In 1787 the Dunkeld agent of the Perth Banking Co. was paid commissions of ¹/₈ per cent on Glasgow bills and ¼ per cent on all others. In 1813, however, the Perth directors decided to place all branch agents on a fixed salary rather than a commission and the levels decided upon were tied to the rates of pay under the old system. The new rates were: Dunkeld £350, Coupar Angus £400, Auchtermuchty £250.[42]

These rates were sometimes higher than those paid to cashiers at head office; for example, in 1821 the Inverness agent of the Perth Banking Co. received £500[43] while the cashier was paid £400. It must be remembered, however, that the agent had usually to maintain his establishment out of his salary. Occasionally an allowance was made for the office or for a clerk but more usually the agent had to pay for these himself so that his net salary was quite a bit less than his gross one.

Other rates of pay for agents included £200 for the Forres agent of the Aberdeen Banking Co. and £100 for the Elgin agent in 1787;[44] £100 for the Hamilton agent

N

of the Paisley Union Banking Co. and £25 for the Greenock man in 1796 and £500 for their Glasgow agent in 1829;[45] and £150 for the Brechin agent of the Montrose Banking Co. in 1815, plus a promise of another £50 the following year if the business was successful.[46]

Branch agents, like members of staff, were required to sign bonds of fidelity, as security for their intromissions. The extent of the bond was anything from 10 to 20 times the amount of the salary. Clearly the agent's situation was often precarious, for one or two bad bills could wipe out his salary for the year. The Aberdeen Banking Co. informed its agent in Leith that

> As to the risk you run in discounting, you have it entirely in your own power to discount none but where the security is undoubted.[47]

Thomas Joplin wrote of the agents that

> The great sum required as security, the business character he possesses, and the risk he himself runs, naturally remove all suspicion as to the prudence of his transactions.[48]

This was sometimes far from the truth, for even the most prudent of agents made mistakes – good bills could easily become bad bills. Most agents bore their losses manfully but some resorted to criminal means to recoup their bad debts. Others became criminals even if they had no losses. The Hamilton branch of the Paisley Union Banking Co. provides only one of several examples of defalcations by agents. In 1815 the bills protested were twice the bills not yet due. The agent had forged a signature on bills deposited with him as security and had then discounted them and taken the money.[49] He was, of course, removed from office and his securities were called to pay his bond but his replacement was no more honest. In 1830 he was found to have been discounting fictitious bills and perhaps even forging them himself. Losses to the company exceeded £10,000.[50]

The criminal element amongst branch agents was small but significant. Fortunately for the companies, agents were usually both prudent and honest.

NOTES

1. Dundee New Bank, D.M.B., 13/9/1802
2. Forbes, 1974, No. 102, p. 55n
3. Malcolm, 1950, p. 173
4. Aberdeen Banking Co., D.M.B., 1769–1776
5. Duckham, 1970, p. 181
6. Paisley Union Banking Co., General Ledger 1788–9; and *Old Statistical Account*
7. G.U.L. Murray Collection MU23 B19, Notes by Buchanan, p. 8
8. Glasgow and Ship Banking Co., D.M.B., 17/4/1839
9. *Ibid.*, 12/4/1838
10. Buchanan, 1884, p. 37
11. Perth Banking Co., D.M.B., 23/11/1809
12. Paisley Union Banking Co., Journal, 1795–6
13. Chandler, 1964, vol. 2, p. 298

14. Boase, 1867, p. 238
15. S.R.O. B18/18/14, East Lothian Banking Co., D.M.B., 9/5/1811 and B18/18/16–17, Reports on Bank's affairs, 1827, 1829
16. S.R.O. B18/18/14, East Lothian Banking Co., D.M.B., 10/6/1813
17. Parliamentary Debates, 1824–1828
18. Signet Library, Court of Session Papers, Second Division, A. Scott v J. Ker, 6/12/1827
19. Gilbart, 1849, vol. 2, p. 744
20. Crick and Wadsworth, 1936, p. 121
21. Buchanan, 1884, p. 40
22. S.R.O., CS311–2142, Box 207, Montrose Banking Co., Letters, Dundee Union Banking Co., to Montrose Banking Co., 15/9/1824
23. Cameron, 1967, p. 71
24. Perth Banking Co., D.M.B., 5/12/1808
25. *Ibid.*, 31/3/1829
26. S.R.O., CS96/2357, Stirling Banking Co., sequestration, 15/8/1828
27. Perth Banking Co., D.M.B., 12/11/1816, 4/8/1818, and 25/3/1841
28. Dundee New Bank, D.M.B., 13/12/1803
29. Perth Banking Co., D.M.B., 5/7/1824
30. East Lothian Banking Co., D.M.B., 5/5/1814
31. Dundee New Bank, D.M.B., 12/1/1803
32. East Lothian Banking Co., D.M.B., 5/5/1814
33. Dundee New Bank, D.M.B., 14/3/1803
34. Montrose Banking Co., D.M.B., 16/10/1815
35. *Ibid.*, 18/6/1816 and S.R.O., CS311–2142, Box 207, Montrose Banking Co. to Wm. Findlayson 23/6/1827
36. Joplin, 1827, p. 24
37. Hall, 1898, p. 481
38. Watt, 1833, p. 20
39. East Lothian Banking Co., D.M.B., 2/8/1810
40. Perth Banking Co., D.M.B., 27/10/1795, 24/5/1861
41. Boase, 1867, B/S 32, 1795
42. Perth Banking Co., D.M.B., 9/10/1787, 22/1/1813, 7/7/1813, 28/6/1816
43. *Ibid.*, 4/9/1821
44. Aberdeen Banking Co., Letter Book, 1787
45. Paisley Union Banking Co., Journal 1795–1796 and D.M.B., 30/11/1829
46. Montrose Banking Co., D.M.B., 18/5/1815
47. Aberdeen Banking Co., Letter Book, 10/3/1788
48. Joplin, 1827, p. 25
49. S.R.O., CS233 5/1, Paisley Union Banking Co. v Wm. Fleming
50. Paisley Union Banking Co., D.M.B., 12/4/1830, 19/7/1832

10

The Correspondents

WHEN a new provincial banking company was founded, one of the earliest tasks of the management was to find and appoint suitable men to conduct the company's business in the main centres of commercial activity, chiefly Edinburgh, Glasgow and London. The practice was to call these men *agents*, which is an accurate definition of their legal position. To save confusion with the branch agents, these representatives will be referred to as *correspondents*.

1. Edinburgh and London

The correspondents in Edinburgh and London were appointed from amongst the private bankers in those cities. Very often a partner in a provincial banking company had a business connection with an Edinburgh private banker whom he recommended for the appointment and the Edinburgh banker, in turn, advised that his London friends should be considered for the London position.

The functions of the Edinburgh and London correspondents were, in most respects, similar, but there were two important differences. The Edinburgh man served as the provincial banker's representative at the note exchange from 1771. The notes of other banks which were taken in the course of business were sent to the correspondent who in turn presented them at the exchange and received his constituent's notes in return. It very often occurred, however, that the volume of notes passing through the official exchange was lessened because Edinburgh bankers who were correspondents for more than one provincial company could effect a transfer without sending the notes to the exchange.

The function which was peculiar to the London banker was the purchase of government funds and bills. Holdings of these securities were the effective reserves of many provincial banking companies while others, like the Ship Bank, played the market in a speculative manner, often with great success.[1] Whatever a company's reason for investing in Government stocks, it was the London correspondent who bought and sold the securities. Purchases and sales of this kind were carried out, either in the name of the cashier of the company (by whom the correspondent was furnished with a power of attorney to enable him to make the transfers), or in the name of the correspondent himself who later transferred ownership to the cashier for behoof of the company.

By the early years of the 19th century it was not unusual for a banking company to arrange for transactions in the funds on behalf of its customers; for example, in 1823 Hugh Rose of Glastullich requested the Perth Banking Co. to sell £17,000 of reduced 3 per cent annuities and to purchase Bank of England stock with the proceeds. All of this was accomplished through Messrs. Barclay, Tritton, Bevan and Co.[2] acting as correspondents. Barclays were instructed in 1823 that when the balance of Perth Banking Co. money in their hands exceeded £25,000 they were to purchase Bank of England stock without further intimation.[3] A good London banker, because of his close association with the money market, could be an extremely valuable asset to a provincial banking company and occasionally a correspondent might use his own initiative to save involving his constituents in an unprofitable investment. On one occasion Barclays sold some 3 per cent annuities on behalf of the Perth Banking Co. but delayed purchasing exchequer bills with the proceeds as instructed because of the high price. This action was approved by the directors in Perth.[4] Clearly in an age of such slow communications a high degree of competence and understanding was essential to the financial links between London and the provinces.

Correspondence agreements with Scottish provincial banking companies and English country banks could often be a considerable asset to a London bank. Smith, Payne and Smith, private bankers in London, acted as loan contractors for new issues of Government securities and in this they found their links with country banks in Scotland and England to be particularly helpful. Before a contractor submitted a bid for a new loan he was required to provide the Treasury with a list of subscribers, and Smiths and Co. were able to include most of their country correspondents on their list which, in 1802, included the Thistle Bank of Glasgow.[5] A successful tender for these loans was a source of considerable profit to a bank, but success depended on a well-organised subscription list. Extensive country connections were an undoubted asset in this respect.

In most other ways the functions of the Edinburgh and London correspondents were similar. The principal task was to collect payment of bills discounted in the country and due for payment in the capitals, which was a relatively simple matter. When the bill fell due the accepter was called upon to pay it and the proceeds were credited to the provincial banker in the books of the correspondent.

Both the Edinburgh and London correspondents were useful sources of advice and information, in the provision of which a touch of paternalism can often be discerned. Messrs. Kinnear and Co. were Edinburgh bankers for the Montrose and other banking companies. In 1819 George Kinnear, the senior partner, promised the directors in Montrose that he would 'with pleasure at all times give your company such information and advice as may be in my power'.[6] The London correspondents, in pursuance of their special function, provided information about the movement of stock prices. In 1818, when these were falling, the Perth Banking Co. asked Barclay's advice about possible further falls.[7] Very often the agent's opinion was sought before a purchase was ordered.

The frequently changing state of the law regarding banking business was a source of great trouble to many bankers but the correspondent was usually approached for his opinion, as he was the man closest to the seat of legal authority.

The advice regarding the Act of 7 George IV c.67 whereby banking companies were required to register the names of their partners has already been mentioned in Chapter 5. Although by no means infallible, the correspondents were a source of free legal advice. But at least one provincial bank preferred to pay for these services. The Perth Banking Co. retained legal advisers in both Perth and Edinburgh. The 'law agent' in Perth was paid a retainer £5–5/– per annum, while his counterpart in Edinburgh received £7–7/–.[8]

Occasionally, during periods of crisis, the correspondents drew upon their greater experience and provided advice about how bankers should conduct themselves. In the crisis of 1825–6 Kinnear wrote that

> Bankers in such times ought not to withdraw support from such traders as are entitled to look to them for it, but on the contrary to be liberal in such instances, while on the other hand they should keep themselves independent and be wary of entering upon any new or distant transactions.[9]

As the crisis worsened he wrote that

> Banks ought to do their utmost at the present time to assist their customers, and one another too, but the latter particularly it may not be in their power to do to a great extent for the public are pressing heavily upon all.[10]

This advice was not requested but doubtless Kinnear thought it necessary to offer it to a young bank which had never before endured a very severe crisis.

In addition to providing advice, the correspondents in Edinburgh and London were also useful sources of information. In the slump of 1817 Kinnears informed their provincial customers that the banks in Edinburgh were thinking of reducing the rate of interest allowed on deposits to 3 per cent.[11] In 1822, when the Bank of England began to discount bills at 4 per cent, Barclays wrote immediately to their correspondents informing them of this action.[12] In general the correspondents acted as a clearing house for information which was imparted to the provinces as fast as the mails could carry it, but the flow of information was, of course, two-way. Provincial bankers kept their correspondents in touch with events in their areas and provided credit opinions of people with whom the Edinburgh and London bankers were contemplating a business connection.[13]

Correspondents were often able to exert power on institutions on behalf of their constituents. George Kinnear was a private banker and a director of the Bank of Scotland. He persuaded the board of that Bank to allow its branch agent at Montrose to exchange notes there with the new Montrose Banking Co. He did so despite the fact that such an arrangement effectively diminished the amount of note exchange business done by him and consequently the amount of commission received. He was also instrumental in helping the bank borrow £10,000 from the Bank of Scotland in 1826.[14]

One of the main functions of the Edinburgh and London correspondents was to hold a supply of funds upon which the provincial company could draw when required. But the seasonal nature of many payments meant that it was not always possible for a bank to maintain a credit balance with its correspondents. When a company held discounted bills which were payable in Edinburgh and London it could dispose of them in one of two ways. Firstly if the bills were almost due they were sent to the correspondent. Secondly if the bills had some time to run they could be sold to customers who required negotiable paper to settle accounts in the capitals, although the practice of drawing bills on correspondents was more common. Often the demand for Edinburgh and London paper outstripped the supply. When this happened the company issued drafts on its correspondents, but unless care had been taken to build up credit balances in Edinburgh and London the accounts became overdrawn. Very often provision had been made for this eventuality when the initial agreements had been negotiated and it was understood that this advance would be only a temporary accommodation, but in times of crisis the demand for good paper and the desire of the bankers to meet their customers' needs often led to over-use, if not abuse, of this facility. The response of the correspondents to the increasing debtor balances of their correspondents' accounts was to request, with increasing firmness, a diminution of the balance. In 1815, when the Montrose Banking Co. had overdrawn its account with Kinnears to the extent of about £8,000, George Kinnear wrote, 'We do not wish to put your company to inconvenience, reduce our advance gradually as you propose, and when you have got the account into a proper state keep it so.'[15]

Several months later Barclays, whose account was also in advance, wrote requesting the 'favour . . . to make us such cash remittances as shall reinstate the account and supply it with funds sufficient to meet the demand'.[16] In 1826, when a similar situation prevailed, Barclays, after several gentle admonitions, stated quite bluntly that 'the capital of the company requires enlargements'.[17] It had become clear to the Barclay and Co. partners that the Montrose Banking Co. had been trading on its correspondents' capital rather than its own. Kinnear was less blunt but equally direct: 'Permit me to impress upon you in the strongest manner the necessity of every Bank's relying on its own resources in these times.'[18] Hill, the cashier at Montrose, sent long-dated bills to Kinnears to cover the advance but these were rejected because 'such bills are quite inefficient in our hands as from the length of their date we can neither pass them at the Banks here nor discount them in London'.[19] Interest was paid at the rate of 5 per cent on sums due to correspondents, which may explain why such abuses were tolerated for so long. Furthermore the correspondents knew that the security for the debt, even if it was not covered by a deposit of bills, was ultimately the whole heritable and personal property of all the partners. Generally, however, relationships between bankers and their correspondents were cordial, and only the imposition rendered necessary by a credit crisis placed a strain on the friendship.

Usually, for much of the year provincial bankers' accounts in Edinburgh and London were positive balances. Surplus funds, certainly before 1822, were deposited with correspondents. In 1818 Kinnears informed the Montrose Banking Co. that

the money your Company have deposited with us is always at their command either here or at London tho' we would prefer paying it in London as affording us a chance of some little advantage by the exchange.[20]

Interest was allowed on these balances at 4 per cent until 1822, when this was reduced to 3 per cent, and after that date the rates of interest showed more inclination to vary than they had hitherto done. The superfluity of money in the money market in the early 1820s caused some embarrassment to the private bankers of London and Edinburgh who were correspondents for the provincial banking companies. In August, 1821 Messrs. Glyn and Co. advised the Paisley Union Banking Co. to reduce its credit balance with them as they could not profitably employ the funds,[21] and this request was repeated by other banks in the following two years. In 1823 Barclays restricted the deposit of the Montrose Bank to £5,000.[22] The Perth Banking Co. was to be limited by Barclays to a deposit of £15–£20,000 but the directors asked to be allowed to deposit £25–£30,000 'as being as small a floating balance as can well be supposed necessary to the carrying on of the business of the Bank with ease'.[23] Sir Wm. Forbes, Jas. Hunter and Co., who were correspondents in Edinburgh for the Perth Banking Co., proposed to limit the latter's deposit there to £10,000 but the amount was eventually left to the discretion of the Perth directors although no interest was allowed on balances over £15,000.[24] Faced with their inability to utilise all of their funds, some of the provincial banking companies bought British and foreign securities.

Tables 36 and 37 set out the names of some of the private banks in Edinburgh and London which engaged in correspondences, together with the names of the Scottish provincial banking companies for which they acted at various times.

Table 36
Scottish Provincial Banking Companies:
Edinburgh Correspondents

1. *Sir Wm. Forbes, Jas. Hunter and Co.* – Aberdeen Banking Co; Hunters and Co., Ayr; Dundee Commercial Bank (no. 1); Dundee New Bank; Greenock Banking Co; Paisley Union Banking Co; Perth United Banking Co; Perth Banking Co.
2. *Thos. Kinnear & Son* – Perth Union Banking Co; Montrose Banking Co; Dundee New Bank; Dundee Banking Co; Stirling Banking Co; Fife Banking Co; Thistle Bank; Fife Banking Co; Falkirk Banking Co.
3. *Mansfield, Hunter (Ramsay) and Co.* – Perth United Banking Co.
4. *Allan and Son* – Kilmarnock Banking Co; Shetland Bank
5. *Donald Smith and Co.* – Renfrewshire Banking Co.

Table 37
London Correspondents

1. *Kinloch, Hog and Co.* – Aberdeen Banking Co; Perth United Banking Co; Perth Banking Co.
2. *Barclay and Co.* – Montrose Banking Co; Perth Banking Co.
3. *Smith, Payne and Smith* – Glasgow Banking Co; Ship Bank; Thistle Bank; Paisley Banking Co.
4. *Glyn and Co.* – Aberdeen Banking Co; Arbroath Banking Co; Paisley Union Banking Co; Dundee Union Banking Co.
5. *Coutts and Co.* – Aberdeen Banking Co.
6. *Ransom, Morland and Co.* – Dundee New Bank; Dundee Banking Co; Glasgow Banking Co.

Tables 36 and 37 are by no means comprehensive but reflect the present state of knowledge on the subject with respect to the better-known firms; however, some banking companies chose non-bankers to be their correspondents. For example the

East Lothian Banking Co. appointed Messrs. Thomson and Co., merchants and insurance brokers, to be their Edinburgh correspondent.[25] The Kilmarnock Banking Co. chose Wm. Fairlie, merchant, an uncle of one of the partners, to be London correspondent.[26] Prior to 1772 the banking companies tended to change their correspondents frequently or to have more than one London account. This was probably a reflection on the instability of the banking system at this time, and after 1772 the system gradually stabilised and bankers changed their correspondents infrequently, and then only after major disagreements. Generally most differences of opinion between banker and correspondent could be easily compromised.

There were three ways in which a correspondent could be paid for his services. In 1825 Messrs. Smith, Payne and Smith suggested the three alternatives which the Dundee Commercial Banking Co. had for paying their correspondents. These were 'a commission charge of 2/– per cent., the maintenance of a stipulated cash balance (interest free) . . . or the payment of an annual fixed charge'. A similar choice was offered to the Paisley Union Banking Co. when it settled with Messrs. Glyn and Co. in 1795.[27] The earliest detail of payments to correspondents which exists is of the arrangement between the Dundee Banking Co. and Messrs. Eadie and Laird, London, in 1765. The correspondents were paid a commission of ¼ per cent on all transactions for the first year, after which it was hoped they would settle for a fixed salary. John Fyffe, the correspondent, was paid a salary of £50 with the use of £2,000 free of interest.[28] As the situation stabilised after 1772, it became common for banks to allow a commission of 1/8th per cent on transactions with correspondents, in addition to which any advances were charged at 5 per cent and deposits were allowed at 3½ or 4 per cent. In the 1820s payments by the Dundee Banking Co. through its Edinburgh and London agents averaged £825,000 and £164,000 per annum respectively.[29] Usually part of the agreement stated that the bank could draw on its correspondents to a certain extent unsecured. In the case of the Paisley Union Bank this was £5,000.[30] By 1800 it had become more common to pay a fixed salary to correspondents. In 1796 the Perth Banking Co. paid £300 to Sir Wm. Forbes and Co.[31] By 1825 Thomas Kinnear thought that 'the salaries of Scotch Country Banks to their Edinburgh agents all run from £200 to £300 per annum and the latter is a much more common rate than the former'.[32]

The system of maintaining correspondents in London and Edinburgh was essential to the proper functioning of the Scottish provincial banking mechanism, as these men were the link which kept the flow of funds and information running. As such they were an integral part of the system.

2. Glasgow and Others

The pattern of economic development in the industrial revolution made Glasgow the centre of industrial activity, and for that reason most of the banking companies found it necessary to have correspondents in that city.

Table 38 sets out the list of banking companies which corresponded with Glasgow in 1802 and 1825.

Table 38
Scottish Provincial Banking Companies:
Companies corresponding with Glasgow in 1802 and 1825[33]

1802	1825
Greenock Banking Co.	Aberdeen Banking Co.
Stirling Banking Co.	Greenock Banking Co.
Kilmarnock Banking Co.	Stirling Banking Co.
Leith Banking Co.	Dundee Union Banking Co.
Perth Banking Co.	Leith Banking Co.
Hunters and Co., Ayr	Dundee New Bank
	Hunters and Co., Ayr
	Perth Banking Co.
	Perth Union Banking Co.

The Northern Bank of Belfast also corresponded with Glasgow in 1825. Some provincial banking companies maintained branches in the city, and these were mentioned in Chapter 9.

The functions of these correspondents were to retire bank notes which had found their way into Glasgow and to collect payment of discounted bills which had been drawn on Glasgow. Occasionally bankers drew bills on these correspondents which they sold to their customers in just the same way as they operated on Edinburgh and London accounts. The firm of J. & R. Watson, private bankers in Glasgow, specialised in that type of work. Throughout the long life of that concern, c.1763 to 1832, a large number of banking companies corresponded with it.

The Perth United Banking Co. corresponded with Watsons until the Royal Bank opened its Glasgow branch in 1783, whereupon the account was transferred to Scott Moncrieff, and when the Perth Banking Co. was formed in 1787 the business was continued. Glasgow bills discounted in Perth were sent to him usually eight days before they were due for payment. Scott Moncrieff was required to remit bills on Edinburgh at four days' date for all bills sent him, for which he was paid a commission of 1/8th per cent.[34] When John More succeeded Scott Moncrieff in 1803 it was decided to pay him a salary of £150 p.a. rather than a commission.[35] Scott Moncrieff forecast, rather inelegantly, at the time that it would be 'the pleasantest and easiest got money he ever got'.[36]

In some cases the correspondence was two-way. In 1814 the Montrose Banking Co. entered an agreement with the Glasgow Banking Co. under which there was to be a mutual collection of bills. Commission was to be charged at 1/8th per cent and balances were to grow to £500 before a transfer was made in Edinburgh at the correspondent's there. Meanwhile, while these balances were growing, interest was to accrue at the rate of 4 per cent.[37]

Generally, correspondences were established where the business required it. For example, the Shetland Banking Co. kept an account with the Montrose Banking Co.,[38] but no further details are known about this business.

There was also a movement to establish accounts with English country banks. In 1793 the Perth Banking Co. asked Messrs. Baker, Hedley and Co. of Newcastle to negotiate their bills without commission, and in return a reciprocal facility was offered, which was agreed to.[39] The movement generally, however, did not make progress until the 1830s, and in 1832 the Dundee New Bank opened an account with the Liverpool Commercial Banking Co.[40] Two years later the Paisley Union Banking Co. found it

> in some cases disadvantageous to the company and inconvenient to some of their customers that the Bank had no correspondent in Manchester on whom they could draw.

Consequently an account was opened with Jones, Lloyd and Co.[41] In 1841 the directors of the Perth Banking Co. decided to open accounts with bankers in Manchester, Liverpool, Birmingham, Newcastle and Sunderland.[42]

The appointment of correspondents in various parts of the country gave fluidity to the payment of debts and therefore encouraged people to incur debts in other places. In the early years of banking development it was sufficient for a provincial banking company to keep accounts in Edinburgh and London, as these were the main financial centres of the country. But as the pace of development quickened it became increasingly necessary for banking companies to keep accounts on which they could draw and on which they could obtain payments for their bills, in the main centres of industrial activity. The establishment of a number of these accounts helped create a national money market in which customers could obtain drafts on the places where they were doing business. The willingness of the bankers to provide this service must be seen as an accelerator to the rate of growth.

NOTES

1. Ship Bank Investments Journal, 1785–1836
2. Perth Banking Co., D.M.B., 22/12/1823
3. *Ibid.*, 2/12/1823
4. *Ibid.*, 30/12/1823
5. Leighton-Boyce, 1958, pp. 93–4
6. S.R.O. CS311/2142 Box 207, Montrose Banking Co., Letter George Kinnear to Montrose Bank, 10/2/1819
7. Perth Banking Co., D.M.B., 21/8/1818
8. *Ibid.*, 3/11/1798 and 6/8/1807
9. S.R.O. CS311/2142 Box 207, Thos. Kinnear to David Hill, 20/12/1825
10. *Ibid.*, 9/1/1826
11. *Ibid.*, Geo. Kinnear to Jas. Austin, 12/5/1817
12. *Ibid.*, Barclay and Co. to David Hill, 3/7/1822
13. *Ibid.*, 8/2/1825
14. *Ibid.*, Geo. Kinnear to Jas. Austin, 11/10/1814, 31/1/1815 and Thos. Kinnear to David Hill, 3/4/1826
15. *Ibid.*, Geo. Kinnear to Jas. Austin, 31/1/1815
16. *Ibid.*, Barclay and Co. to Jas. Austin, 12/8/1815
17. *Ibid.*, Barclay and Co. to David Hill, 21/2/1826
18. *Ibid.*, Thos. Kinnear to David Hill, 2/3/1826

19. *Ibid.*, 15/3/1826
20. *Ibid.*, Geo. Kinnear to Jas. Austin, 3/7/1818
21. Paisley Union Banking Co., Sederunt Book, 1819–1838, 20/8/1821
22. S.R.O. CS311/2142 Box 207, Barclay and Co. to David Hill, 11/10/1823
23. Perth Banking Co., Sederunt Book, 16/10/1823
24. *Ibid.*, 10/11/1823, 13/11/1823 and 13/1/1824
25. S.L. CSP. vol. 501, 1817, case 34
26. Pollok-Morris MSS., Fairlie Letter Book, 23/11/1818
27. Leighton-Boyce, 1956, p. 116; and Fulford, 1953, p. 100
28. Dundee Banking Co., D.M.B., 16/9/1765 and 20/9/1764
29. Boase, 1867
30. Freebairn, 1924
31. Perth Banking Co., D.M.B., 23/9/1796
32. S.R.O. CS311/2142 Box 207, Thos. Kinnear to David Hill, 10/5/1825
33. Post Office Directories
34. Perth Banking Co., D.M.B., 26/4/1787
35. *Ibid.*, 28/11/1803
36. R.B.S., Scott Moncrieff Letters, 13/12/1803
37. S.R.O. CS311–2142, Box 207, Glasgow Banking Co. to Montrose Banking Co., 13/6/1814
38. N.L.S. acc 3250, Hay to Hayfield MSS., Box 27 f2, Box 39 f4
39. Perth Banking Co., D.M.B., 22/1/1793, 29/1/1793
40. R.B.S., Dundee New Bank, miscellaneous documents
41. Paisley Union Banking Co., D.M.B., 17/2/1834
42. Perth Banking Co., D.M.B., 25/3/1841

Part Three

FINANCING THE ECONOMY

11

Business Finance

THIS section demonstrates, by example, the way in which the banking companies provided credit for the various sectors of the economy. For convenience these sectors are considered under five headings. Chapters 11 to 15 deal with general considerations; with agriculture and fishing; with trade and transport; with industry; and with local government and public utilities.

To some extent these sectoral divisions are rather arbitrary, especially where customers had varied business interests. A bank advance, ostensibly to finance investment in one sector, might be used in other ways. This underlines the basic difficulty of using bank ledgers. The researcher can often only speculate about the use to which bank credit was put. For example, Robert McNair had an outstanding balance on cash account with the Ship Bank of £555 in 1752. His business interests included tobacco, sugar, glass and fish;[1] such diversity creates great difficulty where a sectoral analysis of bank advances is to be attempted. Nevertheless it must be borne in mind that there was often a spill-over effect from bank credit in that an advance in one sector enabled the businessman to spend his own capital more freely in other areas.

During the industrial revolution the amount of fixed capital formation by the business world was small in relation to the amount of working capital used to purchase raw materials, pay wages and finance stocks. The sole exception to this was probably the public utilities. 'The main problem for the early industrialist . . . was of finding circulating capital'.[2] Chapter 6 revealed the possibility of longer-term advances on cash account, and it is clear that some banking companies were prepared to make special provisions for selected customers. Nevertheless the bulk of bank finance was short-term. Here again the point must be made that although bank loans seldom constituted a major source of business finance for individual firms, the flexibility attached to bank credit must have been the means by which firms overcame their liquidity crises. Bank finance was often the all-important marginal money, and firms, thus helped, could continue trading.

The banking companies were prepared to finance a very wide range of business activities and even, in some cases, a few non-business activities. For example, in 1761 Wm. McDowall had borrowed £1,356 on cash account from the Ship Bank to finance his new house.[3] The Paisley Union Banking Co. even authorised cash credits for churches in the 1820s and 1830s. Table 39 sets out a list of some of the cash credits awarded by the Aberdeen Banking Co. between 1767 and 1818. These have been chosen, not at random, but to show the great diversity of businesses and other enterprises which the company was prepared to finance.

Table 39
Aberdeen Banking Co., Cash Credits⁴

Customer	Date	Limit of credit
Aberdeen Town Treasurer	1767	£ 1,000
Aberdeen Dean of Guild		1,000
Earl of Aboyne		1,000
Earl of Errol		500
Archd. Grant of Monymusk		500
Theo Ogilvie, Collector of Customs		500
Tannery Co.		1,000
Green Glass House, Alloa		1,000
Francis Peacock, Dancing Master		100
Arthur Gibson, Shipbuilder	1772	500
Leys, Still & Co., Manufacturers	1773	1,000
Aberdeen Sugarhouse Co.	1776	1,000
Wm. Burnett and Co., Brewers	1777	1,000
Alex. Smith, Papermaker	1781	200
John Gordon, Flaxdresser, Fraserburgh	1784	300
Whale Fishing Co.	1785	1,000
T. Bannerman & Co., Merchants		1,000
Clayhills Brickworks	1787	300
J. Chalmers, Printer	1788	150
Garden of Troup, Senator of the College of Justice	1790	1,000
Alex. Smith, Ironmonger	1791	300
B. Johnston, Thread Manufacturer, Cruden	1792	300
Deeside Road	1796	1,800
Whale Fishing Co., Peterhead	1803	1,000
Aberdeen Infirmary	1804	500
Aberdeen Bridewell	1805	2,500
John Milne, Hairdresser & Perfumer	1806	200
Aberdeen Ropework Co.	1808	1,000
Patrick Seller, Writer in Elgin	1810	900
John Smith, Housebuilder, Banff		400
Aberdeen Harbour Improvement Trustees	1812	5,000
Aberdeen Lime Co.	1813	1,000
Marykirk Bridge		1,000
Glentanner Wood Concern		1,000
Lunatic Asylum		300
Shipmaster Society of Aberdeen	1818	500

The Aberdeen Banking Co. was in no sense atypical. This type of list could be repeated from the ledgers and registers of other companies.

In some cases it has been possible to make a sectoral analysis of cash account advances, and these have been incorporated as Tables 40 to 44. The reservations expressed above about the uses made of credits must, however, be borne in mind.

The predominance of the merchants in all cases is the most notable feature of these Tables, but the lack of definition for this group makes further comment difficult. Generally, it may be said that the banking companies were prepared to finance, with cash accounts, all manner of business activities, but there appears to have been a strong concentration on trading interests. The shortfall of information on discounting has already been lamented in Chapter 6, but Chapters 12 to 15 provide some further examples of the types and extent of finance provided by the banking companies.

Table 40
Aberdeen Banking Co., Cash Credits[5] (the first 100), 1767–8

Customers	Authorised limits	Per cent	No. of accounts	Average
Landowners	£ 11,600	21	18	£ 644
Merchants	33,700	62	62	544
Manufacturers	2,960	5	7	422
Professions	4,500	8	11	409
Local Authorities	2,000	4	2	1,000
	£ 54,760	100	100	£ 548

Table 41
Dundee Banking Co., Cash Credits 1763–7[6] (the first 162)

Customers	Authorised limits	Per cent	No. of accounts	Average
Landowners	£ 9,200	19	30	£ 307
Farmers	1,200	2	6	200
Merchants	29,150	59	82	355
Manufacturers	1,100	2	6	183
Professions	4,015	8	15	268
Local Authorities	500	1	2	250
Others	4,620	9	21	220
	£ 49,785	100	162	£ 307

Table 42
Dundee New Bank, Cash Credits 1802–5[7] (the first 156)

Customers	Authorised limits	Per cent	No. of accounts	Average
Landowners	£ 6,850	14	16	£ 428
Farmers	5,800	12	18	322
Merchants	21,450	42	59	364
Manufacturers	7,150	14	24	298
Professions	1,650	3	7	236
Others	7,600	15	32	238
	£ 50,500	100	156	£ 324

The large number in the *others* category consists largely of shopkeepers.

Table 43
Perth Banking Co. Cash Credits[8] 1787 (the first 100)

Customers	Authorised limits	Per cent	No. of accounts	Average
Landowners	£ 9,800	18	16	£ 613
Farmers	1,500	3	4	375
Merchants	20,250	38	44	460
Manufacturers	7,200	14	7	1,028
Professions	1,900	4	7	271
Public Utilities	2,000	4	2	1,000
Others	9,850	19	20	429
	£ 52,500	100	100	£ 525

Table 44
Ship Bank, Glasgow, Cash Accounts[9] at 8/7/1752

Customers	Balances outstanding	Per cent	No. of accounts	Average
Landowners	£ 177	0.5	1	£ 177
Tobacco Merchants	17,023	46	48	355
Merchants	6,416	17	19	338
Professions	176	0.5	1	176
Others	1,613	4	7	230
Unidentified	12,065	32	46	262
	£ 37,470	100	122	£ 307

(Note: This example deals with balances actually drawn and not authorised credits.) The professional in this case was none other than Dr. Wm. Cullen, the discoverer of the principle of latent heat.

NOTES

1. Ship Bank Balance Ledger, 1752; and S.R.A., list of 18th century merchants
2. Crouzet, 1972, p. 45
3. Ship Bank, Balance Ledger, 1761
4. Aberdeen Banking Co., Bond Registers
5. *Ibid.*
6. Boase, 1867
7. Dundee New Bank, D.M.B., 1802–5
8. Perth Banking Co., Bond Register, 1787
9. Ship Bank, Balance Ledger, 1752

P

12

The Finance of Agriculture and Fishing

1. Agriculture

THE preparedness of bankers to make advances to agriculturalists is attested by the formation of banking companies in agricultural areas and by the frequent references in the records to the sending of representatives to markets and trysts.

Some companies, however, were extremely cautious about giving advances to farmers. The nature of the credit required tended, in most cases, to be longer term than the bankers – who had their liquidity to consider – were prepared to provide. For this reason the Perth Banking Co. told its Coupar Angus agent in 1809 that it did not consider 'cash accounts granted to people who are merely farmers as advantageous to the Bank',[1] i.e. tenant farmers, but other companies were less squeamish. For example, the Montrose Banking Co.[2] and the East Lothian Banking Co.[3] both awarded numerous cash accounts to tenant farmers, and very often the signatories to the bonds were also farmers. These, too, were usually tenants and not landowners. It is difficult to appreciate how farmers were able to meet the bankers' requirements of frequent withdrawals and pay-ins to keep the banknotes circulating, but the arrangement does seem to have worked. It may, however, be speculated that the highly active accounts of merchants enabled the banking companies to carry a few less active farming accounts so, in the absence of any cash flow statements from bankers, this question will remain unanswered.

The same ambivalence may be noted in the attitude of the banking companies to landowners. In 1802 the Dundee New Bank refused a loan for estate improvement to John Ochterlony of Guind because advances of this nature were thought to be 'improper'.[4] It may be conceded that landowners were more likely to keep accounts with the private bankers in Edinburgh and even London, where they were able to secure mortgages. Nevertheless some major landowners did use the provincial banking companies; for example, the Dukes of Atholl maintained a long connection, usually as borrowers, with the Perth Banking Co. In 1853 the Duke borrowed £20,000, and the sole condition for this loan was that all his estate business should be transacted via the Perth Banking Co.[5] but unfortunately the term of this loan was not stated. The Aberdeen Banking Co. also made advances to landowners or their factors. The Duke of Gordon borrowed £839 by August, 1770 and his factor was asked to pay the estate improvement workers only in the company's notes.[6] Robert Barclay of Urie and the Earl of Errol,[7] both noted improvers, had each borrowed £500 by 1771, although the latter was none too successful in his estate management.

The planned village must also be mentioned in the context of estate finance. These villages were often designed by landowners who hoped that they would absorb and employ surplus rural labour. Quite often, however, the 'moving spirit in the creation of the village was . . . the businessman in charge of the bleachfield rather than the local landed proprietor'.[8] Other villages were developed in terms of economic growth but were not 'planned'. George Dempster of Dunnichen, founding partner of both the Dundee and Perth United Banking Companies and founder of the Stanley Cotton Co., was a noted improver. He built the village of Letham on his estate, but unfortunately there is no evidence to suggest how this was financed. One of the most famous of the planned villages was Laurencekirk on the estate of Lord Gardenstone. The village was endowed with 'bleachfields, a printfield, linen workers, stocking knitters, cabinet makers, smiths and other sorts of country tradesmen'.[9] Gardenstone 'never claimed to do much more than grant favourable leases' to promote the village,[10] but his influence was much greater than this, for the bond registers of the Aberdeen Banking Co. reveal that he was prepared to stand as guarantor on cash account bonds for the merchants and manufacturers who set up business in Laurencekirk, and the importance of this for the development of these villages cannot be overstated. Without Gardenstone's name on the bonds it is doubtful that the credits would have been granted. Without these the businesses might never have been set up. Gardenstone was not the only landowner to provide guarantees for his tenants' loans; others who did so included Sir Alex. MacDonald of MacDonald for Portree and Sir James Grant of Grant for Granton.[11] Landowners, it would seem, seldom had sufficient resources of their own to finance this sort of development.

Although some companies had reservations about advances to farmers and landowners, the attitude towards dealers in farm products seems to have been easier. One of Scotland's staple trades was in black cattle sold in England, and the banking companies were generally prepared to finance this business. The earliest reference was in 1775 when the Aberdeen Banking Co. sought credit-worthiness references for several drovers before discounting their bills.[12] By 1788 the directors had begun to exercise caution over these discounts because the cattle dealers had been 'going about discounting with all the agents in the north and raising sums far beyond what they are entitled to'. It was feared that if anything went wrong the company 'would be taken in deeply';[13] seemingly the finance provided for these dealers was quite extensive. This type of finance was attractive to bankers because the bills offered for discount were usually drawn on London and the note issues were scattered widely, which kept them in circulation, so inevitably this created rivalry amongst the bankers. In 1809 the Dumfries agent of the Bank of Scotland complained about the activities of the Galloway Banking Co., which had allegedly

endeavoured to entice away the Bank's old customers in the cattle and grain trade by offering them higher terms for their bills on London than the Bank's Agent could give.[14]

The Galloway Banking Co's desire to have this business was the cause of its downfall and it had to retire in 1821 after an advance of £55,000 to McClellan and Campbell, cattle drovers, went bad. Bills to that extent had been discounted without any further security and the drovers had been forced to sell when prices were low.[15] It was a particularly acute example of bad banking, but it serves to illustrate the ease with which these men could obtain credit especially if they had London bills. Much of the accommodation given to cattle dealers was in the form of discounts, but there was one example of a cash account being awarded. In 1821 the Montrose Banking Co. awarded a credit of £200 to a cattle dealer from Brechin on the guarantee of a manufacturer and a woman.[16] This kind of business, however, was difficult to control as bankers found trouble in trying to assess credit-worthiness and then remaining informed of the business activities of their itinerant customers.

The grain trade has already been mentioned, and generally it enjoyed the same favours as the cattle trade. Grain dealers, maltsters and distillers were particularly 'encouraged by the facility of discounts given by the banks'.[17]

One of the most notorious and historically important features of Scottish agriculture and land management was the Highland clearances, but evidence of bank finance for this is scanty. The cash account awarded to Robert Barclay of Urie has already been mentioned. Table 39 revealed that Patrick Sellar, the most infamous of the clearers, was awarded a credit for £900 by the Aberdeen Banking Co. in 1810.[18] It is of course impossible to say what Sellar did with the money, or even how much of it he used, but the timing of the advance coincided with the beginning of his activities in the Highlands, suggesting that the money was used for clearances.

There is some evidence to suggest that the banking companies were prepared to finance other 'improvements'. B. C. Skinner has calculated that £400 was required to erect a lime kiln and its attendant buildings.[19] Unfortunately he did not suggest how much working capital was required. Some banking companies financed this industry with cash credits and possibly discounts. Table 11.1 revealed that the Aberdeen Banking Co. awarded a credit of £1,000 to the Aberdeen Lime Co. in 1813. In 1812 the Perth Banking Co. had opened a credit for £500 in the name of Patrick Bisset, tacksman of the lime works at Gourday.[20] Clearly these accounts constituted a substantial proportion of the capital requirements of businesses in the lime industry.

Examples of banking companies providing finance for various parts of the agricultural industry are numerous, but occasionally these advances were some-what irregular. In 1814 the Selkirk agent of the East Lothian Banking Co. was found to have been making 'large accommodations . . . to certain individuals as loans on land and to enable them to stock large farms, and it was thought that this was 'quite foreign to the principles of banking',[21] for fixed-term loans were usually anathema to the bankers. There was a split in the management of Hunters and Co., Ayr in 1830 because some accommodation bills had been discounted for farmers,[22] and these advances were clearly unorthodox. It must further be admitted that many of the banking companies which specialised in agricultural finance were in the long run unsuccessful. The Galloway Banking Co. has been hailed as 'an important means of mobilising capital and providing credit to land-owners, farmers and merchants in South-West Scotland',[23] but it was ultimately badly managed and had to retire. The Merchant Bank of Stirling 'speculated pretty extensively in discounting bills principally to graziers and agriculturalists',[24] but it failed in 1805, although possibly as much because of crooked management as bad business. The East Lothian Banking Co. shared a similar fate in 1822. The Falkirk Union Banking Co. failed in 1816 and it had been lending to 'men possessing large farms, store farmers, also jobbers in cattle, who bought of the feeders of stock to sell in the south'.[25] The Fife Banking Co. and Stirling Banking Co. closed in the crisis of 1825–6. Both had been making loans to agriculturalists. The Montrose Banking Co. was in poor condition when it sold out in 1829. Only the Perth Banking Co., which had fought shy of agriculture in the early 19th century, derived any gain from its farming customers. In 1855 the directors delighted in the fact that 'no small proportion' of their profits came from agriculture.[26] The message seems clear: it was easy to make mistakes with the accounts of agriculturalists.

The writings of Sir John Sinclair of Ulbster, President of the Board of Agriculture in 1793–8 and 1806–13, on this subject are interesting for their treatment of banking. Sinclair realised that one of the factors which inhibited agricultural growth was the shortage of capital, and he suggested two remedies. The first was that landowners should provide the necessary finance, and the second was that public companies should be formed 'for specific objects of improvement'. No mention was made of the possibilities of bank credit. When he discussed the banks he confined himself to a brief historical narrative of the emergence of banking and the assessment that banks were useful in augmenting the circulating medium, giving security to the transmission of property and enabling merchants and others to transact their business 'with great facility'.[27] Clearly Sinclair had a limited view of the role played by the banks and banking companies in the finance of agriculture. Perhaps his abortive efforts at forming a public bank in Glasgow in 1793 had soured his views on banking.

2. Fishing

A few companies were prepared to finance the fishing industry, the most important part of which was herring fishing. The industry required boats, barrels, salt, etc. at the beginning of the season which were often purchased with credits granted by the banking companies. The Renfrewshire and Shetland Banking Companies were the most active in this business. In the case of the latter, finance was very closely tied to the merchanting side of the business of Messrs. Hay and Ogilvy, the principal partners in the bank. Fishermen borrowed from the bank to buy supplies from the store, but such was the nature of the organisation that this developed into the store borrowing from the bank to provide supplies on credit for the fishermen.[28]

The Renfrewshire Banking Co, provided advances on cash account and upon bills drawn by the fishermen on the curers in Greenock. Roger Aytoun, manager of the company, claimed that the capital of the fishermen had generally been expended in purchasing vessels and erecting stores and that credit facilities were therefore necessary to provide them with working capital.[29] Both the Shetland and Renfrewshire Banking Companies failed in 1842 after a series of bad fishings (see Chapter 5).

The whalefishing industry also received a number of credits from banking companies and these, so far as known, are listed in Table 45.

Table 45
Scottish Provincial Banking Companies:
Cash Account Advances to Whale Fishers

Banking Co.	Fishing Co.	Date	Authorised amount
Dundee Banking Co.	Dundee Whalefishing Co.	1763	£ 500
Aberdeen Banking Co.	Whalefishing Co., Aberdeen	1785	1,000
Aberdeen Banking Co.	Whalefishing Co., Peterhead	1803	1,000
Montrose Banking Co.	Montrose Whalefishing Co.	1815	2,000
Montrose Banking Co.	Montrose Union Co.	1815	3,000
Montrose Banking Co.	New Whalefishing Co.	1820	1,000
Perth Banking Co.	Dundee Union Whalefishing Co.	1829	2,000

(Source: Minute books and bond registers)

These credits were larger than average and are undoubtedly a reflection of the capital requirements of the industry. But despite the dangerous nature of the trade the rewards could be high. The bankers were encouraged to lend in this way because of the nature of the businesses which were organised as large partnerships where all members were bound for the repayment of debts. In the case of the Montrose advances this meant that about twelve people were signatories on the bond and so the security for repayment was better than usual.

The kelp industry must also be mentioned in the context of this Chapter. There is a suggestion in the evidence of Roger Aytoun to the 1826 Promissory Notes Committee that the Renfrewshire Banking Co. was providing advances to support kelp production.[30] The industry certainly received finance from the Shetland Banking Co.,[31] but in neither case was the volume or the nature of the credit revealed. The advance of £15,000 by the Dundee Banking Co. in 1822, secured on the island of Barra, to finance the industry has already been mentioned in Chapter 6. When the duty on imported barilla was reduced in the 1820s the price of kelp declined until the industry became profitless and the money advanced by the Dundee Banking Co. was lost.[32]

NOTES

1. Perth Banking Co., D.M.B., 23/11/1809
2. Montrose Banking Co., D.M.B., *passim*
3. East Lothian Banking Co., D.M.B., *passim*
4. Dundee New Bank, D.M.B., 21/6/1802

5. Perth Banking Co., D.M.B., 4/7/1853
6. Aberdeen Banking Co., Cash a/c Ledger and D.M.B., 16/11/1770
7. Aberdeen Banking Co., Cash a/c Ledger, 1771
8. B. Lenman and E. Gauldie, Sources of Capital for Industrial Growth in East Central Scotland ... unpublished article, p. 6
9. D. Loch, *A Tour through most of the Trading Towns and Villages of Scotland, 1788,* quoted in T. C. Smout, 'The Landowner and the Planned Village in Scotland 1730–1830', in Phillipson and Mitchison (eds), 1970, p. 94
10. Lenman and Gauldie, *op. cit.*, p. 5
11. Aberdeen Banking Co., Bond Registers
12. Aberdeen Banking Co., D.M.B., 10/10/1775
13. *Ibid.*, Letter Book, 10/3/1788
14. B.S., D.M.B., 10/4/1809
15. P.P. Select Committee on Promissory Notes ... 1826, evidence of John Commelin, p. 173
16. Montrose Banking Co., D.M.B., 11/6/1821
17. B.S., Edinburgh Miscellaneous documents, reports on provincial banking companies
18. Aberdeen Banking Co., Bond Register
19. Skinner, 1969, p. 27
20. Perth Banking Co., D.M.B., 21/4/1812
21. East Lothian Banking Co., D.M.B., 5/5/1814
22. Rait, 1930, p. 181
23. Donnachie and MacLeod, 1974, p. 87
24. Cook, 1900, vol. 2
25. P.P. Select Committee on Promissory Notes ... 1826, evidence of T. Kinnear, p. 128
26. Perth Banking Co., D.M.B., 9/7/1855
27. Sinclair, 1814, vol. 3, pp. 324, 374, 445
28. N.L.S., Hay of Hayfield MSS., Acc. 3250, Box 27, f3, Box 41, f1
29. P.P. Select Committee on Promissory Notes ... 1826, evidence of Roger Aytoun, p. 191
30. *Ibid.*, p. 197
31. N.L.S., Hay of Hayfield MSS., Box 27, f1
32. Boase, 1867; B.S. 1822

13

The Finance of Trade and Transport

1. Trade

THE ill-defined and ubiquitous merchant class was the most active group in terms of share ownership – they were also the heaviest borrowers (see Tables 39 to 44). Despite the fact that these men had a wide variety of business interests, often including manufacturing, it would seem appropriate to suggest that a large part of the credit awarded to them was used to finance the movement and holding of goods rather than productive processes.

Much of this finance must have been used to assist trade at local, regional and national levels, but there was also an element devoted to the finance of international trade. The early records of the Aberdeen Banking Co. made frequent mention of the trade with Holland but, unfortunately, no reference was made to the volume of discounts or to the nature of the commodities in question.[1] In October, 1774 the Aberdeen directors also agreed to a loan of £2,000 for six months to the Edinburgh Sugar House.[2] In view of the impending war it may be guessed that this was to enable speculation to take place. At the same time the Thistle Bank was financing the warehousing of West Indian sugar in Campbeltown which was destined for re-export to Ireland.[3]

In the early 1820s the rising market for British goods was South America, where manufacturers sent goods on consignment to agents and in turn received bills accepted by the British partners of the agents. These bills were frequently at six months after sight and were discounted by the bankers, who waited on returns to be made on the sale of the goods before payment was made, which often involved renewal of the bills after the first period of six months.[4] The Glasgow Banking Co. in particular was involved in this business, and many of the bills created have survived in the archives. This type of finance was, of course, antithetical to the canons of sound banking. Nevertheless it seems that some companies were prepared to engage in it, perhaps as they had built up large balances of deposits which, because they were not likely to be so vulnerable to runs as banknotes, enabled the directors to commit some of their resources to longer-term lending. Liquidity was clearly less of a problem for the large banking companies than for the smaller ones, particularly those with little in the way of deposits.

The economy of the West of Scotland rose to prominence in the 18th century on the basis of the tobacco trade with North America; the role of the banks in financing this trade has recently been the subject of some scholarly attention. Professor Jacob Price reckoned that the banks and banking companies, although active in financing the trade, were not important in volume terms.[5] Dr. T. Devine reached a similar conclusion. He looked at the borrowings of two firms in the tobacco trade – Bogle Somervell and Co. in 1768 and Buchanan Hastie and Co. in 1777. The figures are reproduced here in Tables 46 and 47.

Table 46
Sums borrowed by Bogle, Somervell and Co. at July, 1768

Creditor	Value of loan £
Robert Lawson, late from Virginia	1,300
John Anderson, portioner of little Govan	1,000
James Graham, surgeon in Paisley	1,000
John Bell of Autermoney	1,000
James Russell, commissary clerk of Dunblain	600
Cochrane, Murdoch and Co., Bankers (Arms Bank)	500
Christina McGilchrist, relict of Robert Cross, Merchant in Glasgow	500
Mary Maxwell, daughter of deceased James Maxwell of Bogtown	433
Margaret Buchanan, daughter of deceased William Buchanan of Carbeth	300
Henry Wardrop, portioner of Dalmarnock	330
John Sym, writer in Glasgow	150
Martha Bogle, relict of Andrew Leitch, merchant	100
	Total £ 7,113

Source: Register of Deeds, B.10/15/8043, S.R.A.

Table 47
Abstract of sums owed by Buchanan, Hastie and Co. to 1777 with interest calculated to 1783

Creditor	Sums owed £		
Merchants, industrial firms, craftsmen	18,201	19	5
Banks in Glasgow	9,201	9	11
Landowners in Scotland	7,780	9	5
Trust funds of widows, orphans, spinsters, institutions	7,492	2	5
Professional groups (doctors, lawyers, clergymen, army and naval officers)	5,388	8	11
Creditors with addresses in England	2,015	16	0
Unclassified	12,165	0	0
Total	£ 62,245	6	1

Source: Currie Dal Sequestration Bt/1, Buchanan, Hastie and Co. (1777), S.R.O.

The bank cash credit bond required frequent movement of funds and must not be confused with long-term fixed borrowing from individuals. The sums borrowed from banks were 7 and 15 per cent respectively. Dr. Devine therefore concluded (Tables 46 and 47) that 'bank finance was not of central importance to either firm'.[6] Clearly there is room for disagreement on the meaning of 'central importance', but, more fundamentally, there is also a possibility that the Tables might not reflect the total extent of bank finance.

Table 46 indicates the value of loans received, but the rounded amounts involved suggest that these figures are all borrowings on bond and do not include discounts or trade credit. Furthermore, with the exception of the bank bond, all of these amounts were likely to have been medium to long-term borrowing.

This problem and indeed the figures of Table 47 raise the question of when and how does a discount at a bank appear in a firm's books as such? The drawer of a bill, having received it back accepted, might decide to hold it until maturity, in which case it would appear in his books under trade debtors or bills receivable. If he decided to discount it at a bank it would then appear in his books as cash. Thereafter he would have no more to do with the bill unless the acceptor failed to pay it. In the acceptor's books the bill would appear as trade creditors or bills payable. He would have no means of knowing what the drawer had done with it unless informed. The point to be made is that in neither case would a bill appear in the trader's final accounts books as a bank discount. Therefore traders' accounts are unreliable as a guide to bank borrowing, and Table 46 probably does, and Table 47 might, understate the extent of bank finance.

This is not, of course, to suggest that the banks were providing a large part of the capital of trading or any other firms; probably they were not. Nevertheless the view which looks at borrowing in aggregate terms, although the most popular, is not the only perspective – of equal importance to the quantity of credit was its quality. The problem of liquidity was, and is, ever present in the minds of businessmen and the great advantage of bank credit, particularly the cash account, was its flexibility, for customers could borrow and repay when they pleased. Furthermore discounts on good trade bills could be obtained easily when required. The sole exception to this was when the banker himself was caught short and lending had to be curtailed. Generally, however, the banker was an important factor in business finance and a relatively small, short-term loan from a bank could be the difference between trading and closing. No other source of business finance could provide the same degree of flexibility. The point was summed up by Dr. Devine in another article:

> partnership links between several of the tobacco firms and the Glasgow banks which were important purveyors of short-term credit for the trade, helped to exert a stabilising influence and to avert the dangers of a liquidity crisis.[7]

This rather understates the case, for it was more than just the partners and relatives of the bankers who received credit.

In all matters of business finance there are two major considerations – the volume of long-term capital to be borrowed, and the sources of short-term capital. To consider one without the other is to tell only half of the story.

2. Transport

The banking companies were prepared to give cash accounts to those responsible for the building of many of Scotland's roads. The earliest of these loans was made in 1754 when the council in Glasgow authorised the treasurer to borrow 'from any of the banks in the city for road works'. An account for £1,000 was negotiated with the Arms Bank in which Provost George Murdoch was a partner.[8] Road building was more usually undertaken by turnpike trusts, and the records of the banking companies contain numerous references regarding loans to these bodies. The trusts usually consisted of the landowners through whose property the road was to run; for example, in 1811 the Thistle Bank opened a credit for £400 for the Garscube Road on the bond of Sir Ilay Campbell of Garscube, the Hon. Archibald Campbell, Senator of the College of Justice, and John Maxwell of Dargavel, W.S.[9] For this reason the security was undoubted. The banking companies were keen to make this type of advance, and the amounts involved were often the maximum permissible in the terms of the banking company's contract. Although there was little in the way of return until the road was built, these accounts proved to be useful sources of coin once traffic was flowing through the tolls, and in some cases banking companies were prepared to make special terms for these credits. In 1829 the directors of the Perth Banking Co. approved a loan of £12,000 for the Gleneagles Road on the bond of the Duke of Atholl, Lord Strathallan, Sir Patrick Murray and several other landowners.[10] James Gibson Craig, who gave evidence to the 1826 Parliamentary Committee, believed that nearly all of the road trusts had cash accounts 'for the purpose of carrying on their operations'.[11]

Bridges came into the same category as roads. In some cases the banking companies received the public subscriptions for bridge building, and interest was allowed on these accounts. In December, 1792 the Aberdeen Banking Co. agreed to allow interest at 5 per cent on the deposit money of the Spey Bridge up to a limit of £3,000. If the balance exceeded this figure, then the rate on the excess was reduced to 4 per cent.[12] More often, however, the need was for credit. In 1765 an Act was passed authorising the building of a new bridge across the Tay at Perth. This was to be financed by public subscriptions and by a grant of £4,000 from the Board of Forfeited Estates.[13] By 1768 a cash account had been opened with the Perth United Banking Co. in the name of Patrick Miller, Burgh Chamberlain, for the Perth Bridge. The outstanding balance was £930 in 1771 and £894 in 1781.[14]

The story of the financing of the bridge is rather complicated. Seemingly the final cost was over £26,000 against an estimate by Smeaton, the architect, of £10,000, and this involved the trustees, led by the Earl of Kinnoul, in heavy borrowing. The source of the finance was not revealed but Kinnoul confessed in 1770 that he was 'personally bound to the several creditors'[15] and the toll was his security. It seems likely that the money was borrowed on the personal bond market. In 1778, however, the Perth United Banking Co. opened a credit in Kinnoul's name for £8,000. Seemingly the personal bonds had been paid off and the banking company had undertaken to make the loan. This account was kept separate from the Perth Bridge account into which the tolls were paid and from which the interest on the Kinnoul account together with parts of the principle sum were transferred annually. By 1781 there was £894 outstanding on the bridge account and £4,078 on the Kinnoul account. These sums represented 18.3 per cent of advances on cash account and 9 per cent of total advances.[16] Clearly the

Perth United had made an important contribution to the developing infrastructure of Perthshire. Although it was not the prime lender, the facilities which it was prepared to provide proved of great assistance to the trustees.

The Perth Bridge marked the greatest involvement of a banking company in a project of this nature. Other companies, however, were prepared to provide bridge trustees with credits in the same way as the road trustees. For example, in 1813 the Aberdeen Banking Co. authorised a credit of £1,000 to the trustees of the Marykirk Bridge (see Table 39).

Very little can be said about the finance of canals. These never achieved in Scotland the same importance for economic development as their counterparts in England. Between 1816 and 1837 a cash account in the name of the Monkland Navigation, arguably Scotland's most important canal, was in operation at the Glasgow Banking Co. The figures which are available are set out in Table 48.

Table 48

Sums Deposited and Borrowed for Monkland Canal from
the Glasgow Banking Co., 1816–1837[17]

	Deposited		Borrowed	
Year	High	Low	High	Low
1816	3496	805		
1817	3390	2209		
1818	138		4219	
1819	265		5256	
1820			7710	2383
1821			8011	2770
1822			7132	2985
—				
1825			11072	6621
1826			11975	6326
1827			16173	9957
1828			16900	10416
1829			15462	10461
—				
1833			17200	13990
1834			16250	7725
1835			8165	4595
1836	980		9645	
1837	2830		305	

The account was still open in the books of the Glasgow and Ship Bank in 1841 under the name of the Monkland Canal Co.[18]

The Ship Bank, Glasgow, advanced money for the construction of reservoirs on the Crinan Canal in 1808. This appears to have been a long-term loan, for the money was not recalled until 1816.[19]

The banking companies also made loans for harbour improvements. In 1774 the Aberdeen Banking Co. awarded a credit of £1,000 for the improvement of Aberdeen Harbour, and in 1812 a credit of £5,000 was given for the same purpose. There was also a credit of £1,000 in 1774 for Peterhead Harbour.[20]

By the time the railways were beginning to develop, the provincial banking companies had begun to disappear. Nevertheless at least one banking company provided finance for railways. The Coupar Angus agent of the Perth Banking Co. was warned in 1836 that no advances were to be made to the Coupar Angus and Newtyle Railway Company until a bond 'to the satisfaction of the Directors' was given for their repayment.[21] By the mid-1840s the banking company held a number of railway accounts, and in 1846 staff were given salary increases because of increases in responsibility and duty due to 'the Railway accounts and general business'. The following year the directors became aware that note issues had grown because of 'railway labourers' wages and other payments'.[22] The first clear evidence of lending occurred in 1849 when the Scottish Central Railway asked for an overdraft of £60,000 on security of debentures. There was an implied threat behind this application that if the credit was refused, then the account would be taken elsewhere, and as it was a potenially profitable account the credit was granted. In May, 1850 the railway came back for another £19,000 on the security of debentures. It is not known if the first amount had been repaid by this time, but again the loan was granted.[23] Similarly the Scottish Midland Junction Railway Company was awarded a loan of £10,000 for three years on the security of 3½ per cent debentures. This company kept two bank accounts, one with the Perth Banking Co. and the other with the joint-stock Central Bank of Scotland, also based in Perth. The Perth Banking Co. directors felt that the loan was 'likely to give the bank a better hold of the Railway Company for the continuance of their banking business'.[24] Given the situation of competitive banking, it was often the customer who could exert pressure on his banker rather than vice versa.

Only one example of a loan to a shipping company has survived. In 1841 the Perth Banking Co. awarded a cash account for £1,000 to the Dundee and Perth Steam Packet Co.[25]

The general conclusion about the provision of bank finance for the transport sector must be that the banking companies were prepared to finance a wide variety of projects. Many of these received larger than average credits, either because of the better than average security provided or because the account holder was able to exert some leverage on his banker. The transport sector was of vital importance to the process of economic development and the banking companies played an important role in helping to finance it.

NOTES

1. Aberdeen Banking Co., D.M.B., 13/9/1771, 18/10/1771, 7/6/1774
2. *Ibid.*, October, 1774
3. R.B.S., D.M.B., 1/3/1775
4. P.P. Select Committee on Promissory Notes . . . 1826, evidence of Kirkman Finlay, p. 62
5. Price, in Platt and Skaggs, 1971, p. 23; and Price, 1973, Chapter 24
6. T. M. Devine, *Business History*, 1974, p. 125
7. T. M. Devine, *S.H.R.*, 1973, p. 72
8. Renwick, vol. 6, pp. 389, 400
9. B.S. Glasgow, Thistle Bank Papers

10. Perth Banking Co., D.M.B., 12/3/1829, 8/9/1829
11. P.P. Select Committee on Promissory Notes . . . 1826, evidence of J. G. Craig, p. 265
12. Aberdeen Banking Co., Letter book, December, 1792
13. Mure of Caldwell, 1885, Part 2, vol. 2, Letters Lord Privy Seal to Mure, 5/2/1765, 23/7/1765, 21/7/1770
14. Perth United Banking Co., General Ledgers
15. Mure, *op. cit.*, Kinnoul to Mure, 21/7/1770
16. Perth United Banking Co., General Ledgers
17. Glasgow Banking Co., Cash Account Ledgers, 1816–1837
18. Glasgow and Ship Bank, Management Report, 1841
19. Lindsay, 1968, p. 126
20. Aberdeen Banking Co., D.M.B., 13/10/1774, 29/12/1774, and Bond Registers
21. Perth Banking Co., D.M.B., 7/9/1836
22. *Ibid.*, 30/11/1846, 30/11/1847
23. *Ibid.*, 3/3/1849, 31/5/1850
24. *Ibid.*, 22/7/1853
25. *Ibid.*, 11/11/1841

14

The Finance of Industry

1. Introduction

VERY many entries occurred in the cash account ledgers and discount books in the names of individuals and firms who were described as manufacturers. In many cases it has been impossible to discover the nature of their product. For example, in 1770 the Aberdeen Banking Co. decided to grant especially favourable terms on the bills of the Portsoy[1] manufacturers, but the products remain unidentified although the reference is probably to the marble business.

In other cases it has been possible to be more certain of the product, and these instances reveal that the banking companies financed a wide range of manufacturing industries. Many of these goods were standard necessities which, because they did not undergo revolutions in their organisation or technology, tend to be ignored by commentators. A few examples will serve to illustrate the range of businesses involved. In 1794 the Thistle Bank awarded a credit for £500 to the Tanwork Co. in name of Archibald Speirs of Elderslie.[2] The Montrose Banking Co. awarded a credit for £500 to a rope and sail maker in 1815, £500 to a saddler in 1820 and £400 to a shipbuilder in 1821.[3] A Montrose brewer received a credit for £350 in 1815 and an Arbroath brewer got £300 in 1821.[4]

There was even a case in 1772 where the Aberdeen Banking Co. granted a cash account for £1,000 to a manufacturer about to start up in England.[5] Furthermore the branches of the banking companies in the North of England must not be forgotten in this context. Wm. Holme and Co., manufacturers in Carlisle, requested facilities for the discounting of Glasgow bills with the East Lothian Banking Co. in 1810. The extent of this business was about £500 weekly and the banking company's notes were circulated amongst the manufacturer's employees. A similar agreement was negotiated with Messrs. Elliot and Foster, cotton manufacturers in Carlisle, the following year.[6] If these discounts are assumed to be three-month bills, then the total amount for both firms in the hands of the bank at any one time would be in the region of £13,000 (i.e. £1,000 per week for 13 weeks before the first bills were paid).

2. The Textile Industry

There were three main sectors in the textile industry – linen, cotton and wool. Very little is known about bank finance for the last of these, and the first two were so closely related in many ways that it has not always been possible to separate them for the purpose of analysis. An attempt will be made to look at each stage of production in turn.

In 1787 the Perth Banking Co. authorised its Coupar Angus agent to discount bills up to three months to yarn merchants in the Highlands.[7] In 1825 the Montrose Banking Co. was prepared to discount six-month bills for the importation of flax. A worry was expressed at the time that if the Montrose Banking Co. did not discount these long-dated bills, then the newly formed Arbroath Banking Co. would get the business[8] – not always the best reason for taking on new accounts, but obviously an important one in an age of competitive banking.

It was once said in the east of Scotland that 'the banks would not discount flax spinners' bills' because flax spinning was 'a low, mean and disreputable trade'.[9] But although this may have been the case in Dundee, there is ample evidence to show that in other areas and even in Dundee at an earlier stage spinning was not frowned upon by the bankers. In 1790 James Ivory and Co., yarn spinners of Mill of Brighton near Glammis, were awarded a cash account for £500 by the Dundee Banking Co. They were only the second flax spinners in Scotland to use power, and in 1790 they spent £1,000 erecting machinery.[10] The Baxter family in Dundee also received credits and became involved in the Dundee Commercial Banking Co. and then the Dundee New Bank. The principal trade financed by the Arbroath Banking Co. was the manufacture of flax-yarn and cloth.[11]

The best documented cases of bank finance for textiles exist in the records of the Perth United and Perth Banking Companies. The ledgers of the former revealed a large increase in total advances in the mid-1780s. The reason for this is suggested in the *Old Statistical Account*, which gives the impression of an upsurge in economic activity in the years immediately prior to its compilation in the early 1790s. The Stanley Cotton Company went into operation in 1785, and in July of that year a cash account was opened with the Perth United in the name of 'William Marshall for the Stanley Cotton Company'. This was a very active account which has been discussed in Chapter 6. Clearly the banking company was providing an important part of the firm's short-term credit needs and part of its long-term capital requirements. In addition to the cotton industry the bank was providing finance for the linen industry. The first ledger, for 1768–9, contained an account in the name of William Sandeman and Co. at Luncarty. Of the three large bleachfields in the Perth area, Luncarty was the biggest, and there were also accounts in the names of the operators of the other two bleachfields at Huntingtower and Stormont. Thomas and John Borland, the proprietors of Stormont, also owned a small cotton mill for spinning twist. There were three textile printing works located at Ruthven, Cromwell Park and Tulloch. The Perth United had made advances to at least some of the proprietors of all these works, although it is impossible to say if the money thus advanced was being used directly in the finance of these enterprises. Advances were also made to 'Macvicar and Black, Manufacturers, Perth'.[12] The product of the latter's activities has not been recorded. The *Old Statistical Account* recorded that there were 1500 looms in the city and its suburbs, the product of which was worth £100,000 annually. It also recorded that £120,000 worth of linen passed through Perth market every year and therefore through the hands of the Perth merchants. Business was booming in the 1780s, with the result that 'the town has been much enlarged of late'.[13] The participation of the Perth United in this boom was very marked, although it did not have a monopoly of banking services, for the Bank of Scotland had opened a branch in the town in 1785.

One of the very few pieces of evidence regarding bill discounts has survived in the records of the Perth Banking Co. From this it has been possible to give a more extensive picture of the pattern of advances. In the examples given the first figure in brackets refers to the cash account limit, the second figure refers to the discounts outstanding in midsummer 1808.[14] The following are examples of advances made to particular customers. To Sandeman, Turnbull and Co., bleacher, Luncarty (£1,000, £4,300). To Turnbull, Sandeman and Co., calico printers, Tulloch (£1,000, £5,200). These figures afford a good example of how the same people under different firm names could secure extra credit facilities. To Richardson and Co., bleachers, Huntingtower (£1,000, £2,000). The John Richardson who was principal in this bond owned the estate of Pitfour. Possibly this is an example of land purchase by a merchant following economic success. To Young, Ross, Richardson and Co., calico printers, Ruthven (£1,000, £39,300). This was by far the largest discount account. It seems surprising that such a large account should be permitted in a bank the paid-up capital of which was only £44,000 at the time. Six people were bound for the cash account, including James Paton, Sheriff Clerk of Perthshire. In 1824 the bank adopted the form of cash account bond used by the Bank of Scotland which stated explicitly that the amount outstanding on any unpaid bills could be debited to a cash account where 'the primary obligant on the bond shall be either drawer, acceptors or indorsers'.[15] This had the effect of making the securities on the bond responsible for the unpaid bill. It was not revealed how often, if at all, use was made of this clause. To James Fitchie, manufacturer, Perth (£500, £3,700). The two securities on this bond were a London-based umbrella maker and tinplate worker. Perth sent a lot of the umbrella cloth which was made there to Manchester and London. Fitchie was also a bleacher at Meigle. To Thomas Kennedy and Co., manufacturers, Perth (£500, £2,000). The obligants on this bond were other members of the Sandeman and Turnbull families. Most of these customers were also partners.

Other advances to textile manufacturers included £300 on cash account by the Dundee New Bank in 1802 to Alex. Melville, cotton manufacturer and £200 to Thos. Wemyss, bleacher at Balgillo;[16] £500 by the Thistle Bank in 1793 to David Marshall and Co., inkle (ribbon) manufacturers;[17] £200 by the Paisley Union Banking Co. in 1821 to a thread manufacturer;[18] and £3,000 by the Glasgow Banking Co. in 1835 to the Culcreuch Cotton Co.[19]

Research on capital formation in the cotton industry is in progress, and it may be that the specific examples of bank finance given above may be set in the context of total capital. But until that time the historian must content himself with the knowledge that the cost of setting up a cotton mill in the industrial revolution was relatively small:

> A small spinning mill, using horsepower, was never valued at more than £1,000, an Arkwright type watermill of the 1780's between £3,000 and £5,000; the large multi-storied steam mills, which appeared in the 1790's alone were worth £10,000 to £15,000.[20]

Some firms of course rented their building, a practice which substantially reduced their fixed capital requirements. Much capital was accumulated on a ploughed-back profits basis, but clearly the banking companies were prepared to go a long way to meet the capital requirements of textile manufacturers.

Bankers were less important as lenders to the woollen industry than to linen and cotton. Banks 'seem to have played only a small part in the Scottish woollen industry before the 1820's' but from then on they played 'an important role by injecting credit into the system by discounting bills of exchange'.[21] Unfortunately it is impossible to say what part the provincial banking companies played in this.

Clearly the banking companies were prepared to finance at least some sections of the textile industry on a quite extensive scale.

3. The Iron Industry

The iron industry in Scotland was also the recipient of bank finance. The most striking development in this industry in the 18th century was the formation and development of the Carron Iron Co.

Carron first received finance from the Royal Bank in the early 1760s, but as the company's policy was to raise money by a chain of bills it became the practice to borrow from several banks and banking companies. An account was opened with Mansfield, Hunter and Co., private bankers in Edinburgh, from whom Carron borrowed £7,000, later increased to £15,000. The Thistle Bank in Glasgow 'offered £200 weekly to be settled by acceptance at four months, with the possibility of this being extended to six months, giving altogether £5,600'. When the Ayr Bank (Douglas, Heron and Co.) opened for business in 1769 it awarded a credit of £5,000 to Carron which was later extended to £8,400. In 1769 the Carron Iron Co. owed £28,255 to bankers, and from 1769 to 1772 'the Company was predominantly financed by the circulation of bills'.[22]

At a later date the Thistle Bank seems to have concluded a similar arrangement with the Wilsontown Ironworks. In the year to March 1799 the sum of £6,500 was sent and in 1801 the remittances were £5,800. The money was sent in parcels of between £300 and £600 usually at monthly intervals.[23] Unfortunately the method of settlement and the total credit involved are not known.

The Balgonie Iron Co., which failed in 1811, kept accounts with the Cupar Banking Co., the British Linen Co. Cupar Branch, the Commercial Bank of Scotland, Edinburgh, and a London private banker. This company raised cash by the familiar chain of bills method. The Cupar Banking Co. in particular discounted these bills, giving either cash for them or paying 'to the order of the company as they had occasion for money'.[24] The scale of this business is not known, but it seems that the Cupar Banking Co. had managed to extricate itself from the business before the sequestration. In 1811 the iron company owed only £405 on ten bills to the banking company. Nevertheless the latter retired from business in that year.

In 1843 the Monkland Steel Co. owed money to the Glasgow and Ship Banking Co. but the extent of the advance was not revealed.[25]

Apart from finance for iron and steel production, the banking companies were also prepared to provide finance for iron foundries. The records of the banking companies revealed cash accounts in the name of foundries in nearly every town. For example, the Perth Banking Co., by summer 1808, had awarded a cash account for £500 to the Perth Foundry Co. and had discounted bills to the extent of £900.[26]

4. The Coal Industry

The lack of information given on customers' business ventures in bank records renders analysis of bank finance for industry extremely difficult. This is especially so of the coal industry where development was usually undertaken by individuals or simple partnerships rather than companies, as in the iron industry. Nevertheless it is possible to speculate that the coal industry did receive bank finance, because a number of coalmasters were heavily involved as partners and borrowers in the banking companies. For example, George Houston of Johnstone was a partner in the Paisley Union Banking Co., Andrew Thomson of Faskin was a partner in the Paisley Banking Co. and later formed his own private banking company in Glasgow, and James Dunlop of Garnkirk was a partner in the Greenock Banking Co. and was its Glasgow manager until his failure in 1793. At this time Dunlop owed £32,387 to the Greenock Banking Co. and £9,100 to the Royal Bank.[27] It seems likely that Dunlop had used at least some of this money to finance his coal interests.

It is possible to be more specific in a few cases. In 1790 Messrs. Cunninghame and Walker received two loans at 4½ per cent for £2,332 and £2,200 on the joint bond of the partners from Hunters and Co., Ayr. Wm. Taylor received £6,000 from the same firm to finance his coal interests at Nethermains.[28] In 1810 the East Lothian Banking Co. awarded a cash account for £1,000 to John Grieve of Sheriffhall Colliery.[29]

5. The Whisky and Brewing Industries

It would be wrong to conclude this chapter without some mention of the whisky industry which, although it was not a major activity in the industrial revolution period, has since grown to be one of Scotland's most important industrial activities.

The Renfrewshire Banking Co. was particularly important to this industry. Finance was provided for distilleries 'in Argyleshire, and in the Islands and at

Greenock'. In particular, it was claimed that the distilleries of Argyleshire depended almost entirely upon the branches of the Renfrewshire Banking Co. for their supplies of cash.[30]

Robert More and Co., distillers at Underwood near Denny in Stirlingshire, received a cash credit from the Glasgow Banking Co. for £1,000 in 1825.[31] Other Stirlingshire distillers received credit, some of it unauthorised, from the Stirling Banking Co.; for example, Messrs Forrester and Buchanan, grocers in Stirling and distillers at Greenloaning, discounted bills to the extent of £20,000 in the early 1820s.[32] Generally the grain dealers, maltsters and distillers in the area 'were encouraged by the facility of discounts given by the banks'.[33]

The historian of the Scottish brewing industry discovered that 'banks had a considerable interest in making credit available to breweries'.[34] Most of the credit provided was on bill discounts, and banks in all corners of the country were involved in financing this industry.

NOTES

1. Aberdeen Banking Co., D.M.B., 9/3/1770
2. Thistle Banking Co., Cash Credit Bonds
3. Montrose Banking Co., D.M.B., 20/10/1815, 8/11/1820, 30/1/1821
4. *Ibid.*, 3/12/1817, 11/5/1821
5. Aberdeen Banking Co., D.M.B., 25/12/1772
6. East Lothian Banking Co., D.M.B., 20/8/1810, 9/5/1811
7. Perth Banking Co., D.M.B., 20/4/1787
8. S.R.O., CS311–2142, Box 207, Arbroath Branch to Montrose Banking Co., 2/5/1825
9. Quoted by Lenman and Gauldie (1973) from Lamb Collection, Douglastown MSS., 196 (19), 'Flax spinning by machinery prior to 1832'
10. Boase, 1867, b.s.28; and Lenman and Gauldie, 1968, pp. 163–4
11. P.P., Select Committee on Promissory Notes . . . 1826, evidence of Hugh Watt, p. 188
12. Perth United Banking Co., General Ledgers, 1768–1787
13. *Old Statistical Account*, Perth
14. Perth Banking Co., Bill book and bond register, 1808
15. *Ibid.*, D.M.B., 17/3/1824
16. Dundee New Bank, D.M.B., 21/5/1802, 10/7/1802
17. B.S., Glasgow, Thistle Bank bonds
18. Paisley Union Banking Co., D.M.B., 20/8/1821
19. B.S. Glasgow, Miscellaneous Papers
20. Crouzet, 1972, p. 37
21. Gulvin, 1973, p. 62
22. Campbell, 1961, pp. 129–32
23. B.S., Glasgow, Miscellaneous Papers
24. S.R.O., CS96/203, Sequestration book of Balgonie Iron Co.
25. Glasgow and Ship Banking Co., D.M.B., 1/2/1843
26. Perth Banking Co., Bond Register and Discount Book
27. G.U.L., Murray Collection Mu23 B19, notes by J. Buchanan
28. Duckham, vol. 1, 1970, p. 194
29. East Lothian Banking Co., D.M.B., 22/11/1810
30. P.P., Select Committee on Promissory Notes . . . 1826, evidence of Roger Aytoun, p. 199, and Lords Committee, p. 129
31. B.S., Glasgow, Glasgow Banking Co., Cash account bonds
32. S.R.O., CS96/2346, Stirling Banking Co. Sequestration book, p. 541
33. B.S., Edinburgh, miscellaneous documents
34. Donnachie, 1979, Ch. 4, especially Table 32

15

The Finance of Local Government
and Public Utilities

THE century under review saw many developments in the growth of local government and the provision of public utilities – notably in the establishment of gas, water and paving services and in the maintenance of public order. The banking companies financed some of this development on a fairly extensive scale, although here again the banks were not the major lenders.

The maintenance of public order was particularly difficult at times, and local authorities had few qualms about calling in the army to quell unrest. Early in 1812 the cashier of the East Lothian Banking Co. set off

> for Glasgow to make arrangements for paying the different Regiments that are ordered to that city in consequence of some disturbances among the Weavers.[1]

The period of the Napoleonic Wars was an active time for the formation of regiments and the movement of troops. In Scotland large numbers of troops were stationed in East Lothian, and the local banking company captured most of the business of financing these units.[2] The formation of regiments of volunteers was also financed by the banking companies; for example, the Perth Banking Co. awarded a cash credit for £100 in 1794 for the raising of the Perthshire Fencible Cavalry by the Duke of Atholl. Similarly the Earl of Kinnoul's contribution, the Perthshire Regiment of Gentlemen and Yeomen, received a cash account for £500 in 1799.[3]

The town councils of Scotland have a long history of borrowing from banks and banking companies as well as from private individuals. In 1754 the Glasgow Council borrowed £1,000 from the Arms Bank – money which was earmarked for expenditure on the roads (see Chapter 13) but which was spent on 'general purposes'. The credit was authorised for 'what sums the town shall stand in need of'.[4] By 1757 the town had credits at both the Ship and Arms Banks for £1,500 each, and thereafter the story is one of frequent borrowing from the banks as the need arose. In 1767 £550 was borrowed from the Arms Bank on the magistrates' joint bill to discharge pressing debts owed by the town, and the first income received was earmarked for the repayment of this loan.[5]

Also in the Glasgow area the Burgh of Calton borrowed £250 from the Glasgow and Ship Bank in 1842. Of this the Police Department received £187–10/–, and the remainder went to the Statute Labour Department.[6]

Water was supplied by private companies, and in 1830 the Glasgow Water Works Co. had a credit for £30,000 with the Glasgow Banking Co.[7]

In Aberdeen the town treasurer and the dean of guild each received credits for £1,000 from the newly formed Aberdeen Banking Co. in 1767,[8] and in the following year the Aberdeen bankers cast their credit further afield and provided a cash account for £500 to the magistrates of Montrose.[9]

The Dundee Banking Co. authorised an advance of £100 to the town of Dundee in 1768, and in 1773 this was formalised into a regular cash account. In 1795 the Town Council borrowed £500 for the purpose of raising men for the navy. Credits were also provided in 1767 for the Burgh of Brechin, and £400 and £100 for the City of St. Andrews.[10] In 1832 the Dundee magistrates borrowed £550 from the Dundee New Bank to enable them to enforce the new Cholera Acts and Orders of the Privy Council. The assessment was to be the security.[11]

In Perth the Perth United Banking Co. provided accounts for Patrick Miller, burgh chamberlain, but this account was seldom overdrawn. This was in addition to his account for the Perth Bridge mentioned in Chapter 13. Patrick Miller, sheriff clerk of Perthshire, and Robert Oliphant of Rossie, Postmaster General, had cash accounts but these were likely to have been personal accounts. In 1776 a loan of £4,500 was made in name of 'the community of Perth' and this was paid off in 1783.[12]

When the Perth Banking Co. replaced the Perth United in 1787, the practice of lending to the local authority continued unabated. In 1811 an account for £500 was awarded for street paving and lighting and in 1815 a discount of £3,000 was made to finance the building of a new jail, which was followed in 1816 by an agreement to provide up to £13,000 for the erection of new County Public Buildings. In 1829 special loans were made of £250 to the King James Hospital and £2,500 to the Gas Light Co.[13]

In 1813 the Dunbar Council borrowed £500 on bond from the East Lothian Banking Co. Under the heading 'Resolutions anent Economy' the Council, on which several of the banking companies' directors figured prominently, resolved that

the town should have a cash account with one of the Banks for £500 in the name of the Chamberlain who shall have the exclusive right to draw.

Most of this money was used to pave a new street and repair others. The remainder was used in the purchase of the army barracks which were later converted into a cotton factory.[14]

In Dumfries the burgh opened a credit with the local branch of the Ayr Bank in November, 1770. There was a steady stream of withdrawals which had reached £1,185 by September 1771, and when the Bank failed in June, 1772 the burgh owed £3,637. This sum was repaid at Michaelmas 1772. Rather mysteriously the relevant account pages have been torn from the burgh chamberlain's account book for that year.[15]

Many banking companies were prepared, in times of food shortage and high prices, to make special loans to local authorities to provide food for the poor.

These were often interest-free or at least at a reduced rate of interest. In January, 1783 the Aberdeen Banking Co. lent £3,000 to the City of Aberdeen and £500 each to the burghs of Banff, Elgin, Forres and Inverness to help in feeding the poor.[16] At the same time the Dundee Banking Co. made similar loans, i.e. £1,500 for Dundee and £500 each for Forfar and Arbroath.[17] In Perth, the bankers agreed to pay the duty on the importation of oats at their 'patriotic effort' to help feed the poor.[18] A similar situation arose in 1795–6 when the bankers responded in the same way.

Clearly the banking companies were prepared to finance local government and public utilities on a fairly extensive scale. Many municipal corporations, however, were badly, and sometimes corruptly, managed. The Commission appointed to enquire into the administration of these corporations in 1835 reported that the borrowing powers of local authorities were extensive and might be quite useful,

> yet the practice is in its own nature, of such a dangerous tendency, that if not absolutely prohibited, it ought at least to be placed under rigid control.[19]

By that time, however, the days of the Scottish provincial banking companies were almost at an end.

NOTES

1. East Lothian Banking Co., D.M.B., 13/2/1812
2. *Ibid.*, 12/3/1812
3. Perth Banking Co., D.M.B., 16/4/1794, 12/2/1799
4. Renwick, *Extracts from the Records of the Burgh of Glasgow*, vol. 6, p. 400
5. *Ibid.*, vol. 7
6. B.S., Glasgow, Miscellaneous Papers
7. *Ibid.*, Minutes of Committee of Management, Glasgow Water Works Co., 5/5/1830
8. See Table 29
9. Aberdeen Banking Co., Bond Registers
10. Boase, 1867, pp. 70. 90. 187 and b.s.8
11. Dundee New Bank, Miscellaneous documents
12. Perth United Banking Co., General Ledgers, 1768–87
13. Perth Banking Co., D.M.B., 28/6/1811, 26/9/1815, 4/12/1816, 11/5/1829
14. S.R.O., B18/13/7, Dunbar Council Minute Book, 29/10/1813 and July, 1819
15. Dumfries burgh chamberlain's account books, 1770–1772
16. Aberdeen Banking Co., Agenda Note Books, 1783
17. Boase, 1867, p. 129
18. Rait, 1930, p. 133
19. P.P., General Report of the Commissioners on the Municipal Corporations of Scotland, 1835, p. 37

Conclusion

Were the Scottish Provincial Banking Companies Successful?

THE selection of criteria by which to assess a banking system is always a difficult task. In this case four have been chosen: two businessmen's yardsticks and two historians' measurements. Survival and return on capital employed are the principal means by which a businessman might judge a system. An historian on the other hand might be more concerned with the contribution to the growth of the economy and the alacrity with which bankers met the needs of their customers. All four criteria can be reviewed in terms of the extent to which they contributed towards or undermined the stability of the economy.

The literature on Scottish banking generally between 1820 and 1870 is replete with praise of Scottish banking. Anyone who read it and was then asked if Scottish banking was successful would be bound to answer an unhesitating 'yes' on all counts. The eulogies on Scottish banking and the hagiographies of bankers which form the bulk of the literature began with Thomas Joplin in 1822. He claimed that

> the Scotch banks never fail, nor is any danger ever apprehended from them; and . . . in consequence Banking is carried on in that kingdom to an extent unknown, and of course, with advantages totally unfelt in our own.[1]

Joplin's essay was highly polemical, but he was not alone in holding the Scottish banking system in high regard. The prospectus of many an English and Irish joint-stock bank, founded following the legislation of 1826 and 1833, paid tribute to the system of banking which had developed in Scotland; for example, the Huddersfield Banking Co. prospectus stated that 'the prosperity of the Bank of England and the Bank of Ireland is very well known; and that of the Scottish banks has not been at all inferior'.[2] This praise was translated into practical terms by the recruitment of many Scottish-trained bankers into the service of the English and Irish joint-stock banks.

A writer in the *Bankers' Magazine* of 1845 expressed his gratitude to the Scottish people

> for having fostered and firmly established the soundest and most beneficial system of banking and currency, that has ever been in existence, during a century and a half.[3]

Nor were the Scots unaware of their own successes. The directors of the Perth Banking Co. thought Scottish banking to be 'the most perfect system of banking and currency which has ever been exhibited in the world'.[4] Perhaps the greatest compliment to Scottish banking was paid by the Bank of England which excluded Scotsmen from its senior managment, it is said, for fear that, once admitted, they would soon engross the whole concern. It would seem that, in some circles, the success achieved by Scotsmen was in inverse proportion to their popularity. Praise of the Scottish system became less vociferous and less enthusiastic after the failure of the joint-stock Western Bank of Scotland in 1857; and when the City of Glasgow Bank stopped in 1878 the praises died, at least for a time. The reason for this was not just that the Scottish system had been seen to be fallible, but also that the English joint-stock banking system had grown to maturity and had achieved successes of its own. There was no longer a need to study and copy the Scots. The French and Japanese came to study banking in Scotland, but that is another story, for by that time the provincial banking companies, with which this book is concerned, were extinct.

Between 1747 and 1836 no fewer than 45 provincial banking companies were founded. Of these, 26 – i.e. 58 per cent – were partnerships of twelve or fewer members and 19 – i.e. 42 per cent – were co-partneries with thirteen or more shareholders. Nevertheless, despite their numerical inferiority, it was principally around the co-partneries in company with the public banks that the image of respectability, stability and profitability was constructed. It remains to be seen how justified was this characterisation.

Table 49 sets out the names of the provincial banks, together with their dates of opening and closure, the number of partners at close (or nearest date known), the fate of the banks, their condition at closure, and losses sustained by the public in cases of failure, if any.

The first criterion to be considered is success in terms of survival, especially freedom from failure. This of course may not properly be considered to be an historian's judgement, as failures are an expected feature of any group of business enterprises, and often serve a process of renewal. Consequently no moral censure is intended. The freedom from failure of a business is very much an entrepreneur's criterion of success and it is largely from his point of view that this section must be viewed. More particularly the following remarks are aimed at correcting the historical records by disproving Joplin's statement that there were no failures and by outlining the pattern of closure experienced by the provincial banking companies.

Comparisons will be made where possible between the two types of Scottish provincial banking companies and between the Scottish and English systems. The first company was opened in 1747 and the last closed in 1864, and between those two dates there was a wide variety of experience. Looking firstly at the negative side, of the 45 banks, 15 failed, i.e. 33 per cent of bank formations in this group. This statistic, by itself, goes a long way to dent the image. Comparisons with England are full of hazard, but it seems that of approximately 1,000 country bank formations before 1830, about 340, i.e. one third, failed. This compares with a failure rate of one fifth for Scotland in the same period, i.e. before 1830.

Table 49

Scottish Provincial Banking Companies 1747–1864

Name	Opened	Closed	No. of partners at close	Fate	Conditions at close	Debts
1) Banking Co. at Aberdeen	1747	1753	4	retired	declining	paid in full
2) Aberdeen Banking Co.	1767	1849	424	merged Union Bank	declining	paid in full
3) Commercial Banking Co. of Aberdeen	1788	1833	15	merged National Bank	declining	loss to public £116,000
4) John Maberly & Co., Aberdeen	1818	1832	1	failed		
5) Arbroath Banking Co.	1825	1844	80	merged Commercial Bank	good	
6) McAdam and Co., Ayr	1763	1771	15	merged Ayr Bank	declining	paid in full
7) Douglas, Heron and Co., Ayr	1769	1772	241	failed		
8) Hunters and Co., Ayr	1773	1843	11	merged Union Bank	declining	paid in full
9) Caithness Banking Co.	1812	1825	1	merged Commercial Bank	unknown	
10) Cupar Banking Co.	1802	1811	3	retired	declining	paid in full
11) Johnston, Lawson and Co., Dumfries	1766	1771	19	merged Ayr Bank	declining	
12) Dumfries Commercial Bank	1804	1808	3	failed	declining	paid 10/- per £1, loss to public c. £10,000
13) Dundee Banking Co.	1763	1864	80	merged Royal	declining	
14) Dundee Commercial Bank No. 1	1792	1802	4	re-formed as Dundee New	declining	
15) Dundee New Bank	1802	1838	5	merged Dundee Banking Co.	declining	
16) Dundee Union Bank	1809	1844	98	merged Western	declining	
17) Dundee Commercial Bank No. 2	1825	1838	140	retired	declining	paid in full
18) East Lothian Banking Co.	1810	1822	58	failed	criminal mismanagement	paid in full

Name	Opened	Closed	No. of partners at close	Fate	Conditions at closure	Debts
19) Falkirk Banking Co.	1787	1826	5	retired	good	paid in full
20) Falkirk Union Banking Co.	1803	1816	6	failed		paid 9/6 per £1, loss to public c. £26,000
21) Fife Banking Co.	1802	1825	48	failed	criminal mismanagement	paid in full
22) Galloway Banking Co.	1806	1821	4	retired	declining	paid in full
23) Ship Bank, Glasgow	1750	1838	6	merged Glasgow Bank	good	paid in full
24) Arms Bank, Glasgow	1750	1793	4	failed		paid in full
25) Thistle Bank, Glasgow	1761	1836	8	merged Union Bank	declining	
26) Watsons, Glasgow	1763	1832	2	failed		paid 4/9 per £1, loss to public c. £60,000
27) Merchant Bank of Glasgow	1769	1798	48	failed		paid in full
28) Thomsons, Glasgow	1785	1793	3	failed		paid in full
29) Glasgow Bank	1809	1836	14	merged Ship Bank	good	
30) Glasgow and Ship	1836	1843	28	merged Union Bank	declining	
31) Greenock Banking Co.	1785	1843	6	merged Western Bank	declining	
32) Kilmarnock Banking Co.	1802	1821	4	merged Hunters and Co.	declining	
33) Leith Banking Co.	1792	1842	4	failed	declining	paid 3/7 per £1, loss to public c. £42,000
34) Montrose Banking Co.	1814	1829	98	merged National Bank	declining	
35) Paisley Banking Co.	1783	1837	4	merged British Linen	declining	
36) Paisley Union Banking Co.	1788	1838	3	merged Union Bank	good	
37) Perth United Banking Co.	1766	1787	87	re-formed as Perth Banking Co.	good	
38) General Bank of Perth	1767	1772	42	retired	not known	
39) Perth Banking Co.	1787	1857	177	merged Union Bank	good	paid in full

Table 49

Scottish Provincial Banking Companies 1747–1864 – *contd.*

Name	Opened	Closed	No. of partners at close	Fate	Conditions at closure	Debts
40) Perth Union Bank	1810	1836	73	merged National Bank	declining	paid 9/3 per £1, loss to public £122,000
41) Renfrewshire Banking Co.	1802	1842	3	failed		
42) Shetland Bank	1821	1842	2	failed		paid 3/- per £1, loss to public £55,000
43) Stirling Banking Co.	1777	1826	7	failed		paid in full
44) Merchant Bank of Stirling	1784	1805	7	failed	criminal	paid 14/9 per £1, loss to public £13,000
45) Campbell, Thomson and Co.	1787	1798	4	retired	mismanagement not known	paid in full

Table 49
Scottish Provincial Banking Companies 1747–1864 – *contd.*

Number of Banks 45

Failures	a)	business	12
	b)	criminal	3

$$\overline{15} = 33\%$$

Mergers	a)	good	5
	b)	declining	15
	c)	unknown	1

$$\overline{21} = 47\%$$

Retirals	a)	good	1
	b)	declining	4
	c)	unknown	2

$$\overline{7} = 16\%$$

Re-formed 2

$$\overline{2} = 4\%$$

N.B. Declining = profits and/or demand liabilities decreasing

Failures	*Number*	*% of total*	*% of group*
Partnerships	11	73	42
Co-partneries	4	27	21

Lifespan	*Average in years*
Partnerships	34
Co-partneries	29
Overall	32

There were failures in Lerwick 1, Aberdeen 1, Stirling 2, Cupar 1, Falkirk 1, Leith 1, Dunbar 1, Dumfries 1, Ayr 1, Greenock 1, and Glasgow 4. There does not appear to be any geographical pattern to these occurrences, for failures happened in rural areas, market towns, ports and industrial centres. It is to the types of business conducted and to the effects of trade cycles that one must look for the causes of collapse. Commercial slumps precipitated the demise of several banks. The Ayr Bank (Douglas, Heron and Co.) failed in 1772 and must be thought to have been in some measure responsible for the crisis of that year. Two Glasgow companies failed in 1793, at least one of which had been involved in making long-term advances to the building industry, and a third Glasgow company collapsed in 1798. The Falkirk Union Banking Co. failed in 1816. Its partners, who were also substantial debtors, were involved in agriculture and distilling. They suffered from the decline in prices of their products. The Stirling Banking Co. collapsed in the crisis of 1825–6. Messrs. J. & R. Watson, the Glasgow-based private bank, failed in 1832 because it had over-extended itself to one customer by whom it incurred substantial bad debts. The reasons for the closures of the Dumfries Commercial Banking Co. in 1808 and John Maberly and Co. in 1832 are not known. Three companies, namely Shetland, Renfrewshire and Leith, failed in 1842 – all had been involved in making substantial advances to the fishing industry which had suffered a series of poor catches and had recently lost the West Indies market. Lastly, three banks collapsed for the very good reason that the cashiers ran off with the money. In short, it may be stated that the underlying causes of most of the failures which did occur were cyclical trade pressures and bad management; structural weaknesses were a lesser, though possibly still important, element.

In terms of the sub-division of provincial banking companies, the co-partneries performed better than the partnerships. The former group incurred four failures while the latter had eleven. In percentage terms these were 27 per cent and 73 per cent of total failures respectively. Co-partneries as a group had a 21 per cent failure rate, while 42 per cent of partnerships failed. Total losses to the public from failures were about £440,000, all from partnerships, but losses to the public from bank failures are a banker's rather than an economic historian's criterion of judgement. In fact losses to partners, although unquantifiable, were much greater. The loss to a partner of his share of the capital was often worsened by further calls on capital or even by sequestration of his estate. As partners in banking companies were often the leading citizens of an area, particularly in terms of that area's economic development, financial loss or sequestration would have a stultifying effect on growth.

Herbert Heaton has suggested that the collapse of some of the English country banks left whole areas utterly devoid of banking services,[5] but this never really happened in Scotland. Even when the Ayr Bank collapsed in 1772, moves were already afoot to form another local bank in that town. Hunters and Co. was founded in 1773. Dumfries, where Douglas, Heron and Co. had a branch, was the site chosen by the Bank of Scotland for one of its first branches in 1774. There was always a local or national initiative ready to fill gaps in the provision of financial services caused by failures or retirals.

Mergers caused the disappearance of 21 banking companies. Of these, fifteen had ceased, or were about to cease, to be viable business enterprises (i.e. profits and/or demand liabilities were decreasing). A further five were in good condition and the state of one is unknown. The most noteworthy aspect of this movement is its timing. Thirteen provincials disappeared and one appeared as a result of mergers in the period 1833–1844, and no fewer than ten of these were absorbed by public and, more often, joint-stock banks. The other mergers were between provincial banks which combined with one another in an attempt to meet the competition from the arrivistes. The Edinburgh private banks also disappeared in this period. The major causes of this decline (i.e. loss of profits and circulation) have been discussed in Chapter 5. It seems that, once weakened, a company did not take long to find a way out, for there was little chance to retreat into a protective cocoon. Evidently, if many of these companies had not been taken over, they would have failed. Generally, in terms of freedom from failure, it must be acknowledged that the co-partneries fared better than the partnerships, although the former were by no means exempt from the pressures to which Scottish banking was subject. Many of them escaped losses and failures only by entering the embrace of larger business organisations whose economies of scale enabled them to withstand the pressures. The result of the 'principle of combination and of rivalry . . . had been to weed out the weak concerns and to leave the strong institutions in possession of the field'.[6]

Looked at more positively, however, the pattern of success is somewhat different if the lifespans of the banks are taken into consideration. The average of all provincial companies was 32 years. That of the co-partneries was 29 years and that of the partnerships was 34 years. Unfortunately, no comparable figures are available for the English country banks. The Scottish figures suggest that the partnerships survived longer than the co-partneries, but this suggestion must be somewhat qualified. Given that a concentrated period of decline did not occur until the 1830s, the seeming superiority of the partnerships may be explained, quite naturally, by the early start theory. Of the 26 concerns formed before 1800, sixteen were partnerships and ten were co-partneries, and the survival of many of these banks into the 1830s has tended to augment the average lifespan of the partnerships because they were a majority of the early formations. Nevertheless, although these figures do not prove that the partnerships were in any way superior to the co-partneries, they do suggest that there was nothing inherently inferior about the partnership form of organisation. Partnerships, given sound management, could survive just as well as the larger co-partneries.

Much of the praise heaped upon the Scottish banking system stemmed from the crisis of 1825–6 in which 60 English country banks failed – only two Scots banks collapsed, both of them towards the end of the crisis. In particular, the 1826 Parliamentary enquiry into the working of the Scottish banking system gave to bankers from north of the border the opportunity to extol the virtues of their system. Most of those questioned about the extent of failure were either ill-informed or conveniently forgot about half of the eight failures which had occurred before 1825, and the publicity given to the achievements of the system by Sir Walter Scott, alias Malachi Malagrowther, added to the image of success. In fact the percentage of failures amongst provincial banking companies when Scott wrote had reached 19. Clearly some of the failures amongst small banks had caused barely a ripple. The major successes, however, and the factor which most impressed the English commentators, were the public banks, together with the Commercial Bank which had extended branch offices throughout Scotland. The provincial companies, particularly the co-partneries, which were closest to the public banks in organisational form, were a secondary, though still significant, consideration.

Comparisons between Scottish provincial banking companies and English country banks are particularly difficult. The relative sizes of the two systems indicate something of the problem. At the end of the Napoleonic wars each of the counties of Yorkshire, Somerset and Devon had more banks than the whole of the Scottish provinces excluding branches. The Scots banks were able to issue £1 notes which, with the exception of the 1797–1826 period, were not allowed in England. Deposits at interest were generally accepted by the Scots before the practice became common in England, and the same can be said of branch extensions. Comparisons in terms of failure rates are not particularly fruitful because the structures of the two systems were so different for much of the period; for example, there were no public banks operating in the English provinces as there were in Scotland.

2. Profitability

The question of profitability has been discussed in Chapter 6 and the relevant figures were reproduced in Tables 12 to 17.

The conclusion was that profits tended to be higher than those of the Bank of England and Bank of Scotland but lower than those of the English country banks. It was argued that the greater inter-bank competition in Scotland placed constraints on the charges which bankers were able to levy compared to England, and of course the corollary of this was that customers of the Scottish banks and banking companies paid less for their credit than did those of the English country banks.

3. Customer Satisfaction

Customer satisfaction is a qualitative criterion rather than a quantitative measure of success, and the treatment of this aspect of banking performance must therefore be somewhat impressionistic.

The first provincial banking company was founded in Aberdeen in 1747 and this was quickly followed by two formations in Glasgow, both of which opened in 1750. From there the system spread in the following two decades to cover the major provincial towns – Dundee, Dumfries, Ayr, Stirling and Perth. Later decades witnessed further formations in the lesser burghs and second formations in the larger towns. It was essentially customer demand which called these banking companies into being. Faced with the early unwillingness of the public banks to provide banking services, the provincial merchants and manufacturers exercised their own initiative and set up a series of banks throughout the country. In many cases the partners were the first customers, so that banking company formations may be characterised as self-help by merchants with financial problems. But the monetary needs of others were not ignored. Of the first hundred cash accounts awarded by the Aberdeen Banking Company, 46 went to non-partners.[7] The records of other companies tell similar tales.

In general the provincial banking system was prepared to provide short-term credit and cash facilities to a wide variety of sizes and types of business enterprises on condition that, in the case of cash credits, the signatories to the bond were thought to be 'good', and in the case of discounts that the bill was 'real'. The provincial bankers tended to devote more of their resources to advances than did the public banks, which invested heavily in government securities. This policy of the public banks was often criticised by commentators as being contrary to the common good, and seems to have been a contributing factor to the establishment of the freer-lending Commercial Bank in 1810. Nevertheless, the public banks were the system's reserve and were often asked for loans by provincial banks which found themselves with liquidity problems. Although individual banks both in Edinburgh and the provinces might occasionally have been criticised for tight lending policies, the system was always sufficiently flexible, in the years from 1760 to 1845, to generate new banks which supplied the demand for credit.

The banking companies provided further valuable services for customers by taking their deposits at interest, providing inter-town money transfer facilities and issuing banknotes. The supply of a circulating medium was a great boon to a country which was so often short of specie because of its precarious balance of payments and the poor state of the coinage. Consequently, notes found a ready acceptance. In particular, the £1 note was highly valued, as is attested by the evidence of Scottish bankers to the 1826 Committees. These Committees were set up as a result of pressure from North Britain when the Government proposed to forbid the issue of notes under £5 in Scotland for the sake of uniformity with England. The issuing of small notes was 'found compatible with the highest degree of solidity'. The cash credit system which it fostered 'had the best effects upon the people of Scotland'.[8]

The generally larger size of the banking companies and greater resources ensured that the performance of the Scottish provincial banking companies in terms of customer satisfaction was more impressive than that of the English country banks.

4. Economic Growth

No study of country banking in Scotland would be complete without some assessment of the contribution which the system made to economic growth. Unfortunately two factors militate against such an estimate in the case of Scotland.

Firstly, and most importantly, no one has, as yet, produced a set of national income statistics for Scotland. Secondly, the banking companies formed only a part, mostly a minor one, of the Scottish banking system. The Tables produced by Professor Checkland show that only in 1772 were the provincial companies, including the Ayr Bank, larger in terms of total liabilities than the rest of the banking sector.[9] Any consideration of the role played by the banking companies must therefore be somewhat impressionistic and will inevitably overlap with the activities of the other sectors of the banking system.

The few figures which exist suggest that growth in some areas, for example urbanisation and iron in the 19th century, was faster than in England. Professor Cameron's contention that Scottish banking played a major role in Scotland's more rapid industrialisation has been criticised by Professor Crouzet on the grounds that Cameron overlooked the very low level from which Scottish industry started. Crouzet futher alleged that Cameron had not really demonstrated the contribution which the banks had made to capital formation.[10] Hopefully, this book has established the ways in which the banking companies contributed towards capital formation, mobilised resources and otherwise helped their customers to remain in business.

Crouzet's criticism of Cameron on the low-level start principle may be turned back on him by pointing out that although Scotland was a much poorer country than England in 1750 (in *per capita* terms), by 1850 Scotland was 'nearing the peak of its greatest relative prosperity'[11] and had achieved a national income per head that was almost certainly the equal of England's, which is to say that growth must have been faster. It is to the role of the banks and particularly the banking companies in this growth that attention must now turn.

In European or global considerations of economic growth the case of Scotland is often ignored or subsumed under that of England. Scotland, in fact, was the second industrial nation. Its spurt of growth in the 1780s was contemporaneous with that of England, which makes the application of Alexander Gerschenkron's growth model[12] rather difficult. According to the model, Scotland must be considered an advanced economy because its spurt occurred at the same time as England's and therefore its banking system should have been similar.

England, however, was certainly a richer country than Scotland in the 1780s, although the latter's wealth relative to that of the former probably improved after 1750. In other respects the two countries had similar opportunities and resources.

Given the relative poverty of Scotland, it is perhaps significant that one of the two major differences between the countries lay in the types of banking system which they evolved.[13] Nevertheless it must be borne in mind that the structure of the English system might have been different if the laws restricting English country banks to six partners and limiting their note issue to nothing smaller than £5 notes had not been in force. This restrictive legislation complicates the analysis.

Apart from their structures, the major differences between the two systems lay in the instruments developed to serve customers, i.e. cash credits, deposits at interest and branches.

Cash credits were not unknown in England but they never developed to the same extent as they did in Scotland. Two reasons may be considered for this. In 1826 the Scots argued that without small notes they could not operate cash credits, and it may be inferred that the English realised this from an early date. But even when small notes were permitted in England – between 1797 and 1826 – cash accounts did not prove to be a popular credit device. In view of this it must be considered that there was little or no demand for this service. It has already been said that England was a richer country than Scotland, and furthermore it did not suffer to the same extent from balance of payments problems. Given these factors, it seems likely that there was no need for cash accounts and that there was not the same shortage of capital as there was in Scotland.

The same might be said about deposit taking at interest, which began in Scotland, particularly in growth areas, before it developed elsewhere. Arguably there was a greater need to mobilise resources in capital-scarce Scotland, and it was necessary to offer a cash inducement, i.e. interest, in order to attract deposits.

The active participation of the public banks in the Scottish provinces after 1774 introduced a new element of competition into the banking business – an element which was lacking in England. Many provincial banking companies followed the lead of the public banks and set up branches, often in satellite towns. These branch-owning banking companies were often the larger co-partneries, and it is arguable that they were only able to expand in this way because of their larger resources of capital and deposits. English country banks, not being such highly capitalised organisations and not having the same deposit resources, were prevented from engaging in branch extensions to the same extent.

Scotland, then, was able to develop a more efficient system of banking for three reasons. Firstly the public banks both stimulated competition and exercised some control, through the note exchange, over the system. Secondly the legislative constraints on English banks, principally the six-partner law, prevented the development of larger-scale country banks, and thirdly, relative poverty in the Scottish situation encouraged the more efficient use of resources, i.e. deposit taking at interest, which was in turn an important factor in the continued growth of the banking system and, therefore, of the economy.

The main part of provincial bank lending was in the form of discounted bills, but a sizeable part took the form of cash accounts. It has been demonstrated in Chapter 6 and Part Three how these credits could often become long-term loans, and in this way the banking companies can be compared to the German banks of the second half of the 19th century. Gershenkron claims for the German banks that they 'successfully combined the basic idea of the credit mobilier with the short term activities of commercial banks'.[14] He seems unaware that the Scottish banks and banking companies had operated in this way a century earlier. Certainly there was not so much demand for fixed capital in the late 18th century, but the banking system was able to make a contribution towards its formation.

A question often asked of banking systems is whether they were passive or permissive, or whether they performed an active growth-inducing role.

Perhaps one of the most satisfactory ways of assessing the contribution of banking to growth is to consider the views of historical figures in this connection. In 1776 Adam Smith published his *Wealth of Nations*, in which he considered the parallel development of trade and banking. He confessed that he was unable to unravel all the reasons for the growth which had taken place but concluded that

> the trade and industry of Scotland . . . have increased very considerably . . . and that the banks have contributed a good deal to this increase cannot be doubted.[15]

Kirkman Finlay, a leading Glasgow merchant, when asked in 1826 if he thought that the facilities afforded by the banks had conduced to the prosperity of Scotland in the past thirty years, answered:

> I think that is one of the main ingredients, and perhaps I should say the principal ingredient, of the prosperity of the country.[16]

Certainly there was an air of polemic about many of the arguments, but generally the enormous enthusiasm with which the system was defended in 1826 is a significant indicator of the role which the banks and banking companies were playing in economic development. In 1831 the Frenchman Emile Pereire thought Britain's financial system to be the secret of its industrial and political power. The basis of the financial system he took to be the note issue and a large number of banks.[17] In this case the Scots had to share the glory with the English, but there were many Englishmen who thought the Scots system to be superior to their own. Daniel Hardcastle, Jnr., felt that

> the good the Scotch Banks have done and the wealth they had produced, appear . . . to show an admirable system, worthy of all praise and close imitation.[18]

Clearly the banking sector had an important role to play in economic development, but unfortunately none of these quotations reveals the exact nature of the contribution which the banks made to growth.

Certainly some bankers were very growth-minded. Sir Wm. Douglas, founder of the Galloway Banking Co., set up an industrial empire which included 'two cotton spinning mills, woollen and carpet mills, tanneries, breweries, domestic spinning and hand loom weaving; the construction of turnpike roads, canals and harbours'.[19]

The proprietors of the Shetland Banking Co. were prepared to provide copies of *The Practical Farmers' Manual* for free distribution to local farmers, provided that the expense was not too great.[20] The difficulty in interpreting these facts lies in the process of determining whether these activities were undertaken because the actors in the scene were bankers or because they were industrialists. Given the very close links between industry and banking, the usefulness of the distinction between the active and passive roles of the banks becomes doubtful. Professor Crouzet realised something of this when he suggested that

> The old idea of a separation between banking and industry must give way to that of a partial intermingling of the two sectors.[21]

In the case of the Scottish banking companies, however, the intermingling was much more than partial. The banking and business sectors did not have separate life forces. In the industrial revolution a large number of Scotland's leading entrepreneurs were the proprietors of banking company stock and many of them were bank directors. Others were involved with the public banks in similar ways. Perhaps this is one reason why the charges for banking services were kept so low.

It is therefore misleading to talk about the banks and banking companies playing active or passive parts in the process of economic development, as if they had an existence wholly independent of the business units which they served. Rather they were an integral part of the business community sharing its fortunes and misfortunes. The banking companies as such did not, usually, undertake extra-banking economic activity except when enterprises came into their possession in payment of bad debts. Nevertheless, the proprietors and directors of the banking companies were in the forefront of economic development, and bank credit was used by these men at every stage of the growth of their firms. Very many other non-bank linked enterprises also made use of bank finance. There is a discussion in Part Three and Chapter 6 of the ease with which businessmen could obtain credit and thus promote the growth of their undertakings. There could be no easy remedy for the problems of development, but the credit and other services provided by the bankers were important facilitating factors in the process of economic growth.

5. Stability

Any consideration of the contribution which a banking system makes to an economy would be incomplete without entering into the debate about whether or not stability was important.[22] This debate was rehearsed in 1965 in the pages of the *Scottish Journal of Political Economy*, where Professor R.H. Campbell argued that there was no necessary relationship between growth and stability, while Mr. F.S. Taylor, then Secretary of the Institute of Bankers in Scotland, took the opposite view that stability was an important condition for growth.

Scotland was fortunate in the extent to which the government left it free to develop its own banking system in line with the requirements of the economy. Apart from stamp duties, the only real limitations on banking were those imposed by the legislation of 1765 whereby notes under £1 had been forbidden, the option clause had been prohibited and the principle of protestation by summary diligence on unpaid notes had been established. But this was not restrictive legislation, it was regulatory. Its effect was to remove not only the dangerous fringe element which had arisen in the banking system but also to guarantee that the note issues should be freely convertible into specie – an important consideration in the light of the experience of other banking systems. In other respects, apart from commercial law, Scottish banking was free of legislation. In particular there was freedom of note issue and freedom of entry. But more especially there was no restriction on association. The six-partner law in England had deprived that country of 'a banking system commensurate with a period of rapid economic growth'.[23] Scotland, on the other hand, was able to develop a relatively sophisticated system of banking which, because it was free of restrictive legislation and because it was largely established by its customers, must be thought to have been particularly suited for the task required of it.

That task has been considered in terms of survival, profitability, customer satisfaction and contribution to economic growth. It must be acknowledged, however, that these criteria of performance were often at variance with one another and some, if too energetically pursued, were likely to undermine the stability of the economy.

If a banker, anxious to maintain his own survival in a crisis, cut back his lending he might be in danger of driving his customers out of business. If he was concerned with maximising his profits he might be encouraged into speculations both in the funds and with his customers. If he was concerned with satisfying all of his customers' requirements, real and imagined, he would be tempted into over-trading. Similarly, if he was intent on maximising growth either at the micro or macro level, he would be inclined to neglect his reserve requirements. Clearly the banker's prime task was to maintain his own survival and that of his customers. Profitability was a secondary consideration, dependent on survival. But the economist, J.R. McCulloch, criticised the Scottish system of banking on the grounds that it was

> fitted only for a period of prosperity; because the moment alarm and discredit began to make their appearance, the Scotch bankers ceased in a great measure to discount, and provided for their own security by ruining thousands of their own customers.[24]

This is clearly a gross exaggeration. If thousands of customers had been ruined at each crisis, then there would have been little or nothing left. This objection to McCulloch's statement gives rise to doubts about how accurate is the remainder of it or if it has any foundation in fact.

Certainly in the crisis of 1793 the banks and banking companies did largely cease to discount. It is also true that numerous people and several banks were ruined. The difficult question arises whether the stop to new bank credit caused the business failures, or were they caused by bad management on the part of the bankrupts, or a combination of both? Some consideration must be given to the position of the bankers in the light of this.

Given that there was a run on the banks for specie and London paper, they could do nothing but restrict discounts. The London and Edinburgh balances and the specie which the banks obtained when bills were paid soon passed out over the counter in payment of notes and deposits as the run continued. If the banks had gone on discounting, the effect would have been to increase the potential demand for specie and bills on Edinburgh and London. Such an action would merely have intensified the bankers' liquidity problems and would probably have caused more bank and business closures, as happened in 1772.

Bank collapses would usually involve the failure of the partners, and as these men were often the leading traders and industrialists in an area, the consequences for economic growth would have been serious. It has been argued that 'an economy may achieve the maximum rate of growth only by running occasionally into inflation and financial crisis'.[25] Certainly it is true that crises can have beneficial effects in that they may weed out the weaker firms, leaving the stronger in possession of the field. (The financially weaker are sometimes the most technically efficient, for financial weakness is often caused by high rates of capital investment). But in an economy like that of Scotland, where there were such close links between banks and industry, any crisis which involved bank failures would also involve the failure or at least the retardation of growth of the leading firms.

This identity of interests between bankers and industrialists was given a more realistic expression in the liquidity crisis of 1797 when in Edinburgh and Glasgow (possibly also in other areas) the leading merchants and industrialists entered into an understanding whereby they undertook not to make runs on the banks and banking companies.[26] There were, of course, those who continued to do so, but commercial crises in Scotland were never thereafter felt with the same intensity as they were in England.[27] The fact that many leading industrialists were the proprietors of bank stock was a second factor which helped reduce the possible effects of a crisis. These men were usually given special help by the banking companies in which they owned stock because they could be relied upon not to circulate notes in a way which would be damaging to their bank. The co-partnery form of organisation was especially important in this respect, for not only did a large number of shareholders increase the security of the bank, it also increased the inter-dependence factor. Even men who were business rivals might be bound not to undermine general business confidence because of their common interest in the continued existence of their banking company.

Furthermore it was in the interests of the banks and banking companies to be as helpful to their customers as possible in times of crisis, both to promote a quick recovery and to encourage retention of their accounts. The competitive nature of Scottish banking helped to ensure that the needs of the customers were not ignored. But of course the extent to which bankers could help their customers in times of difficulty was conditioned by the extent to which the cusomers helped the banker, i.e. by being prepared to hold notes and deposits.

It is clear, therefore, that stability was important to the growth of the economy, given the nature of the links between banks and industry. Some of the small partnership banking companies were the weak link in the system, and any losses to the public caused by banking company failures occurred as a result of partnership closures. Nevertheless the system, in all its parts, compared favourably with that of England.

Imitation is perhaps the sincerest form of flattery, and this was especially so in the banking world of the 19th century. The legislation to permit the formation of joint-stock banks in England and Ireland was passed as a result of pressure from people who held the Scottish system in high regard, although it is sometimes difficult to determine whether the factor which most impressed these observers was the public banks or the co-partneries. The Scottish system of banking was studied by politicians, economists and bankers from all over the world, and many of them returned home to implement similar systems. In 1855 the French economist J.G. Courcelle-Seneuil became economic adviser to the government of Chile. He was 'an admirer of the old free banks of Escocia and in general a fervent partizan of free banking'.[28] As a result of his influence a free banking regime was instituted. Similarly the Frenchman Emile Pereire believed that 'where one wishes to develop an economic system based on bank currency, it is preferable to have a multiplicity of . . . banks of issue'.[29]

It is impossible to unravel the contributions made by the two main elements in Scottish banking, i.e. the public banks and the banking companies. To a large extent they competed with one another, and the result of this was better and cheaper services for the customers. But there was also a sense in which they were complementary. The public banks, with a higher portion of their assets in gold and government bonds, were the reserve of the system – prepared to lend to the freer-lending provincials in times of difficulty. They instituted and dominated the note exchange which had such beneficial effects on stability. The effect of the combination of these separate elements was to produce, as Pereire put it, a system which 'represented the best adaptations of structure and function to the growth requirements'[30] of the economy.

That it was so was due to many factors – economic, social and political. Political interference in the system had been minimal and had been confined largely to regulatory controls rather than restrictive legislation. In particular Scottish provincial banking companies were fortunate in not being restricted to six partners. It may be speculated that the absence of this control was due to the non-existence of central government in Edinburgh. In London and Dublin monopolies of the Bank of England and Bank of Ireland had to be protected, whereas in Edinburgh the monopoly granted by the old Scottish parliament to the Bank of Scotland in 1695 had been allowed to lapse by the British parliament several years after the Union and at a time when the Jacobites (largely Scots) threatened the Hanoverian succession. When the free banking system which evolved was challenged in 1765, the banking companies were able to muster sufficient political muscle to fight off the threat, and thereafter the Scottish banking system was left to develop without further political interference in its structure and organisation until the challenge of 1826 – a challenge which was again rebuffed. Freedom from legislative interference was therefore a major permissive factor in the development of the system.

In the social sphere the absence of politically imposed controls enabled the system to evolve a cohesion which was a significant dynamic element in development. At the level of the individual firm whole urban elites, despite business rivalries, were able to combine to form banks in many towns. This gave a common identity and commitment to partners so that the banks were made to work, and work efficiently, for the benefit of all who brought their custom to the bank. Where some were dissatisfied, or impatient, the remedy of forming another bank was often accepted with alacrity. At the level of the system the bankers, after initial misunderstandings and difficulties, came to appreciate that their independence could only be guaranteed by a realisation of their mutual inter-dependence.

Competition for business was one thing, but undermining the business of another bank was something different. This realisation was manifest in the note exchange and particularly in the crises of 1797 and 1825–6 when mutual tolerance and co-operative effort helped to minimise the effects of commercial distress.

In the economic sense the system was competitive in response to the demands placed upon it, but the basis of competition was not prices – it was service, particularly the availability of credit. The cost of credit was common in all banks but, because of the extent of competition, it was also low. Branches had the effect of sharpening the competitive edge of the business, and rapid responses to customers' demands were the result, at least in the system, if not always in individual companies.

The product of the combination of these economic, social and political factors was a system of banking which, in its day, was unique. It was, however, a system which was temporary – as indeed all systems are. Continued growth in the economy eventually rendered the provincial banking companies and the Edinburgh private bankers uneconomic, and they were replaced by a new generation of companies – the joint-stock banks. So the bankers with which this book has been concerned had sown the seeds of their own destruction. By meeting the growth requirements of their customers they had raised economic activity to a new height which rendered their own structure obsolete. But, although their business units became redundant, the bankers themselves and the techniques which they had evolved found employment in the new joint-stock banks, not just in Scotland, but throughout the United Kingdom and in many other countries of the world.

NOTES

1. Joplin, 1827, p. 16
2. Huddersfield Banking Co., Minute book, Midland Bank archives
3. *Bankers' Magazine*, May 1845, p. 89
4. Perth Banking Co., D.M.B., 14/7/1845
5. Heaton, 'Financing the Industrial Revolution', in Crouzet, 1972, p. 85
6. Thomas, 1934, p. 104
7. Aberdeen Banking Co., Bond Register and list of partners
8. P.P. Lords Committee on Promissory Notes . . . 1826, Report, p. 4
9. S. G. Checkland, 1975, Tables 7, 8, 14, 15
10. Crouzet, 1972, p. 46, n.5
11. Cameron, 1967, p. 94
12. Gerschenkron, 1962. For some discussion see Checkland, 1975, pp. 233–6
13. The other major difference was the educational system
14. Gerschenkron, 1962, p. 13
15. A. Smith, 1970, p. 394
16. P.P. Select Committee on Promissory Notes . . . 1825, p. 69
17. Quoted in Cameron 1965, p. 128
18. Hardcastle, 1843, p. 345
19. Donnachie and Macleod, 1974, p. 86
20. N.L.S., Hay of Hayfield, Acc.3250, Vol. 61, Letter to W. McPhun, 8/12/1841
21. Crouzet, 1972, p. 47
22. See Taylor and Campbell, 1965; Checkland, 1975, pp. 213–215

23. Pressnell, 1956, pp. 4–5; and Ashton, pp. 100–5
24. McCulloch, 1832, quoted in Thomas, 1935, p. 104
25. Campbell, 1965, p. 44
26. See copies in B.S., Glasgow Archives
27. At least during the life cycle of the banking companies
28. Subercaseaux, 1922, pp. 68–72
29. Cameron, 1965, p. 128
30. Ibid., p. 290

Appendices

Appendix A

Note. All figures to nearest £1,000

APPENDIX A.1

Aberdeen Banking Company, 1767–1849

Balance Sheets 1768–1787

Source: Balance and Cash Books
Bank of Scotland, Aberdeen

Notes: Branch figures are sums due by agents.
All dates at end of February.

Appendix A.1: Aberdeen Banking Company

	1768 Total	%	1769 Total	%	1770 Total	%	1771 Total	%	1772 Total	%	1773 Total	%	1774 Total	%	1775 Total	%	1776 Total	%
Assets																		
Advances																		
Cash a/cs.	29	36	53	42	54	52	66	59	70	57	76	63	79	54	66	43	75	45
Bills	11	14	6	5	9	9.	19	17	18	15	14	12	18	12	19	12	21	13
Others	8	10	4	3	1	1	1	1	5	4	5	4	9	6	12	8	9	5
Total	48	60	63	50	64	62	86	77	93	76	95	79	106	72	97	63	105	63
Branches	—		4	3	3	3	2	2	3	2	3	2	3	2	1	1	8	5
Investments	—														10	6	13	8
Sundry	3	4	7	5	2	2	10	9	11	9	8	7	17	12	24	15	22	13
Cash	29	36	53	42	34	33	14	12	15	13	15	12	20	14	23	15	18	11
Total	80	100	127	100	103	100	112	100	122	100	121	100	146	100	155	100	166	100
Liabilities																		
Notes with public	43	54	48	38	55	53	68	61	79	65	74	61	105	72	114	74	126	76
Deposits					10	10	11	10	5	4	7	6	5	3	4	3	4	2
To public	43	54	48	38	65	63	79	71	84	69	81	67	110	75	118	77	130	78
Sundry	18	23	50	39	8	8	1	1	3	2	7	6	2	1	—		1	1
Capital Paid	19	23	29	23	30	29	30	27	30	25	30	25	30	21	30	19	30	18
Reserves							2	1	5	4	3	2	4	3	7	4	5	3
Total	80	100	127	100	103	100	112	100	122	100	121	100	146	100	155	100	166	100

	1777 Total	%	1778 Total	%	1779 Total	%	1780 Total	%	1781 Total	%	1782 Total	%	1783 Total	%	1784 Total	%	1785 Total	%
Assets																		
Advances	72	41	83	48	85	57	83	61	82	48	77	42	82	41	87	44	83	40
Cash a/cs.	29	16	41	23	18	12	23	17	47	27	50	27	69	34	49	25	51	24
Bills	14	8	15	9	7	5	4	3	4	2	8	4	4	2	12	6	16	8
Others																		
Total	115	65	139	80	110	74	110	81	133	77	135	73	155	77	148	75	150	72
Branches	8	5	7	4	5	3	7	5	12	7	14	8	23	11	23	12	25	12
Investments	17	10	7	4	11	7	11	8	16	9	25	14	14	7	19	10	17	8
Sundry	26	15	10	6	7	5	3	2	7	4	4	2	4	2	3	1	7	3
Cash	10	5	10	6	17	11	5	4	5	3	5	3	5	3	5	2	11	5
Total	176	100	173	100	150	100	136	100	173	100	183	100	201	100	198	100	210	100
Liabilities																		
Notes with public	134	76	131	76	107	71	92	68	126	73	130	71	136	68	118	59	118	56
Deposits	3	2	4	2	4	3	3	2	6	3	8	4	13	6	29	15	37	18
To public	137	78	135	78	111	74	95	70	132	76	138	75	149	74	147	74	155	74
Sundry	1	1	—		1	1	4	3	3	2	5	3	11	5	7	4	11	5
Capital Paid	30	17	30	17	30	20	30	22	30	17	32	18	34	17	36	18	42	20
Reserves	8	4	8	5	8	5	7	5	8	5	8	4	7	4	8	4	2	1
Total	176	100	173	100	150	100	136	100	173	100	183	100	201	100	198	100	210	100

Appendix A.1: Aberdeen Banking Company – *contd.*

	1786		1787																
	Total	%	Total	%	Total	%	Total	%	Total	%	Total	%	Total	%	Total	%	Total	%
Assets																			
Advances	84	37	81	34															
Cash a/cs.	72	31	73	31															
Bills	4	2	4	2															
Others																			
Total	160	70	158	67															
Branches	36	16	47	20															
Investments	19	8	—																
Sundry	2	1	20	8															
Cash	11	5	11	5															
Total	228	100	236	100															
Liabilities																			
Notes with public	126	55	134	57															
Deposits	36	16	29	12															
To public	162	71	163	69															
Sundry	21	9	21	8															
Capital Paid	42	19	43	18															
Reserves	3	1	9	4															
Total	228	100	236	100															

APPENDIX A.2

Arbroath Banking Company, 1825–1844

Partial Balance Sheets 1826–1843

Source: Boase, 1867

Notes: All dates at end of June

S

Appendix A.2: Arbroath Banking Company

	1826 Total %	1827 Total %	1828 Total %	1829 Total %	1830 Total %	1831 Total %	1832 Total %	1833 Total %	1834 Total %
Assets									
Advances									
Cash a/cs.	2	34	3	8	11	14	11	14	13
Bills	45	68	82	86	92	105	94	88	87
Others	2	1	2	3	4	4	4	8	8
Total	49	103	87	97	107	123	109	110	108
Branches									
Investments									
Sundry									
Cash									
Total									
Liabilities									
Notes with public	10	17	19	23	22	18	20	18	15
Deposits	24	32	59	80	86	83	88	84	93
To public	34	49	78	103	108	101	108	102	108
Sundry									
Capital Paid	60	60	60	60	60	60	60	60	60
Reserves									
Total									

	1835 Total	%	1836 Total	%	1837 Total	%	1838 Total	%	1839 Total	%	1840 Total	%	1841 Total	%	1842 Total	%	1843 Total	%
Assets																		
Advances																		
Cash a/cs.	13		9		13		12		17		13		18		21		20	
Bills	95		100		110		108		103		112		114		101		106	
Others	8		8		15		13		16		21		26		24		27	
Total	116		117		138		133		136		146		158		146		153	
Branches																		
Investments																		
Sundry																		
Cash																		
Total																		
Liabilities																		
Notes with public	17		20		23		20		20		15		13		16		13	
Deposits	100		106		116		118		130		141		157		142		148	
To public	117		126		139		138		150		156		170		158		161	
Sundry																		
Capital																		
Paid	60		60		60		60		60		60		60		60		60	
Reserves																		
Total																		

APPENDIX A.3

Dundee Banking Company, 1764–1864

Balance Sheets at Five Yearly Intervals.

Source: Boase, 1867

Notes: Full range of balance sheets given in Boase, 1867.
Branch figures on assets side are total advances
at branches.
Deposit figures on the liabilities side include
deposits at branches.
All dates *c*. 20th February.

Appendix A.3: Dundee Banking Company

	1765 Total	%	1770 Total	%	1775 Total	%	1780 Total	%	1785 Total	%	1790 Total	%	1795 Total	%	1800 Total	%	1805 Total	%
Assets																		
Advances																		
Cash a/cs.	19	54	38	78	25	57	22	44	31	43	40	57	45	25	39	18	24	8
Bills	11	31	7	14	11	25	10	20	31	43	17	24	54	31	68	31	79	27
Others	1	3																
Total	31	88	45	92	36	82	32	64	62	86	57	81	99	56	107	49	103	35
Branches													54	31	86	39	79	27
Investments																	93	32
Sundry	1	3	1	2	4	9	10	20	2	3	4	6	15	8	10	4	10	3
Cash	3	9	3	6	4	9	8	16	8	11	9	13	8	5	19	8	9	3
Total	35	100	49	100	44	100	50	100	72	100	70	100	176	100	222	100	294	100
Liabilities																		
Notes with public	34	97	27	55	36	82	40	80	55	76	43	61	69	39	61	27	67	23
Deposits			9	19									74	42	119	54	198	68
To public	34	97	36	74	36	82	40	80	55	76	43	61	143	81	180	81	265	91
Sundry			6	12					4	6	4	6	32	18	6	3	15	5
Capital Paid	1	3	7	14	7	16	9	18	11	15	21	30	1	1	32	14	13	4
Reserves					1	2	1	2	2	3	2	3			4	2	1	—
Total	35	100	49	100	44	100	50	100	72	100	70	100	176	100	222	100	294	100

Appendix A.3: Dundee Banking Company – contd.

	1810		1815		1820		1825		1830		1835		1840		1845		1850	
	Total	*%*	*Total*	*%*	*Total*	*%*	*Total*	*%*	*Total*	*%*	*Total*	*%*	*Total*	*%*	*Total*	*%*	*Total*	*%*
Assets																		
Advances	38	8	27	4	28	7	36	8	53	11	58	11	84	14	53	9	47	6
Cash a/cs.	160	33	192	32	103	27	143	31	134	28	182	33	247	41	198	32	410	56
Bills			1	–	2	1	147	31	205	43	187	34	125	21	229	37	185	25
Others																		
Total	198	41	220	36	133	35	326	70	392	82	427	78	456	76	480	78	642	87
Branches	114	24	130	22	42	11	–		–		–		43	7	23	3	7	1
Investments	138	29	221	37	190	49	130	28	71	15	67	12	9	2	30	5	28	4
Sundry	18	4	21	3	11	3	6	1	9	2	42	8	81	13	74	12	52	7
Cash	11	2	9	2	10	2	6	1	5	1	11	2	14	2	11	2	11	1
Total	479	100	601	100	386	100	468	100	477	100	547	100	603	100	618	100	740	100
Liabilities																		
Notes with public	58	12	44	7	32	8	31	7	26	6	32	6	31	5	31	5	28	4
Deposits	337	70	478	80	332	86	398	85	420	88	486	89	501	83	514	83	624	84
To public	395	82	522	87	364	94	429	92	446	94	518	95	532	88	545	88	652	88
Sundry	44	9	38	6	4	1	10	2	1	–	1	–	6	1	8	1	9	1
Capital Paid	36	8	35	6	16	4	23	5	25	5	25	5	60	10	60	10	60	8
Reserves	4	1	6	1	2	1	6	1	5	1	3	–	5	1	5	1	19	3
Total	479	100	601	100	386	100	468	100	477	100	547	100	603	100	618	100	740	100

	1855 Total	%	1860 Total	%	1864 Total	%	Total	%	Total	%	Total	%	Total	%	Total	%	Total	%
Assets																		
Advances																		
Cash a/cs.	33	4	53	5	74	9												
Bills	342	43	455	47	345	41												
Others	228	28	229	23	263	31												
Total	603	75	737	75	682	81												
Branches	9	1	17	2	25	3												
Investments	28	4	76	8	56	7												
Sundry	121	15	106	11	44	5												
Cash	41	5	43	4	36	4												
Total	802	100	979	100	843	100												
Liabilities																		
Notes with public	38	5	41	4	41	5												
Deposits	670	84	819	84	685	81												
To public	708	89	860	88	726	86												
Sundry	2	—	60	6	100	12												
Capital Paid	60	7	59	6	17	2												
Reserves	32	4																
Total	802	100	979	100	843	100												

APPENDIX A.4

Dundee Commercial Banking Company No.1, 1792–1802

Balance Sheets 1792–1801

Source: Boase, 1867

Notes: All dates at end of December

Appendix A.4: Dundee Commercial Banking Company No.1

	1792		1793		1794		1795		1796		1797		1798		1799		1800	
	Total	%	Total	%	Total	%	Total	%	Total	%	Total	%	Total	%	Total	%	Total	%
Assets																		
Advances																		
Cash a/cs.	15	37	8	35	8	20	6	11	11	25	8	18	7	13	8	11	6	6
Bills	20	49	11	48	28	68	33	58	25	57	25	54	35	65	51	70	58	58
Others	—		—		—		—										2	2
Total	35	86	19	83	36	88	39	69	36	82	33	72	42	78	59	81	66	66
Branches																		
Investments																		
Sundry	3	7	1	4	1	2	6	10	3	7	5	11	5	9	12	16	30	30
Cash	3	7	3	13	4	10	12	21	5	11	8	17	7	13	2	3	4	4
Total	41	100	23	100	41	100	57	100	44	100	46	100	54	100	73	100	100	100
Liabilities																		
Notes with public	26	63	11	48	24	59	25	44	19	43	15	33	14	26	18	25	30	30
Deposits	9	22	4	17	11	27	23	40	22	50	23	50	27	50	43	59	68	68
To public	35	85	15	65	35	86	48	84	41	93	38	83	41	76	61	84	98	98
Sundry	2	5	4	18	2	5	6	10	2	5	6	13	11	20	9	12	2	2
Capital Paid	4	10	4	17	4	9	2	4	1	2	2	4	2	4	2	3		
Reserves							1	2							1	1		
Total	41	100	23	100	41	100	57	100	44	100	46	100	54	100	73	100	100	100

Appendix A.4: Dundee Commercial Banking Company No.1 – *contd.*

	1801		*Total*	%	*Total*	%	*Total*	%	*Total*	%	*Total*	%	*Total*	%	*Total*	%	*Total*	%
	Total	%																
Assets																		
Advances																		
Cash a/cs.	5	5																
Bills	54	53																
Others	3	3																
Total	62	61																
Branches																		
Investments																		
Sundry	36	35																
Cash	4	4																
Total	102	100																
Liabilities																		
Notes with public	25	24																
Deposits	74	73																
To public	99	97																
Sundry																		
Capital Paid	2	2																
Reserves	1	1																
Total	102	100																

APPENDIX A.5

Dundee New Bank, 1802–1838

Balance Sheets at Five-yearly Intervals

Source: Boase, 1867

Notes: Full range of balance sheets given in Boase, 1867.
          Branch figures on assets side are total advances
          at branches.
          Deposit figures on the liabilities side include
          deposits at branches.
          All figures, save 1838, at end of June
          1838 – 1st January.

Appendix A.5: Dundee New Bank

	1802 Total	1802 %	1805 Total	1805 %	1810 Total	1810 %	1815 Total	1815 %	1820 Total	1820 %	1825 Total	1825 %	1830 Total	1830 %	1835 Total	1835 %	1838 Total	1838 %
Assets																		
Advances	12	6	17	5	16	4	15	4	29	10	25	8	14	5	7	3	21	11
Cash a/cs.	122	60	140	46	213	53	191	56	169	60	201	63	177	69	195	77	109	56
Bills	6	3	5	2	11	3	10	3	6	2	4	1	5	2	7	3		
Others																		
Total	140	69	162	53	240	60	216	63	204	72	230	72	196	76	209	83	130	67
Branches	35	17	63	20	82	20	70	20	39	14	32	10	31	12	19	7	22	11
Investments					30	8	30	9	—									
Sundry	25	12	76	25	37	9	17	5	33	11	52	16	22	9	14	6	32	16
Cash	3	2	5	2	13	3	10	3	8	3	6	2	7	3	11	4	11	6
Total	203	100	306	100	402	100	343	100	284	100	320	100	256	100	253	100	195	100
Liabilities																		
Notes with public	58	29	100	33	97	24	55	16	50	18	50	16	26	10	30	12	19	10
Deposits	141	69	205	67	282	70	251	73	219	77	247	77	212	83	177	70	139	71
To public	199	98	305	100	379	94	306	89	269	95	297	93	238	93	207	82	158	81
Sundry	2	1			4	1	10	3	4	1	6	2	4	2	17	7	7	3
Capital Paid	2	1	1	—	17	4	25	7	11	4	11	3	14	5	28	11	19	10
Reserves					2	1	2	1			6	2			1	—	11	6
Total	203	100	306	100	402	100	343	100	284	100	320	100	256	100	253	100	195	100

APPENDIX A.6

Dundee New Bank, Branch Balance Sheets, 1806–1837

Royal Bank of Scotland, Dundee
Forfar, 1806–1837
Arbroath, 1806–1817
Brechin, 1806–1817

Source: Branch balance sheets

Notes: All dates at end of 30th June

Dundee New Bank, Forfar Branch
Balance Sheets, 1806–37 (All figures in £1,000s)

	Liabilities		Assets					
Year	Deposits	To Head Office	Cash a/cs.	Bill Discounts	Total Advances	Sundry	Cash	Total
1806	9.7	27.9	13.2	21.0	34.2	—	3.4	37.6
7	9.0	28.1	14.3	16.1	30.4	—	6.7	37.1
8	10.0	18.5	2.8	20.4	23.2	0.1	5.2	28.5
9	14.8	17.4	4.1	23.5	27.6	0.1	4.5	32.2
1810	19.2	14.3	6.5	22.0	28.5	—	5.0	33.5
1	12.0	12.6	4.9	14.6	19.5	—	5.1	24.6
2	13.6	15.9	5.0	19.3	24.3	—	5.2	29.5
3	15.5	13.3	5.6	17.8	23.4	—	5.3	28.8
4	21.2	n.a.	4.9	n.a.			n.a.	
5	23.4	10.0	6.2	22.8	29.0	—	4.4	33.4
6	13.6	8.2	4.0	13.7	17.7	—	4.1	21.8
7	22.3	1.9	4.5	16.1	20.6	—	3.6	24.2
8	30.7	5.2	7.9	23.2	31.1	0.1	4.7	35.9
9	33.0	11.3	9.3	28.0	37.3	—	7.0	44.3
1820	37.3	11.1	8.9	29.7	38.6	—	9.8	48.4
1	36.3	16.6	10.6	31.3	41.9	0.1	10.9	52.9
2	38.9	15.5	12.1	30.6	42.7	0.1	11.6	54.4
3	30.7	20.4	13.2	26.3	39.5	—	11.6	51.1
4	32.3	9.3	10.7	20.8	31.5	0.2	9.9	41.6
5	33.9	7.1	8.8	23.4	32.2	—	8.8	41.0
6	24.7	12.2	7.8	20.8	28.6	—	8.3	36.9
7	24.6	13.8	7.5	22.1	29.6	0.1	8.7	38.4
8	25.8	12.3	8.4	22.9	31.3	—	6.8	38.1
9	30.2	9.3	8.4	23.9	32.3	—	7.2	39.5
1830	31.2	6.7	9.1	21.8	30.9	0.4	6.6	37.9
1	30.3	1.7	6.9	20.3	27.2	0.2	4.6	32.0
2	33.2	—	6.9	22.5	29.4	0.2	3.6	33.2
3	35.5	3.2	9.3	23.5	32.8	—	5.9	38.7
4	30.7	5.5	11.8	18.9	30.7	0.2	5.3	36.2
5	30.8	—	8.2	15.6	23.8	3.8	3.2	30.8
6	32.5	—	9.1	8.5	17.6	8.8	6.1	32.5
7	29.3	—	9.6	16.1	25.7	—	3.6	29.3

Dundee New Bank, Arbroath Branch
Balance Sheets, 1806–17 (All figures in £1,000s)

Liabilities		Assets						
		To Head	Cash	Bill	Total			
Year	Deposits	Office	a/cs.	Discounts	Advances	Sundry	Cash	Total
1806	10.5	24.8	3.1	26.9	30.0	0.1	5.2	35.3
7	13.0	27.6	3.9	30.7	34.6	0.1	5.9	40.6
8	15.2	7.1	3.5	14.4	17.9	1.9	2.5	22.3
9	18.9	9.7	4.5	19.5	24.0	0.3	4.3	28.6
1810	16.3	15.4	4.9	23.0	27.9	—	3.8	31.7
1	14.2	8.8	4.1	13.3	17.4	1.6	4.0	23.0
2	17.0	7.6	2.9	14.4	17.3	0.6	6.7	24.6
3	16.1	13.7	4.1	19.5	23.6	0.3	5.9	29.8
4	20.4	7.9	3.1	18.2	21.3	0.6	6.4	28.3
5	19.2	11.1	3.6	19.6	23.2	1.2	5.9	30.3
6	12.6	5.8	3.0	9.7	12.7	0.9	4.8	18.4
7	11.7	—	2.9	2.5	5.4	1.3	5.0	11.7

Brechin Branch

Year	Deposits	To Head Office	Cash a/cs.	Bill Discounts	Total Advances	Sundry	Cash	Total
1806	9.1	9.4	3.6	11.7	15.3	0.1	3.1	18.5
7	10.8	15.4	5.4	14.7	20.1	—	6.1	26.2
8	16.4	7.4	2.8	14.8	17.6	0.1	6.1	23.8
9	18.0	11.7	2.8	22.5	25.3	—	4.4	29.7
1810	17.0	12.5	3.5	22.2	25.7	—	3.8	29.5
1	10.5	8.0	3.3	11.3	14.6	—	3.9	18.5
2	20.4	—	3.5	13.3	16.8	3.0	0.6	20.4
3	14.2	16.5	3.5	23.6	27.1	—	3.6	30.7
4	11.7	17.8	5.7	18.4	24.1	—	5.4	29.5
5	14.0	11.7	5.1	14.6	19.7	0.1	5.9	25.7
6	12.5	6.6	3.7	10.8	14.5	—	4.6	19.1
7[1]	9.0	n.a.	3.6	1.1	4.7		n.a.	

Source: Branch Balance Sheets, Royal Bank of Scotland, Dundee
Notes: 1 Taken from C. W. Boase, *Century of Banking in Dundee*.
        2 All dates as at 30th June.

APPENDIX A.7

Dundee Commercial Banking Company No. 2, 1825–1838

Balance Sheets 1836–1838

Source: Boase, 1867

Notes: All dates at end of June

Appendix A.7: Dundee Commercial Banking Company No. 2

	1836 Total	%	1837 Total	%	1838 Total	%	Total	%	Total	%	Total	%	Total	%	Total	%
Assets																
Advances																
Cash a/cs.	45	10	44	12	50	14										
Bills	341	72	243	68	231	65										
Others	39	8	28	8	39	11										
Total	425	90	315	88	320	90										
Branches																
Investments																
Sundry	40	8	28	8	21	6										
Cash	7	2	14	4	12	4										
Total	472	100	357	100	353	100										
Liabilities																
Notes with public	37	8	36	10	31	9										
Deposits	339	72	245	69	241	68										
To public	376	80	281	79	272	77										
Sundry	22	4	16	4	26	7										
Capital																
Paid	50	11	50	14	50	14										
Reserves	24	5	10	3	5	2										
Total	472	100	357	100	353	100										

APPENDIX A.8

Ship Bank Glasgow, 1749–1836

Balance Sheets 1752–1761

Source: Balance Book
           Bank of Scotland, Glasgow

Notes: Cash Balance taken to be half the sum in the
           hands of the cashier. The note issue figure
           has been adjusted accordingly.
           All figures at end of July.

Appendix A.8: Ship Bank, Glasgow

	1752 Total	%	1753 Total	%	1754 Total	%	1755 Total	%	1756 Total	%	1757 Total	%	1758 Total	%	1759 Total	%	1760 Total	%
Assets																		
Advances																		
Cash a/cs.	38	69	39	62	43	63	46	66	48	59	45	54	51	52	54	48	70	50
Bills	9	16	13	20	19	28	18	26	20	25	20	24	36	37	43	38	56	40
Others																		
Total	47	85	52	82	62	91	64	92	68	84	65	78	87	89	97	86	126	90
Branches																		
Investments																		
Sundry			3	5	1	2	1	1	2	2	9	11	2	2	5	5	3	2
Cash	8	15	8	13	5	7	5	7	11	14	9	11	9	9	10	9	11	8
Total	55	100	63	100	68	100	70	100	81	100	83	100	98	100	112	100	140	100
Liabilities																		
Notes with public	25	45	32	51	34	50	31	44	28	35	41	49	40	41	47	42	60	43
Deposits	20	36	17	27	24	35	27	39	38	47	38	46	39	40	40	36	39	28
To public	45	81	49	78	58	85	58	83	66	82	79	95	79	81	87	78	99	71
Sundry	8	15	10	16	8	12	9	13	11	13	—		11	11	16	14	30	21
Capital Paid	2	4	4	6	2	3	3	4	4	5	4	5	8	8	9	8	11	8
Reserves																		
Total	55	100	63	100	68	100	70	100	81	100	83	100	98	100	112	100	140	100

Appendix A.8: Ship Bank, Glasgow – *contd.*

	1761 Total	%	Total	%	Total	%	Total	%	Total	%	Total	%	Total	%	Total	%	Total	%
Assets																		
Advances																		
Cash a/cs.	85	46																
Bills	82	45																
Others																		
Total	167	91																
Branches																		
Investments																		
Sundry	3	2																
Cash	13	7																
Total	183	100																
Liabilities																		
Notes with																		
public	82	45																
Deposits	47	26																
To public	129	71																
Sundry	41	22																
Capital																		
Paid	13	7																
Reserves																		
Total	183	100																

APPENDIX A.9

Thistle Bank, Glasgow, 1761–1836

Balance Sheets 1786–1792

Source: Balance Book
Bank of Scotland, Glasgow

Notes: Cash balances have been assumed to be 5 per cent
of note issues. The latter figure has
been adjusted accordingly.
All figures at end of March.

Appendix A.9: Thistle Bank, Glasgow

	1786		1787		1788		1789		1790		1791		1792					
	Total	%	Total	%	Total	%	Total	%	Total	%	Total	%	Total	%	Total	%	Total	%
Assets																		
Advances																		
Cash a/cs.	15	7	17	7	15	6	10	5	26	10	14	5	24	8				
Bills	104	47	185	78	191	79	145	66	149	60	188	67	225	71				
Others	35	16	8	4	10	4	26	12	10	4	23	8	37	12				
Total	154	70	210	89	216	89	181	83	185	74	225	80	286	91				
Branches																		
Investments	47	22	10	4	—		20	9	20	8	10	3	11	3				
Sundry	15	7	14	6	21	9	16	7	44	17	44	16	17	5				
Cash	3	1	3	1	4	2	2	1	2	1	3	1	4	1				
Total	219	100	237	100	241	100	219	100	251	100	282	100	318	100				
Liabilities																		
Notes with public	34	16	27	11	31	13	12	5	13	5	14	5	18	6				
Deposits	143	65	168	71	165	68	162	74	200	80	217	77	245	77				
To public	177	81	195	82	196	81	174	79	213	85	231	82	263	83				
Sundry	19	9	20	9	22	9	23	11	16	6	30	11	34	11				
Capital Paid																		
Reserves	23	10	22	9	23	10	22	10	22	9	21	7	21	6				
Total	219	100	237	100	241	100	219	100	251	100	282	100	318	100				

APPENDIX A.10

Glasgow Banking Company, 1809–1836

Balance Sheets 1810–1819

Source: Boase, 1867.

Notes: Cash and note circulation balances were
          calculated by C. W. Boase. The basis
          of assessment was not revealed.
          Figures for 1815 were not revealed.
          No details available on nature of
          branch figures.
          All figures at end of June.

Appendix A.10: Glasgow Banking Company

	1810 Total	%	1811 Total	%	1812 Total	%	1813 Total	%	1814 Total	%	1816 Total	%	1817 Total	%	1818 Total	%	1819 Total	%
Assets																		
Advances Cash a/cs.	—	—													40	3	98	8
Bills	432	90	366	83	461	85	540	87	655	89	665	89	659	86	1320	92	986	80
Others	—		5	1	17	3	8	1	4	1	19	2	21	3				
Total	432	90	371	84	478	88	548	88	659	90	684	91	680	89	1360	95	1084	88
Branches	23	5	18	4	24	4	38	6	14	2	14	2	14	2			10	1
Investments			3	—	10	2	10	1	12	2					7	—	14	1
Sundry	12	3	30	7	12	2	12	2	36	5	18	2	34	4	24	2	88	7
Cash	11	2	21	5	20	4	16	3	11	1	35	5	37	5	48	3	41	3
Total	478	100	443	100	544	100	624	100	732	100	751	100	765	100	1439	100	1237	100
Liabilities																		
Notes with public	111	23	90	20	93	17	122	20	135	18	142	19	129	17	190	13	154	12
Deposits	226	47	213	48	295	54	331	53	401	55	362	48	418	55	940	65	778	63
To public	337	70	303	68	388	71	453	73	536	73	504	67	547	72	1130	78	932	75
Sundry	28	6	19	4	24	5	25	4	32	4	51	7	6	1	31	2	7	1
Capital Paid	100	21	113	26	120	22	131	21	144	20	174	23	190	24	238	17	266	22
Reserves	13	3	8	2	12	2	15	2	20	3	22	3	22	3	40	3	32	2
Total	478	100	443	100	544	100	624	100	732	100	751	100	765	100	1439	100	1237	100

APPENDIX A.11

Greenock Banking Company, 1785–1843

Partial Balance Sheets 1814–1828

Source: Balance Books
             Royal Bank of Scotland, Edinburgh

Notes: All dates at end of June.

Appendix A.11: Greenock Banking Company

	1814 Total	%	1815 Total	%	1816 Total	%	1817 Total	%	1818 Total	%	1819 Total	%	1820 Total	%	1821 Total	%	1822 Total	%
Assets																		
Advances																		
Cash a/cs.																		
Bills	316		370		229		216		239		247		222		202		150	
Others																		
Total																		
Branches																		
Investments																		
Sundry																		
Cash	3		3		3		2		2		2		2		2		2	
Total																		
Liabilities																		
Notes with public	103		105		77		64		74		80		69		69		67	
Deposits	168		173		162		159		166		175		172		175		174	
To public	271		278		239		223		240		255		241		244		241	
Sundry																		
Capital Paid																		
Reserves																		
Total																		

	1823 Total	%	1824 Total	%	1825 Total	%	1826 Total	%	1827 Total	%	1828 Total	%	Total	%	Total	%	Total	%
Assets																		
Advances																		
Cash a/cs.																		
Bills	127		158		176		185		185		186							
Others																		
Total																		
Branches																		
Investments																		
Sundry																		
Cash	2		1		1		2		3		2							
Total																		
Liabilities																		
Notes with public	67		65		81		73		63		58							
Deposits	159		161		164		174		176		177							
To public	226		226		245		247		239		235							
Sundry																		
Capital																		
Paid																		
Reserves																		
Total																		

APPENDIX A.12

Montrose Banking Company, 1814–1829

Partial Balance Sheets 1816–1822

Source: Minute Book
          Bank of Scotland, Edinburgh.

Notes: Cash account advances have been estimated at
          60 per cent of authorised credits.
          All figures at end of April.

Appendix A.12: Montrose Banking Company

	1816 Total	%	1817 Total	%	1818 Total	%	1819 Total	%	1820 Total	%	1821 Total	%	1822 Total	%	Total	%	Total	%
Assets																		
Advances																		
Cash a/cs.	11		12		13		14		17		18		20					
Bills	37		29		49		55		90		87		94					
Others																		
Total	48		41		62		69		107		105		114					
Branches																		
Investments																		
Sundry																		
Cash																		
Total																		
Liabilities																		
Notes with public																		
Deposits																		
To public																		
Sundry																		
Capital																		
Paid	17		17		18		18		18		18		19					
Reserves	1		1		1		1		1		1		2					
Total																		

APPENDIX A.13

Paisley Union Banking Company, 1788–1838

Balance Sheets 1789, 1795–6, 1820, 1836

Source: Journal Ledger and Minute Books
Bank of Scotland, Glasgow

Notes: No details are available on the nature of
the branch figures.
All dates at end of June.

Appendix A.13: Paisley Union Banking Company

	1789 Total	%	1795 Total	%	1796 Total	%	1820 Total	%	1836 Total	%	Total	%	Total	%	Total	%
Assets																
Advances																
Cash a/cs.	9	13	16	18	12	8	128	20	79	15						
Bills	29	41	42	46	102	64	372	57	354	65						
Others																
Total	38	54	58	64	114	72	500	77	433	80						
Branches	28	39	22	24	19	12	42	6	30	5						
Investments					15	9	42	6	14	3						
Sundry	4	6	10	11	9	6	52	8	35	6						
Cash	1	1	1	1	1	1	15	3	32	6						
Total	71	100	91	100	158	100	651	100	544	100						
Liabilities																
Notes with public	50	71	38	42	64	41	107	16	108	20						
Deposits	10	14	39	43	78	49	488	75	397	73						
To public	60	85	77	85	142	90	595	91	505	93						
Sundry	1	1	3	3	3	2	1	—								
Capital Paid	10	14	11	12	13	8	40	6	24	4						
Reserves							15	3	15	3						
Total	71	100	91	100	158	100	651	100	544	100						

APPENDIX A.14

Perth United Banking Company, 1766–1787

Balance Sheets 1767–1786

Source: General Ledgers Bank of Scotland, Edinburgh
and Glasgow.

Notes: All dates at end of September

Appendix A.14: Perth United Banking Company

	1767 Total	%	1768 Total	%	1769 Total	%	1770 Total	%	1771 Total	%	1772 Total	%	1773 Total	%	1774 Total	%	1775 Total	%
Assets																		
Advances	46	61	48	57	40	51	35	52	28	36	31	54	24	47	21	44	20	34
Cash a/cs.	15	20	18	21	19	24	18	27	18	23	2	4	6	12	7	15	8	14
Bills	3	4	4	5	7	9	3	5	2	3	1	2	1	2	1	2	—	
Others																		
Total	64	85	70	83	66	84	56	84	48	62	35	60	31	61	29	61	28	48
Branches Investments																		
Sundry	3	4	4	5	3	4	7	10	8	11	11	20	9	18	14	29	26	44
Cash	8	11	10	12	9	12	4	6	21	27	11	20	11	21	5	10	5	8
Total	75	100	84	100	78	100	67	100	77	100	57	100	51	100	48	100	59	100
Liabilities																		
Notes with public	55	74	44	52	44	56	40	60	49	64	31	54	24	47	32	67	43	73
Deposits			3	4	10	13	10	15	1	1	2	4	2	4	2	4	1	2
To public	55	74	47	56	54	69	50	75	50	65	33	58	26	51	34	71	44	75
Sundry			25	30	11	14	3	5	12	16	10	18	11	22	—		1	2
Capital Paid	10	13	12	14	13	17	14	20	15	19	14	24	14	27	14	29	14	23
Reserves	10	13																
Total	75	100	84	100	78	100	67	100	77	100	57	100	51	100	48	100	59	100

U

Appendix A.14: Perth United Banking Company – contd.

	1776 Total	%	1777 Total	%	1778 Total	%	1779 Total	%	1780 Total	%	1781 Total	%	1782 Total	%	1783 Total	%	1784 Total	%
Assets																		
Advances																		
Cash a/cs.	26	39	35	46	39	60	37	59	32	46	27	38	25	36	23	33	24	28
Bills	14	21	15	20	12	18	11	17	17	25	26	36	24	35	24	35	30	35
Others	5	7	4	5	—		—		3	4	3	4	4	5	6	9	10	12
Total	45	67	54	71	51	78	48	76	52	75	56	78	53	76	53	77	64	75
Branches																		
Investments																		
Sundry	18	27	15	20	4	6	9	14	11	16	7	10	8	12	9	13	9	10
Cash	4	6	7	9	10	16	6	10	6	9	9	12	8	12	7	10	13	15
Total	67	100	76	100	65	100	63	100	69	100	72	100	69	100	69	100	86	100
Liabilities																		
Notes with public	50	75	55	72	46	71	47	75	53	77	56	78	53	77	51	74	67	78
Deposits	1	1	—		—		—		—		—		—		1	1	—	
To public	51	76	55	72	46	71	47	75	53	77	56	78	53	77	52	75	67	78
Sundry	2	3	7	9	5	8	2	3	2	3	1	1	1	1	2	3	4	5
Capital Paid Reserves	14	21	14	19	14	21	14	22	14	20	15	21	15	22	15	22	15	17
Total	67	100	76	100	65	100	63	100	69	100	72	100	69	100	69	100	86	100

	1785 Total	%	1786 Total	%	Total	%	Total	%	Total	%	Total	%	Total	%	Total	%	Total	%	Total	%
Assets																				
Advances																				
Cash a/cs.	26	28	28	34																
Bills	56	60	31	38																
Others																				
Total	82	88	59	72																
Branches																				
Investments																				
Sundry	5	5	14	17																
Cash	7	7	9	11																
Total	94	100	82	100																
Liabilities																				
Notes with public	70	74	65	80																
Deposits			1	1																
To public	70	74	66	81																
Sundry	9	10	1	1																
Capital																				
Paid																				
Reserves	15	16	15	18																
Total	94	100	82	100																

APPENDIX A.15

Perth Banking Company, 1787–1857

Balance Sheets 1788–1789, 1830–1857

Source: General Ledger, Progressive Ledger, Minute Books
Bank of Scotland, Edinburgh and Glasgow.

Notes: Cash balances for the years 1830–9 are estimated
as 2 per cent of demand liabilities. The balances
under *Sundry* include balances due by branches and
correspondents. It has not been possible to
separate the two.
1788–9 at end of September.
All other dates at end of May.

Appendix A.15: Perth Banking Company

	1788 Total	%	1789 Total	%	Total	%	1830 Total	%	1831 Total	%	1832 Total	%	1833 Total	%	1834 Total	%	1835 Total	%
Assets																		
Advances																		
Cash a/cs.	30	36	31	38			100	17	95	17	138	25	148	28	163	32	155	31
Bills	30	36	37	46			310	54	277	48	202	37	197	38	180	36	188	38
Others	5	6																
Total	65	78	68	84			410	71	372	65	340	62	345	66	343	68	343	69
Branches	3	4	3	4														
Investments							134	23	164	29	155	28	128	25	110	22	110	22
Sundry	2	2					23	4	29	5	45	8	41	8	46	9	34	7
Cash	13	16	10	12			9	2	9	1	8	2	8	1	8	1	8	2
Total	83	100	81	100			576	100	574	100	548	100	522	100	507	100	495	100
Liabilities																		
Notes with public	51	61	48	59			64	11	75	13	70	13	56	11	59	12	58	12
Deposits	3	4	3	4			403	70	399	70	375	69	373	71	353	70	339	68
To public	54	65	51	63			467	81	474	83	445	82	429	82	412	82	397	80
Sundry	14	17	14	17			37	6	20	3	18	3	3	1	2	—	2	—
Capital Paid	14	17	14	17			66	12	66	11	67	12	67	13	67	13	83	17
Reserves	1	1	2	3			6	1	14	3	18	3	23	4	26	5	13	3
Total	83	100	81	100			576	100	574	100	548	100	522	100	507	100	495	100

Appendix A.15: Perth Banking Company – contd.

	1836 Total	1836 %	1837 Total	1837 %	1838 Total	1838 %	1839 Total	1839 %	1840 Total	1840 %	1841 Total	1841 %	1842 Total	1842 %	1843 Total	1843 %	1844 Total	1844 %
Assets																		
Advances																		
Cash a/cs.	125	26	168	33	139	26	168	32	159	31	148	29	176	32	185	34	163	30
Bills	192	41	129	25	93	17	66	13	55	11	67	13	91	16	66	12	76	14
Others																		
Total	317	67	297	58	232	43	234	45	214	42	215	42	267	48	251	46	239	44
Branches																		
Investments	92	19	137	27	231	43	252	48	252	50	251	50	262	47	265	49	294	54
Sundry	57	12	67	13	70	13	29	6	32	6	29	6	22	4	21	4	58	11
Cash	7	2	8	2	8	1	8	1	7	2	8	2	3	1	3	1	3	1
Total	473	100	509	100	541	100	523	100	505	100	503	100	554	100	540	100	594	100
Liabilities																		
Notes with public	32	7	48	10	56	10	52	10	45	9	41	8	42	8	39	7	43	8
Deposits	340	72	353	69	376	70	360	69	348	69	342	68	351	63	354	66	388	72
To public	372	79	401	79	432	80	412	79	393	78	383	76	393	71	393	73	431	80
Sundry	2	—	6	1	2	—	3	1	2	—	2	—	42	8	23	4	35	6
Capital																		
Paid	83	18	83	16	83	15	100	19	100	20	100	20	100	18	100	19	100	19
Reserves	16	3	19	4	24	5	8	1	10	2	18	4	19	3	24	4	28	5
Total	473	100	509	100	541	100	523	100	505	100	503	100	554	100	540	100	594	100

	1845 Total	%	1846 Total	%	1847 Total	%	1848 Total	%	1849 Total	%	1850 Total	%	1851 Total	%	1852 Total	%	1853 Total	%
Assets																		
Advances																		
Cash a/cs.	169	26	142	23	161	25	257	38	309	43	296	41	274	40	257	39	252	35
Bills	85	13	131	21	153	23	105	15	105	15	115	16	100	14	102	15	106	15
Others																		
Total	254	39	273	44	314	48	362	53	414	58	411	57	374	54	359	54	358	50
Branches																		
Investments	304	46	298	48	271	41	253	37	254	35	256	36	259	37	264	39	261	37
Sundry	95	14	43	7	59	9	51	8	38	5	40	6	53	8	37	6	80	11
Cash	9	1	11	1	12	2	11	2	11	2	11	1	9	1	9	1	16	2
Total	662	100	625	100	656	100	677	100	717	100	718	100	695	100	669	100	715	100
Liabilities																		
Notes with public	48	8	46	7	45	7	47	7	43	6	44	6	44	7	42	6	50	7
Deposits	472	71	437	70	444	68	475	70	465	65	488	68	474	68	439	66	472	66
To public	520	79	483	77	489	75	522	77	508	71	532	74	518	75	481	72	522	73
Sundry	10	1	6	1	24	4	7	1	55	8	27	4	14	2	22	3	25	3
Capital																		
Paid	100	15	100	16	100	15	100	15	100	14	100	14	100	14	100	15	100	14
Reserves	32	5	36	6	43	6	48	7	54	7	59	8	63	9	66	10	68	10
Total	662	100	625	100	656	100	677	100	717	100	718	100	695	100	669	100	715	100

Appendix A.15: Perth Banking Company – *contd.*

	1854 Total	%	1855 Total	%	1856 Total	%	1857 Total	%	Total	%	Total	%	Total	%	Total	%
Assets																
Advances																
Cash a/cs.	267	37	296	40	284	36	213	26								
Bills	131	18	116	16	200	26	252	30								
Others																
Total	398	55	412	56	484	62	465	56								
Branches																
Investments	242	34	230	32	214	28	252	30								
Sundry	56	8	67	9	58	7	82	10								
Cash	21	3	22	3	24	3	30	4								
Total	717	100	731	100	779	100	829	100								
Liabilities																
Notes with public	56	8	58	8	56	7	55	7								
Deposits	462	64	491	67	536	69	589	71								
To public	518	72	549	75	592	76	644	78								
Sundry	29	4	15	2	17	2	29	3								
Capital Paid	100	14	100	14	100	13	100	12								
Reserves	70	10	67	9	70	9	56	7								
Total	717	100	731	100	779	100	829	100								

Appendix B

SUSPENSION OF PAYMENTS HANDBILL (see Chapter 3, part 1)

Edinburgh, *March 1, 1797.*

THE following ORDER of the PRIVY COUNCIL has been received this Morning, by Express, from London, viz.

'Upon the Representation of the Chancellor of the Exchequer, stating, That from the result of the Information which he has received, and of the Enquiries which it has been his Duty to make, respecting the effect of the unusual *Demands for Specie* that have been made upon the Metropolis, in consequence of ill-founded or exaggerated alarms in different parts of the Country, it appears, That unless some Measure is immediately taken, there may be reason to apprehend a want of a sufficient Supply of Cash to answer the exigencies of the Public Service; it is the unanimous Opinion of the Board, That it is indispensably necessary for the Public Service, that the Directors of the Bank of England should forbear issuing any Cash in payment, until the Sense of Parliament should be taken on that Subject, and the proper Measures adopted thereupon for maintaining the means of Circulation, and Supporting the Public and Commercial Credit of the Country at this important juncture: And it is ordered that a Copy of this Minute be transmitted to the Directors of the Bank of England; and they are hereby required, on the grounds of the exigency of the case, to conform thereto until the sense of Parliament can be taken as aforesaid.

(Signed) W. FAWKENER.'

In pursuance of the above Order, the Bank of Scotland, the Royal Bank of Scotland, the British Linen Company, Sir William Forbes, James Hunter and Company, and the Leith Banking Company, hereby INTIMATE, That they are to forbear Issuing any SPECIE in Payments, until the Sense of Parliament shall be known on that Subject. IN EVERY OTHER RESPECT, Business will be carried on as usual by the above Companies, *in all their Offices* in Town and Country.

JAMES FRASER, Treasurer,
For *The Bank of Scotland.*
WALTER HOG, Manager,
For *The British Linen Company.*
Wm FORBES, JAMES HUNTER, & Co.

WILLIAM SIMPSON, Cashier,
For *The Royal Bank of Scotland.*
JAMES KER, Manager,
For *The Leith Banking Company.*

Appendix C

CASH CREDIT BOND (see Chapter 6, part 3)

Source.   Bank of Scotland, Glasgow.   Thistle Bank Papers.

WE Robert Muirheid Merchant in Glasgow John Buchanan of Ardoch and James Dunlop of Househill. Whereas the Thistle Bank Company of Glasgow have agreed to allow us Credit upon a Cash Account to be kept in their books in the name of the said Robert Muirheid to the amount of Five Hundred pounds Sterling upon our granting these presents Therefore we the saids Robert Muirheid John Buchanan and James Dunlop Bind and oblige us conjunctly and severally our Heirs Executors and Successors whatsoever to Content and pay to John Campbell of Clathick Robert Scot of Aikenhead Henry Ritchie of Busby James Rowan of Bellahouston and Archibald Graham Banker in Glasgow the partners of the said Company or to the Survivor or Survivors of them or to the said Archibald Grahame their Cashier or to any other Cashier to be appointed by them for the use of the said Company or to the Assignees of any one of them the foregoing sum of Five hundred pounds Sterling or such part or parts thereof as he the said Robert Muirheid shall draw out by drafts or orders on their Cashier in Virtue of the foresaid credit over and above what of the proper cash of the said Robert Muirheid may happen to be lodged on the said Cash Account and that at any time the same shall be demanded after Six months from the date hereof with the due and lawful interest thereof from the time of the said advance until the same is repaid with Twenty pounds money foresaid of penalty for every hundred pounds in case of faillzie and proportionally for more or less. And it is hereby declared that a Stated Account made out from such orders or drafts as shall be drawn by the said Robert Muirheid on the Cashier of the said Company and signed by their Accountant shall be sufficient to Constitute and Ascertain a balance and Charge against us, And that no suspension shall pass at our instance of a charge so ascertained but on Consignation only, Consenting to the registration hereof in the books of Council and Session or any other Competent to have the strength of a Decreet interponed thereto that letters of Horning on six days and all other execution necessary pay pass hereupon as effeirs and to that effect we Constitute Our Prors.

In witness whereof these presents written on stamped paper by John Kemp Clerk to the said Company are subscribed by us as follows viz. At Glasgow the Fifth day of November One thousand eight hundred years by the saids Robert Muirheid and James Dunlop before these witnesses John Graham Clerk to the said Company and the said John Kemp, And by the said John Buchanan at Glasgow the thirteenth day of said month of November and year foresaid before these witnesses the saids John Graham and John Kemp.

John Graham	*Witness*	Robert Muirheid
John Kemp	*Witness*	James Dunlop
John Graham	*Witness*	John Buchanan
John Kemp	*Witness*	

Appendix D

COMPARATIVE SIZES OF SCOTTISH PROVINCIAL BANKING
COMPANIES AND ENGLISH COUNTRY BANKS

SOME indication of the comparative size of the average units in the Scottish and English banking systems can be obtained by reference to the paid-up capitals of banks and this has been discussed in Chapter 6.

A further attempt was made to compare the average size of units in the two systems by reference to the number of units and the size of population for the year 1825.

The population census for 1821 revealed that the population of England and Wales was greater than that of Scotland by a factor of 6 (12 m and 2 m).

In 1825 there were 23 banking companies, 3 public banks, 3 joint-stock banks and 7 Edinburgh-based private banks – a total of 36 institutions. The number of institutions in England and Wales at the same time was in the region of 650. If it is assumed that the demand for banking services was roughly equal in both countries, then the number of banks in Scotland could be grossed by the population factor, i.e. 6, which suggests that there would have been 216 banks in Scotland compared with 650 in England and Wales. This in turn suggests that Scottish banks were on average three times the size of their English counterparts, a figure which compares exactly with the comparison between paid-up capitals of Scottish provincial banking companies and English country banks.

This analysis, however, is rendered unsatisfactory for two reasons. Firstly, the number of assumptions involved in the calculation, for example that of equal demand for services, undermines its usefulness. Secondly, the entirely different structures of the two systems makes it impossible to compare like with like at the macro level. There was not the same homogeneity amongst Scottish banks as there was in England. There were no public banks active in the English provinces as there were in Scotland. Furthermore, the Scottish system of branches provided a much wider range of banking offices, so that any Scottish/English comparison would have to incorporate this.

Bibliography

1. Manuscripts

The principal manuscripts used for this book are in the collections of the three Scottish Banks, all of which have been surveyed by the National Register of Archives (Scotland) NRA(S). The survey numbers are:

No.945   Bank of Scotland
No.226   Royal Bank of Scotland
No.349   National Commercial (now merged with Royal Bank)
No.452   The Clydesdale Bank

Further material on banking may be traced in the NRA(S) source list No.13.
The major items used in this work are listed below.

Bank of Scotland:	Directors' Minute Books
	Miscellaneous documents – Edinburgh
	Miscellaneous documents – Glasgow
British Linen Bank:	Directors' Minute Books
Commercial Bank of Scotland:	Directors' Minute Books
	Letter Books
National Bank of Scotland:	Directors' Minute Books
Royal Bank of Scotland:	Directors' Minute Books
	Scott-Moncrieff Letters

(The minute books and letters mentioned above have been prepared in transcript form by Mrs. E. O. A. Checkland. It was this source which was mainly used).
Balfour of Balfour and Trenabie, NRA(S) 627
Buccleuch MSS, SRO GD 244/666/–
Bute, Marquis of, NRA(S) 631
Campbell of Succoth, GCA TD 99
Dr. J. Campbell NRA(S) 657
Edinburgh University Library, Miscellaneous letters on banking
Glasgow Quasi bankers, SRA B10/15/7145
Harvard College Library, Lee Letters, copy in SRA
Home of Wedderburn, SRO GD 627
Houston of Johnstone, NRA(S) 935
Hunter-Blair MSS
Innes of Stow, SRO GD 113/270
Lawson, James, SRA TD 172/2
Mansfield, Earl of, NRA(S) 776
Melville Collection: SRO GD 51
                       NLS
                       Bank of Scotland
Murray Collection, Glasgow University Library, MU 23 B 19
Preston, Lt. Col. R.C., NRA(S) 934
Saltoun MSS, NLS

Speirs of Elderslie, NRA(S) 607
Steel-Maitland, SRO GD 193
The Registers of Deeds and files of Court Processes at the Scottish Record Office have also been
fruitful sources of subsidiary material.

Aberdeen Banking Co.

Prospectus 1765, CBS Glasgow
Contracts 1767 and 1806, Aberdeen Public Library
Cash account and bond registers, 1767–1818, 4 vols., BoS Aberdeen
Stock Transfer Journal, 1767–1785, BoS Aberdeen
Dividend Receipt Book, 1772–1832, BoS Aberdeen
Cashier's Letter Book, 1767, BoS Aberdeen
Principal General Ledger, 1767–69, BoS Aberdeen
Progressive General Ledger, 1767–69, BoS Aberdeen
Weekly States of Cash, 1768–1777, 3 vols., BoS Aberdeen
Specie and Note Reserve Book, 1767–1803, BoS Aberdeen
Weekly abstracts of balances, 1768–1787, BoS Aberdeen
Directors' Minute Book, 1769–1776, BoS Aberdeen
Scroll Minute Books, 1770–99, 4 vols., BoS Aberdeen
Letter Book, 1767–71 and 1782–94, BoS Aberdeen
Cashier's Account Book, 1767–68, BoS Aberdeen
Teller's Cash Book, 1768–69, BoS Aberdeen
Post Bills Register, 1768–1773, BoS Aberdeen
General Ledger, 1769, BoS Aberdeen
Cash Account Progressive Ledger, 1769–71, BoS Aberdeen
Bills Book, 1771–72, BoS Aberdeen
Bills of Exchange Book, 1772–1777, BoS Aberdeen
Forms of Deeds n.d., BoS Aberdeen
Cash Account Progressive Ledger, 1792–94, BoS Aberdeen
Interest Receipt Ledger, 1798–1800, BoS Aberdeen
Cashier's Private Journal, 1840–42, BoS Aberdeen
Cash Book, 1845–47, BoS Aberdeen
Deposit Receipt Ledger, 1848–50, BoS Aberdeen
Bills book, 1848–57 Banchory Branch, BoS Aberdeen
Deposit Receipt Book, Banchory Branch, BoS Aberdeen

Ayr Bank (Douglas, Heron and Co.)

List of Partners, Ewart Library, Dumfries
Dumfries Burgh Chamberlain Account Book, Dumfries Burgh Archives
Fettercairn papers, NLS Acc. 4796 2nd series, Box 54, Outline history of Ayr Bank

Dundee Banking Co.

Sederunt Book, 1763–67, RBS Dundee
List of Partners, 1826 and 1858, Dundee Public Library
Contract, 1826 and 1863, Dundee Public Library
Papers re proposed takeover by UBS, BoS Glasgow

Dundee Commercial Banking Co. No. 1

Letters and Documents, 1792–1802, RBS Dundee

Dundee New Bank

Letters and Documents, 1802–38, RBS Dundee
Trial Balance Book, 1806–10, 1817–38, RBS Dundee
Sederunt Book, 1802–6, RBS Dundee
Private Letter Book, 1802–4, RBS Dundee

Register of Notes, 1802–3, RBS Dundee
Note Plate Impression Record, 1802–3, RBS Dundee
Private Journal, 1802–6, RBS Dundee
Private Ledger, 1802–6, RBS Dundee
Memo of Notes Burned, 1805, RBS Dundee
Contract, 1806, 1828, 1837, RBS Dundee
Sederunt Book, 1806–1837, RBS Dundee
Proposals and agreements on sale, 1838, RBS Dundee
Liquidation Papers post, 1838, RBS Dundee
Papers re Bells and Kinnaird, 1808, RBS Dundee

Dundee Commercial Banking Co. No.2

Contract, 1825, Dundee Public Library

East Lothian Banking Co.

Sederunt Book, 1809–14, SRO
Committee of Accounts – Record Book, 1823, SRO
Reports on Affairs, 1827, 1829, SRO

Ship Bank, Glasgow

Balance Book, 1752–61, BoS Glasgow
Journal, 1785–1836, BoS Glasgow
Cash Account Ledgers, 1785–1836 incomplete, BoS Glasgow
Bonds and Commission, 1750–1775, SRA B10/15/–

Arms Bank, Glasgow

Bonds and commissions, 1750–1765, SRA B10/15/–

Thistle Bank, Glasgow

Cash Account ledgers, 1769–1836 incomplete, BoS Glasgow
Journals, 1778–9, 1797–8, BoS Glasgow
Balance Ledger, 1786–92, BoS Glasgow
Letter Books to Edinburgh correspondent, 1834–6, 3 vols., BoS Edinburgh
Mure of Caldwell MSS., NLS
Acc. 4942
Bonds and Commissions, SRA B10/15/–
Cash Credit and other bonds, Miscellaneous papers, 2 boxes, BoS Glasgow

Merchant Banking Co. of Glasgow

Bonds and Commissions, 1769–72, SRA B10/15/–

Glasgow Banking Co.

Cash account ledgers, 1809–1837, BoS Glasgow
Sederunt Book and Dividend Book, 1809–1843, BoS Glasgow
Miscellaneous Papers, 1809–37, BoS Glasgow

Glasgow and Ship Bank

Minute Book of Management Committee, 1842–3, BoS Glasgow
Miscellaneous Papers, 1837–43, BoS Glasgow

Greenock Banking Co.

Journal, 1786, RBS Edinburgh
State Book, 1813–28, 2 vols., RBS Edinburgh

Kilmarnock Banking Co.

Contract of Co-partnery, 1802, Pollok-Morris MSS, NRA(S) 905
Letter Book, 1802–19, Pollok-Morris MSS, NRA(S) 905

Montrose Banking Co.

Minute Book, 1814–22, BoS Edinburgh
Letter Book, 1814–16, BoS Edinburgh
Stock Ledger, 1814–29, BoS Edinburgh

Paisley Banking Co.

Papers re Dundee branch, 1790, RBS Dundee

Paisley Union Banking Co.

General Ledger, 1788–9, BoS Glasgow
Journal, 1795–6, BoS Glasgow
Minute Book, 1819–38, BoS Glasgow

Perth United Banking Co.

General Ledgers, 1766–87, 21 vols., BoS Glasgow

Perth Banking Co.

Minute Book, 1785–1811, BoS Glasgow
Stock Ledger, 1787–1810, BoS Glasgow
Stock Journal, 1787–1810, BoS Glasgow
Dividend Journal, 1787–1808, BoS Glasgow
Contract of Co-partnery, 1787, BoS Edinburgh
Progressive Ledger, 1787–9, BoS Edinburgh
General Ledger, 1787–9, BoS Edinburgh
Bills Books, 4 vols., 1787–94, BoS Glasgow
Cash Book, Coupar Angus Branch, 1795–1808, BoS Glasgow
Contract of Co-partnery, 1808, BoS Glasgow
Minute Book, 1807–32, BoS Glasgow
Stock Ledger, 1808–29, BoS Glasgow
Dividend Book, 1809–32, BoS Glasgow
Bond Register, 1808–32, BoS Glasgow
Bill Accounts Book, 1808–9, BoS Glasgow
Letter Book, Coupar Angus Branch, 1809–11, BoS Glasgow
Ledger Dunkeld Branch, 1818–22, BoS Glasgow
Branch Control Ledger, 1819, BoS Glasgow
Interest Receipts Balance List, 1823–30, BoS Glasgow
Contract of Co-partnery, 1829, BoS Glasgow
Minute Book, 1828–72, 2 vols., BoS Glasgow
Bond Register, 1829–57, BoS Glasgow
Dividend Ledger, 1831–57, BoS Glasgow
Stock Journal, 1829–57, BoS Glasgow
Stock Ledger, 1829–57, BoS Glasgow
Letter Book, 1829–31, BoS Glasgow
Note Circulation Book, 1840–57, 3 vols., BoS Glasgow
Investment Register, 1841–57, BoS Edinburgh
Deposit Receipt Register, 1841–44, BoS Glasgow
Deposit Receipt Register Coupar Angus Branch, 1841–57, BoS Glasgow

Shetland Banking Co.

Hay of Hayfield MSS, NLS Accession 3250

Stirling Banking Co.

Sequestration Report, 1829, Clydesdale Bank, Glasgow

2. Court Processes

1760	Court of Session (CS). Trotter v Arms Bank. See Morison 14607.
1805	CS96/2349–53 Merchant Banking Co. of Stirling-Sequestration Journals.
1808–	CS232 C15/41 C16/57 C16/92 C16/105 Campbell, Thomson and Co. Winding up papers.
1811	CS96/203 Balgonie Iron Co. – Sequestration Journal.
1815	CS96/935–7. Sequestration Journals of William Hamilton, agent for Paisley Union Banking Co. at Hamilton.
1816	CS233 1 Inglis F/5/1 Fleming, Leiper agt. Paisley Union Bkg. Co.
1816	CS233 1 Inglis F/1/27. Falkirk Union Banking Co. – Sequestration Papers.
1816	CS96/987–8 Falkirk Union Banking Co. Sequestration divisions.
1816	CS96/869 Falkirk Union Banking Co. Sequestration Journals.
1816/36	CS96/326–332 Borthwick and Goudie. Sequestration Journals.
1819	CS96/848 Robert Kent. Sequestration Journal.
1822	CS44 Box 75. Merchant Bank of Stirling. Extracted process.
1826	CS96/2346–8 and 2345–9 Stirling Banking Co. Sequestration Journals.
1827	CS Second Division 6/18/1827. A. Scot agt. J. Ker. (Leith Bkg. Co.).
1827	CS96/692 Andrew Christie-Sequestration Journal.
1828	CS96/835 Robert Ballingall-Sequestration Journal.
1829	CS311/2142 Box 207 Private Correspondence of Montrose Banking Co. 1814–31.
1831	CS96/683 John Ferguson-Sequestration Journal.
1832	CS231 1 Currie Mack W/2/17. J. and R. Watson-unextracted process.
1832	CS96/450 J. & R. Watson. Sequestration Journal.
1832	PRO B/3/3641–2. John Maberly Sequestrations.
1842	CS279/1089, 2425 and 285/52. Shetland Banking Co. Sequestration processes.

General

1842   SRO CS 283 Sequestration Returns.

3. Newspapers and Magazines

Arbroath Guide
Bankers Magazine
The Bee
Blackwoods Edinburgh Magazine
Caledonian Mercury
The Dundee Magazine and Journal of the Times
The Dundee Weekly Advertiser and Angus-shire Intelligencer
Edinburgh Advertiser
Edinburgh Almanac
Edinburgh Courant
Edinburgh Gazette
Edinburgh Magazine
General Almanac of Scotland
Glasgow Advertiser
Glasgow Courant
Glasgow Courier
Glasgow Herald
Glasgow Journal
Glasgow Mercury
Greenock Advertiser
Montrose Review
Scots Magazine
Scotsman
Scottish Bankers Magazine

4. Parliamentary Papers and Acts

Debates   Hansard, especially 1826–8

Acts

5 Geo.III	c.49 Option Clause and Small Notes Act
12 Geo.III	c.72 Scottish Bankruptcy Act
14 Geo.III	c.21 Ayr Bank Redemption of Annuities Act
15 Geo.III	c.51 English Small Notes Act
17 Geo.III	c.30 English Small Notes Act
33 Geo.III	c.74 Scottish Bankruptcy Act
7 Geo.IV	c.67 Scottish Banking Companies (Entitlement to Sue) Act

v

Reports

1793	Commercial Credit 1826 (23) 111
1797	Outstanding Demands on the Bank of England 1826 (26) 111
1797	Lords' Committee of Secrecy 1810 (17) 111
1804	Circulating Paper, The Specie and the Current Coin of Ireland. 1803–4 (86) IV
1810	High Price of Bullion. 1810 (349) 111
1812	Country Bank Licences 1812–3 (183) XIII
1819	Resumption of Cash Payments. 1819 (202, 282) 111
1819	Lord's Committee of Secrecy. 1819 (291) 111
1826	Promissory Notes in Scotland and Ireland. Commons. 1826–7 (402) 111
1826	Promissory Notes in Scotland and Ireland. Lords 1826–7 (245) VI
1832	Bank Charter 1831–2 (722) VI
1835	Municipal Corporations of Scotland 1835–6 (29)
1836	Joint-Stock Banks. 1836 (591) IX
1837	Joint-Stock Banks. 1837 (531) XIV
1840	Banks of Issue. 1840 (602) IV
1841	Banks of Issue. 1841 (366, 410) V
1857	Bank Acts. 1857 (220) X
1858	Bank Acts. 1858 (381) V

Applications

1826	To Treasury re Scottish Notes in England. 1826–7 (24) XIV

Others

1827–	Inland Revenue (Scotland). Returns of Scottish Banking Companies

5. Books and Pamphlets

Anon.	1841	An Account of the Constitution, Objects and Practice of the Bank of Scotland. Edinburgh
	1755	An Address to the Town and County of Aberdeen upon the present state of Trade and Manufacturers. n.p.
	1840	No Title – subject, banking profits. Edinburgh
	1762	A Letter on the Conduct of the Banks. Edinburgh
	1752	A Letter from a Gentleman in Glasgow to his Friend in Edinburgh concerning Bank Notes and Paper Credit. Glasgow
	1860	A Short Memoir of James Young, merchant burgess of Aberdeen. Aberdeen
	1842	Mercantile Embarrassments and the Banking System. Edinburgh
	n.d.	Montrosiana. Montrose
	n.d.	Old Country Houses of the Old Glasgow Gentry. Glasgow
Attwood, T.	1828	The Scotch Banker, London
(Ayr Bank)	1788	The Precipitation and Fall of Messrs. Douglas, Heron and Co., late Bankers in Ayr. Edinburgh
Anderson, J. L.	1910	The Story of the Commercial Bank of Scotland. Edinburgh
Bell, R.	1815	A Dictionary of the Law of Scotland. Edinburgh
Bird, P.	1971	The Interpretation of Published Accounts. London
Boase, C. W.	1867	A Century of banking in Dundee. Edinburgh
Burke	1970	Peerage and Baronetage. London
Buchanan, J. (Glasguensis)	1884	Banking in Glasgow During the Olden Time. Glasgow
Cannan, E.	1925	The Paper Pound. London
Cameron, R. (ed)	1967	Banking in the Early Stages of Industrialisation. Oxford
Cameron, R. (ed)	1972	Banking and Economic Development: Some Lessons of History. Oxford

Campbell, R. H.	1961	Carron Company. Edinburgh
	1971	Scotland Since 1707. Oxford
Chandler, G.	1964	Four Centuries of Banking. London
Checkland, S. G.	1975	Scottish Banking: A History 1695–1973. Glasgow
Clapham, J.	1944	The Bank of England. London
Cockburn, H.	1856	Memorials of His Time. Edinburgh
Cook, W. B. (ed)	1900	The Stirling Antiquary. Stirling
Cook, W. B. and Morris, D. B. (eds)	1916	Extracts from the Records of the Merchant Guild of Stirling. Stirling
Crathorne, N. 1973	1973	Tennant's Stalk. London
Crick, W. F. and Wadsworth, J. E.	1936	A Hundred Years of Joint-Stock Banking. London
Crouzet, F. (ed)	1972	Capital Formation in the Industrial Revolution. London
Deane, P.	1967	British Economic Growth 1688–1959. Trends and Structure. Cambridge
Defoe, D.	1709	The History of the Union of Great Britain. Edinburgh
Devine, T. M.	1975	The Tobacco Lords. Edinburgh
Donnachie, I. and Macleod I.	1974	Old Galloway. Newton Abbot
Donnachie, I.	1979	A History of the Brewing Industry in Scotland. Edinburgh
Duckham, B. F.	1970	A History of the Scottish Coal Industry, 1700–1815. Newton Abbot
Fairman, W.	1824	An Account of the Public Funds. London
Feaveryear, A.	1963	The Pound Sterling. Oxford
Fetter, F. W.	1965	The Development of British Monetary Orthodoxy, 1797–1875. Harvard
Fleming, J. S.	1877	Scottish Banking; A Historical Sketch. Edinburgh
Forbes, Sir Wm.	1860	Memoirs of a Banking House. Edinburgh
Fortune	1824	Epitome of the Stocks and Public Funds. London
Francis, S.	1961	The Hannays of Sorbie. n.p.
Fulford, R.	1953	Glyn's 1753–1953. London
Fuller, J.	n.d.	The History of Berwick-upon-Tweed. Berwick
Gairdner, C. D.	1902	Autobiography. Kilmarnock
Gayer, A. D., Rostow, W. W. and Schwartz, A. N.	1953	The Growth and Fluctuations of the British Economy 1790–1850. Oxford
Gerschenkron, A.	1962	Economic Backwardness in Historical Perspective. Harvard
Gibson, J. C.	1930	The Old Private Banks of Stirling. Stirling
Gilbart, J. W.	1849	Practical Treatise on Banking. London
Glen, W.	1807	A Treatise on the Law of Bills of Exchange . . . in Scotland. Glasgow
Graham, W.	1886	The One Pound Note in Scotland. Edinburgh
Greener, M.	1968	Between the Lines of the Balance Sheet. London
Gregory, T. E.	1836	The Westminster Bank. London
Gulvin, C.	1973	The Tweedmakers. Newton Abbot
Haldane, A. R. B.	1973	The Drove Roads of Scotland. Newton Abbot
Hall, R.	1898	History of Galashiels. Galashiels
Hamilton, H.	1932	The Industrial Revolution in Scotland. Oxford
	1963	An Economic History of Scotland in the Eighteenth Century. Oxford
Hardcastle, D.	1843	Banks and Bankers. London
Holgate, H. C. F.	1948	English Bank Accounting and its Historical Background. London
Horne, H. O.	1947	A History of Savings Banks. Oxford
Homer, S.	1963	A History of Interest Rates. Rutgers
Hume, D.		See Rotwein
Hunt, B. C.	1936	The Development of the Business Corporation in England. Cambridge, Mass.
Joplin, T.	1827	An Essay on Banking in England and Scotland. London
Keith, A.	1936	The North of Scotland Bank. Aberdeen
Kerr, A. W.	1926	History of Banking in Scotland. London

King, W. T. C.	1936	History of the London Discount Market. London
Law, J.	1750	Money and Trade Considered. Glasgow
Leighton-Boyce, J.	1958	Smiths the Bankers. London
Lindsay, J.	1968	The Canals of Scotland. Newton Abbot
Logan, W. H.	1844	The Scotch Banker. Edinburgh
McCulloch, J. R.	1857	Select Tracts on Paper Currency and Banking. London
McCulloch, J. R.	1832	The Bank Question. London
McGregor, G.	1881	The History of Glasgow. Glasgow
MacLeod, H. D.	1883	Theory and Practice of Banking. London
MacLeod, H. D.	1891	The Elements of Banking. London
Maitland, J. (Earl of Lauderdale)	1804	An Enquiry into the Nature and Origin of Public Wealth. New York (1962 edition)
Malcolm, C. A.	1945	The Bank of Scotland. Edinburgh
	n.d.	The Bank of Scotland in Dumfries. n.p.
	1950	The British Linen Bank. Edinburgh
Marshall, T. H.	1849	The History of Perth. Perth
Matthews, P. W.	1926	History of Barclays Bank Ltd. London
Mitchell, D.	1866	The History of Montrose. Montrose
Mitchell, J. O.	1905	Old Glasgow Essays. Glasgow
Mitchell, B. R. and Dean, P.	1971	Abstract of British Historical Statistics. Cambridge
Mitchison, R.	1962	Agricultural Sir John. London
Morrison	—	Dictionary of Decisions. Edinburgh
Munro, N.	1928	The History of the Royal Bank of Scotland. Edinburgh
Mure, W. of Caldwell	1883–5	Selections from the Family Papers preserved at Caldwell. Edinburgh
Myers, M. G.	1970	A Financial History of the United States. London
New York	1837	Bank Commissioners' Report. New York
Parker, G.	1973	The Emergence of Modern Finance in Europe. London
The Parliamentary History of England 1814. London		
Payne, P. L. (ed)	1967	Studies in Scottish Business History. London
Payne, P. L.	1974	British Entrepreneurship in the Nineteenth Century. London
Phillips, M.	1894	A History of Banks, Bankers and Banking in Northumberland, Durham and North Yorkshire. London
Phillipson, N. T. and Mitchison, R. (eds)	1970	Scotland in the Age of Improvement. Edinburgh
Pollard, S.	1968	The Genesis of Modern Management. Harmondsworth
Porteous, A.	1912	The History of Crieff. Edinburgh
Powell, E. T.	1966	The Evolution of the Money Market. London
Pressnell, L. S.	1956	Country Banking in the Industrial Revolution. Oxford
Price, J.	1973	France and the Chesapeake. Ann Arbor
Rae, G.	1885	The Country Banker. London
Rait, R. S.	1930	The History of the Union Bank of Scotland. Glasgow
Reed, M.	1975	A History of James Capel and Co. London
Reid, J. M.	1938	The History of the Clydesdale Bank. Glasgow
Renwick, R.	—	Extracts from the Records of the Burgh of Glasgow. Edinburgh
Rotwein, E. (ed)	1955	Hume's Writings on Economics. Edinburgh
Sayers, R. S.	1957	Lloyd's Bank in the History of English Banking. Oxford
Scott, Sir Walter	1826	Thoughts on the Proposed Change in Currency by Malachi Malagrowther. Edinburgh
Sen, S. R.	1957	The Economics of Sir James Steuart. London
Senex	1884	Glasgow Past and Present. Glasgow
Sinclair, Sir J.	1814	General Report of the Agricultural State and Political Circumstances of Scotland. Edinburgh
Sinclair, Sir J. and Attwood, T.	1826	The Late Prosperity and the Present Adversity of the Country Explained. London
Statistical Account	1790's	(Old)
Statistical Account	1840's	(New)
Skinner, B. C.	1969	The Lime Industry in the Lothians. Edinburgh

Slaven, A.	1975	The Development of the West of Scotland. London
Smith, A.	1776	The Wealth of Nations (ed. A Skinner 1970). Harmondsworth
Smith, R. M.	1921	The History of Greenock. Greenock
Smout, T. C.	1963	Scottish Trade on the Eve of Union. Edinburgh
	1969	History of the Scottish People. London
Somers, R.	1873	The Scottish Banks and System of Issue. Edinburgh
Steuart, Sir J.	1767	An Enquiry into the Principles of Political Oeconomy (ed. A. Skinner 1966). Edinburgh
Stewart, G.	1881	Curiosities of Glasgow Citizenship. Glasgow
Subercaseaux, G.	1922	Monetary and Banking Policy in Chile. Oxford
Thomas, S. E.	1934	The Rise and Growth of Joint-Stock Banking. London
Thomson, G. G.	1903	An Old Glasgow Family of Thomson. Glasgow
Thomson, R.	1825	A Treatise on the Law of Bills of Exchange in Scotland. Edinburgh
Thornton, H.	1802	An Enquiry into the Nature and Effects of the Paper Credit of Great Britain. London
Ward. J. T. and Wilson, R. G. (eds)	1971	Land and Industry. Newton Abbot
Watt, H.	1833	The Practice of Banking in England and Scotland. London
Webb, B.	1767	The Complete Negociator of the Exchanges. London
Wilson, C. H.	1941	Anglo-Dutch Commerce and Finance in the Eighteenth Century. Cambridge

6. Articles

Anon.	1963	Early Banking in Dundee. TBR
	1960	The Glasgow Financial Scene: Early 19th Century. TBR
	1961	The Rise of Glasgow's West India Trade. TBR
	1962	An Early Glasgow-West India Miscellany. TBR
	1958	The Royal Bank and the London-Edinburgh Exchange Rate in the 18th Century. TBR
Anderson, B. L.	1969	Provincial Aspects of the Financial Revolution of the 18th Century. BH
	1970	Money and the Structure of Credit in the 18th Century. BH
Ashton, T. S.	1945	The Bill of Exchange and Private Banks in Lancashire 1790–1830. EcHR
Cameron, R.	1963	The Banker as Entrepreneur. ExEH
Campbell, R. H.	1964	An Economic History of Scotland in the 18th Century: Review SJPE
	1965	A Rejoinder to F. S. Taylor. SJPE
	1965	The Industrial Revolution: A Revision Article. SJPE
Checkland, S. G.	1954	The Liverpool Bill System and its Liverpool Protagonists 1810–1827. Economica
	1968	Banking History and Economic Development: Seven Systems: Review. SJPE
Christie, J. R.	1909	Joint-Stock Enterprise in Scotland before the Companies Acts. Juridical Review
Devine, T. M.	1973	Glasgow Merchants and the Collapse of the Tobacco Trade, 1775–1783. SHR
Devine, T. M.	1974	Sources of Capital for the Glasgow Tobacco Trade, 1740–1780. BH
Ernst, J. A.	1965	Genesis of the Currency Act of 1764. Wm. and Mary Quarterly
Evans, E. G.	1962	Planter Indebtedness and the Coming of the Revolution in Virgina. Wm. and Mary Quarterly
Forbes, R. N.	1974	Early Banking Excursions. TBR
Freebairn, C. F.	1924	An Old Banking Institution: The Paisley Union Bank. SBM

Good, D. F.	1973	Backwardness and the Role of Banking in 19th Century European Industrialisation. JEcH
Gourvish, T. R.	1969	The Bank of Scotland, 1830–45. SJPE
Hamilton, H.	1952	Scotland's Balance of Payments Problem in 1752. EcHR
Jardine, W. M.	1900	Old Glasgow Banks and Bankers. Old Glasgow Club
Kellett, J. R.	1961	Property Speculators and the Building of Glasgow, 1780–1830. SJPE
Lenman, B. P. and Gauldie, E. E.	1968	The Industrial History of the Dundee Region from the 18th to the Early 20th Century. British Association
	—	Sources of Capital for Industrial Growth in East Central Scotland before the Mid 19th Century. Unpublished
Munn, C. W.	1975	Origins of the Scottish Note Exchange. TBR
Price, J. M.	1967	The Rise of Glasgow in the Chesapeake Tobacco Trade, 1707–1775, in P. L. Payne (ed), Studies in Scottish Business History
	1971	Capital and Credit in the British Chesapeake Trade, 1750–75, in V. B. Platt and D. C. Skaggs (eds), Of Mother Country and Plantations, Ohio
Rockoff, H. T.	1975	Varieties of Banking and Regional Economic Development in the United States 1840–60. JEcH
Roover, R. A. de.	1954	New Interpretations of the History of Banking. JWH
Sheridan, R. B.	1960	The British Credit Crisis of 1772 and the American Colonies. JEcH
Smout, T. C.	1964	Scottish Landowners and Economic Growth 1650–1850. SJPE
	1970	The Landowner and the Planned Village in Scotland, 1730–1830, in Phillipson and Mitchison (eds), Scotland in the Age of Improvement
Soltow, J. H.	1959	Scottish Traders in Virginia. EcHR
Taylor, F. S.	1965	Scottish Banks in the 18th Century. SJPE
Turner, W. H. K.	1968	Rural Settlements. British Association
Ward, J. T.	1968	Charles W. Boase, Banker and Bishop Abertay Historical Society

7. Unpublished Writings

| Munn, C. W. | 1972 | The East Lothian Bank. Strathclyde B.A. dissertation |
| McNaughtan, D. P. | 1972 | The Royal Bank of Scotland 1780–1800. Strathclyde B.A. dissertation |

Index